WORLD CIVILIZATIONS

Sources, Images, and Interpretations

VOLUME II

Edited by
Dennis Sherman
JOHN JAY COLLEGE OF CRIMINAL JUSTICE, CITY UNIVERSITY OF NEW YORK

A. Tom Grunfeld
EMPIRE STATE COLLEGE, STATE UNIVERSITY OF NEW YORK

Gerald Markowitz
JOHN JAY COLLEGE OF CRIMINAL JUSTICE, CITY UNIVERSITY OF NEW YORK

David Rosner
BARUCH COLLEGE, CITY UNIVERSITY OF NEW YORK

Linda Heywood
HOWARD UNIVERSITY

McGRAW-HILL, INC.
New York   St. Louis   San Francisco   Auckland   Bogotá
Caracas   Lisbon   London   Madrid   Mexico City   Milan
Montreal   New Delhi   San Juan   Singapore   Sydney   Tokyo   Toronto

WORLD CIVILIZATIONS
Sources, Images, and Interpretations
Volume II

 This book is printed on recycled, acid-free paper containing a minimum of 50% total recycled fiber with 10% postconsumer de-inked fiber.

1234567890 DOC DOC 909876543

ISBN 0-07-056833-2

This book was set in Caledonia by Ruttle, Shaw & Wetherill, Inc.
The editor was Pamela Gordon;
the production supervisor was Louise Karam.
The cover was designed by Carla Bauer.
The photo researcher was Barbara Salz.
Project supervision was done by Ruttle, Shaw & Wetherill, Inc.
R. R. Donnelley & Sons Company was printer and binder.

Cover painting: A Scribe. Courtesy of the Arthur M. Sackler Museum. Harvard University Art Museums.

Library of Congress Cataloging-in-Publication Data

World civilizations: sources, images, and interpretations / edited by
   Dennis Sherman; A. Tom Grunfeld . . . [et al.].
      p.   cm.
   Includes bibliographical references.
   ISBN 0-07-056831-6 (v. 1). —ISBN 0-07-056833-2 (v. 2)
   1. Civilization—History—Sources.   2. Civilization—History.
I. Sherman, Dennis.   II. Grunfeld, A. Tom.
CB69.W66   1994
909—dc20   93-34784

ABOUT THE AUTHORS

Dennis Sherman is professor of History at John Jay College of Criminal Justice, the City University of New York. He received his BA (1962) and JD (1965) degrees from the University of California at Berkeley and his PhD (1970) from the University of Michigan. He was visiting Professor at the University of Paris (1978–1979, 1985). He received the Ford Foundation Prize Fellowship (1968–1969, 1969–1970), a fellowship from the Council for Research on Economic History (1971–1972), and fellowships from the National Endowment for the Humanities (1973–1976). His publications include *A Short History of Western Civilization*, Seventh Edition (coauthor), *Western Civilization: Images and Interpretations*, Third Edition, *A Study Guide and Readings for the Western Experience* (1991), a series of introductions in the Garland Library of War and Peace, several articles and reviews on nineteenth-century French economic and social history in American and European journals, and short stories in literary reviews.

A. Tom Grunfeld is an Associate Professor of History at the State University of New York/Empire State College. He received his BA (1972) from the State University of New York/College at Old Westbury, his MA (1973) from the University of London/School of Oriental and African Studies and his PhD (1985) from New York University. He has received travel and research grants from the National Endowment for the Humanities (1984), the Research Foundation of the City University of New York (1985), and the State University of New York (1985, 1987, 1991). His publications include over 60 articles in journals published in a dozen countries, *The Making of Modern Tibet* (1987), and *On Her Own: Journalistic Adventures from the San Francisco Earthquake to the Chinese Revolution 1917–1927* (1993). He has lived in and traveled extensively throughout Asia since 1966.

Gerald Markowitz is Professor of History at the Graduate Center, John Jay College of the City University of New York. He received his PhD from the University of Wisconsin (1971). He received grants from the National Endowment for the Humanities (1975–77, 1987–89, 1992–94). His publications include *The Anti-Imperialists, 1898–1902* (1976), *Democratic Vistas: Post Offices and Public Art in the New Deal* (with Marlene Park) (1984), *Deadly Dust: Silicosis and the Politics of Industrial Disease* (with David Rosner) (1991), *Dying for Work: Safety and Health in the United States* (ed. with D. Rosner) (1987), *"Slaves of the Depression": Workers' Letters about Life on the Job* (ed. with D. Rosner) (1987), as well as numerous articles and reviews on American History.

David Rosner is Professor of History at Baruch College and the Graduate Center of the City University of New York. He received his PhD from Harvard University (1978). He received fellowships and grants from the National Endowment for the Humanities (1982–83, 1987–89, 1992–94), was a Josiah Macy Fellow in the History of Biology and Medicine (1973–1976) and was a John Simon Guggenheim Fellow (1987–88). His publications include *A Once Charitable Enterprise: Hospitals and Health Care in Brooklyn and New York, 1885–1915* (1982), *Deadly Dust: Silicosis and the Politics of Industrial Disease* (with Gerald Markowitz) (1991), *Dying for Work: Safety and Health in the United States* (ed. with G. Markowitz) (1987), *"Slaves of the Depression": Workers' Letters about Life on the Job* (ed. with G. Markowitz) (1987), as well as numerous articles and reviews on American History.

Linda Heywood is Associate Professor of African History at Howard University in Washington, D.C. She received her BA (1973) from Brooklyn College and her PhD (1984) from Columbia University. She was a Visiting Assistant Professor at Cleveland State University (1982–84). She received a Whiting Fellowship (1977) and a grant from Howard University Faculty Humanities Program (1990). Her publications include several articles on the economic and political history of central Angola. She is the coeditor of *Black Diaspora: Africans and Their Descendants in the Wider World*, Parts I and II (1988 revised editions). She is currently completing a manuscript entitled "Thwarted Power: The State and Transformation in Central Angola, 1840–1975."

We Look Backward,
All of Us,
To Know,
All of Us,
If We Can.

CONTENTS IN BRIEF

CONTENTS

TOPICAL CONTENTS

1914 to the Present

ENVIRONMENT AND GEOGRAPHY

1500–1914

1914 to the Present

GOVERNMENT AND POLITICS

1500–1914

1914 to the Present

IMPERIAL EXPANSION AND COLONIALISM

1500–1914

1914 to the Present

RELIGION

1500–1914

1914 to the Present

REVOLUTION AND RESISTANCE

1500–1914

1914 to the Present

SOCIAL LIFE AND SOCIAL STRUCTURE

1500–1914

1914 to the Present

THOUGHT AND CULTURE

1500–1914

1914 to the Present

WAR AND DIPLOMACY

1500–1914

1914 to the Present

WOMEN

1500–1914

1914 to the Present

PREFACE

This book provides a broad introduction to the sources historians use, the kind of interpretations historians make, and the evolution of civilizations throughout the world over the past six thousand years. A large selection of documents, photographs, and maps is presented along with introductions, commentaries, and questions designed to place each selection in a meaningful context and facilitate an understanding of its historical significance. The selections and accompanying notes also provide insights into how historians work and some of the problems they face.

A brief look at the task facing historians will supply a background to what will be covered in this book. To discover what people thought and did and to organize this into a chronological record of the human past, historians must search for evidence—for the sources of history. Most sources are written materials, ranging from government records to gravestone inscriptions, memoirs, and poetry. Other sources include paintings, photographs, sculpture, buildings, maps, pottery, and oral traditions. In searching for sources, historians usually have something in mind—some tentative goals or conclusions that guide their search. Thus, in the process of working with sources, historians must decide which ones to emphasize. What historians ultimately write is a synthesis of the questions posed, the sources used, and their own ideas.

The perspective in this book is not from western civilization or indeed from any particular civilization. The perspective is the course of human history as a whole, as it ebbs and flows over various parts of the globe. At the same time, the focus in each chapter will usually be on particular civilizations as they have arisen, developed, and interacted with other civilizations of the world. The sources have been selected to provide an overall balance between political, economic, social, intellectual, religious, and cultural history. However, most chapters also stress certain topics of particular importance for understanding the history of a civilization. Therefore, for example, some chapters will have more sources on social and women's history, while others will emphasize political and religious history.

Structure of the Book

This book is divided into manageable chapters, the divisions based on how the different civilizations of the world have developed over time and within certain geographical contexts. There is also a **topical table of contents** that further facilitates cross-chapter comparisons between different civilizations and over time. All the chapters are organized the same way. Each chapter is broken into sections consisting of the following features:

Each chapter opens with a **chapter introduction,** in which the period of history and the general topics to be dealt with in the chapter are described. The introduction provides a brief sketch of some of the most important developments, but no effort is made to cover the period. Instead, the purpose is to introduce the topics, issues, and questions that the sources in the chapter focus on, and to place these sources in the historical context of the civilizations being examined.

The introduction is followed by a **time line,** showing the relevant dates, people, events, and developments of the period, to provide a historical context for the selections in the chapter.

The chapter time line is followed by the **primary sources.** These are documents written by individuals involved in the matter under investigation. Historians consider these documents their main building blocks for learning about and interpreting the past. They are pieces of evidence that show what people thought, how they acted, and what they accomplished. At the same time historians must criticize these sources both externally—to attempt to uncover forgeries and errors—and internally—to find the authors' motives, inconsistencies within the documents, and different meanings of words and phrases.

Each document is preceded by a **headnote.** The headnote provides some information on the nature of the source, places it in a specific historical context, and indicates its particular focus.

The headnotes end with suggestions of **points to consider.** These points are not simply facts to be searched for in the selection. Rather, they are designed to stimulate analytical thought about the selections and to indicate some of the uses of each source.

The primary sources are followed by visual sources, including maps, and then by **secondary sources.**

Secondary sources are documents written by scholars about the time in question. Usually, they are interpretations of what occurred based on examination of numerous primary documents and other sources. They reflect choices the authors have made and their own particular understandings of what has happened. Often there are important differences of opinion among scholars about how to understand significant historical developments. Secondary sources should therefore be read with these questions in mind: What sort of evidence does the author use? Does the author's argument make sense? What political or ideological preferences are revealed in the author's interpretation? How might one argue against the interpretation presented by the author? At times the distinction between primary and secondary documents becomes blurred, as when the author is a contemporary of the events he or she is interpreting. If a document by that author is read as an interpretation of what occurred, it would be a secondary source. As evidence for the assumption and attitudes of the author's times, however, the document would be a primary source.

Like the primary documents, all the secondary documents are preceded by headnotes and suggestions for points to consider.

Visual sources are paintings, drawings, sculpture, ceramics, photographs, buildings, monuments, coins, and so forth, that can provide valuable historical insights or information. Although they often include characteristics of secondary documents, they are usually most valuable when used in the same way as primary documents. In this book their purpose is not merely to supplement the documents or provide examples of the great pieces of art throughout history. It is to show how these visual materials can be used as sources of history and to provide insights difficult to gain solely through written documents. To this end, each visual source is accompanied by a relatively extensive interpretive description. Care should be taken in viewing these sources and using these descriptions. By their very nature, visual sources usually have a less clear meaning than written documents. Scholars differ greatly over how sources such as paintings, ceramics, and coins should be interpreted. Therefore, the descriptions accompanying the visual sources are open to debate. They are designed to show how it is possible for historians to use visual materials as sources of history—as unwritten evidence for what people thought and did in the past.

Maps often combine elements of primary documents, secondary documents, and visual sources. However, here they are usually used to help establish relationships, such as the connections between geographical factors and political developments, thereby enabling us to interpret what occurred differently than we could have if we had relied on written sources alone. As is the case with visual sources, each map is accompanied by an interpretive description. These descriptions indicate some of the ways maps might be used by historians.

Each chapter ends with **chapter questions.** These are designed to draw major themes of the chapter together in a challenging way. Answers to these questions require some analytical thought and the use of several of the selections in the chapter and even, occasionally, the use of sources from several chapters.

Since a book of this size can only sample what is available and outline what has occurred, this book is truly an introduction to the human past and its sources. Indeed, it is our hope that the materials presented here will reveal the range of sources that can be used to deepen our understanding of the human past and serve as a jumping-off point for further exploration into history and the historian's discipline.

McGraw-Hill and the authors would like to thank Edward Anson, University of Arkansas at Little Rock; Hines Hall, Auburn University; Udo Heyn, California State, Los Angeles; Thomas Kay, Wheaton College; Gretchen Knapp, State University of New York, Buffalo; Daniel Lewis, San Bernadino Valley College; Marilyn Morris, University of North Texas; Oliver Pollack, University of Nebraska, Omaha; Linda Walton, Portland State University; Lawrence Watkins, University of Kansas; John Weakland, Ball State University; Joseph Whitehorne, Lord Fairfax Community College; and Richard Williams, Washington State University for their many helpful comments and suggestions in reviewing this book.

Dennis Sherman
A. Tom Grunfeld
Gerald Markowitz
David Rosner
Linda Heywood

A NOTE ON CHINESE ROMANIZATION

From the first contacts of Europeans and Chinese there has been a problem in transliterating Chinese characters into the western alphabet. Many varied systems were developed. The romanization system most widely used in the English-speaking world was named after its nineteenth-century British creators, Wade and Giles.

In recent years there has been an attempt to develop a single transliteration which could be used universally. This system, adopted officially in the People's Republic of China in 1979, is known as *pinyin*. This system approximates the Chinese sounds more closely although it uses letters such as *q* and *x* in ways unfamiliar to most English speakers.

In this book we have used *pinyin*, but the first time a word appears, the Wade-Giles form will appear in brackets except for names particularly well known such as Sun Yat-sen, Chiang Kai-shek, Hong Kong, Tibet, etc.

ONE

European Expansion and Global Encounters, 1500–1700

Between the mid-fifteenth and mid-sixteenth centuries much of Europe gained new political, economic, and technological strength. This enabled European states to support a new wave of expansion into the rest of the world. Led by Portugal and then Spain, these states sent explorers, missionaries, merchants, colonists, and armed forces throughout the world. In some cases, as for the civilizations of the Americas, the consequences would be immediate and profound. In other cases, as in China and Japan, the effects would be more indirect. But in the long run, this European expansion would mark a turning point in world history.

In Asia, contacts between Westerners and peoples of south and east Asia extended back for centuries, long before Marco Polo, the most widely known European traveler, reached China in the thirteenth century. Organized by merchants, missionaries, adventurers, or explorers, caravans crossed the vast plateaus of central Asia with the help of the local Turkic inhabitants. By the fifteenth century Arab speaking merchants and bankers had developed a monopoly on the east and south Asia trade. This changed in the fifteenth, sixteenth, and seventeenth centuries as the Portuguese, Spanish, Dutch,

British, and French moved in. During this same period the Russians were advancing eastward through Siberia, conquering as they went. A new Asian-European relationship had the potential of becoming a dialogue rewarding to all, but the relationship was marred from the beginning by ethnocentrism and the Europeans' propensity to force their will on the Asians. The long-established Asian societies were usually able to resist European efforts to establish control over them during this period.

In sub-Saharan Africa, the ability of Europeans to penetrate the continent beyond setting up coastal posts was limited by geographical factors, disease, and resistance from African kingdoms. However, this new contact with Europeans, and particularly the development of the slave trade, would become of importance to both Africans and Europeans.

In the Americas, Christopher Columbus's arrival in 1492 has often been used as the starting point for discussion of American history. Recently, historians have acknowledged that the indigenous peoples of North, Central, and South America had a rich culture that predated Europeans' arrival but

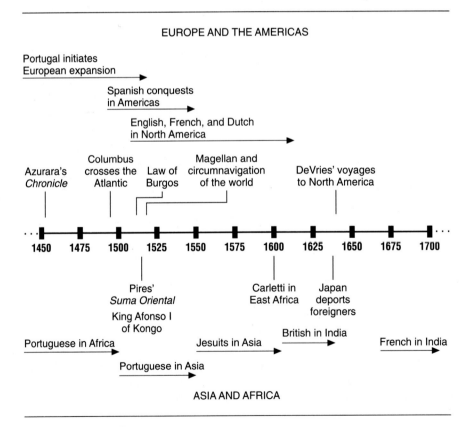

which has been neglected. As they established empires, Europeans from Spain, Portugal, France, Holland, and England had to adapt their own cultures to the existing environment of peoples and places in the western hemisphere. Europeans had to interact with the Native Americans they conquered and the Africans they brought to the Americas as slaves.

The sources in the chapter will examine three main topics. First, what were the motives for the European expansion? What did they have to gain? How did they justify their actions? Second, what observations did the people involved in these cross-cultural contacts make? What do these observations tell us about the societies being observed? What do they reveal about the observer's own assumptions? Third, what were the consequences of these global encounters? What were the effects in Europe? What were the effects outside of Europe?

This last topic will bring us toward a more detailed examination of developments in various parts of the world, which will be the focus of later chapters.

PRIMARY SOURCES

The Chronicle of the Discovery and Conquest of Guinea
Azurara

The great geographic expansion and conquests of the fifteenth and sixteenth centuries were initiated by Prince Henry (the Navigator) of Portugal (1394–1460). Although he did not personally participate in the explorations, he established a naval school and base of operations on the southwestern tip of Portugal from which he sent expeditions down the west coast of Africa. One of the clearest explanations of the motives for this effort has been provided by Gomes Eannes de Azurara, a friend of Prince Henry (referred to as "the Lord Infant"), who chronicled the voyages of 1452–1453 at the request of King Alfonso V.

> **Consider:** *The explanations that sound more like rationalizations than reasons for explorations; whether economic, military, and religious motives are complementary or contradictory; how this document reflects the history of a country engaged with Islam.*

Source: Gomes Eannes de Azurara, *The Chronicle of the Discovery and Conquest of Guinea,* vol. I, trans. Charles Raymond Beazley and Adgar Prestage (London: Hakluyt Society, 1896), pp. 27–29.

We imagine that we know a matter when we are acquainted with the doer of it and the end for which he did it. And since in former chapters we have set forth the Lord Infant as the chief actor in these things, giving as clear an understanding of him as we could, it is meet that in this present chapter we should know his purpose in doing them. And you should note well that the noble spirit of this Prince, by a sort of natural constraint, was ever urging him both to begin and to carry out very great deeds. For which reason, after the taking of Ceuta he always kept ships well armed against the Infidel, both for war, and because he had also a wish to know the land that lay beyond the isles of Canary and that Cape called Bojador, for that up to his time, neither by writings, nor by the memory of man, was known with any certainty the nature of the land beyond that Cape. Some said indeed that Saint Brandan had passed that way; and there was another tale of two galleys rounding the Cape, which never returned. But this doth not appear at all likely to be true, for it is not to be presumed that if the said galleys went there, some other ships would not have endeavoured to learn what voyage they had made. And because the said Lord Infant wished to know the truth of this,—since it seemed to him that if he or some other lord did not endeavour to gain that knowledge, no mariners or merchants would ever dare to attempt it—(for it is clear that none of them ever trouble themselves to sail to a place where there is not a sure and certain hope of profit)—and seeing also that no other prince took any pains in this matter, he sent out his own ships against those parts, to have manifest certainty of them all. And to this he was stirred up by his zeal for the service of God and of the King Edward his Lord and brother, who then reigned. And this was the first reason of his action.

The second reason was that if there chanced to be in those lands some population of Christians, or some havens, into which it would be possible to sail without peril, many kinds of merchandise might be brought to this realm, which would find a ready market, and reasonably so, because no other people of these parts traded with them, nor yet people of any other that were known; and also the products of this realm might be taken there, which traffic would bring great profit to our countrymen.

The third reason was that, as it was said that the power of the Moors in that land of Africa was very much greater than was commonly supposed, and that there were no Christians among them, nor any other race of men; and because every wise man is obliged by natural prudence to wish for a knowledge of the power of his enemy; therefore the said Lord Infant exerted himself to cause this to be fully discovered, and to make it known determinately how far the power of those infidels extended.

The fourth reason was because during the one and thirty years that he had warred against the Moors, he had never found a Christian king, nor a lord outside this land, who for the love of our Lord Jesus Christ would aid him in the said war. Therefore he sought to know if there were in those parts any Christian princes, in whom the charity and the love of Christ was so ingrained that they would aid him against those enemies of the faith.

The fifth reason was his great desire to make increase in the faith of our Lord Jesus Christ and to bring to him all the souls that should be saved,—understanding that all the mystery of the Incarnation, Death, and Passion of our Lord Jesus Christ was for this sole end—namely the salvation of lost souls—whom the said Lord Infant by his travail and spending would fain bring into the true path. For he perceived that no better offering could be made unto the Lord than this; for if God promised to return one hundred goods for one, we may justly believe that for such great benefits, that is to say for so many souls as were saved by the efforts of this Lord, he will have so many hundreds of guerdons in the kingdom of God, by which his spirit may be glorified after this life in the celestial realm. For I that wrote this history saw so many men and women of those parts turned to the holy faith, that even if the Infant had been a heathen, their prayers would have been enough to have obtained his salvation. And not only did I see the first captives, but their children and grandchildren as true Christians as if the Divine grace breathed in them and imparted to them a clear knowledge of itself.

Africa and Europe: The Problems of Alliances
Afonso I of Kongo

The Kingdom of Kongo was the largest and most powerful state in west-central Africa before 1500. The Kongolese met Europeans for the first time when Portuguese sailors led by Diogo Cão reached their country in 1483. By 1491, the ruler (the Mani Kongo) had been baptized and accepted Christianity. King Afonso I, his son (ca. 1485–1543) was instrumental in making his state a Christian country, but often had to deal with a variety of problems, both with his own countrymen and with the Portuguese. Among the fruits of this contact were literacy, new building techniques, bureaucratic styles and titles and a host of lesser cultural infusions. In his attempts to maintain Christianity, Afonso often turned to either Portugal or Rome for assistance. The following selection touches on the conflicts that emerged between various Portuguese factions who had different allies among the Kongolese nobility, and the relationship between the African king and his European ally.

> **Consider:** *What the document reveals about the strengths and weaknesses of this African-European alliance; the Kongolese experience with Christianity.*

Now we wish to tell your Highness about a certain Rui do Rego whom your Highness sent here to teach us and set an example for us, but as soon as he arrived here he wished to be treated like a nobleman and never wanted to teach a single

SOURCE: William H. McNeill and Mitsuko Iriye, *Modern Asia and Africa* (Oxford: 1971), pp. 56–59.

boy. During the Lenten season he came to us and asked for an ox, and we ordered one to be given to him. Then he said he was dying of hunger, and we ordered two sheep to be given to him, but that he was to eat them secretly, so that our people would not see him. Yet he, disregarding this, went and killed the ox in the middle of Lent, in front of all our nobles, and even tempted us with the meat; so that when our people saw it, those who were young and had only been Christians a short time all fled to their lands, and the older ones who remained with us said things that are not to be repeated, stating that we had forbidden them to eat meat, while the white men had plenty of meat, and that we had deceived them and they wanted to kill us. Then we, with much patience and many gifts, were able to pacify them, telling them that they should save their souls and not look at what that man was doing, and that if he wished to go to Hell then they should let him go.

We were so disgusted with all this that we could not see Rui do Rego again and ordered him to go to Chela,[1] so that he could board the first ship that arrived— for he had not taught as your Highness had ordered him to, but had caused to return to idols those whom we, with much fatigue, had converted. So he went and stayed at Chela—and at this time Simão da Silva[2] arrived with two ships and found the said Rui do Rego, who told him so many evil things and so many lies that there is no reckoning them, and that he had been cheated. And then Simão da Silva believed him, through the wrongheadedness of Rui do Rego and what he had said—but Rego did not tell him of the wickedness and heresy that he had practiced here. So that Simão da Silva did not wish to come to where we were (as your Highness had ordered him to) and sent the [ship's] physician with your letters, whom we sheltered as if he had been our brother. A vicar from the island [of São Tomé], who was present here, asked us to let him take the physician to his house to stay with him—but that ecclesiastic spoke so evilly of us to the physician that the physician's mind was changed, and he became persuaded that Simão da Silva should not come [to the capital]. And your Highness will know that it was Fernão de Melo who had ordered all this, since your Highness has no trading station here, and he has tainted goods [to sell?] and always steals from us.

Yet notwithstanding this, Sire, the physician fell ill with fever and could not return to Simão da Silva with an answer, and he wrote him a letter advising him not to come here; that we were a "João Pires" [a "Mr. Nobody," a nonentity], and that we did not deserve any of the things sent by your Highness.[3] The which letter he gave to one of our servants, and it came into our hands and we showed it to all of your Highness' servants who had come in the fleet. When we saw those things we well understood that they had been done at the command of Fernão de Melo—and we gave thanks to our Lord God for having been called a "João

---

[1] A coastal region south of the Zaire River.
[2] In 1512 the king of Portugal sent Simão da Silva, with several ships and many men and supplies, as ambassador to the king of the Congo.
[3] The king of Portugal had sent an impressive diversity of supplies, animals, luxuries, plants, and seeds with his ambassador to the Congo.

Pires" for His love. And all these things, lord and brother, we have suffered with good judgement and prudence, crying many tears—and we have reported nothing to our nobles and people, so that they may not conspire against us.

Then we sent one of our cousins with a young nobleman and wrote to Simão da Silva that, for the love of God, he should come and comfort us, and punish the people who were here, for we would not send him to ask anything of your Highness, except to ask that everyone be treated justly. Because of our entreaties, and those of Dom João our cousin, he left to come, but halfway here the fevers afflicted him with such force that he died. When we heard the news it broke our feet and hands,[4] and we suffered so much vexation that never again, not until this day, have we ever had any pleasure, because of the great disorders and evils later done by the men who came with him.

---

[4] A peculiar expression indicating great anguish.

The Suma Oriental
Tomé Pires

Vasco da Gama's voyage around the southern tip of Africa to India in 1498, ending the Arab monopoly on Indian trade, initiated a massive European expansion into Asia. Soon the Portuguese established a string of outposts and colonies that stretched around much of the world. In Asia alone these posts included Goa, on the west coast of India in 1510, Malacca on the west cast of Malaya in 1511, Macao off the coast of China in 1514, Timor in the eastern tip of Indonesia in 1520, and Japan in 1543.

Portuguese travelers to trading posts and urban centers often wrote about the lands and peoples they encountered, providing us with much of our evidence about these early contacts. Tomé Pires was a Portuguese apothecary to his country's royal family. He was also an explorer and wandered to Asia, living in Goa and Malacca, but also traveling extensively from 1511 to 1517. In 1517 he was dispatched as the Portuguese Ambassador to China where he was arrested after the Chinese authorities heard rumors that the Europeans were enslaving Chinese. He died in a Canton jail. In 1517 he submitted The Suma Oriental *(Account of the East) to the King of Portugal as an account of the trade and political situations in Asia to aid future Portuguese exploitation of Asia. Excerpts from this work follow.*

> **Consider:** *The concerns and attitude of Tomé Pires; the flavor of the trading posts he describes; the mixture of people already present in Asian ports before the Europeans arrived.*

SOURCE: Armando Cortesão, trans., *The Suma Oriental of Tomé Pires. An Account of the East, From the Red Sea to Japan, Written in Malacca and India in 1512–1515*, vol. II (London: Printed for the Hakluyt Society, 1944).

CAMBAY

I now come to the trade of Cambay. . . . All the trade in Cambay is in the hands of the heathen. Their general designation is Gujaratees, and then they are divided into various races—Banians, Brahmans and Pattars. . . . They are men who understand merchandise; they are so properly steeped in the sound and harmony of it, that the Gujaratees say that any offence connected with merchandise is pardonable. . . . They are diligent, quick men in trade. They do their accounts with figures like ours and with our very writing. They are men who do not give away anything that belongs to them, nor do they want anything that belongs to anyone else; wherefore they have been esteemed in Cambay up to the present, practising their idolatry, because they enrich the kingdom greatly with the said trade. There are also some Cairo merchants settled in Cambay, and many Khorasans and Guilans from Aden and Ormuz, all of whom do a great trade in the seaport towns of Cambay. . . .

They trade with the kingdom of the Deccan and Goa and with Malabar, and they have factors everywhere, who live and set up business—as the Genoese do in our part [of the world]— . . . taking back to their own country the kind of merchandise which is valued there. . . .

SIAM

Through the cunning [of the Siamese] the foreign merchants who go to their land and kingdom leave their merchandise in the land and are ill paid; and this happens to them all—but less to the Chinese, on account of their friendship with the king of China. . . .

There are very few Moors in Siam. The Siamese do not like them. There are, however, Arabs, Persians, Bengalees, many Kling, Chinese and other nationalities. And all the Siamese trade is on the China side, and in Pase, Pedir and Bengal. The Moors are in the seaports.

CHINA

They affirm that all those who take merchandise from Canton to the islands make a profit of three, four or five in every ten, and the Chinese have this custom so that the land shall not be taken from them, as well as in order to receive the dues on the merchandise exported as well as imported; and the chief [reason] is for fear lest the city be taken from them, because they say that the city of Canton is a rich one, and corsairs often come up to it. . . .

They say that the Chinese made this law about not being able to go to Canton for fear of the Javanese and Malays, for it is certain that one of these people's junks would rout twenty Chinese junks. They say that China has more than a thousand junks, and each of them trades where it sees fit; but the people are weak, and such is their fear of Malays and Javanese that it is quite certain that one [of our] ship[s] of four hundred tons could depopulate Canton, and this depopulation would bring great loss to China.

Not to rob any country of its glory, it certainly seems that China is an important, good and very wealthy country, and the Governor of Malacca would not need as much force as they say in order to bring it under our rule, because the people are very weak and easy to overcome. . . .

They say that there are people from Tartary (*Tartaria*) in the land of China . . . and these people are very white with red beards. They ride on horseback; they are warlike. And they say that they go from China to the land of the Tartars (*tartaros*) in two months, and that in Tartary they have horses shod with copper shoes, and this must be because China extends a long way on the northern side, and our bombardiers say that in Germany they heard tell of these people and of a city named by the Chinese *Quesechama*, and it seems to them that by this route they could go to their lands in a short time; but they say that by reason of the cold the land is uninhabited.

JAVA

The king of Java is a heathen. . . . These kings of Java have a fantastic idea: they say that their nobility has no equal. The Javanese heathen lords are tall and handsome; they are lavishly adorned about their person, and have richly caparisoned horses. They use krises, swords, and lances of many kinds, all inlaid with gold. They are great hunters and horsemen—stirrups all inlaid with gold, inlaid saddles, such as are not to be found anywhere else in the world. The Javanese lords are so noble and exalted that there is certainly no nation to compare with them over a wide area in these parts. . . .

The lords of Java are revered like gods, with great respect and deep reverence. The land of Java is thickly peopled in the interior, with many cities, and very large ones, including the great city of *Dayo* where the king is in residence and where his court is. They say that the people who frequent the court are without number. The kings do not show themselves to the people except once or twice in the year. They stay in their palace . . . and there they are with all the pleasures and with feasts, with great quantities of wives and concubines. They say that the king of Java has a thousand eunuchs to wait on these women, and these eunuchs are dressed like women and wear their hair dressed in the form of diadems. . . .

MALACCA

Those from Cairo bring the merchandise brought by the galleasses of Venice, to wit, many arms, scarlet-in-grain, coloured woollen cloths, coral, copper, quicksilver, vermilion, nails, silver, glass and other beads, and golden glassware.

Those from Mecca bring a great quantity of opium, rosewater and such like merchandise, and much liquid storax.

Those from Aden bring to Gujarat a great quantity of opium, raisins, madder, indigo, rosewater, silver, seed-pearls, and other dyes, which are of value in Cambay.

In these companies go Parsees, Turks, Turkomans and Armenians, and they come and take up their companies for their cargo in Gujarat, and from there they embark in March and sail direct for Malacca; and on the return journey they call at the Maldive Islands.

Women and Poverty in Japan
Francesco Carletti

The Asian–European relationship had the potential of becoming a dialogue rewarding to all sides, but in fact the relationship was marred from the beginning by each side lacking an understanding of the other's culture. The following selection is from the writings of Francesco Carletti who was born in Florence in 1572. He spent several years traveling with his father around the world, including East Asia in 1597–1598. Carletti is writing for an audience that has virtually no information about the Japanese and is relying on his accounts to formulate their own views. Here Carletti discusses poverty, women, and prostitution in Japan. Notice Carletti's hypocrisy since selling children and prostitution occurred in Europe as well.

> **Consider:** *The image of Japanese civilization this account might produce in European readers' minds; whether this reveals more about European visions of Japanese women than Japanese society; why the author might have chosen to write this account.*

[The Japanese] do not, however, hold in equal esteem the virtue of their daughters and sisters; or rather they take no account of this at all. Indeed it often happens that a girl's own father, mother, or brothers—without any feeling of shame on the part of any of those concerned—will without hesitation sell her as a prostitute before she is married, for a few pence, under the pressure of poverty, which is very severely felt throughout the whole country. And this poverty is the cause of the most shameless immorality—an immorality which is so gross and which takes such different and unusual forms, to pass belief.

But the Portuguese are my witnesses and cannot be gainsaid—especially those who come year by year from China, that is, from the island of Macao. . . . As soon as ever these Portuguese arrive and disembark, the pimps who control this traffic in women call on them in the houses in which they are quartered for the time of their stay, and enquire whether they would like to purchase, or acquire in any other method they please, a girl, for the period of their sojourn, or to keep her for so many months, or for a night, or for a day, or for an hour, a contract being

SOURCE: Bishop Trollope, trans. "The Carletti Discourse" published in *The Transactons of the Asiatic Society of Japan*, second series, vol. IX, 1932.

first made with these brokers, or an agreement entered into with the girl's relations, and the money paid down. And if they prefer it they will take them to the girl's house, in order that they may see her first, or else they will take them to see her on their own premises, which are usually situated in certain hamlets or villages outside the city. And many of these Portuguese, upon whose testimony I am relying, fall in with this custom as the fancy takes them, driving the best bargain they can for a few pence. And so it often happens that they will get hold of a pretty little girl of fourteen or fifteen years of age, for three or four *scudi*, or a little more or less, according to the time during which they wish to have her at their disposal, with no other responsibility beyond that of sending her back home when done with. Nor does this practice in any way interfere with a girl's chances of marriage. Indeed many of them would never get married, if they had not by this means acquired a dowry, by accumulating 30 or 40 *scudi*, given to them from time to time by these Portuguese, who have kept them in their houses for seven or eight months on end, and who have in some cases married them themselves. And when these women are hired by the day, it is enough to give them the merest trifle, nor do they ever refuse to be hired on account of a variation in the price, which is hardly ever refused by their relations, or by those who keep them as a sort of stock in trade for these purposes in their houses, and to whom the money is paid—the women being in effect all slaves sold for these purposes. And there are, moreover, some of them who, by agreement with the brokers, ask for no more than their food and clothing—neither of which costs much—while the whole of their earnings go to the men who keep them.

To sum up, the country is more plentifully supplied than any other with these sort of means of gratifying the passion for sexual indulgence, just as it abounds in every other sort of vice, in which it surpasses every other place in the world.

Laws of the Burgos:
The Spanish Colonize Central
and South America

As the first colonists in the New World, Spaniards sought to exploit the wealth of Central and South America through the use of forced labor. This "encomienda" system, a system of forced labor on extensive plantations, permitted Spanish settlers to compel native peoples to labor in gold and silver mines, agriculture, and in the home. This excerpt is from a set of laws developed at Burgos, Spain in 1512. They became the basis for the legal system for Spanish America in the early colonial period.

SOURCE: Lesley Byrd Simpson, trans. *The Laws of Burgos of 1512–1513*, (Westport, Conn.: Greenwood Press).

Consider: *Spanish assumptions and concerns about these native peoples; what these laws tell us about how the native population actually lived under Spanish domination.*

Whereas, the King, my Lord and Father, and the Queen, my Mistress and Mother (may she rest in glory!), always desired that the chiefs and Indians of the Island of Española be brought to a knowledge of our Holy Catholic Faith, and, . . .

Whereas, it has become evident through long experience that nothing has sufficed to bring the said chiefs and Indians to a knowledge of our Faith (necessary for their salvation), since by nature they are inclined to idleness and vice, and have no manner of virtue or doctrine (by which Our Lord is disserved), and that the principal obstacle in the way of correcting their vices and having them profit by and impressing them with the doctrine is that their dwellings are remote from the settlements of the Spaniards who go hence to reside in the said Island, because, although at the time the Indians go to serve them they are indoctrinated in and taught the things of our Faith, after serving they return to their dwellings where, because of the distance and their own own evil inclinations, they immediately forget what they have been taught and go back to their customary idleness and vice, . . .

Whereas, this is contrary to our Faith, and,

Whereas, it is our duty to seek a remedy for it in every way possible, . . . the most beneficial thing that could be done at present would be to remove the said chiefs and Indians to the vicinity of the villages and communities of the Spaniards. . . .

First, since it is our determination to remove the said Indians and have them dwell near the Spaniards, we order and command that the persons to whom the said Indians are given, or shall be given, in encomienda, shall at once and forthwith build, for every fifty Indians, four lodges [*bohíos*] of thirty by fifteen feet, and have the Indians plant 5,000 hillocks (3,000 in cassava and 2,000 in yams), 250 pepper plants, and 50 cotton plants . . . and these shall be settled next the estates of the Spaniards who have them in encomienda, well situated and housed, and under the eyes of you, our said Admiral and judges and officers . . . and the persons who have the said Indians in their charge [in encomienda] shall have them sow, in season, half a *fanega* of maize, and shall also give them a dozen hens and a cock to raise and enjoy the fruit thereof, the chickens as well as the eggs; and as soon as the Indians are brought to the estates they shall be given all the aforesaid as their own property. . . .

Also, we order and command that the citizen to whom the said Indians are given in encomienda shall, upon the land that is assigned to him, be obliged to erect a structure to be used for a church. . . . Every Sunday and obligatory feast day they may come there to pray and hear Mass, and also to hear the good advice that the priests who say Mass shall give them; and the priests who say Mass shall teach them the Commandments and the Articles of the Faith, and the other things of the Christian doctrine. Therefore, in order that they be instructed in the things of the Faith and become accustomed to pray and hear Mass, we command that the Spaniards who are on the estates with the said Indians and have charge of them shall be obliged to bring them all together to the said church in the morning and remain with them until after Mass is said; and after Mass they shall bring them back to the estates and give them their pots of cooked meat, in such wise that they eat on that day better than on any other day of the week. . . .

Also, we order and command that, after the Indians have been brought to the estates, all the founding [of gold] that henceforth is done on the said Island shall be done in the manner prescribed below: that is, the said persons who have Indians in encomienda shall extract gold with them for five months in the year and, at the end of these five months, the said Indians shall rest forty days, and the day they cease their labor of extracting gold shall be noted on a certificate, which shall be given to the miners who go to the mines. . . .

Also, we order and command that all those on the said Island who have Indians in encomienda, now or in the future, shall be obliged to give to each of them a hammock in which to sleep continually; and they shall not allow them to sleep on the ground, as hitherto they have been doing. . . .

Voyages from Holland to America: The Dutch Colonize North America
David Pietersz de Vries

The Dutch were the first to colonize the area of the lower Hudson Valley in what are now the states of New York, New Jersey, and Connecticut in the United States. They established large estates and imported tenant farmers to work small parcels of land. Initially, Native Americans and the Dutch farmers traded together and lived in close proximity. Yet, new interests and new administrators led the Dutch to try to displace the Algonquins from their land. This document, about a massacre that took place in February of 1643 reveals the harsh practices of colonists who had little respect for the rights or humanity of those they considered to be "uncivilized."

> **Consider:** *The reasons for the author's opposition to the Governor's actions; whether the Governor's stand was based on self-interest or humanistic concerns.*

. . . So was this business begun between the 25th and 26th of February in the year 1643. I remained that night at the governor's, sitting up. I went and sat in the kitchen, when, about midnight, I heard a great shrieking, and I ran to the ramparts

SOURCE: David Pietersz de Vries, *Voyages From Holland to America*, Henry C. Murphy, trans. (New York, 1853), pp. 167–171.

of the fort, and looked over to Pavonia. Saw nothing but firing, and heard the shrieks of the Indians murdered in their sleep. I returned again to the house by the fire. Having sat there awhile, there came an Indian with his squaw, whom I knew well, and who lived about an hour's walk from my house, and told me that they two had fled in a small skiff; that they had betaken themselves to Pavonia; that the Indians from Fort Orange had surprised them; and that they had come to conceal themselves in the fort. I told them that they must go away immediately; that there was no occasion for them to come to the fort to conceal themselves; that they who had killed their people at Pavonia were not Indians, but the Swannekens, as they call the Dutch, had done it. . . . When it was day, the soldiers returned to the fort, having massacred or murdered eighty Indians, and considering they had done a deed of Roman valour, in murdering so many in their sleep; where infants were torn from their mother's breasts, and hacked to pieces in the presence of the parents, and the pieces thrown into the fire and in the water, and other sucklings were bound to small boards, and then cut, stuck, and pierced, and miserably massacred in a manner to move a heart of stone. . . . After this exploit, the soldiers were rewarded for their services, and Director Kieft thanked them by taking them by the hand and congratulating them. . . .

. . . As soon as the Indians understood that the Swannekens had so treated them, all the men whom they could surprise on the farm-lands, they killed; but we have never heard that they have ever permitted women or children to be killed. They burned all the houses, farms, barns, grain, haystacks, and destroyed everything they could get hold of. So there was an open destructive war begun. . . . When now the Indians had destroyed so many farms and men in revenge for their people, I went to Governor William Kieft, and asked him if it was not as I had said it would be, that he would only effect the spilling of Christian blood. Who would now compensate us for our losses? But he gave me no answer.

A Voyage to South America: Caste and Race in Latin America
Jorge Juan and Antonio de Ulloa

Unlike English North America, which excluded Native Americans from any participation in colonial society and enslaved anyone who had any African ancestors, Spanish and Portuguese South America developed a much more complex social caste and racial system. While the English colonies enforced strict distinctions between blacks and whites, the Spanish developed a more varied set of racial categories, which some historians have argued led to less segregation and racial hostility. This excerpt was written by two

---

SOURCE: Jorge Juan and Antonio de Ulloa, *A Voyage to South America*, vol. I (London, 1772), pp. 29–32.

Spanish officials after their inspection of the caste system of the Caribbean port Cartha-gena.

> **Consider:** *The ways that the South American system allowed for a greater degree of interaction among people of different racial backgrounds; how the caste system reinforced social and class distinctions.*

The inhabitants may be divided into different castes or tribes, who derive their origin from a coalition of Whites, Negroes, and Indians. Of each of these we shall treat particularly.

The Whites may be divided into two classes, the Europeans, and Creoles, or Whites born in the country. The former are commonly called Chapitones, but are not numerous; most of them either return into Spain after acquiring a competent fortune, or remove up into inland provinces in order to increase it. Those who are settled at Carthagena carry on the whole trade of that place, and live in opulence; whilst the other inhabitants are indigent, and reduced to have recourse to mean and hard labor for subsistence. The families of the White Creoles compose the landed interest; some of them have large estates, and are highly respected. . . . Some of these families, in order to keep up their original dignity, have either married their children to their equals in the country, or sent them as officers on board the galleons, but others have greatly declined. Besides these, there are other Whites, in mean circumstances, who either owe their origin to Indian families, or at least to an intermarriage with them, so that there is some mixture in their blood; but when this is not discoverable by their color, the conceit of being Whites alleviates the pressure of every other calamity.

Among the other tribes which are derived from an intermarriage of the Whites with the Negroes, the first are the Mulattos. Next to these the Tercerones, pro-duced from a White and a Mulatto, with some approximation to the former, but not so near as to obliterate their origin. After these follow the Quarterones, proceeding from a White and a Terceron. The last are the Quinterones, who owe their origin to a White and Quarteron. This is the last gradation, there being no visible difference between them and the Whites, either in color or features; nay, they are often fairer than the Spaniards. The children of a White and Quinteron are also called Spaniards, and consider themselves as free from all taint of the Negro race. Every person is so jealous of the order of their tribe or cast, that if, through inadvertence, you call them by a degree lower than what they actually are, they are highly offended, never suffering themselves to be deprived of so valuable a gift of fortune. . . .

These are the most known and common tribes or castes; there are indeed several others proceeding from their intermarriages; but, being so various, even they themselves cannot easily distinguish them. . . .

These castes, from the Mulattos, all affect the Spanish dress, but wear very slight stuffs on account of the heat of the climate. These are the mechanics of the city; the Whites, whether Creoles or Chapitones, disdaining such a mean occu-pation, follow nothing below merchandise. But it being impossible for all to succeed, great numbers not being able to procure sufficient credit, they become poor and miserable from their aversion to those trades they follow in Europe; and, instead of the riches which they flattered themselves with possessing in the Indies, they experience the most complicated wretchedness.

The class of Negroes is not the least numerous, and is divided into two parts; the free and the slaves. These are again subdivided into Creoles and Bozares, part of which are employed in the cultivation of the haciendas, or estancias. Those in the city are obliged to perform the most laborious services, and pay out of their wages a certain quota to their masters, subsisting themselves on the small remainder. The violence of the heat not permitting them to wear any clothes, their only covering is a small piece of cotton stuff about their waist; the female slaves go in the same manner. Some of these live at the estancias, being married to the slaves who work there; while those in the city sell in the markets all kind of eatables. . . .

VISUAL SOURCES

Exploration, Expansion, and Politics

Aside from the various motivations for the voyages of discovery during the fifteenth and sixteenth centuries, a number of factors combined to make those voyages physically possible when earlier they were not. Technological discoveries significantly improved shipbuilding and navigation. But also important was the understanding and mapping of prevailing ocean currents and winds in relation to land masses. It was much easier to sail with, rather than against, currents and winds, and sailors counted on finding land masses for supplies along the way.

The early voyages tended to take advantage of currents and winds as shown in this map. Thus, for example, early voyages to North America usually took a more southerly route westward across the Atlantic and returned on a more northerly route, while Portuguese ships headed east to the Indian Ocean by following winds and currents to Brazil and then crossed the Atlantic farther south. Prevailing currents and winds also explain the difficulty of westward voyages around the tip of South America. These patterns of voyages also shed light on some of the geopolitical results of expansion. For example, even though Portugal's efforts were directed toward an eastern route to the Far East, she acquired Brazil (her only territory in the New World) to the west since it was on a route favored by winds and currents.

Consider: *How this map helps explain the pattern of exploration and colonization by the various European powers.*

Map 1-1 Overseas Explorations

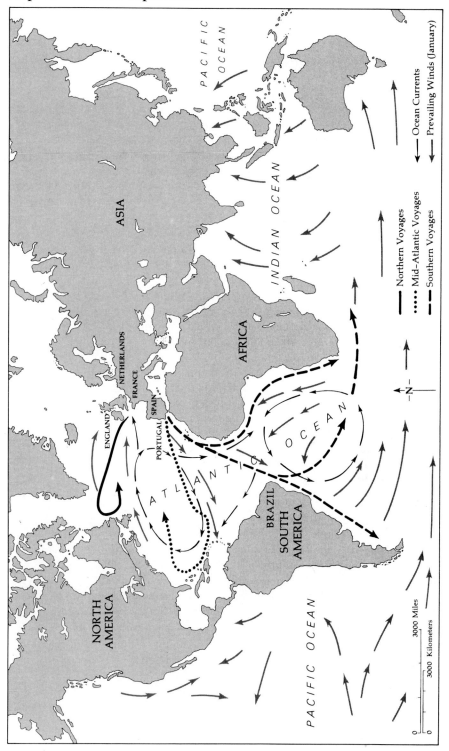

A Buddhist Temple:
European Views of Asia

When the first European travelers returned from Asia they brought with them tales of exotic lands and peoples that were so astonishing as to be barely believable. While Asian cultures were different enough from European cultures to elicit wonderment, travelers tended to exaggerate, and even distort, what they had seen. Europeans were interested in Asia as a source of precious goods (spice, tea, etc.), a market for excess European goods, and fertile ground for missionaries to proselytize. They rarely tried to understand what they were experiencing, and their contempt for non-European culture required distortion of their accounts lest anyone back home think these people were somehow equal to them.

Photo 1-1

From: *Pacific Voyages: The Encyclopedia of Discovery & Exploration* (London: Aldus Books Ltd., 1971).

This illustration is from the 1600s and depicts a Buddhist temple in China. The unknown European artist has seen fit to include two demons that look suspiciously European in origin on either side of the Buddha statue.

> **Consider:** *The impression the artist was trying to create in European viewers' minds.*

SECONDARY SOURCES

The Expansion of Europe
Richard B. Reed

In analyzing the overseas expansion of the fifteenth and sixteenth centuries, historians typically emphasize a combination of economic and religious factors to explain the motivation behind expansion while focusing on the establishment of adequate knowledge and technology as key conditions for its occurrence. In the following selection, Richard B. Reed argues that European expansion was a nationalistic phenomenon, and because of this, Portugal was able to become the early leader.

> **Consider:** *Why Italy and Germany did not participate in overseas expansion; how one might attack Reed's argument that Portugal was in a better position to initiate expansion than any other country; other factors that might help explain why Portugal led in overseas expansion.*

The expansion of Europe was an intensely nationalistic phenomenon. It was an aspect of the trend, most evident in the late fifteenth and early sixteenth centuries, toward the establishment of strong centralized authority in the "new monarchies," as they have been called, and the emergence of the nation-state. A policy of overseas expansion required a degree of internal stability and national conscious-ness that only a powerful central government could command. Portugal achieved this position long before her eventual competitors, and under the leadership of the dynamic house of Avis became a consolidated kingdom comparatively free from feudal divisions before the end of the fifteenth century. While Spain was still divided into a number of conflicting political jurisdictions, England and France

SOURCE: Richard B. Reed, "The Expansion of Europe," in *The Meaning of the Renaissance and Reformation*, ed. Richard L. DeMolen (Boston: Houghton Mifflin, 1974), p. 299. Reprinted by permission.

were preoccupied with their own and each other's affairs, and the Dutch were still an appendage of the Empire, the Portuguese combined the advantages of their natural geographic situation with their political and economic stability to initiate the age of discovery. Spain in the sixteenth century, and England, France, and the Netherlands in the seventeenth century, became active colonial powers only after each had matured into strong national entities, independent of feudal political and economic restrictions. . . .

The importance of the nation-state in Renaissance expansion is particularly apparent when the Italian city-states are considered. Venice and Genoa, cities that had contributed so many of the medieval travelers and early Renaissance geographers and mapmakers, did not participate directly in Europe's overseas expansion. Yet Italian names dominated the rolls of the early voyagers. Prince Henry employed Venetians and Florentines in his naval establishment, while Columbus, Vespucci, Verrazano, the Cabots, and many others sailed for Spain, France, and England. Italian cartography was the best in Europe until the second half of the sixteenth century, and a high proportion of the books and pamphlets that chronicled new discoveries emanated from the presses of Vicenza, Venice, Rome, and Florence. Italian bankers and merchants were also very active in the commercial life of the principal Iberian cities. A divided Italy was instrumental in making Renaissance expansion possible, but it could not take full advantage of its own endowments. Germans, too, figured prominently in the expansion of the sixteenth century, as the names of Federmann, Staden, Welser, and Fugger attest. But Germany, like Italy, was not united, and the emergence of these two nations as colonial powers had to wait until their respective consolidations in the nineteenth century.

While every nationality in Western Europe was represented in Renaissance expansion, it was by no means an international venture. On the contrary, it was very much an expression of that nationalistic fervor that characterized political developments in the fifteenth and sixteenth centuries. It was primarily a state enterprise, often financed privately but controlled and protected by the governments of the concerned powers. There was no cooperation between nations, and even after the upheaval of the Protestant Reformation, when political loyalties and alignments were conditioned by religious sympathies, there were no colonial alliances that provided for mutual Protestant or Catholic overseas policies.

The Changing Ecology of New England

William Cronon

Along with new habits, technologies and cultures, Europeans brought entirely new economic systems to New England. Together, these dramatically affected the environment of both the Native Americans and the colonists. We tend to think of ecological damage as being a product of twentieth century industrialism. In this excerpt, William Cronon summarizes the changes that New England underwent in the first two hundred years of contact between colonists and Native Americans. Both groups changed the "natural" environment. Significantly, he does not see all these changes as being beneficial or even benign.

> **Consider:** *Cronon's view that Americans, in addition to being "the people of plenty, were a people of waste"; the significance of ecological changes.*

New England in 1800 was far different from the land the earliest European visitors had described. By 1800, the Indians who had been its first human inhabitants were reduced to a small fraction of their former numbers, and had been forced onto less and less desirable agricultural lands. Their ability to move about the landscape in search of ecological abundance had become severely constrained, so that their earlier ways of interacting with the environment were no longer feasible and their earlier sources of food were less easy to find. Disease and malnutrition had become facts of life for them.

Large areas particularly of southern New England were now devoid of animals which had once been common: beaver, deer, bear, turkey, wolf, and others had vanished. In their place were hordes of European grazing animals which constituted a heavier burden on New England plants and soils. Their presence had brought hundreds of miles of fences. With fences had come the weeds: dandelion and rat alike joined alien grasses as they made their way across the landscape. New England's forests still exceeded its cleared land in 1800, but, especially near settled areas, the remaining forest had been significantly altered by grazing, burning, and cutting. The greatest of the oaks and white pines were gone, and cedar had become scarce. Hickory had been reduced because of its attractiveness as a fuel. Clear-cutting had shifted forest composition in favor of those trees that were capable of sprouting from stumps, with the result that the forests of 1800 were physically smaller than they had been at the time of European settlement. The cutting of upland species such as beech and maple, which were accustomed to moist sites, produced drying that encouraged species such as the oaks, which preferred drier soils.

Deforestation had in general affected the region by making local temperatures more erratic, soils drier, and drainage patterns less constant. A number of smaller streams and springs no longer flowed year-round, and some larger rivers were dammed and no longer accessible to the fish which had once spawned in them. Water and wind erosion were taking place with varyng severity, and flooding had become more common. Soil exhaustion was occurring in many areas as a result of poor husbandry, and the first of many European pests and crop diseases had already begun to appear. These changes had taken place primarily in the settled areas, and it was still possible to find extensive regions in the north where they did not apply. Nevertheless, they heralded the future. . . .

The implications of this . . . ecological contradiction stretched well beyond the colonial period. Although we often tend to associate ecological changes primarily with the cities and factories of the nineteenth and twentieth centuries, it should by now be clear that changes with similar roots took place just as profoundly in the farms and countrysides of the colonial period. The transition to capitalism alienated the products of the land as much as the products of human labor, and so transformed natural communities as profoundly as it did human ones. By integrating New England ecosystems into an ultimately global capitalist economy, colonists and Indians together began a dynamic and unstable process of ecological change which had in no way ended by 1800. We live with their legacy today. When the geographer Carl Sauer wrote in the twentieth century that Americans had "not yet learned the difference between yield and loot," he was describing one of the most longstanding tendencies of their way of life. Ecological abundance and economic prodigality went hand in hand: the people of plenty were a people of waste.

China's Response to the West
John K. Fairbank and Ssu-yu Teng

At first China welcomed Europeans. The Chinese view was that their civilization was superior and non-Chinese had been coming for centuries looking to acquire aspects of this superior culture. The Europeans, the Chinese believed, were just the latest of these visitors. What the Chinese discovered, however, was that these travelers were different. They believed their own civilization was better and brought technologically advanced goods to prove it. Moreover they tried to convert the Chinese to Christianity, to Europeanize them, and to trade with them as equals. All this confused the Chinese court.

While the earliest Portuguese arrivals did not endear themselves to the Chinese, the Jesuits, particularly Matteo Ricci who became an advisor to the Emperor, respected and incorporated Confucian practices into Christian belief in a strategy designed to make

SOURCE: Ssu-yu Teng and John K. Fairbank, *Response to the West*, Cambridge, Mass.: Harvard University Press, Copyright © 1954, 1979 by the President and Fellows of Harvard College, © renewed 1982. Reprinted by permission.

conversion to Christianity appealing to the Chinese elite. Other orders, the Dominicans for example, opposed any dilution of Christian beliefs and the opposing factions contested their views in the Vatican. This struggle came to be known as the Rites Controversy which the Jesuits ultimately lost, leading to the expulsion of all missionaries from China.

This reading is by two of the more prominent American historians of China, John K. Fairbank and Ssu-yu Teng, and explores how the Chinese officials met these early European challenges and what influences these Europeans left in their wake.

> **Consider:** *What it was about these new Europeans that made the Chinese uncomfortable and why; how Westerners influenced China; why that influence was not greater.*

The first extensive cultural contact between China and Europe began near the end of the sixteenth century, when the Jesuit missionaries, in the wake of the Portuguese, reached China by sea. Their dual function is well known: they not only diffused Western ideas in China, including elements of mathematics, astronomy, geography, hydraulics, the calendar, and the manufacture of cannon, but they also introduced Chinese (particularly Confucian) ideas into Europe. The Jesuits found it easier to influence China's science than her religion. Perceiving this, they used their scientific knowledge as a means of approach to Chinese scholars. Although a small number of their Chinese converts took part in the translation and compilation of religious and scientific books, the majority of the native scholars, entrenched in their ethnocentric cultural tradition, were not seriously affected by the new elements of Western thought. . . .

. . . [T]he immediate Jesuit influence in China was through items of practical significance, such as cannon, the calendar, or Ricci's map of the world. Why is so little trace of Christian doctrine to be found in the writings of Chinese scholars in the subsequent century? If this is to be explained by the fact that government suppression cut off contact and the relatively few professed converts had few successors, we still face the question why the minds of the non-Christian scholars were not more permanently influenced by Western knowledge or ideas. . . .

Opposition to the Jesuits and other Western missionaries was motivated partly by the xenophobic suspicion that foreigners were spies; partly by ethical scruples against Christian religious ceremonies which seemed contrary to Chinese customs such as the veneration of Heaven, ancestors and Confucius; and partly by professional jealousy, on the assumption that if Catholicism were to become prevalent in China, the decline of the doctrines of Confucius, Buddha, and Lao-tzu would damage the position of their protagonists. . . .

The Chinese Buddhist leadership appears to have been vehemently anti-Catholic. Meanwhile most Chinese scholars remained dogmatically opposed to the Westerners' religion. Lacking enthusiasm for their religion, they also disliked their science. . . . The conservatives objected to Western scientific instruments, arguing that clocks were expensive but useless, that cannon could not annihilate enemies but usually burned the gunners first, and that on Ricci's map of the globe China was not in the very center and was not large enough. They also objected to Western painting because it lacked forceful strokes. . . .

Behind all this condemnation of Western learning lay the basic political fact that the Manchu rulers of China could not tolerate the propagation of a foreign religion which asserted the spiritual supremacy of Rome over Peking. By 1640 Japan, under the Tokugawa, had proscribed Christianity and foreign contact (except for the Dutch in Nagasaki) as politically dangerous. In China by the end of the seventeenth century there were Catholic congregations in all but two of the provinces; the Roman Catholic faith was banned in the Yongzheng (Yung-cheng) period (1723–1735). . . .

All in all, the residual influence of the Western technology made available to China through the early missionaries seems to have been rather slight. Even when present, it was seldom acknowledged. Meanwhile an anti-Western political tradition had become well established.

The Closing of Japan
G. B. Sansom

In 1640, Japan deported all Europeans (except a handful of Dutch traders restricted to the island of Deshima in Nagasaki Bay) and forbid Japanese from leaving the country. There were also widespread persecutions of Japanese Christians. This has often been portrayed as a case of religious persecution. While it was certainly that, there were other factors as well. The reading which follows is from noted British Japanologist G. B. Sansom. Here he argues that the expulsion of Christianity from Japan was a political, rather than a religious, affair.

> **Consider:** *The motives, according to Sansom, for the anti-Christian acts; how missionary activity might be related to economic, military, and political activity.*

It will be seen that here was no consistent antagonism to a foreign creed, but a variable attitude based upon political grounds. . . . [T]he successes and failures of the Roman Catholic Church in India, China, and Japan have been closely related to the degree of political support that in the estimate of those countries was enjoyed by the missionaries. It is reasons such as these that best explain the apparent vacillations and inconsistencies of the Japanese ruling class in their treatment of Christian propaganda during the period we have been considering.

The action taken by Japan against Christianity cannot be considered separately from the exclusion policy to which it was a prelude. . . . [T]he anti-Christian edict of 1616 was inspired in part at least by fear of Spanish intervention in the domestic

SOURCE: George B. Sansom, *The Western World and Japan. A Study in the Interaction of European and Asiatic Culture* (1950), pp. 177–179.

affairs of Japan. The edict was re-enacted in 1624 because the Shogun had further grounds for suspecting Spain, or at any rate the Spanish in the Philippines, of aggressive designs; and this new edict was accompanied not only by the expulsion of all Spaniards but also by the stoppage of overseas travel by Japanese. The door was gradually being closed to both ingress and egress. The Shimabara rising that began in 1637 evidently caused further misgivings to the Shogunate, for it was followed in 1638 by the expulsion of all Portuguese, whether priests or traders. At the same time the prohibition of foreign travel was strengthened by imposing the death penalty on any Japanese who should attempt to leave the country or, having left it, should return. This embargo was extended to foreign trade by a law that forbade the building of any ship of more than 2,500 bushels' capacity and consequently prevented ocean voyages. Thus Japan deliberately cut herself off from intercourse with other nations rather than face the dangers it involved. In the history of relations between Europe and Asia this was the most decided rejection ever given by an Asiatic people to an approach by the Western world. . . .

. . . It is at first sight hard to understand why the Asiatic people who gave Europeans the most friendly welcome should have also given them the most violent dismissal. . . . It was clearly not due to a peculiar distaste for foreign intercourse, since that was resumed with remarkable alacrity once the country was reopened at a later date. It is true that, since the civilization of Japan was self-contained and her economy self-supporting, there was no compelling reason for cultural or commercial exchanges; and conservative sentiment, in Japan as in other countries, was naturally opposed to foreign influences, because to most people what is foreign is also disturbing. But the intense distrust which drove the Tokugawa shoguns to close their doors arose from no ordinary conservatism. They were moved by fear, and fear not of the contamination of national customs . . . but rather of domestic uprising against themselves.

By 1615 Ieyasu, the first Tokugawa Shogun, had after long struggle imposed the authority of his family upon all his feudal rivals. But neither he nor his successors felt entirely secure for several decades, and it was a cardinal feature of their policy to take every possible precaution against rebellion by one or more of the still powerful western feudatories. . . .

In 1637 the Tokugawa government had good reason to fear that one or [an]other of these great families might conspire with foreigners—Spanish, Portuguese, or Dutch—trade with them for firearms, get their help in procuring artillery and ships, and even call upon them for military or naval support. The leaders of the ruling house, firmly estabished as it was, did not feel strong enough to face this risk; and they took steps to remove it by closing the country to foreign influence, so far as that was possible.

The Effects of Expansion on the Non-European World

M. L. Bush

While the expansion of Europe was of great significance for European history, it was of even greater consequence for the non-European world touched by the explorers. However, its effects differed greatly in the New World, where the Spanish dominated, and the East, where the Portuguese were the leaders. In the following selection, M. L. Bush analyzes these differences.

> **Consider:** *Internal factors in non-Western societies that help explain these differences; contrasts between Portugal and Spain that help explain the different consequences for non-Western societies.*

The Castilian Empire in the West and the Portuguese Empire in the East had very different effects upon the world outside of Europe. In the first place, the Castilian expansion westwards precipitated a series of overseas migrations which were unparalleled in earlier times. For most of the sixteenth century, 1,000 or 2,000 Spaniards settled in the New World each year. Later this was followed by a large wave of emigrants from northwestern Europe, fleeing from persecution at home to the Atlantic sea-board of North America and the Caribbean, and a final wave of Africans forced into slavery in the West Indies and in Brazil. On the other hand, in the East, there was virtually no settlement in the sixteenth century. Europe impressed itself only by fort, factory and church, by colonial official, trader and missionary.

In the second place, the settlement of the New World had a severe effect upon native peoples, whereas in the East, European influence was very slight until much later times.

In the early 1520s, the conquistadors brought with them smallpox and typhoid. Between them these European diseases soon decimated the Indian population, particularly in the great epidemics of the 1520s, 1540s and 1570s. In central Mexico, for example, an Indian population which numbered 11,000,000 in 1519 numbered no more than 2,500,000 by the end of the century. In addition, the Indian was beset by enormous grazing herds of horned cattle which the white settler introduced. He escaped the herds by working for the white settler, but if this led him to the crowded labour settlements, as it quite often did, he stood less chance of escaping infection. Either through falling hopelessly in debt as a result of desiring the goods of the white man, or through entering the labour settlements on a permanent basis to avoid the herds and also the system of obligatory labour

---

SOURCE: M. L. Bush, *Renaissance, Reformation and the Outer World* (New York: Harper & Row, 1967), pp. 143–145. London: Blanford Press, Ltd., 1967.

introduced by the Spaniard,[1] there was a strong tendency for the Indian to become europeanised. He became a wage-earner, a debtor and a Christian. The Indian was exploited. But in the law he remained free. Enslavement was practised, but it was not officially tolerated. Moreover, the Franciscan order, a powerful missionary force in the New World, did its best to save the Indian from the evil ways of the white man. In Barthlomew de Las Casas and Francisco de Vitoria, the Indian found influential defenders; and through their schemes for separate Indian Christian communities, he found a partial escape from the white man. But the Indian mission towns, which were permitted by Charles V, were objected to by his successor, Philip II, and they only survived in remote areas.

With few exceptions, the way of life of the surviving Indians was basically changed by the coming of the white man. The outstanding exception was in Portuguese Brazil where the more primitive, nomadic Indians had a greater opportunity to retreat into the bush. There was also less settlement in Brazil, and generally less impression was made because of Portuguese preoccupations elsewhere, and also because of their lack of resources for empire-building on the Spanish scale. Furthermore, within the Spanish Empire, the European impressed himself less on the Incas in Peru than upon the Aztecs in Mexico. Because of the slow subjection of Peru, several Inca risings, the nature of the terrain, the smallness of the Spanish community, the process of europeanisation was much slower, and in the long run much less complete. The remnants of the Inca aristocracy became Spanish in their habits and Catholic in their religion, but the peasantry tended to remain pagan. In contrast to these developments, the westernisation of the East was a development of more modern times.

The West impinged upon the East in the sixteenth century mainly through the missionary. With the arrival of St. Francis Xavier in 1542 in India, an impressive process of conversion was begun. Concentrating upon the poor fishermen of the Cape Comorin coast, within ten years he had secured, it was said, 60,000 converts. The Jesuits fixed their attention on the East, choosing Goa as their main headquarters outside of Rome. Little was accomplished in Malaya, Sumatra and China in the sixteenth century, and Christianity soon suffered setbacks in the Moluccas after a promising start, but in Ceylon the conversion of the young king of Kotte in 1557 was a signal triumph, and so were the conversions in Japan. In the 1580s Jesuit missionaries in Japan claimed to have converted 150,000, most of whom, however, were inhabitants of the island of Kyushu.

Christianity was not a new religion in the East. There were extensive communities of Nestorian Christians, but they were regarded as alien as the Muslim by the Europeans. The new Christians by 1583 were supposed to number 600,000. But compared with the expansion of Islam in the East—a process which was taking place at the same time—the expansion of Christianity was a minute achievement.

---

[1] This system depended upon every Indian village offering a proportion of its menfolk or labour service for a limited amount of time throughout the year.

Finally, the Portuguese sea empire did little to transport Portuguese habits abroad. Their empire was essentially formed in response to local conditions. On the other hand, the Spanish land empire was to a much greater extent reflective of Castilian ways.

In the New World a carefully developed and regulated system of government was established in which it was seen that the care taken to limit the independent power of feudal aristocrats in the Old World should also be applied to the New. There was a firm insistence upon government officials being royal servants. However, the government of the New World became much more regulated from the centre than that of the old. There was less respect for aristocratic privilege. Less power was unreservedly placed in the hands of the nobility. In the New World, in fact, the weaknesses of government, at first, did not lie in the powers and privileges of the nobility but rather in the cumbersome nature of the government machinery. Nevertheless, in spite of these precautions, the New World, by the early seventeenth century, had become a land of great feudal magnates enjoying, in practice, untrammelled power.

Chapter Questions

1. Analyze the motives for the European expansion and the forces that stimulated and enabled the Europeans to carry out this expansion.
2. Compare the consequences of the new encounters in Asia, Africa, and the Americas. How do you explain the differences?
3. Drawing on the sources in this and the previous chapter, discuss what the observations made by Europeans tell us about the Europeans themselves and their own societies in addition to the societies they are observing.

TWO

Europe's Early Modern Era, 1500–1789

The Renaissance and the overseas expansion of Europe were two signs that Western civilization was emerging from the Middle Ages into a new era, stretching from the sixteenth to the eighteenth century, which Western historians have come to call Early Modern. There were several other signs. New monarchs created powerful national states that would endure for centuries. These states benefited from and took advantage of new economic developments such as the growth of commerce and the spread of capitalistic practices. The aristocracy, though still socially and culturally dominant, underwent internal changes and was challenged by a new middle class of merchants and entrepreneurs. The Roman Catholic Church, in decline during the last two centuries of the Middle Ages, was split apart by the Protestant Reformation. New ideas and ways of thinking about the world and the human condition led to the intellectual revolutions known as the Scientific Revolution and the Enlightenment.

In this chapter we will focus on three of these developments. The first is the Reformation. Initiated in 1517 by Martin Luther's challenges to official Church doctrine and papal authority, the Reformation spread in Germany, northern Europe, and other parts of Europe during the sixteenth century. The passion involved in the Reformation and the historical significance of this division in the western Christian Church have made the Reformation the object of intensive study. Here we will focus on the nature and appeal of the Protestant challenge and the Catholic response, the much debated question of causes, and the possible significance of the Reformation.

The second development is the rise of early modern political institutions. Emphasis will be on the competition over the source and exercise of political power—both in theory and in practice. Here the conflict was usually between monarchs and the nobility or, particularly in England, between royal and parliamentary authority. This will lead us to examine connections between political struggle, economic policy, and religious conflict. Additionally, some developments in intellectual history will be touched on, particularly as they relate to political theory.

The third development is the nature of Early Modern society. Although wars, economic development, and urbanization were forces of change, the structure of society changed little during these centuries. At the base of society were commoners—mostly the peasantry—and at the top was the still dominant aristocracy. Sources in this chapter will examine these groups as well as the Early Modern family and the position of women.

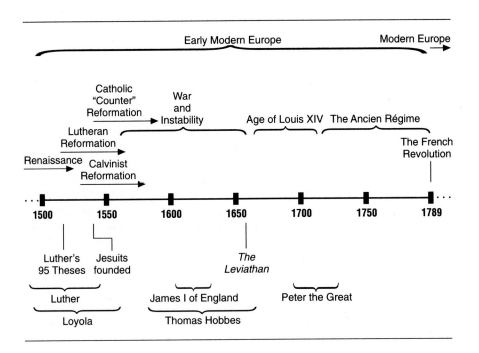

PRIMARY SOURCES

Justification by Faith
Martin Luther

The early leader of the Reformation was Martin Luther (1483–1546). Born in Germany to a wealthy peasant family, Luther became an Augustinian monk and a professor of theology at the University of Wittenberg. While at this post in 1517, he became involved in the indulgence problem with Tetzel and issued rather academic challenges in his ninety-five theses. News of this act quickly spread, and a major controversy developed. Although originally intending to stimulate only modest reforms within the Catholic Church, Luther soon found himself espousing doctrines markedly differing from those authorized by the Church and taking actions that eventually resulted in his expulsion from the Church.

Luther himself attributed his spiritual evolution to certain crucial experiences. The most important of these was his first formulation of the doctrines of "justification by faith," which constituted the core of his beliefs and much of the basis for Protestantism. In the following excerpts from his autobiographical writings, Luther describes this experience.

> **Consider:** *What Luther meant by "justification by faith"; why this doctrine might have been so appealing to many Catholics; why this doctrine might have been threatening to the Catholic Church.*

I greatly longed to understand Paul's Epistle to the Romans and nothing stood in the way but that one expression, "the justice of God," because I took it to mean that justice whereby God is just and deals justly in punishing the unjust. My situation was that, although an impeccable monk, I stood before God as a sinner troubled in conscience, and I had no confidence that my merit would assuage him. Therefore I did not love a just and angry God, but rather hated and murmured against Him. Yet I clung to the dear Paul and had a great yearning to know what he meant.

Night and day I pondered until I saw the connection between the justice of God and the statement that "the just shall live by his faith." Then I grasped that the justice of God is that righteousness by which through grace and sheer mercy God justifies us through faith. Thereupon I felt myself to be reborn and to have gone through open doors into paradise. The whole of Scripture took on a new meaning, and whereas before the "justice of God" had filled me with hate, now it became to me inexpressibly sweet in greater love. This passage of Paul became to me a gate to heaven. . . .

SOURCE: From Roland H. Bainton, *The Age of Reformation* (New York: D. Van Nostrand Co., Inc., 1956), pp. 97–98. Reprinted by permission.

If you have a true faith that Christ is your Saviour, then at once you have a gracious God, for faith leads you in and opens up God's heart and will, that you should see pure grace and overflowing love. This it is to behold God in faith that you should look upon His fatherly, friendly heart, in which there is no anger nor ungraciousness. He who sees God as angry does not see Him rightly but looks only on a curtain, as if a dark cloud had been drawn across his face.

Constitution of the Society of Jesus

The Catholic Church was not passive in the face of the challenges from Protestant reform-ers. In a variety of ways the Church reformed itself from within and took the offensive against Protestants in doctrine and deed. Probably the most effective weapons of the Catholic Counter Reformation was the Society of Jesus (the Jesuits) founded by Ignatius Loyola (1491–1556). Loyola, a soldier who had turned to the religious life while recover-ing from wounds, attracted a group of highly disciplined followers who offered their ser-vices to the pope. In 1540, the pope formally accepted their offer. The Jesuits became an arm of the Church in combating Protestantism, spreading Catholicism to foreign lands and gaining influence within Catholic areas of Europe. The following is an excerpt from the Constitution of the Society of Jesus, approved by Pope Paul III in 1540.

Consider: *The characteristics of this organization that help explain its success; how, in tone and content, this document differs from Luther's document.*

He who desires to fight for God under the banner of the cross in our society,— which we wish to distinguish by the name of Jesus,—and to serve God alone and the Roman pontiff, his vicar on earth, after a solemn vow of perpetual chastity, shall set this thought before his mind, that he is a part of a society founded for the especial purpose of providing for the advancement of souls in Christian life and doctrine and for the propagation of faith through public preaching and the ministry of the word of God, spiritual exercises and deeds of charity, and in particular through the training of the young and ignorant in Christianity and through the spiritual consolation of the faithful of Christ in hearing confessions; and he shall take care to keep first God and next the purpose of this organization always before his eyes. . . .

All the members shall realize, and shall recall daily, as long as they live, that this society as a whole and in every part is fighting for God under faithful obedience to one most holy lord, the pope, and to the other Roman pontiffs who succeed him. And although we are taught in the gospel and through the orthodox faith to recognize and steadfastly profess that all the faithful of Christ are subject to the Roman pontiff as their head and as the vicar of Jesus Christ, yet we have adjudged

SOURCE: James Harvey Robinson, ed., *Readings in European History*, vol. II (Boston: Ginn, 1904), pp. 162–163.

that, for the special promotion of greater humility in our society and the perfect mortification of every individual and the sacrifice of our own wills, we should each be bound by a peculiar vow, in addition to the general obligation, that whatever the present Roman pontiff, or any future one, may from time to time decree regarding the welfare of souls and the propagation of the faith, we are pledged to obey without evasion or excuse, instantly, so far as in us lies, whether he send us to the Turks or any other infidels, even to those who inhabit the regions men call the Indies; whether to heretics or schismatics, or, on the other hand, to certain of the faithful.

The Powers of the Monarch in England
James I

Turmoil, instability, and war (often civil war) characterized much of the period between the mid-sixteenth and mid-seventeenth centuries. In England, friction between the monarchy and Parliament increased under the Stuart kings, starting with James I. Already the Scottish monarch, James became King of England on the death of Elizabeth in 1603. James had a scholarly background and a reputation for his strong views about the monarchy. One of his clearest presentations of these views was in a speech to Parliament made in 1610. In it, he comments on the nature of the king's power, not simply in England but everywhere.

Consider: *How James justifies the high position and vast powers he feels should rightly belong to kings; the limits to monarchical powers.*

The state of Monarchy is the supremest thing upon earth; for kings are not only God's lieutenants upon earth and sit upon God's throne, but even by God himself they are called gods. There be three principal similitudes that illustrate the state of Monarchy: one taken out of the Word of God and the other two out of the grounds of policy and philosophy. In the Scriptures kings are called gods, and so their power after a certain relation compared to the Divine power. Kings are also compared to the fathers of families, for a king is truly *parens patriae*, the politic father of his people. And lastly, kings are compared to the head of his microcosm of the body of man.

Kings are justly called gods for that they exercise a manner or resemblance of Divine power upon earth; for if you will consider the attributes to God you shall see how they agree in the person of a king. God hath power to create or destroy, make or unmake, at his pleasure; to give life or send death; to judge all, and to be judged nor accomptable to none; to raise low things and to make high things low

SOURCE: From J. R. Tanner, *Constitutional Documents of the Reign of James I, A.D. 1603–1625* (Cambridge, England: Cambridge University Press, 1930), pp. 15–16. Reprinted by permission.

at his pleasure; and to God are both soul and body due. And the like power have kings; they make and unmake their subjects; they have power of raising and casting down; of life and death; judges over all their subjects and in all causes, and yet accomptable to none but God only. They have power to exalt low things and abase high things, and make of their subjects like men at the chess, a pawn to take a bishop or a knight, and to cry up or down any of their subjects as they do their money. And to the King is due both the affection of the soul and the service of the body of his subjects. . . .

As for the father of a family, they had of old under the Law of Nature *patriam potestatem,* which was *potestatem vitae et necis,* over their children or family, (I mean such fathers of families as were the lineal heirs of those families whereof kings did originally come), for kings had their first original from them who planted and spread themselves in colonies through the world. Now a father may dispose of his inheritance to his children at his pleasure, yea, even disinherit the eldest upon just occasions and prefer the youngest, according to his liking; make them beggars or rich at his pleasure; restrain or banish out of his presence, as he finds them give cause of offence, or restore them in favour again with the penitent sinner. So may the King deal with his subjects.

And lastly, as for the head of the natural body, the head hath the power of directing all the members of the body to that use which the judgment in the head think most convenient. . . .

The Powers of Parliament in England
The House of Commons

James's views on monarchical powers were not accepted by members of Parliament. Indeed, from the beginnng of his reign through the reign of his son Charles I, king and Parliament struggled over their relative powers. Along with other problems, this struggle culminated in the 1640s with the outbreak of civil war and the eventual beheading of Charles I. The nature of this struggle is partially revealed in the following statements issued by the House of Commons in 1604 to the new king, James I.

> **Consider:** *The powers over which the House of Commons and the king differed; the justifications used by James I and the House of Commons for their claims; any ways in which compromise was possible between these two positions.*

Now concerning the ancient rights of the subjects of this realm, chiefly consisting in the privileges of this House of Parliament, the misinformation openly delivered to your Majesty hath been in three things:

Source: From J. R. Tanner, *Constitutional Documents of the Reign of James I, A.D. 1603–1625* (Cambridge, England: Cambridge University Press, 1930), pp. 220–222. Reprinted by permission.

First, That we held not privileges of right, but of grace only, renewed every Parliament by way of donature upon petition, and so to be limited.

Second, That we are no Court of Record, nor yet a Court that can command view of records, but that our proceedings here are only to acts and memorials, and that the attendance with the records is courtesy, not duty.

Thirdly and lastly, That the examination of the return of writs for knights and burgesses is without our compass, and due to the Chancery.

Against which assertions, most gracious Sovereign, tending directly and apparently to the utter overthrow of the very fundamental privileges of our House, and therein of the rights and liberties of the whole Commons of your realm of England which they and their ancestors from time immemorable have undoubtedly enjoyed under your Majesty's most noble progenitors, we, the knights, citizens, and burgesses of the House of Commons assembled in Parliament, and in the name of the whole commons of the realm of England, with uniform consent for ourselves and our posterity, do expressly protest, as being derogatory in the highest degree to the true dignity, liberty, and authority of your Majesty's High Court of Parliament, and consequently to the rights of all your Majesty's said subjects and the whole body of this your kingdom: And desire that this our protestation may be recorded to all posterity.

And contrariwise, with all humble and due respect to your Majesty our Sovereign Lord and Head, against those misinformations we most truly avouch,

First, That our privileges and liberties are our right and due inheritance, no less than our very lands and goods.

Secondly, That they cannot be withheld from us, denied, or impaired, but with apparent wrong to the whole state of the realm.

Thirdly, And that our making of request in the entrance of Parliament to enjoy our privilege is an act only of manners, and doth weaken our right no more than our suing to the King for our lands by petition. . . .

Fourthly, We avouch also, That our House is a Court of Record, and so ever esteemed.

Fifthly, That there is not the highest standing Court in this land that ought to enter into competency, either for dignity or authority, with this High Court of Parliament, which with your Majesty's royal assent gives laws to other Courts but from other Courts receives neither laws nor orders.

Sixthly and lastly, We avouch that the House of Commons is the sole proper judge of return of all such writs and of the election of all such members as belong to it, without which the freedom of election were not entire: And that the Chancery, though a standing Court under your Majesty, be to send out those writs and receive the returns and to preserve them, yet the same is done only for the use of the Parliament, over which neither the Chancery nor any other Court ever had or ought to have any manner of jurisdiction.

From these misinformed positions, most gracious Sovereign, the greatest part of our troubles, distrusts, and jealousies have risen. . . .

Austria Over All If She Only Will: Mercantilism
Philipp W. von Hornick

Mercantilism, a loose set of economic ideas and corresponding government policies, was a common component of political absolutism during the seventeenth century. Typical mercantilist goals were the acquisition of bullion, a positive balance of trade, and economic self-sufficiency. An unusually clear and influential statement of mercantilist policies was published in 1684 by Philipp Wilhelm von Hornick. A lawyer and later a government official, Hornick set down what he considered to be the nine principal rules for a proper economic policy. These are excerpted here.

> **Consider:** *The political and military purposes served by encouraging mercantilist policies; the foreign policy decisions such economic policies would support; the political and economic circumstances that would make it easiest for a country to adhere to and benefit from mercantilist policies.*

NINE PRINCIPAL RULES OF NATIONAL ECONOMY

If the might and eminence of a country consist in its surplus of gold, silver, and all other things necessary or convenient for its *subsistence,* derived, so far as possible, from its own resources, without *dependence* upon other countries, and in the proper fostering, use, and application of these, then it follows that a general national *economy* (*Landes-Oeconomie*) should consider how such a surplus, fostering, and enjoyment can be brought about, without *dependence* upon others, or where this is not feasible in every respect, with as little *dependence* as possible upon foreign countries, and sparing use of the country's own cash. For this purpose the following nine rules are especially serviceable.

First, to inspect the country's soil with the greatest care, and not to leave the agricultural possibilities or a single corner or clod of earth unconsidered. Every useful form of *plant* under the sun should be experimented with, to see whether it is adapted to the country, for the distance or nearness of the sun is not all that counts. Above all, no trouble or expense should be spared to discover gold and silver.

Second, all commodities found in a country, which cannot be used in their natural state, should be worked up within the country; since the payment for *manufacturing* generally exceeds the value of the raw material by two, three, ten, twenty, and even a hundred fold, and the neglect of this is an abomination to prudent managers.

SOURCE: Philipp W. von Hornick, "Austria Over All If She Only Will," in Arthur Eli Monroe, ed., *Early Economic Thought*. Reprinted by permission of Harvard University Press (Cambridge, Mass., 1927), pp. 223–225. Copyright © 1924 by The President and Fellows of Harvard College.

Third, for carrying out the above two rules, there will be need of people, both for producing and cultivating the raw materials and for working them up. Therefore, attention should be given to the population, that it may be as large as the country can support, this being a well-ordered state's most important concern, but, unfortunately, one that is often neglected. And the people should be turned by all possible means from idleness to remunerative *professions;* instructed and encouraged in all kinds of *inventions,* arts, and trades; and, if necessary, instructors should be brought in from foreign countries for this.

Fourth, gold and silver once in the country, whether from its own mines or obtained by *industry* from foreign countries, are under no circumstances to be taken out for any purpose, so far as possible, or allowed to be buried in chests or coffers, but must always remain in *cirulation;* nor should much be permitted in uses where they are at once *destroyed* and cannot be utilized again. For under these conditions, it will be impossible for a country that has once acquired a considerable supply of cash, especially one that possesses gold and silver mines, ever to sink into poverty; indeed, it is impossible that it should not continually increase in wealth and property. Therefore,

Fifth, the inhabitants of the country should make every effort to get along with their domestic products, to confine their luxury to these alone, and to do without foreign products as far as possible (except where great need leaves no alternative, or if not need, wide-spread, unavoidable abuse, of which Indian spices are an example). And so on.

Sixth, in case the said purchases were indispensable because of necessity or *irremediable* abuse, they should be obtained from these foreigners at first hand, so far as possible, and not for gold or silver, but in exchange for other domestic wares.

Seventh, such foreign commodities should in this case be imported in unfinished form, and worked up within the country, thus earning the wages of *manufacture* there.

Eighth, opportunities should be sought night and day for selling the country's superfluous goods to these foreigners in manufactured form, so far as this is necessary, and for gold and silver; and to this end, *consumption,* so to speak, must be sought in the farthest ends of the earth, and developed in every possible way.

Ninth, except for important considerations, no importation should be allowed under any circumstances of commodities of which there is sufficient supply of suitable quality at home; and in this matter neither sympathy nor compassion should be shown foreigners, be they friends, kinsfolk, *allies,* or enemies. For all friendship ceases, when it involves my own weakness and ruin. And this holds good, even if the domestic commodities are of poorer quality, or even higher priced. For it would be better to pay for an article two dollars which remain in the country than only one which goes out, however strange this may seem to the ill-informed.

Decree on the Invitation of Foreigners

Peter the Great

Russia stood on the eastern edge of Europe and spread well into Asia. By the sixteenth century, Russia had expelled the Mongols and begun a vast expansion. A century later the Russian Empire extended to the Pacific, but ambitious tsars continued to feel thwarted in their efforts to expand Russia westward. Many people perceived Russia to be behind technological and other developments occurring farther west in Europe. Tsar Peter the Great (1682–1725) was one of those who called for Russia to adopt certain western European institutions and practices. This is illustrated in the Decree on the Invitation of Foreigners, issued in 1702.

> **Consider:** *How Peter is trying to promote changes in Russia; Peter's motives for the changes he wants; problems Peter anticipates in getting people to accept foreigners.*

It is sufficiently known in all the lands which the Almighty has placed under our rule, that since our accession to the throne all our efforts and intentions have tended to govern this realm in such a way that all of our subjects should, through our care for the general good, become more and more prosperous. For this end we have always tried to maintain internal order, to defend the State against invasion, and in every possible way to improve and to extend trade. With this purpose we have been compelled to make some necessary and salutary changes in the administration, in order that our subjects might more easily gain a knowledge of matters of which they were before ignorant, and become more skillful in their commercial relations. We have therefore given orders, made dispositions, and founded institutions indispensable for increasing our trade with foreigners, and shall do the same in future. Nevertheless, we fear that matters are not in such a good condition as we desire, and that our subjects cannot in perfect quietness enjoy the fruits of our labors, and we have therefore considered still other means to protect our frontier from the invasion of the enemy, and to preserve the rights and privileges of our State, and the general peace of all Christians, as is incumbent on a Christian monarch to do. To attain these worthy aims, we have endeavored to improve our military forces, which are the protection of our State, so that our troops may consist of well-drilled men, maintained in perfect order and discipline. In order to obtain greater improvement in this respect, and to encourage foreigners, who are able to assist us in this way, as well as artists and artisans profitable to the State, to come in numbers to our country, we have issued this manifesto, and have ordered printed copies of it to be sent throughout Europe. And as in our residence of Moscow, the free exercise of religion of all other sects, although

---

SOURCE: George Vernadsky, ed., *A Source Book for Russian History From Early Times to 1917* (New Haven: Yale University Press, 1972), p. 347 as excerpted.

not agreeing with our church, is already allowed, so shall this be hereby confirmed anew in such wise that we, by the power granted to us by the Almighty, shall exercise no compulsion over the consciences of men, and shall gladly allow every Christian to care for his own salvation at his own risk.

Women of the Third Estate

The vast majority of eighteenth-century Europeans were not members of the aristocracy. Over 90 percent were peasants, artisans, domestics, and laborers—often referred to in France as members of the Third Estate. While both men and women of the Third Estate shared much, women's positions and grievances often differed from those of men. Articulate records of these women's grievances are difficult to find, but the flood of formal petitions preceding the French Revoluton of 1789 provides us with some rich sources. The following is a "Petition of the Women of the Third Estate to the King," dated several months prior to the outbreak of the French Revolution.

> **Consider:** *What options seem available to women; the problems identified and solutions proposed; ways in which men's interests and women's interests might clash.*

1 January 1789. Almost all women of the Third Estate are born poor. Their education is either neglected or misconceived, for it consists in sending them to learn from teachers who do not themselves know the first word of the language they are supposed to be teaching. . . . At the age of fifteen or sixteen, girls can earn five or six sous a day. If nature has not granted them good looks, they get married, without a dowry, to unfortunate artisans and drag out a grueling existence in the depths of the provinces, producing children whom they are unable to bring up. If, on the other hand, they are born pretty, being without culture, principles, or any notion of morality, they fall prey to the first seducer, make one slip, come to Paris to conceal it, go totally to the bad here, and end up dying as victims of debauchery.

Today, when the difficulty of earning a living forces thousands of women to offer themselves to the highest bidder and men prefer buying them for a spell to winning them for good, any woman drawn to virtue, eager to educate herself, and with natural taste . . . is faced with the choice either of casting herself into a cloister which will accept a modest dowry or of going into domestic service. . . .

If old age overtakes unmarried women, they spend it in tears and as objects of contempt for their nearest relatives.

To counter such misfortunes, Sire, we ask that men be excluded from practicing those crafts that are women's prerogative, such as dressmaking, embroidery, mil-

---

SOURCE: Excerpts from *Not In God's Image* by Julia O'Faolain and Lauro Martines. Copyright © 1973 by Julia O'Faolain and Lauro Martines. Reprinted by permission of Harper & Row, Publishers, Inc.

inery, etc. Let them leave us the needle and the spindle and we pledge our word never to handle the compass or the set-square.

We ask, Sire . . . to be instructed and given jobs, not that we may usurp men's authority but so that we may have a means of livelihood, and so that the weaker among us who are dazzled by luxury and led astray by example should not be forced to join the ranks of the wretched who encumber the streets and whose lewd audacity disgraces both our sex and the men who frequent them.

VISUAL SOURCES

The Leviathan: Political Order and Political Theory
Thomas Hobbes

Although England avoided the Thirty Years' War, she had her own experiences with passionate war and disruption of authority. Between 1640 and 1660 England endured the civil war, the trial and execution of her king, Charles I, the rise to power of Oliver Cromwell, and the return to power of the Stuart king, Charles II. These events stimulated Thomas Hobbes (1588–1679) to formulate one of the most important statements of political theory in history.

Hobbes supported the royalist cause during the civil war and served as tutor to the future Charles II. Applying some of the new philosophical and scientific concepts being developed during the seventeenth century, he presented a theory for the origins and proper functioning of the state and political authority. His main ideas appear in Leviathan *(1651), the title page of which appears here. It shows a giant monarchical figure, with symbols of power and authority, presiding over a well-ordered city and surrounding lands. On close examination one can see that the monarch's body is composed of the citizens of this commonwealth who, according to Hobbes's theory, have mutually agreed to give up their independence to an all-powerful sovereign who will keep order. This is explained in the following selection from Hobbes's book, in which he relates the reasons for the formation of a commonwealth to the nature of authority in that commonwealth.*

> **Consider:** *Why men form such a commonwealth and why they give such power to the sovereign; how Hobbes's argument compares with that of James I; why both those favoring more power for the House of Commons and those favoring increased monarchical power might criticize this argument.*

Source: Thomas Hobbes, *The Leviathan*, vol. III of *The English Works of Thomas Hobbes*, ed. Sir William Molesworth (London: John Bohn, 1889), pp. 113, 151–153, 157, 159.

Photo 2-1

Whatsoever therefore is consequent to a time of war, where every man is enemy to every man; the same is consequent to the time, wherein men live without other security, than what their own strength, and their own invention shall furnish them withal. In such condition, there is no place for industry; because the fruit thereof is uncertain: and consequently no culture of the earth; no navigation, nor use of the commodities that may be imported by sea; no commodious building; no instruments of moving, and removing, such things as require much force; no knowledge of the face of the earth; no account of time; no arts; no letters; no society; and which is worst of all, continual fear, and danger of violent death; and the life of man, solitary, poor, nasty, brutish, and short. . . .

The final cause, end, or design of men who naturally love liberty, and dominion over others, in the introduction of that restraint upon themselves, in which we see them live in commonwealths, is the foresight of their own preservation, and of a more contented life thereby; that is to say, of getting themselves out from that miserable condition of war, which is necessarily consequent . . . to the natural passions of men, when there is no visible power to keep them in awe, and tie them by fear of punishment to the performance of their covenants, and observation of those laws of nature set down. . . .

For the laws of nature, as *justice, equity, modesty, mercy,* and, in sum, doing to others as we would be done to, of themselves, without the terror of some power to cause them to be observed, are contrary to our natural passions, that carry us to partiality, pride, revenge, and the like. And covenants, without the sword, are but words, and of no strength to secure a man at all. . . .

The only way to erect such a common power, as may be able to defend them from the invasion of foreigners, and the injuries of one another, and thereby to secure them in such sort, as that by their own industry, and by the fruits of the earth, they may nourish themselves and live contentedly; is, to confer all their power and strength upon one man, or upon one assembly of men, that may reduce all their wills, by plurality of voices, unto one will: which is as much as to say, to appoint one man, or assembly of men, to bear their person; and every one to own, and acknowledge himself to be author of whatsoever he that so beareth their person, shall act, or cause to be acted, in those things which concern the common peace and safety; and therein to submit their wills, every one to his will, and their judgments to his judgment. This is more than consent, or concord; it is a real unity of them all, in one and the same person, made by covenant of every man with every man, in such manner, as if every man should say to every man, *I authorise and give up my right of governing myself, to this man, or to this assembly of men, on this condition, that thou give up thy right to him, and authorise all his actions in like manner.* This done, the multitude so united in one person, is called a COMMONWEATH, . . . This is the generation of that great Leviathan, or rather, to speak more reverently, of that *mortal god,* to which we owe under the *immortal God,* our peace and defence. For by this authority, given him by every particular man in the commonwealth, he hath the use of so much power and strength conferred on him, that by terror thereof, he is enabled to perform the wills of them all, to peace at home, and mutual aid against their enemies abroad. And in him consisteth the essence of the commonwealth; which to define it, is *one person, of whose acts a great multitude, by mutual covenants one with another, have made themselves every one the author, to the end he may use the strength and means of them all, as he shall think expedient, for their peace and common defence.*

And he that carrieth this person, is called SOVEREIGN, and said to have *sovereign power;* and every one besides, his SUBJECT.

Happy Accidents of the Swing
Jean-Honoré Fragonard

The aristocracy remained dominant culturally during the Ancien Régime, commissioning most of the art of the period. It is not surprising, then, that the art reflected aristocratic values and tastes. Happy Accidents of the Swing *by Jean-Honoré Fragonard exemplifies a type of painting quite popular among France's eighteenth-century aristocracy.*

Fragonard was commissioned by Baron de Saint-Julien in 1767 to paint a picture of his mistress on a swing being pushed by a bishop who did not know that the woman was the baron's mistress, with the baron himself watching from a strategic place of hiding. In the picture the woman on the swing seems well aware of what is happening, flinging off her shoe toward a statue of the god of discretion in such a way as to cause her gown to billow out revealingly.

This painting reflects a certain religious irreverence on the part of the eighteenth-century aristocracy, for the joke is on the unknowing bishop. The significance of this irreverence is magnified by the fact that Saint-Julien had numerous dealings with the clergy, since he was at this time a government official responsible for overseeing clerical wealth.

The lush setting of the painting and the tenor of the scene suggest the love of romantic luxury and concern for sensual indulgence by this most privileged but soon to be declining part of society.

> **Consider:** *The evidence in this picture of the attitudes and lifestyle of the eighteenth-century French aristocracy.*

Photo 2-2

The Wallace Collection

SECONDARY SOURCES

The Continental Reformation: A Religious Interpretation
John M. Headley

Since the Reformation's occurrence in the sixteenth century, scholars have sought to explain it. Why did it occur? Why did some people convert to Protestantism while others did not? Answers to these questions have been colored by religious preference as well as by interpretive biases. The oldest, most traditional interpretation of the causes of the Reformation is a religious one, focusing on the doctrinal and spiritual factors involved. While many of the older religious interpretations have been modified to take account of economic, social, and political factors, many historians still stress religious causes as being most fundamental in the Reformation. This is reflected in the following selection by John M. Headley of the University of North Carolina.

> **Consider:** *The ways in which Lutheranism satisfied "men thirsting for God in a society saturated with religion"; connections that can be made between the Reformation and the Renaissance.*

The Reformation grew out of the depths of a church that sacramentally and legally embraced all of society. If the progress of this movement was shaped by the social-political currents of the age, its point of origin is to be found in a question of authority raised by a troubled conscience and not in particular abuses. The late medieval church, through a process of excessive institutionalization, had sacrificed spirit to structure and had come to confuse authority with its own practices and judgments. Confusion over the actual tradition of the church was aggravated in the schools by the rending of scripture into a collection of arguments and propositions for philosophical inquiry. In each process scripture, the ultimate source of knowledge of the faith, had lost its unity and integrity. A jumble of competing images cluttered people's minds, as well as the naves of churches. Luther's insight had the effect of restoring to the center of Christian experience not simply the unity and authority of scripture but also the overriding fact of Christ as personal Savior. At Augsburg, Leipzig, and Worms, he exalted scripture above all other authorities, patristic, canonistic, and papal, defying a church grown overly confident in the exercise of its massive power.

To a religiously-starved generation Christ now appeared neither as a pious

SOURCE: John M. Headley, "The Continental Reformation," in *The Meaning of the Renaissance and Reformation*, ed. Richard L. DeMolen (Boston: Houghton Mifflin, 1974), pp. 204–205. Reprinted by permission.

memory nor as a symbol in the mass but in the full and present reality of His person, communicated to the believer preeminently through the Bible—freshly and pungently translated and widely disseminated by the printing press. The direct encounter between Christ and the Christian who takes on the person of Christ was no longer a subject-object relationship, but one between persons in which Christ is always the same, a continuing reality. Here Luther and the Reformation struck a modern note and capitalized upon a strain in the experience of the Renaissance. What Catholic historians call "subjectivism," the profoundly spiritual event of personal appropriation, first emerged in the humanism of Petrarch, was shifted by Lorenzo Valla from classical texts to those of the early church, refocused by Erasmus on the example of Christ, and altered again by Luther to pertain to the gift of Christ. An essentially doctrinal reform, Christocentric and theocentric in character, it had an immense and immediate impact upon men thirsting for God in a society saturated with religion.

A Political Interpretation of the Reformation
G. R. Elton

In more recent times the religious interpretation of the Reformation has been challenged by political historians. This view is illustrated by the following selection from the highly authoritative New Cambridge Modern History. *Here, G. R. Elton of Canmbridge argues that while spiritual and other factors are relevant, primary importance for explaining why the Reformation did not did not take hold rests with political history.*

Consider: *How Elton supports his argument; the ways in which Headley might refute this interpretation.*

The desire for spiritual nourishment was great in many parts of Europe, and movements of thought which gave intellectual content to what in so many ways was an inchoate search for God have their own dignity. Neither of these, however, comes first in explaining why the Reformation took root here and vanished there— why, in fact, this complex of antipapal 'heresies' led to a permanent division within the Church that had looked to Rome. This particular place is occupied by politics and the play of secular ambitions. In short, the Reformation maintained itself wherever the lay power (prince or magistrates) favoured it; it could not survive where the authorities decided to suppress it. Scandinavia, the German principalities, Geneva, in its own peculiar way also England, demonstrate the first; Spain, Italy, the Habsburg lands in the east, and also (though not as yet conclusively) France, the second. The famous phrase behind the settlement of 1555—*cuius*

SOURCE: From G. R. Elton, ed., *The New Cambridge Modern History*, vol. II, *The Reformation* Cambridge, England: Cambridge University Press, 1958), p. 5. Reprinted by permission.

regio eius religio—was a practical commonplace long before anyone put it into words. For this was the age of uniformity, an age which held at all times and everywhere that one political unit could not comprehend within itself two forms of belief or worship.

The tenet rested on simple fact: as long as membership of a secular polity involved membership of an ecclesiastical organisation, religious dissent stood equal to political disaffection and even treason. Hence governments enforced uniformity, and hence the religion of the ruler was that of his country. England provided the extreme example of this doctrine in action, with its rapid official switches from Henrician Catholicism without the pope, through Edwardian Protestantism on the Swiss model and Marian papalism, to Elizabethan Protestantism of a more specifically English brand. But other countries fared similarly. Nor need this cause distress or annoyed disbelief. Princes and governments, no more than the governed, do not act from unmixed motives, and to ignore the spiritual factor in the conversion of at least some princes is as false as to see nothing but purity in the desires of the populace. The Reformation was successful beyond the dreams of earlier, potentially similar, movements not so much because (as the phrase goes) the time was ripe for it, but rather because it found favour with the secular arm. Desire for Church lands, resistance to imperial and papal claims, the ambition to create self-contained and independent states, all played their part in this, but so quite often did a genuine attachment to the teachings of the reformers.

The World We Have Lost:
The Early Modern Family
Peter Laslett

The family is a tremendously important institution in any society. Changes in its structure and functions occur very slowly and gradually. With the passage of centuries since Early Modern times, we can see some sharp differences between the family of that period and the family of today. In the following selection Peter Laslett, a social historian from Cambridge who has written extensively on the Early Modern period, points out the differences.

> **Consider:** *The economic and social functions of the family revealed in this selection; how the structure of this family differs from that of a typical twentieth-century family.*

In the year 1619 the bakers of London applied to the authorities for an increase in the price of bread. They sent in support of their claim a complete description of a bakery and an account of its weekly costs. There were thirteen or fourteen

---

SOURCE: Excerpt from *The World We Have Lost* by Peter Laslett. Copyright © 1965 by Peter Laslett. Reprinted by permission of Charles Scribner's Sons.

people in such an establishment; the baker and his wife, four paid employees who were called journeymen, two apprentices, two maidservants and the three or four children of the master baker himself. . . .

The only word used at that time to describe such a group of people was "family." The man at the head of the group, the entrepreneur, the employer, or the manager, was then known as the master or head of the family. He was father to some of its members and in place of father to the rest. There was no sharp distinction between his domestic and his economic functions. His wife was both his partner and his subordinate, a partner because she ran the family, took charge of the food and managed the women-servants, a subordinate because she was woman and wife, mother and in place of mother to the rest.

The paid servants of both sexes had their specified and familiar position in the family, as much part of it as the children but not quite in the same position. At that time the family was not one society only but three societies fused together: the society of man and wife, of parents and children and of master and servant. But when they were young, and servants were, for the most part, young, unmarried people, they were very close to children in their status and their function. . . .

Apprentices, therefore, were workers who were also children, extra sons or extra daughters (for girls could be apprenticed too), clothed and educated as well as fed, obliged to obedience and forbidden to marry, unpaid and absolutely dependent until the age of twenty-one. If apprentices were workers in the position of sons and daughters, the sons and daughters of the house were workers too. John Locke laid it down in 1697 that the children of the poor must work for some part of the day when they reached the age of three. The sons and daughters of a London baker were not free to go to school for many years of their young lives, or even to play as they wished when they came back home. Soon they would find themselves doing what they could do in *bolting,* that is sieving flour, or in helping the maidservant with her panniers of loaves on the way to the market stall, or in playing their small parts in preparing the never-ending succession of meals for the whole household.

We may see at once, therefore, that the world we have lost, as I have chosen to call it, was no paradise or golden age of equality, tolerance or loving kindness. It is so important that I should not be misunderstood on this point that I will say at once that the coming of industry cannot be shown to have brought economic oppression and exploitation along with it. It was there already. The patriarchal arrangements which we have begun to explore were not new in the England of Shakespeare and Elizabeth. They were as old as the Greeks, as old as European history, and not confined to Europe. And it may well be that they abused and enslaved people quite as remorselessly as the economic arrangements which had replaced them in the England of Blake and Victoria. When people could expect to live for only thirty years in all, how must a man have felt when he realized that so much of his adult life, perhaps all, must go in working for his keep and very little more in someone's else's family?

Lords and Peasants
Jerome Blum

*The aristocracy made up a small percentage of Europe's population. Some 80 to 90 per-
cent of the people were still peasants. While peasants lived in a variety of different circumstances, most lived at not much more than a subsistence level. They were usually
thought of as at the bottom of society. In the following selection, Jerome Blum analyzes
attitudes held toward the peasants by seigniors (lords) and by peasants themselves.*

> **Consider:** *How lords viewed peasants in relation to themselves; how the lords'
> attitudes reflected actual social conditions; possible consequences of the negative
> attitudes held about peasants.*

With the ownership of land went power and authority over the peasants who
lived on the land. There were a multitude of variations in the nature of that
authority and in the nature of the peasants' subservience to their seigniors, in the
compass of the seigniors' supervision and control, and in the obligations that the
peasants had to pay their lords. The peasants themselves were known by many
different names, and so, too, were the obligations they owed the seigniors. But,
whatever the differences, the status of the peasant everywhere in the servile lands
was associated with unfreedom and constraint. In the hierarchical ladder of the
traditional order he stood on the bottom rung. He was "the stepchild of the age,
the broad, patient back who bore the weight of the entire social pyramid . . . the
clumsy lout who was deprived and mocked by court, noble and city." . . .

The subservience of the peasant and his dependence upon his lord were mir-
rored in the attitudes and opinions of the seigniors of east and west alike. They
believed that the natural order of things had divided humankind into masters and
servants, those who commanded and those who obeyed. They believed themselves
to be naturally superior beings and looked upon those who they believed were
destined to serve them as their natural inferiors. At best their attitude toward the
peasantry was the condescension of paternalism. More often it was disdain and
contempt. Contemporary expressions of opinion repeatedly stressed the ignorance, irresponsibility, laziness, and general worthlessness of the peasantry, and
in the eastern lands the free use of the whip was recommended as the only way
to get things done. The peasant was considered some lesser and sub-human form
of life; "a hybrid between animal and human" was the way a Bavarian official put
it in 1737. An eyewitness of a rural rising in Provence in 1752 described the
peasant as "an evil animal, cunning, a ferocious half-civilized beast; he has neither
heart nor honesty. . . ." The Moldavian Basil Balsch reported that the peasants of

SOURCE: Jerome Blum, *The End of the Old Order in Rural Europe.* Copyright © 1978 Princeton
University Press. Excerpt, pp. 29–31, 44–49, reprinted with permission of Princeton University
Press.

his land were "strangers to any discipline, order, economy or cleanliness. . . ; a thoroughly lazy, mendacious . . . people who are accustomed to do the little work that they do only under invectives or blows." A counselor of the duke of Mecklenburg in an official statement in 1750 described the peasant there as a "head of cattle" and declared that he must be treated accordingly. . . .

The conviction of their own superiority harbored by the seigniors was often compounded by ethnic and religious differences between lord and peasant. In many parts of central and eastern Europe the masters belonged to a conquering people who had established their domination over the native population. German seigniors ruled over Slavic peasants in Bohemia, Galicia, East Prussia and Silesia, and over Letts and Estonians in the Baltic lands; Polish lords were the masters of Ukrainian, Lithuanian, and White Russian peasants; Great Russians owned manors peopled by Ukrainians and Lithuanians and Poles; Magyars lorded it over Slovaks and Romanians and Slovenes—to list only some of the macroethnic differences. Few peoples of the rest of the world can match Europeans in their awareness of and, generally, contempt for or at least disdain for other ethnic and religious groups. . . . The dominant group, though greatly outnumbered, successfully maintained its cultural identity precisely because it considered the peasants over whom it ruled as lesser breeds of mankind, even pariahs. . . .

Schooling for most peasants was, at best, pitifully inadequate and usually entirely absent, even where laws declared elementary education compulsory. . . . [B]y far the greatest part of Europe's peasantry lived out their lives in darkest ignorance.

The peasants themselves, oppressed, contemned, and kept in ignorance by their social betters, accepted the stamp of inferiority pressed upon them. "I am only a serf" the peasant would reply when asked to identity himself. They seemed without pride or self-respect, dirty, lazy, crafty, and always suspicious of their masters and of the world that lay outside their village. Even friendly observers were put off by the way they looked and by their behavior. One commentator complained in the 1760's that "one would have more pity for them if their wild and brutish appearance did not seem to justify their hard lot."

Chapter Questions

1. Using the sources in this chapter, explain the Reformation and its spread in sixteenth-century Europe.

2. What arguments and tactics might someone supporting monarchical absolutism and someone opposing it use against each other?

3. How might sources in this chapter be used to compare the life of the aristocracy with that of commoners?

4. Speculate on how a history of Europe during this time might be written and understood by readers if historians drew primarily from sources dealing with the lives of commoners, such as some of the sources in this chapter.

THREE

Asia, 1500–1700

While these centuries marked major changes in the West and new encounters between East and West, it was not a period of major transformation in much of Asia. However, within the different Asian societies, important developments were taking place.

In China, the Ming Dynasty was characterized by relative stability and prosperity. Major building projects, such as the early fifteenth-century construction of the Forbidden City in Beijing (Peking), were undertaken. All cultural productions, and literature in particular, flourished—though more in quantity than in originality. The government fostered rigidity and remained relatively inward looking, apart from the vigilance needed against attack from Japanese pirates along the coast and from Mongols and Manchus from the north. By the mid-seventeenth century, the Manchus were victorious and established their own dynasty. They adopted the Confucian bureaucracy and ways of governing, were generally accepted by the Chinese, and eventually extended Chinese rule as far as Tibet.

In contrast, this period was one of greater change for Japan. The sixteenth century witnessed the emergence of strong military leaders. By 1600, Japan was unified by the Tokugawa house that created the Shogunate in 1603 and would rule for the next two hundred and fifty years. It outlawed Christianity, cut Japan off from the world, and established a centralized feudal state. Increasingly the samurai became, through education, government bureaucrats. And as the economy developed, a merchant class grew.

In India, the first Muslim rulers, the Delhi Sultanate (1211–1504), became ineffectual and were replaced by the Islamic Mogul (also Mughal—originally a Persian word for Mongols, but in the sixteenth century referred to the fierce Turkish tribe that conquered north India) Dynasty in 1526. Under Akbar, this rule was conciliatory toward the Hindus and encouraging of the arts. However, his seventeenth-century successors followed less tolerant policies and made costly attempts to expand their rule to the south, eventually leading to the collapse of Mogul power by the beginning of the eighteenth century and the spread of British power over India.

Finally, in the Middle East, Islamic powers not only remained strong but expanded their control. Most striking was the continued rise of the Ottoman

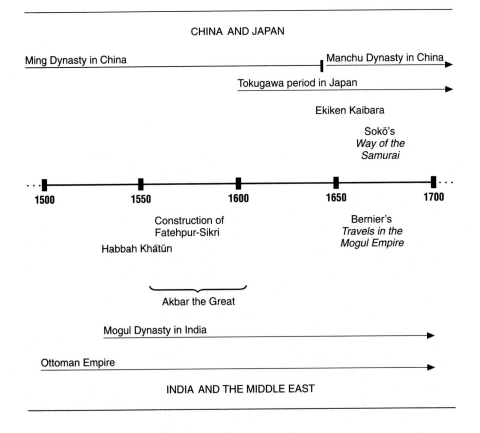

Empire, which by the last decades of the seventeenth century included all the southern and eastern Mediterranean basin and extended well into eastern Europe. However, the Ottomans themselves were under pressure from the expanding Russian Empire to the north and from the rise of the Islamic Safavid state in Iran. By the eighteenth century these Islamic powers had already begun a long-term process of decline.

The sources in this chapter focus on three topics. The first is social and political life in China and Japan. Here there is a particular focus on the role of women and the developing role of the samurai in Japan, as well as on family life in China. The second is Indian civilization, here also with some focus on women as well as the broader aspects of Indian culture. Finally, some sources will deal with Islamic civilizations, particularly the Ottoman Empire, which rose to heights during this period but also showed signs of long-term decline.

PRIMARY SOURCES

The Way of the Samurai
Yamaga Sokō

In the course of the seventeenth century, Confucianism became a greater influence as Japanese intellectuals began to develop an intellectual paradigm which was more reflective of their own culture. One of the first to do so was Yamaga Sokō (1622–1685). A man of enormous intellect and independence of thought, Yamaga became interested not only in the major philosophies of his day, but in military science as well.

Worried about the continual inaction of samurai under peaceful Tokugawa rule, Yamaga tried to forge a new identity for these warriors. This was markedly different from China where soldiers had very low status. Bringing together the ethics of Confucianism and the Japanese feudal tradition, Yamaga's writings are acknowledged as the beginnings of a creed known as bushido (the way of the warriors). Yamaga's writings on the samurai also symbolize the transformation of the samurai in this period from a military aristocracy to government bureaucrats and political and intellectual leaders. The following excerpts are from The Way of the Samurai, *which was the first attempt by Yamaga to develop his thoughts on this subject.*

SOURCE: *Sources of Japanese Tradition*, Ryusaku Tsuneda, et al., eds. (New York: Columbia University Press, 1961), pp. 398–401.

Consider: *The nature of a society that requires such strict codes of behavior from its people; how Yamaga justifies this description of the samurai's duties.*

The master once said: The generation of all men and of all things in the universe is accomplished by means of the marvelous interaction of the two forces [yin and yang]. Man is the most highly endowed of all creatures, and all things culminate in man. Generation after generation men have taken their livelihood from tilling the soil, or devised and manufactured tools, or produced profit from mutual trade, so that peoples' needs were satisfied. Thus the occupations of farmer, artisan, and merchant necessarily grew up as complementary to one another. However, the samurai eats food without growing it, uses utensils without manufacturing them, and profits without buying or selling. What is the justification for this? . . . The samurai is one who does not cultivate, does not manufacture, and does not engage in trade, but it cannot be that he has no function at all as a samurai. He who satisfied his needs without performing any function at all would more properly be called an idler. Therefore one must devote all one's mind to the detailed examination of one's calling.

Human beings aside, does any creature in the land—bird or animal, lowly fish or insect, or insentient plant or tree—fulfill its nature by being idle? Birds and beasts fly and run to find their own food; fish and insects seek their food as they go about with one another; plants and trees put their roots ever deeper into the earth. . . . All things are thus. Among men, the farmers, artisans, and merchants also do the same. One who lives his whole life without working should be called a rebel against heaven. Hence we ask ourselves how it can be that the samurai should have no occupation; and it is only then as we inquire into the function of the samurai, that [the nature of] his calling becomes apparent. . . .

If one deeply fixes his attention on what I have said and examines closely one's own function, it will become clear what the business of the samurai is. The business of the samurai consists in reflecting on his own station in life, in discharging loyal service to his master if he has one, in deepening his fidelity in associations with friends, and, with due consideration of his own position, in devoting himself to duty above all. However, in one's own life, one becomes unavoidably involved in obligations between father and child, older and younger brother, and husband and wife. Though these are also the fundamental moral obligations of everyone in the land, the farmers, artisans, and merchants have no leisure from their occupations, and so they cannot constantly act in accordance with them and fully exemplify the Way. The samurai dispenses with the business of the farmer, artisan, and merchant and confines himself to practicing this Way; should there be someone in the three classes of the common people who transgresses against these moral principles, the samurai summarily punishes him and thus upholds proper moral principles in the land. It would not do for the samurai to know the martial and civil virtues without manifesting them. Since this is the case, outwardly he stands in physical readiness for any call to service and inwardly he strives to fulfill the Way of the lord and subject, friend and friend, father and son, older and younger brother, and husband and wife. Within his heart he keeps to the ways of peace, but without he keeps his weapons ready for use. The three classes of the common people make him their teacher and respect him. By following his teachings, they are enabled to understand what is fundamental and what is secondary.

Herein lies the Way of the samurai, the means by which he earns his clothing, food, and shelter; and by which his heart is put at ease, and he is enabled to pay back at length his obligation to his lord and the kindness of his parents. . . . But if perchance one should wish public service and desire to remain a samurai, he should sustain his life by performing menial functions, he should accept a small income, he should limit his obligation to his master, and he should do easy tasks [such as] gate-keeping and nightwatch duty. This then is [the samurai's] calling. The man who takes or seeks the pay of a samurai and is covetous of salary without in the slightest degree comprehending his function must feel shame in his heart. Therefore I say that that which the samurai should take as his fundamental aim is to know his own function.

Greater Learning for Women
Ekiken Kaibara

There is some evidence which leads us to believe that in its earliest years, women enjoyed a fairly high status in Japanese society. With the introduction of feudalism and the emergence of a military society, along with the influence of Confucianism and Buddhism, that status deteriorated since militarization and both sets of beliefs denigrated women. Japan was soon emulating its neighbors and relegating women to a very low status.

The following excerpts are from a book entitled Greater Learning for Women *by Ekiken Kaibara, a seventeenth century intellectual, and purports to spell out the duties and functions of women in Japanese life. Until late in the nineteenth century, this book was widely used.*

> **Consider:** *Why these guidelines are so rigid; how men profit from these rules; what this reveals about Japanese society in general; the similarities with Ban Zhao's rules for women in China (Chapter 8, Volume I).*

From her earliest youth a girl should observe the line of demarcation separating women from men, and never, even for an instant, should she be allowed to see or hear the least impropriety. The customs of antiquity did not allow men and women to sit in the same apartment, to keep their wearing apparel in the same place, to bathe in the same place, or to transmit to each other anything directly from hand to hand. . . . It is written likewise in the *Lesser Learning* that a woman must form no friendship and no intimacy except when ordered to do so by her

SOURCE: *Women and Wisdom of Japan (Greater Learning for Women)*, Ekiken Kaibara, trans. (London: John Murray, 1905), pp. 33–46.

parents or by middlemen. Even at the peril of her life must she harden her heart like rock or metal and observe the rules of propriety.

✿

In China marriage is called "returning," for the reason that a woman must consider her husband's home as her own, and that, when she marries, she is therefore returning to her own home. However low and needy her husband's position may be, she must find no fault with him, but consider the poverty of the household which it has pleased Heaven to give her as the ordering of an unpropitious fate. The sage of old taught that, once married, she must never leave her husband's house. Should she forsake the "way" and be divorced, shame shall cover her till her latest hour. With regard to this point, there are seven faults which are termed the "Seven Reasons for Divorce":

(i) A woman shall be divorced for disobedience to her father-in-law or mother-in-law. (ii) A woman shall be divorced if she fails to bear children, . . . (iii) Lewdness is a reason for divorce. (iv) Jealousy is a reason for divorce. (v) Leprosy or any like foul disease is a reason for divorce. (vi) A woman shall be divorced who, by talking overmuch and prattling disrespectfully, disturbs the harmony of kinsmen and brings trouble on her household. (vii) A woman shall be divorced who is addicted to stealing. . . .

✿

It is the chief duty of a girl living in the parental house to practise filial piety towards her father and mother. But after marriage her duty is to honour her father-in-law and mother-in-law, to honour them beyond her father and mother, to love and reverence them with all ardour, and to tend them with practice of every filial piety. . . .

✿

A woman has no particular lord. She must look to her husband as her lord, and must serve him with all worship and reverence, not despising or thinking lightly of him. The great lifelong duty of a woman is obedience. In her dealings with her husband, both the expression of her countenance and style of her address should be courteous, humble, and conciliatory, never peevish and intractable, never rude and arrogant—that should be a woman's first and chiefest care. When the husband issues his instructions, the wife must never disobey them.

✿

The five worst infirmities that afflict the female are indocility, discontent, slander, jealousy, and silliness. Without any doubt, these five infirmities are found in seven or eight out of every ten women, and it is from these that arises the inferiority of women to men. A woman should cure them by self-inspection and self-reproach.

A Woman's Voice in India
Habbah Khātūn

Habbah Khātūn lived in India during the reign of Akbar in the mid-sixteenth century. We know little of her life except that she was born into a well-to-do family and was married to a man in the same social class. She remained childless, which created difficulties in her marriage. The humiliation she felt in this situation was voiced in songs she sang while working with the other women in the field.

Her remarkable intelligence and talents led her to be ensconced in the palace of the ruling family of Kashmir. She developed her talents, giving a literary form to the Kashmiri language and developing a music system based on Persian and Indian styles. Her songs inspired much anti-Mogul feeling in northwest India. These are two of her songs, still sung today among the people of Kashmir.

> **Consider:** *How women in a male-dominated society can emerge as prominent figures; what these songs reveal about Khātūn's and the life of other women in sixteenth-century India.*

He has pierced every fibre of my body with the
    lightning of love:
I, hapless one, am filled with longing for him.
He glanced at me from the top of the wall—
I wish I could tie a turban round his head.
Why did he then turn his back on me?
I, hapless one, am filled with longing for him.
He glanced at me through my door—

Who told him where I lived?
Why has he left me in such anguish?
I, hapless one, am filled with longing for him.
He glanced at me through my window,
He who is lovely like my ear-rings;
He has made my heart restless:
I, hapless one, am filled with longing for him.
He glanced at me through the crevice in my roof,
Sang like a bird that I may look at him,
Then, soft-footed, vanished from my sight:
I, hapless one, am filled with longing for him.
He glanced at me while I was drawing water,
I withered like a red rose,
My body and soul were ablaze with love:

SOURCE: M. Mujeeb, *The Indian Muslims* (London: George Allen & Unwin, Ltd., 1967), pp. 328–329.

I, hapless one, am longing for him.
He glanced at me in the waning moonlight of early dawn,
Stalked after me like one obsessed.
Why did he stoop so low?
I, hapless one, am filled with longing for him!

                         ✿

I thought I was indulging in play, and lost myself.
   Oh for the day that is dying!
At home I was secluded, unknown,
When I left home, my fame spread far and wide,
The pious laid all their merit at my feet.
   Oh for the day that is dying!
Me beauty was like a warehouse filled with rare merchandise,
Which drew men from all the four quarters;
Now my richness is gone, I have no worth:
   Oh for the day that is dying!
My father's people were of high standing,
I became known as Habbah Khātūn:
   Oh for the day that is dying!

Travels in the Mogul Empire: Politics and Society in India

Francois Bernier

Francois Bernier (1620–1688) was a French physician who traveled widely through the Middle East and India from 1654 to 1669. He spent about twelve years in Mogul [Mughal] India, including time traveling with and observing the court of the Mogul ruler, Aurangzeb. Upon his return to France, he published his writings and letters on his travels.

In this undated (1670?) letter to French Finance Minister Jean Baptiste Colbert, Bernier describes some of his adventures and observations while traveling with Aurangzeb. This excerpt attempts to explain one of the major problems the Mogul rulers had with social stratification and the consequences of allowing a small elite too much power.

> **Consider:** *The connections between Indian politics, economics, and society revealed in this letter; how this letter might reflect Bernier's own concerns and assumptions.*

SOURCE: François Bernier, *Travels in the Mogul Empire* A.D. *1656–1668* (London: Oxford University Press, 1983), pp. 300–303.

. . . The *King*, as proprietor of the land, makes over a certain quantity to military men, as an equivalent for their pay; and this grant is called *jah-ghir*, or, as in Turkey, *timar*; the word *jah-ghir* signifying the spot from which to draw, or the place of salary. Similar grants are made to governors, in lieu of their salary, and also for the support of their troops, on condition that they pay a certain sum annually to the King out of any surplus revenue that the land may yield. The lands not so granted are retained by the King as the peculiar domains of his house, and are seldom, if ever, given in the way of *jah-ghir*; and upon these domains he keeps contractors, who are also bound to pay him an annual rent.

The persons thus put in possession of the land, whether as *timariots*, governors, or contractors, have an authority almost absolute over the peasantry, and nearly as much over the artisans and merchants of the towns and villages within their district; and nothing can be imagined more cruel and oppressive than the manner in which it is exercised. There is no one before whom the injured peasant, artisan, or tradesman can pour out his just complaints; no great lords, parliaments, or judges of local courts exist, as in *France*, to restrain the wickedness of those merciless oppressors, and the *Kadis*, or judges, are not invested with sufficient power to redress the wrongs of these unhappy people. This sad abuse of the royal authority may not be felt in the same degree near capital cities such as *Dehly* and *Agra*, or in the vicinity of large towns and seaports, because in those places acts of gross injustice cannot easily be concealed from the court.

This debasing state of slavery obstructs the progress of trade and influences the manners and mode of life of every individual. There can be little encouragement to engage in commercial pursuits, when the success with which they may be attended, instead of adding to the enjoyments of life, provokes the cupidity of a neighbouring tyrant possessing both power and inclination to deprive any man of the fruits of his industry. When wealth is acquired, as must sometimes be the case, the possessor, so far from living with increased comfort and assuming an air of independence, studies the means by which he may appear indigent: his dress, lodging, and furniture continue to be mean, and he is careful, above all things, never to indulge in the pleasures of the table. In the meantime, his gold and silver remain buried at a great depth in the ground; agreeable to the general practice among the peasantry, artisans and merchants, whether *Mahomeians* or *Gentiles*, but especially among the latter, who possess almost exclusively the trade and wealth of the country, and who believe that the money concealed during life will prove beneficial to them after death. A few individuals alone who derive their income from the King or from the *Omrahs*, or who are protected by a powerful patron, are at no pains to counterfeit poverty, but partake of the comforts and luxuries of life.

I have no doubt that this habit of secretly burying the precious metals, and thus withdrawing them from circulation, is the principal cause of their apparent scarcity in *Hindoustan*.

VISUAL SOURCES

Akbar Inspecting the Construction of Fatehpur-Sikri

Tulsi the Elder, Bandi, and Madhu the Younger

After witnessing the death of two previous male offspring, India's Mogul ruler, Akbar, had his most fervent wish fulfilled when on August 30, 1569 a son and heir-apparent was born. So inspired was he that a decision was made to build a grand edifice on the site of the birth just outside a town called Sikri. This magnificent structure, a classic example of Mogul architecture, became known as Fathabad, later Fatehpur, (City of Victory) and hence the name Fatehpur-Sikri. It became the Mogul capital. Construction took place from 1571–1576 and consisted of palaces, pavilions for various rituals, grand mosques, bazaar areas, gardens, and courtyards.

Akbar was himself interested in architecture and had commissioned many great building projects. This scene, painted in 1590, shows Akbar personally directing the building of the city and conferring with the stone masons while workers go about their business all around him.

Consider: *How people of different rank are distinguished; the role such building projects might play in a civilization.*

Architecture and the Imperial City

Since Confucian thinking created a society of rules of behavior and etiquette, it is not surprising that the architecture would follow this same pattern. Those who could afford it built houses surrounded by high walls, with the buildings around the inside of the walls and the middle left to a courtyard, or several courtyards if the family was wealthy enough. This was not a random architecture but a design of specific purpose and intent (see also the plan for the Chinese house, Chapter 3, Volume I). There were traditions as to where each family member resided.

The imperial family followed these designs and traditions as well. When the Ming Dynasty decided to move the capital of China to Beijing (Peking—northern capital) in the fifteenth century, it had built an Imperial City with an inner Forbidden City, thus named since only members of the court and those on official business could enter. The Ming rulers built themselves residential palaces and ceremonial halls surrounded by a high wall, with a door leading to each point on the compass. This Forbidden City was home to the court and thousands of imperial eunuchs. Outside the gates to the larger Imperial

Photo 3-1

Victoria & Albert Museum, London/Art Resource

Map 3-1   The Imperial City

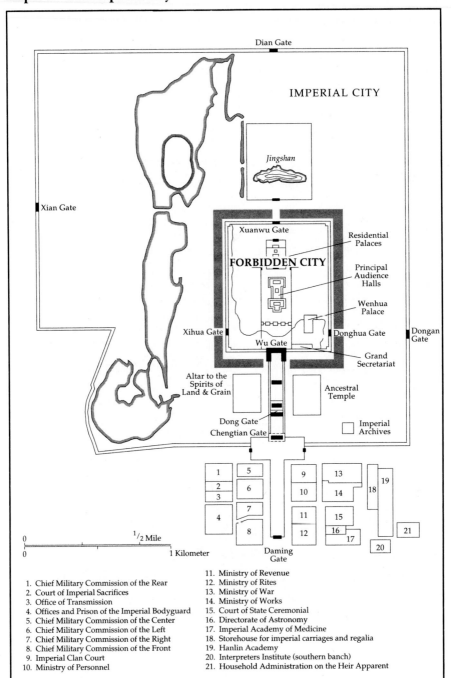

1. Chief Military Commission of the Rear
2. Court of Imperial Sacrifices
3. Office of Transmission
4. Offices and Prison of the Imperial Bodyguard
5. Chief Military Commission of the Center
6. Chief Military Commission of the Left
7. Chief Military Commission of the Right
8. Chief Military Commission of the Front
9. Imperial Clan Court
10. Ministry of Personnel
11. Ministry of Revenue
12. Ministry of Rites
13. Ministry of War
14. Ministry of Works
15. Court of State Ceremonial
16. Directorate of Astronomy
17. Imperial Academy of Medicine
18. Storehouse for imperial carriages and regalia
19. Hanlin Academy
20. Interpreters Institute (southern branch)
21. Household Administration on the Heir Apparent

City stood the offices of the Chinese bureaucracy; each designated a place according to its importance and status.

> **Consider:** *The traditional ideas that influence the design of these buildings; how they are built specifically to the rules of Chinese society.*

SECONDARY SOURCES

Islam in Indonesia
John R. Bowen

Indonesia is the world's largest archipelago stretching some 3,200 miles, encompassing about 13,700 islands of which about 6,000 are inhabited. Originally animist, Indonesians were converted to Hinduism in the third century by merchants and priests who arrived from southern India. From the fifth century, travelers bringing Buddhism, also from India, began arriving as well. From the end of the thirteenth century, Islam began appearing in the archipelago (in the form of Sufi mysticism), also by way of Indian merchants. Islam quickly began to eclipse its predecessors. The conversion to Islam in Indonesia did not, however, mean an end to Hindu-Buddhist beliefs and practices but, rather, a synthesis. Indonesians could embrace Islam without jettisoning their earlier customs, thereby incorporating their earlier beliefs with Islam.

In this selection, John R. Bowen, Professor of Anthropology at Washington University, St. Louis, examines the situation in Java where, more than any place in Indonesia, the Hindu-Javanese culture was kept alive. Bowen looks at two interpretations of what occurred in Java. Today some 85 percent of Indonesia's 190,000,000 people are Muslim, making it the largest Muslim state in the world.

> **Consider:** *The issue of religious synthesis and the ability of religions to adapt to local culture; the distinction between a culture and a religion.*

CASE STUDY: CULTURE AND RELIGION IN JAVA

One issue dividing students of Indonesian Islam is the degree to which some (the more traditional) religious forms are mixtures of Islamic and pre-Islamic ideas. This issue has arisen in particular with regard to Javanese religious life.

SOURCE: John R. Bowen, "Islam in Indonesia," Reprinted with permission from *Asia in the Core Curriculum. Case Studies in the Social Sciences.* Myron L. Cohen, ed. (Armonk, New York, M. E. Sharpe, 1992), pp. 100–102.

One position, developed by Clifford Geertz, is that Javanese society is . . . divided into three streams: the high culture of the Javanese nobles with its stress on mysticism and etiquette, the low culture of Javanese peasants with its many spirits and ritual meals, and the self-consciously Islamic culture of the merchants, students, and scholars, which saw itself as opposed to many features of the Javanese past. In this view, the basic elements of Javanese culture, including ritual meals, the art of shadow puppetry, and the ideas of power and rank suffusing the Javanese kingdoms evolved from indigenous and Hindu ideas, prior to the introduction of Islamic ideas. Islam was adopted as an additional religious layer rather late in Javanese history.

A second position holds that Javanese culture is suffused with Islamic ideas and in fact is the outcome of a process of religious adaptation. Advocates of this position argue that Islamic mystics, known as Sufis, propagated a form of Islam that was in keeping with Javanese interest in spirits and the power of unseen forces. They reinterpreted pre-Islamic ideas in Islamic terms. Thus, these scholars argue, the ritual meal in traditional Javanese culture was modified to conform to the custom as practiced throughout the Islamic world. Even the power of Javanese kings came to be viewed through an Islamic lens: the king was no longer an incarnation of a Hindu deity, but the "shadow of God on earth," an idea taken from Persian Muslim political thought.

What is clear is that Javanese religious life shows the adaptation of Islamic traditions to a particular set of Javanese emphases. Islam entered a Java where large kingdoms had already developed an elaborate court culture based on a mixture of animistic and Hindu ideas. Most Javanese Muslims acknowledge this cultural heritage, in which an emphasis on refinement and self-control is combined with Islamic ideas. For Javanese, authority involves the absorption of power within the self, the capacity to smoothly control others without being flustered or showing emotion. Refinement is epitomized by the lithe heros of shadow puppet theater, who effortlessly defeat giants; it is reflected in one's mastery of the elaborate system of speech levels in the Javanese language, and in the control of desires attained through meditation.

Sufism provided a Muslim framework that validated this idea of inward control. Meditation and abstinence refocus thought away from the outer world and toward one's inner self, and finally toward God. Some Sufi scholars taught that God was present in oneself. Whether or not one sees the present-day Javanese emphasis on self-control as pre-Islamic or as part of Sufism, it seems clear that a fit between indigenous and Sufi ideas was crucial to the propagatiom of Islam on Java.

Muslim rituals also have been shaped to fit indigenous concerns. On Java, the ritual meal, although present throughout the archipelago and indeed in other Muslim societies, takes on a Javanese character. The meal maintains social and emotional equilibrium, a persistent Javanese concern, by involving everyone in a neighborhood or village on an equal basis (despite their otherwise marked social inequalities). "When you give a ritual meal," said one Javanese quoted by Geertz, "nobody feels different from anyone else."

Funerals, though conducted according to Islamic rules, also reveal the Javanese concern for controlling emotion and reaching a state of detachment. The relatives of the deceased pass under his/her body several times when it is on the litter, give away money as a sign of their willingness to let the deceased go, and feature at the funeral meal a large, flattened-out rice cake that symbolizes the flat character of their emotions.

Marriage, Caste, and Society in India
V. P. S. Raghuvanshi

Indian society was in great part structured by the caste system. Determined by birth, one's caste was lifelong, inherited, and unbending. For Hindus, it was universal. No aspect of the caste system was more rigid than the issues of intercaste sexual relations and marriage. They went to the heart of maintaining caste lines. The following excerpt, written by V. P. S. Raghuvanshi, a prominent social historian of India, analyzes the connections between sexual relations, marriage, caste, and society. His focus is on India during the eighteenth century, but his analysis applies to the seventeenth and sixteenth centuries almost as well.

> **Consider:** *How and why marriage rules were so central to caste in Hindu society; the differences between functional castes and nonfunctional high castes.*

Caste governed the code of rules and conventions relating to marriage in Hindu society. In the 18th century, inter-caste matrimonial connections were beyond the comprehension of people and were liable to be visited by the sentence of excommunication. During the period we have evidence that the rules of caste, if violated in other respects, were leniently viewed but those in respect of marriage and sexual intercourse were rigorously enforced. . . . If a girl of high caste in Peshwas' dominions were detected in act of adultery, she could be sold and treated as a slave. In this sense caste implied hereditary continuation of families in the same group and prevented wide inter-mixture of blood. Marriage in the same caste was a social maxim of almost universal applicability among the Hindus. . . . Elsewhere caste suffered from various distinctions of rank even within its own sub-groups and these, in their turn, influenced marriage. As a general rule, among castes whose people were not privileged to be reckoned as "twice-born," the sub-castes had become entirely distinct endogamous groups. In this sense anything like a *Sudra* caste was non-existent. The various artisan and professional castes, loosely termed *Sudra*, by the end of the 18th century had organized themselves into

SOURCE: V. P. S. Raghuvanshi, *Indian Society in the Eighteenth Century* (New Delhi: Associated Publishing House, 1969), pp. 53–56.

separate endogamous[1] units of society. Their sub-divisions had become distinct castes. So strict was the rule that even sexual connection of the woman with a man outside her caste invariably entailed her excommunication from her own. This rule was rigidly observed even by those castes which were considered "altogether vile."

If matrimony within the group be construed as the fundamental test of caste, then the Kayasthas of Northern India, who might have been one caste before, had ceased to be so by the end of the 18th century. Their various sub-divisions like those of Srivastavas, Bhatnagars, Mathurs, Saxenas, Gaurs etc., had formed themselves into separate matrimonial groups and had thus become separate castes. Similarly in South India, the Panchalars, including people of the trades of goldsmiths, black smiths, carpenters, masons, although reckoned as one caste, did not admit of inter-group matrimonial relationship.

The relationship between sub-caste and marriage was, however, not necessarily uniform in the upper castes. In Bengal, the Brahmans, as also the Kayasthas, constituted single castes as distinctions of sub-castes were not material in regulating marriages within the same group. Hence those of higher birth (Kulins) were coveted by all inferior to them. Here Kulinism, although it encouraged a nefarious traffic in women, prevented the formation of rigid endogamous sub-groups. But this was not the case in Northern India or Central India. In Bihar, the Brahmans claiming descent from Kanauj had split into various local sub-divisions like Shukla, Anturvedi, etc., and even among them there were no inter-matrimonial relations. The other Brahman sub-castes, too, were endogamous subgroups. In Central India, also, we find that there was nothing like a uniform Brahman caste. The Brahmans had frittered into endless, strictly endogamous sub-castes. The same was true of the *Vaisya* community in Northern India. It was divided into several sub-divisions which were endogamous. The Rajputs were a solid exception. There sub-groups arranged on clan basis were exogamous, and marriage was regulated primarily on the basis of "purity of descent." This, too, could be overruled as a serious consideration if the girl of the lower class or family belonged to a rich influential family. Marriage outside the broad Rajput kin-group was, however, held in odium. Malcolm cites the degradation of the whole clan of Pamars in the social scale in Central India as their Chief, rulers of Dhar, married his daughter to a Maratha prince with whom "the poorest of the proud Rajput Chiefs" would refrain from eating together.

As such, we may say that caste was necessarily an endogamous group but among the functional castes, the sub-groups were also endogamous everywhere. In the non-functional high castes, the various sub-castes were not necessarily so everywhere, though in Northern India, among the Brahmans, *Vaisyas* and Kayasthas they had become so.

---

[1] "Endogamous" refers to marriage within a particular caste or group in accordance with set custom or law.

The Ottoman Empire and Its Successors

Peter Mansfield

The Ottoman Empire grew rapidly during the fifteenth and sixteenth centuries, reaching its height during the second half of the seventeenth century. Nevertheless, there were already signs of decline in the seventeenth century. In the following excerpt from The Ottoman Empire and Its Successors, *Peter Mansfield analyzes some of the causes for this long-term decline, here focusing on economic factors.*

> **Consider:** *The role of new trade routes and Ottoman taxation policies in the decline of the Empire; what the Ottoman Empire might have done to stem the decline.*

. . . The opening of a new trade route to Asia via the Cape by the Portuguese in the sixteenth century and the establishment of Dutch and British power in Asia in the seventeenth century "deprived Turkey of the greater part of her foreign commerce and left her, together with the countries over which she ruled, in a stagnant backwater through which the life-giving stream of world trade no longer flowed." At the same time the flood of cheap silver from the Spanish colonies in the New World caused a violent inflation, and disastrous devaluation of the currency of the Ottoman Empire. The consequent economic distress was compounded by the government's increasing demands for revenues from the already overtaxed peasantry for the swelling bureaucracy and armed forces. While the economies of the European powers made rapid progress in the seventeenth and eighteenth centuries, that of the Ottoman Empire actually declined. Agriculture deteriorated as the peasantry abandoned the countryside for the towns, but there was no compensating development of industry. Turkey's stagnant science and technology lagged increasingly behind the west, and it lacked any independent entrepreneurial class which might have led an industrial revolution. Western economic superiority was also manifested within the Ottoman Empire. In the sixteenth century, when the Empire was at the height of its powers, the Ottoman sultan granted special privileges to the French, English, Venetians and other non-Muslims, who had established themselves within the Empire to trade. These privileges—known as the Capitulations—exempted them from taxes imposed on Muslim Ottoman subjects and gave them the right to be tried in their own consular courts. As Ottoman power declined the privileges were reinforced. By the nineteenth century there were flourishing European business communities in many parts of the Empire which were virtually above the law.

SOURCE: Peter Mansfield, *The Ottoman Empire and Its Successors* (London: The Macmillan Press Ltd., 1973), p. 7.

Chapter Questions

1. Several sources in this chapter deal with the position of and problems facing women in China, Japan, and India during this period. Is it fair to make comparisons here? How might it be argued that these sources reveal similar circumstances facing women in these civilizations?

2. How might the sources in this chapter be used to support the argument that even though Western civilization was expanding during these two centuries, most Asian civilizations continued to develop in line with their own internal, rather than external, forces?

3. Drawing on sources from this chapter and the previous chapters on the West, how might it be argued that European societies were becoming increasingly dynamic and flexible at the same time that societies such as those in India, China, and the Ottoman Empire were becoming more rigid and tradition bound? How might other sources be used to show that in many ways the lives of people in these civilizations and the problems they faced were similar?

FOUR

The Scientific Revolution and the Enlightenment in Europe

One of the most important intellectual revolutions of Western civilization, an intellectual revolution that would eventually spread throughout the world, occurred in the seventeenth century. Building on some sixteenth-century breakthroughs and a more deeply rooted interest in the workings of the natural world, a small elite of thinkers and scientists—Descartes, Galileo, Newton, Kepler, Bacon, and Boyle—established the foundations for the modern sciences.

In the process of developing the modern sciences, these thinkers challenged the established conception of the universe as well as previous assumptions about knowledge. This ultimately successful challenge, now known as the Scientific Revolution, had a number of key elements. First, the view of the universe as being stable, fixed, and finite, with the earth at its center, gave way to a view of the universe as moving and almost infinite, with the earth merely one of millions of bodies all subject to the laws of nature. Second, earlier methods for ascertaining the truth, which primarily involved referring to traditional authorities such as Aristotle, Ptolemy, and the Church, were replaced by methods that emphasized skepticism, rationalism, and rigorous reasoning based on observed facts and mathematical laws. Third, although these thinkers remained concerned with their own deeply held religious beliefs, the general scientific orientation shifted from theological questions to secular questions that focused on how things worked.

Most of these intellectual developments were known to only a few throughout Europe. In the eighteenth century these scientific ideas and methods became popularized as part of the intellectual ferment of the Enlightenment. A group of thinkers, called the *philosophes*, developed and popularized related sets of ideas that formed a basis for modern thought. Their methods emphasized skepticism, empirical reasoning, and satire. Most believed that Western civilization was on the verge of enlightenment, that reasoning and education could quickly dispel the darkness of the past that had kept people in a state of immaturity. The main objects of their criticisms were institutions, such as governments and the Church, and irrational customs that perpetuated old ways of thinking and thus hindered progress.

For the Scientific Revolution, the primary sources emphasize two broad questions that faced these seventeenth-century scientists. First, how can one ascertain the truth? Second, what is the proper line between science and scriptural authority? The secondary sources concentrate on the nature and causes of the Scientific Revolution as well as its importance for women.

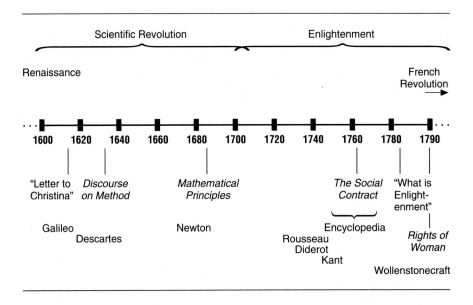

For the Enlightenment, the primary and secondary sources concern three issues. First, what was the nature of Enlightenment thought? Second, how should we characterize the *philosophes*? Finally, how did Enlightenment thought affect eighteenth-century politics before the French Revolution?

Together, the sources reveal an intellectual movement still tied to the traditional society of Early Modern Europe but with strikingly modern characteristics. Toward the end of the eighteenth century this movement would play an important role in the transition to Modern Europe, the subject of the following chapters. During the nineteenth and twentieth centuries, the principles and ideas of this intellectual movement would spread throughout the world.

PRIMARY SOURCES

The Discourse on Method
René Descartes

Seventeenth-century science needed new philosophical and methodological standards for truth to replace those traditionally used to support scientific assumptions. These were forcefully provided by René Descartes (1596–1650) in his Discourse on Method *(1637). Born and educated in France, but spending his most productive years in Holland, Descartes gained fame as a mathematician, physicist, and metaphysical philosopher. The following excerpt from his* Discourse *contains the best-known statement of his approach to discovering truth.*

> **Consider:** *The ways in which Descartes' approach constitutes a break with traditional ways of ascertaining the truth; the weaknesses of this approach and how a modern scientist might criticize this method; how this approach reflects Descartes' background as a mathematician.*

In place of the multitude of precepts of which logic is composed, I believed I should find the four following rules quite sufficient, provided I should firmly and steadfastly resolve not to fail of observing them in a single instance.

The first rule was never to receive anything as a truth which I did not clearly know to be such; that is, to avoid haste and prejudice, and not to comprehend

SOURCE: René Descartes, "The Discourse on Method" in *The Philosophy of Descartes.* Henry A. P. Torrey, ed. and trans. (New York: Henry Holt, 1982), pp. 46–48.

anything more in my judgments than that which should present itself so clearly and so distinctly to my mind that I should have no occasion to entertain a doubt of it.

The second rule was to divide every difficulty which I should examine into as many parts as possible, or as might be required for resolving it.

The third rule was to conduct my thoughts in an orderly manner, beginning with objects the most simple and the easiest to understand, in order to ascend as it were by steps to the knowledge of the most composite, assuming some order to exist even in things which did not appear to be naturally connected.

The last rule was to make enumerations so complete, and reviews so comprehensive, that I should be certain of omitting nothing.

Those long chains of reasoning, quite simple and easy, which geometers are wont to employ in the accomplishment of their most difficult demonstrations, led me to think that everything which might fall under the cognizance of the human mind might be connected together in a similar manner, and that, provided only one should take care not to receive anything as true which was not so, and if one were always careful to preserve the order necessary for deducing one truth from another, there would be none so remote at which he might not at last arrive, nor so concealed which he might not discover. And I had no great difficulty in finding those with which to make a beginning, for I knew already that these must be the simplest and easiest to apprehend; and considering that, among all those who had up to this time made discoveries in the sciences, it was the mathematicians alone who had been able to arrive at demonstrations—that is to say, at proofs certain and evident—I did not doubt that I should begin with the same truths which they investigated.

Letter to Christina of Tuscany: Science and Scripture
Galileo Galilei

The most renowned scientist at the beginning of the seventeenth century was the Italian astronomer, mathematician, and physicist Galileo Galilei (1564–1642). His discoveries about gravity, velocity, and the movement of astronomical bodies were grounded in a scientific method that ran contrary to the accepted standards for truth and authority. In the following excerpt from a letter to the Grand Duchess Christina of Tuscany (1615),

SOURCE: From Galileo Galilei, *Discoveries and Opinions of Galileo*, Stillman Drake, ed. and trans. Reprinted by permission of Doubleday & Company, Inc. (New York, 1957), pp. 182–183. Copyright © 1957 by Stillman Drake.

Galileo defends his ideas and delineates his view of the correct line between science and scriptural authority.

> **Consider:** *According to Galileo's view, the kinds of topics or questions that are appropriately scientific and those that are appropriately theological; how Galileo's views compare with those of Descartes; why Galileo's views are so crucial to the scientific revolution.*

I think that in discussions of physical problems we ought to begin not from the authority of scriptural passage, but from sense-experiences and necessary demonstrations; for the holy Bible and the phenomena of nature proceed alike from the divine Word, the former as the dictate of the Holy Ghost and the latter as the observant executrix of God's commands. It is necessary for the Bible, in order to be accommodated to the understanding of every man, to speak many things which appear to differ from the absolute truth so far as the bare meaning of the words is concerned. But Nature, on the other hand, is inexorable and immutable; she never transgresses the laws imposed upon her, or cares a whit whether her abstruse reasons and methods of operation are understandable to men. For that reason it appears that nothing physical which sense-experience sets before our eyes, or which necessary demonstrations prove to us, ought to be called in question (much less condemned) upon the testimony of biblical passages which may have some different meaning beneath their words. For the Bible is not chained in every expression to conditions as strict as those which govern all physical effects; nor is God any less excellently revealed in Nature's actions than in the sacred statements of the Bible. . . .

From this I do not mean to infer that we need not have an extraordinary esteem for the passage of holy Scripture. On the contrary, having arrived at any certainties in physics, we ought to utilize these as the most appropriate aids in the true exposition of the Bible and in the investigation of those meanings which are necessarily contained therein, for these must be concordant with demonstrated truths. I should judge that the authority of the Bible was designed to persuade men of those articles and propositions which, surpassing all human reasoning, could not be made credible by science, or by any other means than through the very mouth of the Holy Spirit.

Yet even in those propositions which are not matters of faith, this authority ought to be preferred over that of all human writings which are supported only by bare assertions or probable arguments, and not set forth in a demonstrative way. This I hold to be necessary and proper to the same extent that divine wisdom surpasses all human judgment and conjecture.

But I do not feel obliged to believe that that same God who has endowed us with senses, reason, and intellect has intended to forgo their use and by some other means to give us knowledge which we can attain by them.

Mathematical Principles of Natural Philosophy

Sir Isaac Newton

The greatest scientific synthesis of the seventeenth century was made by Isaac Newton (1642–1727), who was born in England and attained a post as professor of mathematics at Cambridge University. Newton made his most important discoveries early in life. By the beginning of the eighteenth century he was the most admired scientific figure in Europe. He made fundamental discoveries concerning gravity, light, and differential calculus. Most important, he synthesized various scientific findings and methods into a description of the universe as working according to measurable, predictable mechanical laws. Newton's most famous work, Mathematical Principles of Natural Philosophy *(1687), contains his theory of universal gravitation. In the following selection from that work, Newton describes his four rules for arriving at knowledge.*

Consider: *Why Newton's rules might be particularly useful for the experimental sciences; ways these rules differ from those of Descartes.*

RULE I

We are to admit no more causes of natural things than such as are both true and sufficient to explain their appearances.

To this purpose the philosophers say that Nature does nothing in vain, and more is in vain when less will serve; for Nature is pleased with simplicity, and affects not the pomp of superfluous causes.

RULE II

Therefore to the same natural effects we must, as far as possible, assign the same causes.

As to respiration in a man and in a beast; the descent of stones in *Europe* and in *America;* the light of our culinary fire and of the sun; the reflection of light in the earth, and in the planets.

RULE III

The qualities of bodies, which admit neither intensification nor remission of degrees, and which are found to belong to all bodies within the reach of our experiments, are to be esteemed the universal qualities of all bodies whatsoever.

SOURCE: Sir Isaac Newton, *Mathematical Principles of Natural Philosophy*, Andrew Motte, trans., revised by Florian Cajori (Berkeley, Calif.: University of California Press, 1947), pp. 398, 400. Copyright © 1934 Renewed 1962 Regents of the University of California. Reprinted by permission of the University of California Press.

For since the qualities of bodies are only known to us by experiments, we are to hold for universal all such as universally agree with experiments; and such as are not liable to diminution can never be quite taken away.

RULE IV

In experimental philosophy we are to look upon propositions inferred by general induction from phenomena as accurately or very nearly true, notwithstanding any contrary hypotheses that may be imagined, till such time as other phenomena occur, by which they may either be made more accurate, or liable to exceptions.

This rule we must follow, that the argument of induction may not be evaded by hypotheses.

What Is Enlightenment?
Immanuel Kant

One of the most pervasive themes among Enlightenment thinkers was a self-conscious sense of a spirit of enlightenment. This is illustrated in the following excerpt from a short essay by Immanuel Kant (1724–1804) of Königsberg in East Prussia. Kant, one of the world's most profound philosophers, is particularly known for his analysis of the human mind and how it relates to nature, as set forth in his Critique of Pure Reason *(1781). In the following essay, written in 1784, Kant defines the spirit of the Enlightenment and describes some of its implications.*

> **Consider:** *What Kant means by "freedom" and why he feels freedom is so central to the Enlightenment; how people can become enlightened and the appropriate environment to facilitate this enlightenment; what Kant would consider "mature"; how Kant relates enlightenment and politics.*

Enlightenment is man's leaving his self-caused immaturity. Immaturity is the incapacity to use one's intelligence without the guidance of another. Such immaturity is self-caused if it is not caused by lack of intelligence, but by lack of determination and courage to use one's intelligence without being guided by another. *Sapere Aude!* Have the courage to use your own intelligence! is therefore the motto of the enlightenment.

Through laziness and cowardice a large part of mankind, even after nature has freed them from alien guidance, gladly remain immature. It is because of laziness and cowardice that it is so easy for others to usurp the role of guardians. It is so comfortable to be a minor! If I have a book which provides meaning for me, a

SOURCE: Immanuel Kant, "What Is Enlightenment?" in *The Philosophy of Kant*, Carl J. Friedrich, ed. Reprinted by permission of Random House, Inc. (New York, 1949), pp. 132–134, 138–139. Copyright © 1949 by Random House, Inc.

pastor who has conscience for me, a doctor who will judge my diet for me and so on, then I do not need to exert myself. I do not have any need to think; if I can pay, others will take over the tedious job for me. The guardians who have kindly undertaken the supervision will see to it that by far the largest part of mankind, including the entire "beautiful sex," should consider the step into maturity, not only as difficult but as very dangerous. . . .

But it is more nearly possible for a public to enlighten itself: this is even inescapable if only the public is given its freedom. . . .

All that is required for this enlightenment is *freedom;* and particularly the least harmful of all that may be called freedom, namely, the freedom for man to make *public use* of his reason in all matters. . . .

The question may now be put: Do we live at present in an enlightened age? The answer is: No, but in an age of enlightenment. Much still prevents men from being placed in a position or even being placed into position to use their own minds securely and well in matters of religion. But we do have very definite indications that this field of endeavor is being opened up for men to work freely and reduce gradually the hindrances preventing a general enlightenment and an escape from self-caused immaturity. In this sense, this age is the age of enlightenment and the age of Frederick (The Great). . . .

I have emphasized the main point of enlightenment, that is of man's release from his self-caused immaturity, primarily *in matters of religion*. I have done this because our rulers have no interest in playing the guardian of their subjects in matters of arts and sciences. Furthermore immaturity in matters of religion is not only most noxious but also most dishonorable. But the point of view of a head of state who favors freedom in the arts and sciences goes even further; for he understands that there is no danger in legislation permitting his subjects to make *public* use of their own reason and to submit *publicly* their thoughts regarding a better framing of such laws together with a frank criticism of existing *legislation*. We have a shining example of this; no prince excels him whom we admire. Only he who is himself enlightened does not fear spectres when he at the same time has a well-disciplined army at his disposal as a guarantee of public peace. Only he can say what (the ruler of a) free state dare not say: *Argue as much as you want and about whatever you want but obey!*

Prospectus for the Encyclopedia of Arts and Sciences

Denis Diderot

More than any other work, the Encyclopedia of Arts and Sciences, *edited by Denis Diderot (1713–1784) and Jean-le-Rond d'Alembert (1717–1783), epitomizes the Enlightenment. Written between 1745 and 1780, it presented to the public the sum of knowledge considered important by Enlightenment thinkers. The critical Enlightenment spirit underlying the* Encyclopedia *led traditional authorities to condemn it and to suppress it more than once. The following is an excerpt from the* Prospectus *that appeared in 1750, announcing the forthcoming* Encyclopedia. *The* Prospectus *was written by Diderot, a philosopher, novelist, and playwright who had already been in trouble with the authorities for his writings. The* Prospectus *apparently aroused widespread expectations; even before the first volume of the* Encyclopedia *appeared, more than a thousand orders for it had been received.*

> **Consider:** *What a reader could hope to gain by purchasing the* Encyclopedia *and how these hopes themselves reflect the spirit of the Enlightenment; how this selection from the* Prospectus *reflects the same ideas expressed by Kant; how the Enlightenment as described here related to the scientific revolution of the seventeenth century.*

It cannot be denied that, since the revival of letters among us, we owe partly to dictionaries the general enlightenment that has spread in society and the germ of science that is gradually preparing men's minds for more profound knowledge. How valuable would it not be, then, to have a book of this kind that one could consult on all subjects and that would serve as much to guide those who have the courage to work at the instruction of others as to enlighten those who only instruct themselves!

This is one advantage we thought of, but it is not the only one. In condensing to dictionary form all that concerns the arts and sciences, it remained necessary to make people aware of the assistance they lend each other; to make use of this assistance to render principles more certain and their consequences clearer; to indicate the distant and close relationships of the beings that make up nature, which have occupied men; to show, by showing the interlacing both of roots and

SOURCE: Denis Diderot, *Prospectus à l'Encyclopédie*, in Diderot, *Oeuvres complètes*, eds. Jules Assézat and Maurice Tourneux, 20 vols. (Paris, 1875–1877), vol. XIII, pp. 129–131, in Richard W. Lyman and Lewis W. Spitz, eds., *Major Crises in Western Civilization*, vol. II, Nina B. Gunzenhauser, trans. (New York: Harcourt, Brace & World, 1965), pp. 11–12. Reprinted by permission of Harcourt Brace Jovanovich, Inc.

of branches, the impossibility of understanding thoroughly some parts of the whole without exploring many others; to produce a general picture of the efforts of the human spirit in all areas and in all centuries; to present these matters with clarity; to give to each the proper scope, and to prove, if possible, our epigraph by our success. . . .

The majority of these works appeared during the last century and were not completely scorned. It was found that if they did not show much talent, they at least bore the marks of labor and of knowledge. But what would these encyclopedias mean to us? What progress have we not made since then in the arts and sciences? How many truths discovered today, which were not foreseen then? True philosophy was in its cradle; the geometry of infinity did not yet exist; experimental physics was just appearing; there was no dialectic at all; the laws of sound criticism were entirely unknown. Descartes, Boyle, Huyghens, Newton, Leibnitz, the Bernoullis, Locke, Bayle, Pascal, Corneille, Racine, Bourdaloue, Bossuet, etc., either had not yet been born or had not yet written. The spirit of research and competition did not motivate the scholars: another spirit, less fecund perhaps, but rarer, that of precision and method, had not yet conquered the various divisions of literature; and the academies, whose efforts have advanced the arts and sciences to such an extent, were not yet established. . . . At the end of this project you will find the tree of human knowledge, indicating the connection of ideas, which has directed us in this vast operation.

A Vindication of the Rights of Woman
Mary Wollstonecraft

While the Enlightenment was dominated by men, there were possibilities for active involvement by women. Several women played particularly important roles as patrons and intellectual contributors to the gatherings of philosophes and members of the upper-middle-class and aristocratic elite held in the salons of Paris and elsewhere. It was, however, far more difficult for a woman to publish serious essays in the Enlightenment tradition. Indeed, Enlightenment thinkers did little to change basic attitudes about the inferiority of women. One person who managed to do both was Mary Wollstonecraft (1759–1797), a British author who in 1792 published A Vindication of the Rights of Woman. *The book was a sharply reasoned attack against the oppression of women and an argument for educational change. In the following excerpt, Wollstonecraft addresses the author of a proposed new constitution for France that, in her opinion, does not adequately deal with the rights of women.*

SOURCE: Mary Wollstonecraft, *The Rights of Woman* (London: J. M. Dent and Sons, Ltd., 1929), pp. 10–11.

Consider: *Why education is so central to her argument; the ways in which this argument reflects the methods and ideals of the Enlightenment.*

Contending for the rights of woman, my main argument is built on this simple principle, that if she be not prepared by education to become the companion of man, she will stop the progress of knowledge and virtue; for truth must be common to all, or it will be inefficacious with respect to its influence on general practice. And how can woman be expected to co-operate unless she knows why she ought to be virtuous? unless freedom strengthens her reason till she comprehends her duty, and see in what manner it is connected with her real good? If children are to be educated to understand the true principle of patriotism, their mother must be a patriot; and the love of mankind, from which an orderly train of virtues spring, can only be produced by considering the moral and civil interest of mankind; but the education and situation of woman at present shuts her out from such investigations.

In this work I have produced many arguments, which to me were conclusive, to prove that the prevailing notion respecting a sexual character was subversive of mortality, and I have contended, that to render the human body and mind more perfect, chastity must more universally prevail, and that chastity will never be respected in the male world till the person of a woman is not, as it were, idolised, when little virtue or sense embellish it with the grand traces of mental beauty, or the interesting simplicity of affection.

Consider, sir, dispassionately these observations, for a glimpse of this truth seemed to open before you when you observed, "that to see one-half of the human race excluded by the other from all participation of government was a political phenomenon, that, according to abstract principles, it was impossible to explain." If so, on what does your constitution rest? If the abstract rights of man will bear discussion and explanation, those of woman, by a parity of reasoning, will not shrink from the same test; though a different opinion prevails in this country, built on the very arguments which you use to justify the oppression of woman—prescription.

Consider—I address you as a legislator—whether, when men contend for their freedom, and to be allowed to judge for themselves respecting their own happiness, it be not inconsistent and unjust to subjugate women, even though you firmly believe that you are acting in the manner best calculated to promote their happiness? Who made man the exclusive judge, if woman partake with him of the gift of reason?

The Social Contract
Jean Jacques Rousseau

More than anyone else, Jean Jacques Rousseau (1712–1778) tested the outer limits of Enlightenment thought and went on to criticize its very foundations. Born in Geneva, he spent much of his life in France (mainly in Paris), where he became one of the philosophes who contributed to the Encyclopedia. *Yet he also undermined Enlightenment thought by holding that social institutions had corrupted people and that human beings in the state of nature were more pure, free, and happy than in modern civilization. This line of thought provided a foundation for the growth of Romanticism in the late eighteenth and early nineteenth centuries. Rousseau's most important political work was* The Social Contract *(1762), in which he argued for popular sovereignty. In the following selection from that work, Rousseau focuses on what he considers the fundamental argument of the book—the passage from the state of nature to the civil state by means of the social contract.*

> **Consider:** *Rousseau's solution to the main problem of* The Social Contract; *the advantages and disadvantages of the social contract; what characteristics of Enlightenment thought are reflected in this selection.*

"The problem is to find a form of association which will defend and protect with the whole common force the person and goods of each associate, and in which each, while uniting himself with all, may still obey himself alone, and remain as free as before." This is the fundamental problem of which *The Social Contract* provides the solution.

The clauses of this contract are so determined by the nature of the act that the slightest modification would make them vain and ineffective; so that, although they have perhaps never been formally set forth, they are everywhere the same and everywhere tacitly admitted and recognised, until, on the violation of the social compact, each regains his original rights and resumes his natural liberty, while losing the conventional liberty in favour of which he renounced it.

These clauses, properly understood, may be reduced to one—the total alienation of each associate, together with all his rights, to the whole community; for, in the first place, as each gives himself absolutely, the conditions are the same for all; and, this being so, no one has any interest in making them burdensome to others.

Moreover, the alienation being without reserve, the union is as perfect as it can be, and no associate has anything more to demand: for, if the individuals retained certain rights, as there would be no common superior to decide between them and the public, each, being on one point his own judge, would ask to be so on all;

SOURCE: Jean Jacques Rousseau, *The Social Contract and Discourses* (London: J. M. Dent, Everyman Library, 1913), pp. 14–15, 18–19.

the state of nature would thus continue, and the association would necessarily become inoperative or tyrannical.

Finally, each man, in giving himself to all, gives himself to nobody; and as there is no associate over whom he does not acquire the same right as he yields others over himself, he gains on equivalent for everything he loses, and an increase of force for the preservation of what he has.

If then we discard from the social compact what is not of its essence, we shall find that it reduces itself to the following terms—

Each of us puts his person and all his power in common under the supreme direction of the general will, and, in our corporate capacity, we receive each member as an indivisible part of the whole.

✿

The passage from the state of nature to the civil state produces a very remarkable change in man, by substituting justice for instinct in his conduct, and giving his actions the morality they had formerly lacked. Then only, when the voice of duty takes the place of physical impulses and right of appetite, does man, who so far had considered only himself, find that he is forced to act on different principles, and to consult his reason before listening to his inclinations. Although, in this state, he deprives himself of some advantages which he got from nature, he gains in return others so great, his faculties are so stimulated and developed, his ideas so extended, his feelings so ennobled, and his whole soul so uplifted, that, did not the abuses of this new condition often degrade him below that which he left, he would be bound to bless continually the happy moment which took him from it for ever, and, instead of a stupid and unimaginative animal, made him an intelligent being and a man.

Let us draw up the whole account in terms easily commensurable. What man loses by the social contract is his natural liberty and an unlimited right to everything he tries to get and succeeds in getting; what he gains is civil liberty and the proprietorship of all he possesses. If we are to avoid mistake in weighing one against the other, we must clearly distinguish natural liberty, which is bounded only by the strength of the individual, from civil liberty, which is limited by the general will; and possession, which is merely the effect of force or the right of the first occupier, from property, which can be founded only on a positive title.

We might, over and above all this, add, to what man acquires in the civil state, moral liberty, which alone makes him truly master of himself; for the mere impulse of appetite is slavery, while obedience to a law which we prescribe to ourselves is liberty. But I have already said too much on this head, and the philosophical meaning of the word liberty does not now concern us.

VISUAL SOURCES

Experiment with an Air Pump
Joseph Wright

Few paintings provide a better image of the Enlightenment than Experiment with an Air Pump *(1768) by the British artist Joseph Wright. The experiment takes place in the center of the picture; its apparent success is evidenced by the dead bird inside a closed glass bowl from which the air has been pumped out. The informally dressed experimenter is carefully observing his work. Around him are members of his family and some well-dressed friends.*

The form and content of this picture symbolize the Enlightenment. A small source of light is sufficient to enlighten humanity and reveal the laws of nature. Science is not just for specialists but something amateurs can understand and practice to obtain practical

Photo 4-1

The Tate Gallery, London

results. That it is a British painting is particularly significant, for the English led in developing useful machines and were identified as having a more pragmatic approach to science and ideas than other peoples. The painting also reveals customary images of the sexes: the experimenter boldly forging on while to his left a friend or associate calmly explains what is happening to a woman and her daughter, whose sensibilities are as appropriately fragile as the dying bird—the main object of their concern.

> **Consider:** *Any common themes in this painting and the documents by Diderot and Kant.*

SECONDARY SOURCES

Early Modern Europe: Motives for the Scientific Revolution
Sir George Clark

By the seventeenth century, certain broad historical developments had set the stage for individuals to make the discoveries we associate with the Scientific Revolution. In addition, these individuals were motivated in ways that medieval people were not and used the new and growing body of techniques, materials, and knowledge to make their discoveries. In the following selection, British historian Sir George Clark, a recognized authority on the seventeenth century, examines some of the motives that led people to engage in scientific work.

> **Consider:** *The distinctions Clark makes among different people engaged in scientific work; why, more than thirteenth- or fourteenth-century people, these seventeenth-century people had a "disinterested desire to know."*

There were an infinite number of motives which led men to engage in scientific work and to clear the scientific point of view from encumbrances; but we may group together some of the most important under general headings, always remembering that in actual life each of them was compounded with the others. There were economic motives. The Portuguese explorers wanted their new instrument for navigation; the German mine-owners asked questions about metal-

---

SOURCE: Sir George Clark, *Early Modern Europe.* Reprinted by permission of The Oxford University Press (Oxford, 1957), pp. 164–165.

lurgy and about machines for lifting and carrying heavy loads; Italian engineers improved their canals and locks and harbours by applying the principles of hydrostatics; English trading companies employed experts who used new methods of drawing charts. Not far removed from the economic motives were those of the physicians and surgeons, who revolutionized anatomy and physiology, and did much more good than harm with their new medicines and new operations, though some of them now seem absurd. Like the doctors, the soldiers called science to their aid in designing and aiming artillery or in planning fortifications. But there were other motives far removed from the economic sphere. Jewellers learnt much about precious and semi-precious stones, but so did magicians. Musicians learnt the mathematics of harmony; painters and architects studied light and colour, substances and proportions, not only as craftsmen but as artists. For a number of reasons religion impelled men to scientific study. The most definite and old-established was the desire to reach absolute correctness in calculating the dates for the annual fixed and movable festivals of the Church: it was a pope who presided over the astronomical researchers by which the calendar was reformed in the sixteenth century. Deeper and stronger was the desire to study the wonders of science, and the order which it unravelled in the universe, as manifestations of the Creator's will. This was closer than any of the other motives to the central impulse which actuated them all, the disinterested desire to know.

No Scientific Revolution for Women

Bonnie S. Anderson and Judith P. Zinsser

The Scientific Revolution was generally carried out by men. A few women participated directly in the Scientific Revolution, but they were the exception rather than the rule. The Scientific Revolution was based on principles such as observing, measuring, experimenting, and coming to reasoned conclusions. Were these principles applied by men to change assumptions about women, particularly about female physiology? Bonnie S. Anderson and Judith P. Zinsser address this question in their interpretative survey of women in European history, A History of Their Own.

> **Consider:** *According to Anderson and Zinsser, why there was no Scientific Revolution for women; how perceptions of female physiology relate to broader assumptions about women and men.*

In the sixteenth and seventeenth centuries Europe's learned men questioned, altered, and dismissed some of the most hallowed precepts of Europe's inherited

SOURCE: Excerpts from *A History of Their Own*, vol. II, by Bonnie Anderson and Judith Zinsser. Copyright © 1988 by Harper & Row, Publishers, Inc. Reprinted by permission of HarperCollins Publishers, Inc.

wisdom. The intellectual upheaval of the Scientific Revolution caused them to examine and describe anew the nature of the universe and its force, the nature of the human body and its functions. Men used telescopes and rejected the traditional insistence on the smooth surface of the moon. Galileo, Leibnitz, and Newton studied and charted the movement of the planets, discovered gravity and the true relationship between the earth and the sun. Fallopio dissected the human body, Harvey discovered the circulation of the blood, and Leeuwenhoek found spermatozoa with his microscope.

For women, however, there was no Scientific Revolution. When men studied female anatomy, when they spoke of female physiology, of women's reproductive organs, of the female role in procreation, they ceased to be scientific. They suspended reason and did not accept the evidence of their senses. Tradition, prejudice, and imagination, not scientific observation, governed their conclusions about women. The writings of the classical authors like Aristotle and Galen continued to carry the same authority as they had when first written, long after they had been discarded in other areas. Men spoke in the name of the new "science" but mouthed words and phrases from the old misogyny. In the name of "science" they gave a supposed physiological basis to the traditional views of women's nature, function, and role. Science affirmed what men had always known, what custom, law, and religion had postulated and justified. With the authority of their "objective," "rational" inquiry they restated ancient premises and arrived at the same traditional conclusions: the innate superiority of the male and the justifiable subordination of the female.

The Age of Reason
Frank Manuel

The Enlightenment owes its substance to the thought of a relatively small group of eighteenth-century philosophes who came from many countries but were centered in France. Although they often argued among themselves, there was a set of approaches and propositions on which most of them agreed. In the following selection Frank E. Manuel, a historian of ideas from Brandeis and New York University, analyzes the philosophes' new moral outlook, an outlook that seems particularly modern.

Consider: *How the primary documents support or contradict Manuel's interpretation; the ways in which the moral outlook described here is overly optimistic and naive; the elements of this outlook that make the most sense for today's world.*

Despite their sharp cleavages and varying interests, there was a common ground on which all the intellectuals could stand, and from their inconsistent and even

SOURCE: Frank E. Manuel, *The Age of Reason*. Reprinted by permission of Cornell University Press (New York, 1951), pp. 46–47. Copyright © 1951 by Cornell University.

incompatible tendencies there emerged a moral outlook distinct from that of the previous age. The eighteenth-century philosophers popularized general precepts of conduct which in time were widely accepted in most civilized societies. They made aggressive war look odious and mocked the ideal of military glory. They preached religious toleration, free speech, a free press. They were in favor of the sanctions of law to protect individual liberties and they were against tyranny which governed by caprice. They wanted equality of all citizens before the law and they were opposed to any recognition of social distinctions when men were brought to justice. They abhorred torture and other barbaric punishments and pleaded for their abolition; they believed that punishment should fit the crime and should be imposed only to restrain potential malefactors. They wanted freedom of movement across state boundaries both for individuals and articles of commerce. Most of them believed that it did not require the threat of eternal torment in hell to make moral ideas generally accepted among mankind. They were convinced that the overwhelming number of men, if their natural goodness were not perverted in childhood, would act in harmony with simple rules and the dictates of rational principles without the necessity for severe restraints and awful punishments.

In summary, though the *philosophes* did not solve the problem of the existence of evil and suffering in the world, they did manage to establish in European society a general consensus about conduct which is evil, a moral attitude which still sustains us. Despite their subservient behavior toward some of the European despots and the social anarchy ultimately inherent in their doctrines of absolute self-interest, the eighteenth-century men of letters did formulate a set of moral principles which to this day remain basic to any discussion of human rights. The deficiencies of their optimistic moral and political outlook are by now visible, but they did venture the first bold examination of reality since the Greeks and they dared to set forth brand-new abstractions about man and the universe. They taught their contemporaries to view the institutions of church and state in the light of reason and to judge them by the simple criterion of human happiness.

Eighteenth-Century Europe: Enlightened Absolutism
M. S. Anderson

Historians have long debated exactly how much the Enlightenment influenced monarchs of the time. Traditionally there has been considerable acceptance of the view that monarchs such as Joseph II of Austria and Frederick II of Prussia were enlightened. In recent years this view has been seriously narrowed and questioned to the point where many

SOURCE: M. S. Anderson, *Eighteenth-Century Europe: 1713–1789*. Reprinted by permission of Oxford University Press (Oxford, 1966), pp. 100–102. Copyright © Oxford University Press.

historians feel that enlightened despotism and enlightened absolutism are no longer terms that can usefully be applied to these eighteenth-century monarchs. M. S. Anderson, of the London School of Economics and Political Science, supports this newer critical view. In the following selection he analyzes the limited ways in which eighteenth-century monarchs can be considered enlightened.

> **Consider:** *The characteristics of enlightened despotism; how enlightened despotism differs from seventeenth-century absolutism and twentieth-century totalitarianism.*

It is generally agreed that in the later eighteenth century, notably in the generation from about 1760 to 1790, many of the monarchies of Europe began to display new characteristics. In one state after another rulers or ministers (Catherine II in Russia, Frederick II in Prussia, Gustavus III in Sweden, Charles III in Spain, Struensee in Denmark, Tanucci in Naples) began to be influenced, or to claim that they were influenced, by the ideas which economists and political philosophers, notably in France, had been proclaiming for several decades. This "enlightened despotism" is in many ways an unsatisfactory subject of study. Except in a few cases—notably those of the Archduke Leopold in Tuscany (1765–90) and his better-known brother Joseph in the Habsburg dominions—it was always largely superficial and contrived. Usually the policies actively pursued by the enlightened despots, however warm the welcome they gave to new theories of government and administration, ran to some extent in traditional channels.

All of them attempted to improve the administration of their states, especially with regard to taxation, and to unify their territories more effectively. Many of them attempted or at least envisaged judicial reforms, notably by the drawing up of elaborate legal codes. The code of civil procedure and the penal code issued by Joseph II in 1781 and 1787, and above all the great Prussian code of 1791, the outcome of many years of labour during the reign of Frederick II, are outstanding examples. With few exceptions the enlightened despots hoped to achieve their ends by increasing their own authority and the power of the central government in their states. But with the partial exception of the desire for legal reform none of these ambitions was new. In differing ways they had been seen in the activities of the 'New Monarchs' of the sixteenth century and in those of Louis XIV and his contemporaries; they were to be seen once more, with greater intensity and effect, in those of Napoleon I. Some elements of novelty can, it is true, be detected in the attitude of several rulers and governments of the later eighteenth century. In particular the growing humanitarianism, which "enlightened" thought and writing had done much to foster, was now inspiring efforts to abolish judicial torture and greater consideration than in the past for the interests of such groups as orphans and old soldiers. But there were few rulers whose policies in practice represented more than the development of ambitions cherished by their predecessors. Thus Frederick II made little real alteration in the administrative system bequeathed him by his father; and most of his territorial ambitions, notably in Poland, were also inherited. Most of the changes which Catherine II attempted or contemplated in Russia—the secularization of church lands in 1764, the reform of local government in 1775, the codification of the law, attempted particularly by the unsuc-cessful Legislative Commission of 1767—had been suggested during the reigns of her predecessors. What distinguished Frederick and Catherine from Frederick William I and Peter the Great was not so much their policies as their explicit justification of them (especially in the case of Catherine) in terms of advanced contemporary thought. It was this appeal to intellectual and moral standards rather than to those of mere expediency that made these rules appear to be doing something new. And this appeal was essentially spurious. No ruler of any major state could allow his policies to be dictated by theory, however attractive. The history, geographical position, and resources of the state he ruled, the power or weakness of its neighbours, and a host of other factors, set limits to what he might reasonably attempt in either internal or external affairs. Joseph II spent his reign in a continuous series of efforts to improve the administration of his territories and the condition of his subjects. More than any other major ruler of the period he was truly inspired by the theories of government then current in enlightened Europe. Yet his disregard of realities in his relations with the Hungarians, with the inhabitants of his Netherlands provinces, and with the Catholic church, and the failure and near-collapse to which this disregard had led by the end of his reign, were the supreme proof that, as always, there was an 'order of possible progress' in politics and all other aspects of life in the eighteenth century, and that this order could be disregarded only to a very limited extent.

Chapter Questions

1. What were the main ways in which the science of the seventeenth century constituted a break from the past? What were some of the main problems facing seventeenth-century scientists in making this break?

2. What core of ideas and attitudes most clearly connects Enlightenment thinkers as revealed in these sources? How do these ideas relate to eighteenth-century society and institutions?

3. What policies would an eighteenth-century ruler have to pursue to fit to the greatest degree the ideas and assumptions of Enlightenment thinkers? What hindrances were faced by monarchs who wanted to be more enlightened?

4. In what ways do the sources support the argument that together, the Scientific Revolution and the Enlightenment constitute a single intellectual revolution of great long-term significance?

FIVE

Revolution, Nationalism, and the State in Europe, 1789–1914

In 1789, the French Revolution ended the relative political and social stability of the Ancien Regime and initiated the period Western historians usually call the Modern Era. Within a few tumultuous years feudalism was abolished, liberal principles echoing Enlightenment thought were formally recognized, Church lands were confiscated, the monarchy was abolished, and government administration was reorganized.

A decade later the turmoil initiated in 1789 was far from over. Napoleon Bonaparte, rising with opportunities presented by the French Revolution, gained power not only in France, but directly and indirectly throughout much of continental Europe. His final fall in 1815 marked the end of a series of wars and the Age of Napoleon.

The European powers crafted a settlement at the Congress of Vienna (1814–1815). Conservatism dominated, rejecting changes instituted during the revolutionary and Napoleonic periods, restoring traditional groups and governments to power, and resisting liberalism and nationalism. Nevertheless, movements for national liberation and liberal reform surfaced during the 1820s, 1830s, and 1840s. Liberalism, encompassing demands for greater freedom, constitutional government, and political rights, was particularly strong in western Europe. A climax came in 1848, when revolutions erupted across Europe—usually in the name of nationalism or liberalism. Victories proved short-lived and soon groups standing for authoritarian rule took advantage of the disunity to regain power.

Between 1850 and 1914 politics in Europe became focused on increased governmental involvement in the economic and social life of the nation and the growth of nationalism. With its roots in the French Revolution and the Napoleonic period, nationalism was capitalized on by national governments and was at the core of the successful unification movements in Italy and Germany.

The sources in this chapter focus on three topics: revolution; conservatism and liberalism; and nationalism. Historians are fascinated by revolutions, through which change is unusually rapid and dramatic. Here several sources deal with the causes and significance of various revolutions during the period, but particularly the French Revolution of 1789. Included is an examination of Napoleon's appeal and the significance of his policies. The nature of con-

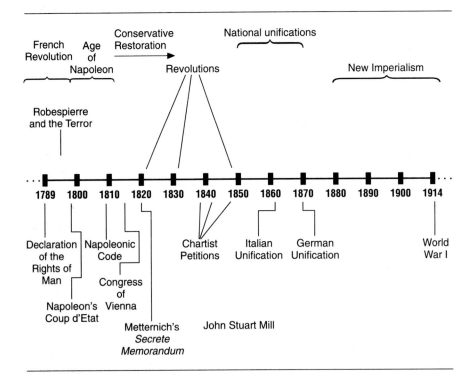

servatism and liberalism will be examined by looking at their doctrines and political policies. Nationalism will be analyzed by examining its common characteristics.

This focus on revolution and political developments in Europe between 1789 and 1914 sets the stage for an examination of the economic, social, and cultural changes that transformed the West during this same period.

PRIMARY SOURCES

The Cahiers: Discontents of the Third Estate

Pressured by discontent and financial problems, Louis XVI called for a meeting of the Estates General in 1789. This representative institution, which had not met for 175 years, reflected the traditional formal divisions in French society: the First Estate, the clergy; the Second Estate, the nobility; and the Third Estate, all the rest from banker and lawyer to peasant. In anticipation of the meeting of the Estates General, the king requested and received cahiers, lists of grievances drawn up by local groups of each of the three Estates. These cahiers have provided historians with an unusually rich source of materials revealing what was bothering people just before the outbreak of the revolution in 1789. The following is an excerpt from a cahier from the Third Estate in Carcassonne.

> **Consider:** *Why these grievances might be revolutionary; the ways in which these grievances are peculiar to the Third Estate and not shared by the First and Second Estates.*

8. Among these rights the following should be especially noted: the nation should hereafter be subject only to such laws and taxes as it shall itself freely ratify.

9. The meetings of the Estates General of the kingdom should be fixed for definite periods, and the subsidies judged necessary for the support of the state and the public service should be noted for no longer a period than to the close of the year in which the next meeting of the Estates General is to occur.

10. In order to assure to the third estate the influence to which it is entitled in view of the number of its members, the amount of its contributions to the public

SOURCE: "Cahier of the Grievances, Complaints, and Protests of the Electoral District of Carcassone. . . ." From James Harvey Robinson, ed., *Readings in European History*, vol. II (Boston: Ginn, 1904), pp. 399–400.

treasury, and the manifold interests which it has to defend or promote in the national assemblies, its votes in the assembly should be taken and counted by head.

11. No order, corporation, or individual citizen may lay claim to any pecuniary exemptions. . . . All taxes should be assessed on the same system throughout the nation.

12. The due exacted from commoners holding fiefs should be abolished, and also the general or particular regulations which exclude members of the third estate from certain positions, offices, and ranks which have hitherto been bestowed on nobles either for life or hereditarily. A law should be passed declaring members of the third estate qualified to fill all such offices for which they are judged to be personally fitted.

13. Since individual liberty is intimately associated with national liberty, his Majesty is hereby petitioned not to permit that it be hereafter interfered with by arbitrary orders for imprisonment. . . .

14. Freedom should be granted also to the press, which should however be subjected, by means of strict regulations, to the principles of religion, morality, and public decency. . . .

The Declaration of the Rights of Man and Citizen

No document better summarizes the ideals underlying the French Revolution than The Declaration of the Rights of Man and Citizen. *After an extended discussion, this document was passed by the National Assembly on August 27, 1789; later a revised version of it was incorporated into the Constitution of 1791. Its provisions are a combination of general statements about human rights and specific statements about what the government should and should not do. This document corresponds to the American* Declaration of Independence. *It is also viewed more broadly as containing the general principles for democratic revolutions in the eighteenth and nineteenth centuries.*

> **Consider:** *How this document reflects ideals of the Enlightenment; at which social groups this document was aimed; who would suffer most from or be most infuriated by its provisions; the ways in which this document is inconsistent with monarchical government; how a monarch might retain meaningful powers while still conforming to this document.*

SOURCE: James Harvey Robinson, ed., "The French Revolution, 1789–1791," in *Translations and Reprints from the Original Sources of European History*, vol. I, no. 5, Department of History of the University of Pennsylvania, ed. (Philadelphia: University of Pennsylvania Press, 1898), pp. 6–8.

The representative of the French people, organized as a National Assembly, believing that the ignorance, neglect or contempt of the rights of man are the sole cause of public calamities and of the corruption of governments, have determined to set forth in a solemn declaration the natural, inalienable and sacred rights of man, in order that this declaration, being constantly before all the members of the social body, shall remind them continually of their rights and duties; in order that the acts of the legislative power, as well as those of the executive power, may be compared at any moment with the ends of all political institutions and may thus be more respected; and, lastly, in order that the grievances of the citizens, based hereafter upon simple and incontestable principles, shall tend to the maintenance of the constitution and redound to the happiness of all. Therefore the National Assembly recognizes and proclaims, in the presence and under the auspices of the Supreme Being, the following rights of man and of the citizen:—

ARTICLE 1. Men are born and remain free and equal in rights. Social distinctions may only be founded upon the general good.

2. The aim of all political association is the preservation of the natural and imprescriptible rights of man. These rights are liberty, property, security and resistance to oppression.

3. The principle of all sovereignty resides essentially in the nation. No body nor individual may exercise any authority which does not proceed directly from the nation.

4. Liberty consists in the freedom to do everything which injures no one else; hence the exercise of the natural rights of each man has no limits except those which assure to the other members of the society the enjoyment of the same rights. These limits can only be determined by law.

5. Law can only prohibit such actions as are hurtful to society. Nothing may be prevented which is not forbidden by law, and no one may be forced to do anything not provided for by law.

6. Law is the expression of the general will. Every citizen has a right to participate personally or through his representative in its formation. It must be the same for all, whether it protects or punishes. All citizens, being equal in the eyes of the law, are equally eligible to all dignities and to all public positions and occupations, according to their abilities, and without distinction except that of their virtues and talents.

7. No person shall be accused, arrested or imprisoned except in the cases and according to the forms prescribed by law. Any one soliciting, transmitting, executing or causing to be executed any arbitrary order shall be punished. But any citizen summoned or arrested in virtue of the law shall submit without delay, as resistance constitutes an offence.

8. The law shall provide for such punishments only as are strictly and obviously necessary, and no one shall suffer punishment except it be legally inflicted in virtue of a law passed and promulgated before the commission of the offence.

9. As all persons are held innocent until they shall have been declared guilty, if

arrest shall be deemed indispensable, all harshness not essential to the securing of the prisoner's person shall be severely repressed by law.

10. No one shall be disquieted on account of his opinions, including his religious views, provided their manifestation does not disturb the public order established by law.

11. The free communication of ideas and opinions is one of the most precious of the rights of man. Every citizen may, accordingly, speak, write and print with freedom, but shall be responsible for such abuses of this freedom as shall be defined by law.

12. The security of the rights of man and of the citizen requires public military force. These forces are, therefore, established for the good of all and not for the personal advantage of those to whom they shall be entrusted.

13. A common contribution is essential for the maintenance of the public forces and for the cost of administration. This should be equitably distributed among all the citizens in proportion to their means.

14. All the citizens have a right to decide, either personally or by their representatives, as to the necessity of the public contribution; to grant this freely; to know to what uses it is put; and to fix the proportion, the mode of assessment, and of collection, and the duration of the taxes.

15. Society has the right to require of every public agent an account of his administration.

16. A society in which the observance of the law is not assured, nor the separation of powers defined, has no constitution at all.

17. Since property is an inviolable and sacred right, no one shall be deprived thereof except where public necessity, legally determined, shall clearly demand it, and then only on condition that the owner shall have been previously and equitably indemnified.

Speech to the National Convention— February 5, 1794: The Terror Justified

Maximilien Robespierre

Between 1793 and 1794, France experienced the most radical phase of the revolution, known as the Reign of Terror. During this period France was essentially ruled by the twelve-member Committee of Public Safety elected by the National Convention every

SOURCE: Raymond P. Stearns, ed., *Pageant of Europe*. Copyright 1947 by Harcourt Brace Jovanovich, Inc. and renewed by Josephine B. Stearns. Reprinted by permission of Harcourt Brace Jovanovich, Inc. (New York, 1947), pp. 404–405.

month. The outstanding member of this committee was Maximilien Robespierre (1758–1794), a provincial lawyer who rose within the Jacobin Club and gained a reputation for incorruptibility and superb oratory. Historians have argued over Robespierre, some singling him out as a bloodthirsty individual with the major responsibility for the executions during the Reign of Terror, others seeing him as a sincere, idealistic, effective revolutionary leader called to the fore by events of the time. In the following speech to the National Convention on February 5, 1794, Robespierre defines the revolution and justifies extreme actions, including terror, in its defense.

> **Consider:** *What Robespierre means when he argues that terror flows from virtue; how the use of terror relates to the essence of the revolution; how this speech might be interpreted as an Enlightenment attack on the Ancien Régime carried to its logical conclusion.*

It is time to mark clearly the aim of the Revolution and the end toward which we wish to move; it is time to take stock of ourselves, of the obstacles which we still face, and of the means which we ought to adopt to attain our objectives. . . .

What is the goal for which we strive? A peaceful enjoyment of liberty and equality, the rule of that eternal justice whose laws are engraved, not upon marble or stone, but in the hearts of all men.

We wish an order of things where all low and cruel passions are enchained by the laws, all beneficent and generous feelings aroused; where ambition is the desire to merit glory and to serve one's fatherland; where distinctions are born only of equality itself; where the citizen is subject to the magistrate, the magistrate to the people, the people to justice; where the nation safeguards the welfare of each individual, and each individual proudly enjoys the prosperity and glory of his fatherland; where all spirits are enlarged by the constant exchange of republican sentiments and by the need of earning the respect of a great people; where the arts are the adornment of liberty, which ennobles them; and where commerce is the source of public wealth, not simply of monstrous opulence for a few families.

In our country we wish to substitute morality for egotism, probity for honor, principles for conventions, duties for etiquette, the empire of reason for the tyranny of customs, contempt for vice for contempt for misfortune, pride for insolence, the love of honor for the love of money . . . that is to say, all the virtues and miracles of the Republic for all the vices and snobbishness of the monarchy.

We wish in a word to fulfill the requirements of nature, to accomplish the destiny of mankind, to make good the promises of philosophy . . . that France, hitherto illustrious among slave states, may eclipse the glory of all free peoples that have existed, become the model of all nations. . . . That is our ambition; that is our aim.

What kind of government can realize these marvels? Only a democratic government. . . . But to found and to consolidate among us this democracy, to realize the peaceable rule of constitutional laws, it is necessary to conclude the war of liberty against tyranny and to pass successfully through the storms of revolution. Such is the aim of the revolutionary system which you have set up. . . .

Now what is the fundamental principle of democratic, or popular government—that is to say, the essential mainspring upon which it depends and which makes it function? It is virtue: I mean public virtue . . . that virtue which is nothing else but love of fatherland and its laws. . . .

The splendor of the goal of the French Revolution is simultaneously the source of our strength and of our weakness: our strength, because it gives us an ascendancy of truth over falsehood, and of public rights over private interests; our weakness, because it rallies against us all vicious men, all those who in their hearts seek to despoil the people. . . . It is necessary to stifle the domestic and foreign enemies of the Republic or perish with them. Now in these circumstances, the first maxim of our politics ought to be to lead the people by means of reason and the enemies of the people by terror.

If the basis of popular government in time of peace is virtue, the basis of popular government in time of revolution is both virtue and terror: virtue without which terror is murderous, terror without which virtue is powerless. Terror is nothing else than swift, severe, indomitable justice; it flows, then, from virtue.

Memoirs: Napoleon's Appeal
Madame de Remusat

Napoleon was neither the candidate of those longing to turn France to a more revolutionary course nor of those who wanted to return France to the legitimacy of the Ancien Régime. He came to power promising to uphold both revolutionary principles and order. Scholars have analyzed the question of why he was able to rise to power. Some see him as a military and political genius; others argue that he was an opportunist who took advantage of circumstances as they arose. One of the earliest analyses of Napoleon's rise to power was written by Madame de Remusat (1780–1821). As a lady in waiting to Empress Josephine and wife of a Napoleonic official, she observed Napoleon firsthand and described him in her Memoirs.

Consider: *Why, according to Remusat, Napoleon was so appealing to the French; the means Napoleon used to secure his power.*

I can understand how it was that men worn out by the turmoil of the Revolution, and afraid of that liberty which had long been associated with death, looked for repose under the dominion of an able ruler on whom fortune was seemingly resolved to smile. I can conceive that they regarded his elevation as a decree of destiny and fondly believed that in the irrevocable they should find peace. I may confidently assert that those persons believed quite sincerely that Bonaparte,

---

SOURCE: From James Harvey Robinson, ed., *Readings in European History*, vol. II (Boston: Ginn, 1904), pp. 491–492.

whether as consul or emperor, would exert his authority to oppose the intrigue of faction and would save us from the perils of anarchy.

None dared to utter the word "republic," so deeply had the Terror stained that name; and the government of the Directory had perished in the contempt with which its chiefs were regarded. The return of the Bourbons could only be brought about by the aid of a revolution; and the slightest disturbance terrified the French people, in whom enthusiasm of every kind seemed dead. Besides, the men in whom they had trusted had one after the other deceived them; and as, this time, they were yielding to force, they were at least certain that they were not deceiving themselves.

The beief, or rather the error, that only despotism could at that epoch maintain order in France was very widespread. It became the mainstay of Bonaparte; and it is due to him to say that he also believed it. The factions played into his hands by imprudent attempts which he turned to his own advantage. He had some grounds for his belief that he was necessary; France believed it, too; and he even succeeded in persuading foreign sovereigns that he constituted a barrier against republican influences, which, but for him, might spread widely. At the moment when Bonaparte placed the imperial crown upon his head there was not a king in Europe who did not believe that he wore his own crown more securely because of that event. Had the new emperor granted a liberal constitution, the peace of nations and of kings might really have been forever secured.

Secret Memorandum to Tsar Alexander I, 1820: Conservative Principles

Prince Klemens von Metternich

The outstanding leader of the conservative tide that rose with the fall of Napoleon was Prince Klemens von Metternich (1773–1859). From his post as Austrian Minister of Foreign Affairs, Metternich hosted the Congress of Vienna and played a dominating role within Austria and among the conservative states of Europe between 1815 and 1848. Both in principle and in practice, he represented a conservatism that rejected the changes wrought by the French Revolution and stood against liberalism and nationalism. The following is an excerpt from a secret memorandum that Metternich sent to Tsar Alexander I of Russia in 1820, explaining his political principles. While not a sophisticated statement of political theory, it does reflect key elements of conservative attitudes and ideas.

SOURCE: Prince Richard Metternich, ed., *Memoirs of Prince Metternich, 1815–1829*, vol. III, Mrs. Alexander Napier, trans. (New York: Charles Scribner's Sons, 1881), pp. 454–455, 458–460, 468–469.

Consider: *What threats Metternich perceives; how Metternich connects "presumption" with the middle class; how this document reflects the experience of the revolutionary and Napoleonic periods; the kinds of policies that would logically flow from these attitudes.*

"L'Europe," a celebrated writer has recently said, *"fait aujourd'hui pitié à l'homme d'esprit et horreur à l'homme vertueux."*[1]

It would be difficult to comprise in a few words a more exact picture of the situation at the time we are writing these lines!

Kings have to calculate the chances of their very existence in the immediate future; passions are let loose, and league together to overthrow everything which society respects as the basis of its existence; religion, public morality, laws, customs, rights, and duties, all are attacked, confounded, overthrown, or called in question. The great mass of the people are tranquil spectators of these attacks and revolutions, and of the absolute want of all means of defense. A few are carried off by the torrent, but the wishes of the immense majority are to maintain a repose which exists no longer, and of which even the first elements seem to be lost. . . .

Having now thrown a rapid glance over the first causes of the present state of society, it is necessary to point out in a more particular manner the evil which threatens to deprive it, at one blow, of the real blessings, the fruits of genuine civilisation, and to disturb it in the midst of its enjoyments. This evil may be described in one word—presumption; the natural effect of the rapid progression of the human mind towards the perfecting of so many things. This it is which at the present day leads so many individuals astray, for it has become an almost universal sentiment.

Religion, morality, legislation, economy, politics, administration, all have become common and accessible to everyone. Knowledge seems to come by inspiration; experience has no value for the presumptuous man; faith is nothing to him; he substitutes for it a pretended individual conviction, and to arrive at this conviction dispenses with all inquiry and with all study; for these means appear too trivial to a mind which believes itself strong enough to embrace at one glance all questions and all facts. Laws have no value for him, because he has not contributed to make them, and it would be beneath a man of his parts to recognise the limits traced by rude and ignorant generations. Power resides in himself; why should he submit himself to that which was only useful for the man deprived of light and knowledge? That which, according to him, was required in an age of weakness cannot be suitable in an age of reason and vigour amounting to universal perfection, which the German innovators designate by the idea, absurd in itself, of the Emancipation of the People! Morality itself he does not attack openly, for without it he could not be sure for a single instant of his own existence; but he interprets

---

[1] Europe . . . is pitied by men of spirit and abhorred by men of virtue.

its essence after his own fashion, and allows every other person to do so likewise, provided that other person neither kills nor robs him.

In thus tracing the character of the presumptuous man, we believe we have traced that of the society of the day, composed of like elements, if the denomination of society is applicable to an order of things which only tends in principle towards individualising all the elements of which society is composed. Presumption makes every man the guide of his own belief, the arbiter of laws according to which he is pleased to govern himself, or to allow some one else to govern him and his neighbours; it makes him, in short, the sole judge of his own faith, his own actions, and the principles according to which he guides them. . . .

The Governments, having lost their balance, are frightened, intimidated, and thrown into confusion by the cries of the intermediary class of society, which, placed between the Kings and their subjects, breaks the sceptre of the monarch, and usurps the cry of the people—the class so often disowned by the people, and nevertheless too much listened to, caressed and feared by those who could with one word reduce it again to nothingness.

We see this intermediary class abandon itself with a blind fury and animosity which proves much more its own fears than any confidence in the success of its enterprises, to all the means which seem proper to assuage its thirst for power, applying itself to the task of persuading Kings that their rights are confined to sitting upon a throne, while those of the people are to govern, and to attack all that centuries have bequeathed as holy and worthy of man's respect—denying, in fact, the value of the past, and declaring themselves the masters of the future. We see this class take all sorts of disguises, uniting and subdividing as occasion offers, helping each other in the hour of danger, and the next day depriving each other of all their conquests. It takes possession of the press, and employs it to promote impiety, disobedience to the laws of religion and the State, and goes so far as to preach murder as a duty for those who desire what is good.

On Liberty
John Stuart Mill

During the second half of the nineteenth century, liberalism in theory and practice started to change. In general it became less wedded to laissez-faire *policies and less optimistic than it was during the first half of the nineteenth century. This change is reflected in the thought of John Stuart Mill (1806–1873). He was the most influential British thinker of the mid-nineteenth century and probably the leading liberal theorist of the period. When he was young he favored the early liberalism of his father, James Mill, a well-known philosopher, and Jeremy Bentham, the author of utilitarianism. Over time he perceived*

SOURCE: John Stuart Mill, *Utilitarianism, Liberty, and Representative Government* (London: J. M. Dent and Sons Ltd., Everyman Liberty, 1910), pp. 66–68.

difficulties with this early liberalism, and new dangers. He modified his liberal ideas, a change that would later be reflected in liberal political policies of the late nineteenth and early twentieth centuries. In the following selection from On Liberty *(1859), his most famous work, Mill analyzes this evolution of liberalism starting with the aims of liberals during the first half of the nineteenth century.*

> **Consider:** *What Mill feels was the essence of early liberalism; what crucial changes occurred to transform liberalism; what Mill means by tyranny of the majority.*

The aim, therefore, of patriots was to set limits to the power which the ruler should be suffered to exercise over the community; and this limitation was what they meant by liberty. It was attempted in two ways. First, by obtaining a recognition of certain immunities, called political liberties or rights, which it was to be regarded as a breach of duty in the ruler to infringe; and which if he did infringe, specific resistance, or general rebellion, was held to be justifiable. A second, and generally a later expedient, was the establishment of constitutional checks, by which the consent of the community, or of a body of some sort, supposed to represent its interests, was made a necessary condition to some of the more important acts of the governing power. To the first of these modes of limitation, the ruling power, in most European countries, was compelled, more or less, to submit. It was not so with the second; and, to attain this, or when already in some degree possessed, to attain it more completely, became everywhere the principal object of the lovers of liberty. And so long as mankind were content to combat one enemy by another, and to be ruled by a master, on condition of being guaranteed more or less efficaciously against his tyranny, they did not carry their aspirations beyond this point.

A time, however, came, in the progress of human affairs, when men ceased to think it a necessity of nature that their governors should be an independent power, opposed in interest to themselves. It appeared to them much better that the various magistrates of the State should be their tenants or delegates, revocable at their pleasure. In that way alone, it seemed, could they have complete security that the powers of government would never be abused to their disadvantage. By degrees this new demand for elective and temporary rulers became the prominent object of the exertions of the popular party, wherever any such party existed; and superseded, to a considerable extent, the previous efforts to limit the power of rulers. As the struggle proceeded for making the ruling power emanate from the periodical choice of the ruled, some persons began to think that too much importance had been attached to the limitation of the power itself. *That* (it might seem) was a resource against rulers whose interests were habitually opposed to those of the people. What was now wanted was, that the rulers should be identified with the people; that their interest and will should be the interest and will of the nation. The nation did not need to be protected against its own will. There was no fear of its tyrannising over itself. Let the rulers be effectually responsible to it, promptly removable by it, and it could afford to trust them with power of which it could itself dictate the use to be made. Their power was but the nation's own power, concentrated, and in a form convenient for exercise. This mode of thought, or rather perhaps of feeling, was common among the last generation of European liberalism, in the Continental section of which it still apparently predominates. . . .

In time, however, a democratic republic came to occupy a large portion of the earth's surface, and made itself felt as one of the most powerful members of the community of nations; and elective and responsible government became subject to the observations and criticisms which wait upon a great existing fact. It was now perceived that such phrases as "self-government," and "the power of the people over themselves," do not express the true state of the case. The "people" who exercise the power are not always the same people with those over whom it is exercised; and the "self-government" spoken of is not the government of each by himself, but of each by all the rest. The will of the people, moreover, practically means the will of the most numerous or the most active *part* of the people; the majority, or those who succeed in making themselves accepted as the majority; the people, consequently *may* desire to oppress a part of their number; and precautions are as much needed against this as against any other abuse of power. The limitation, therefore, of the power of government over individuals loses none of its importance when the holders of power are regularly accountable to the community, that is, to the strongest party therein. This view of things, recommending itself equally to the intelligence of thinkers and to the inclination of those important classes in European society to whose real or supposed interests democracy is adverse, has had no difficulty in establishing itself; and in political speculations "the tyranny of the majority" is now generally included among the evils against which society requires to be on its guard.

Like other tyrannies, the tyranny of the majority was at first, and is still vulgarly, held in dread, chiefly as operating through the acts of the public authorities. But reflecting persons perceived that when society is itself the tyrant—society collectively over the separate individuals who compose it—its means of tyrannising are not restricted to the acts which it may do by the hands of its political functionaries. Society can and does execute its own mandates: and if it issues wrong mandates instead of right, or any mandates at all in things with which it ought not to meddle, it practises a social tyranny more formidable than many kinds of political oppression, since, though not usually upheld by such extreme penalties, it leaves fewer means of escape, penetrating much more deeply into the details of life, and enslaving the soul itself. Protection, therefore, against the tyranny of the magistrate is not enough: there needs protection also against the tyranny of the prevailing opinion and feeling; against the tendency of society to impose, by other means than civil penalties, its own ideas and practices as rules of conduct on those who dissent from them; to fetter the development, and, if possible, prevent the formation, of any individuality not in harmony with its ways, and compel all characters to fashion themselves upon the model of its own. There is a limit to the legitimate interference of collective opinion with individual independence: and to find that limit, and maintain it against encroachment, is as indispensable to a good condition of human affairs, as protection against political despotism.

The First Chartist Petition: Demands for Change in England

Movements for reform occurred throughout Europe between 1815 and 1848 despite the efforts of conservatives to quash them. Eventually almost all countries in Europe experienced the revolutions conservatives feared so much. One exception was England, but even there, political movements threatened to turn into violent revolts against the failure of the government to change. The most important of these was the Chartist movement, made up primarily of members of the working class who wanted reforms for themselves. The following is an excerpt from the first charter presented to the House of Commons in 1838. Subsequent charters were presented in 1842 and 1848. In each case the potential existed for a mass movement to turn into a violent revolt, and in each case Parliament rejected the Chartist demands. Only later in the century were most of these demands met.

Consider: *The nature of the Chartists' demands; by what means the Chartists hoped to achieve their ends; how Metternich might analyze these demands.*

Required, as we are universally, to support and obey the laws, nature and reason entitle us to demand that in the making of the laws the universal voice shall be implicitly listened to. We perform the duties of freemen; we must have the privileges of freemen. Therefore, we demand universal suffrage. The suffrage, to be exempt from the corruption of the wealthy and the violence of the powerful, must be secret. The assertion of our right necessarily involves the power of our uncontrolled exercise. We ask for the reality of a good, not for its semblance, therefore we demand the ballot. The connection between the representatives and the people, to be beneficial, must be intimate. The legislative and constituent powers, for correction and for instruction, ought to be brought into frequent contact. Errors which are comparatively light, when susceptible of a speedy popular remedy, may produce the most disastrous effects when permitted to grow inveterate through years of compulsory endurance. To public safety, as well as public confidence, frequent elections are essential. Therefore, we demand annual parliaments. With power to choose, and freedom in choosing, the range of our choice must be unrestricted. We are compelled, by the existing laws, to take for our representatives men who are incapable of appreciating our difficulties, or have little sympathy with them; merchants who have retired from trade and no longer feel its harrassings; proprietors of land who are alike ignorant of its evils and its cure; lawyers by whom the notoriety of the senate is courted only as a means of obtaining notice in the courts. The labours of a representative who is sedulous in the discharge of his duty are numerous and burdensome. It is neither just, nor reasonable, nor safe, that they should continue to be gratuitously rendered. We

Source: From R. G. Gammage, *History of the Chartist Movement*, 2nd ed. (Newcastle-on-Tyne, England: Browne and Browne, 1894), pp. 88–90.

demand that in the future election of members of your honourable house, the approbation of the constituency shall be the sole qualification, and that to every representative so chosen, shall be assigned out of the public taxes, a fair and adequate remunerative for the time which he is called upon to devote to the public service. The management of his mighty kingdom has hitherto been a subject for contending factions to try their selfish experiments upon. We have felt the consequences in our sorrowful experience. Short glimmerings of uncertain enjoyment, swallowed up by long and dark seasons of suffering. If the self-government of the people should not remove their distresses, it will, at least, remove their repinings. Universal suffrage will, and it alone can, bring true and lasting peace to the nation; we firmly believe that it will also bring prosperity. May it therefore please your honourable house, to take this our petition into your most serious consideration, and to use your utmost endeavours, by all constitutional means, to have a law passed, granting to every male of lawful age, sane mind, and unconvicted of crime, the right of voting for members of parliament, and directing all future elections of members of parliament to be in the way of secret ballot, and ordaining that the duration of parliament, so chosen, shall in no case exceed one year, and abolishing all property qualifications in the members, and providing for their due remuneration while in attendance on their parliamentary duties.

"And your petitioners shall ever pray."

VISUAL SOURCES

Allegory of the Revolution
Jeaurat de Bertray

Jeaurat de Bertray's "Allegory of the Revolution" is literally a jumble of historical and revolutionary symbols. At the top is a portrait of Jean Jacques Rousseau, at the time considered by many the spiritual and intellectual father of the French Revolution even though he never advocated revolution and died eleven years before it began. Below him are the new flags of the French Republic, the one on the left with the nationalistic words "love of country." Farther to the left is a triangular monument to Equality, below it two maidens representing Goodness and Good Faith, and in the center a bundle of rods and arms topped by a red liberty cap, all symbolizing a fair, forceful republican government. Just below is paper money, the assignats, a fair, forceful republican government. Just below is paper money, the assignats, that helped finance the revolution and pay off debts, and in the center right grows a liberty tree. To the right are two unfinished pillars, the first dedicated to the regeneration of morals and The Declaration of the Rights of Man

Photo 5-1

Courtesy, Musée Carnavelet/Photographie Bulloz

and Citizen, *the second to the French Revolution. Just below them and in the background are symbols of forceful determination to uphold and defend the revolution: a guillotine, a cannon, and a soldier. In the right foreground is a peasant wearing a liberty cap and sowing a field. This painting pulls together many symbols and elements of the revolutionary ideology. It was painted in 1794, the time of the most radical phase of the revolution.*

> **Consider:** *Connections between this picture,* The Declaration of the Rights of Man and Citizen, *and the Enlightenment; the ways in which the Ancien Régime is rejected symbolically in this picture.*

Internal Disturbances and the Reign of Terror

Understanding of the Reign of Terror has often been distorted by an image of random and purposeless brutality. One way to gain clearer insights into the Terror is through the use of maps and statistics, which reveal where the Terror occurred, how intensive it was, and who its victims were. The two maps presented here compare the amount of civil disturbance facing government officials and the number of executions occurring in the various departments of France during the period of the Terror. The two pie charts com-

Map 5-1   Internal Disturbances

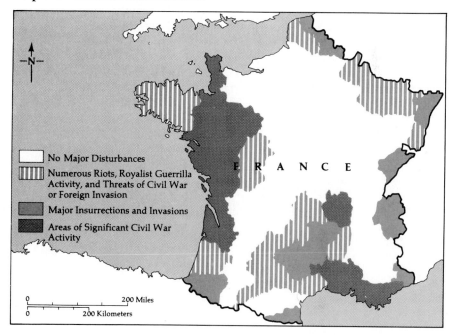

pare the estimated percentages of France's population belonging to the various classes in 1789 and during the Terror from March 1793 to August 1794.

> **Consider:** *How these maps and charts support an argument that the Reign of Terror was not random or purposeless; the hypotheses that might be drawn from these maps and charts about the causes or effects of the Terror.*

Map 5-2   The Incidence of Terror

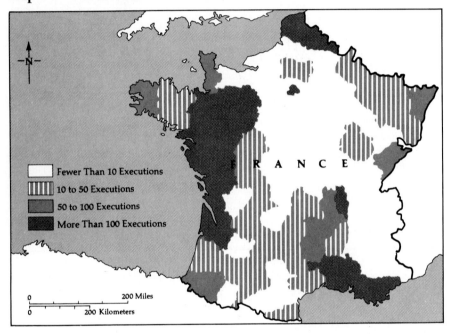

Chart 5-1   Classes in France

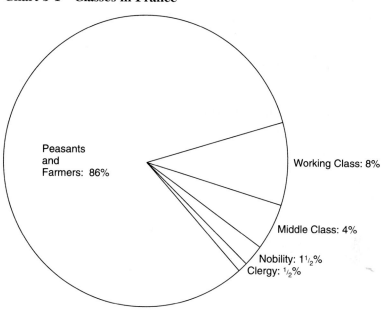

Peasants and Farmers: 86%

Working Class: 8%

Middle Class: 4%

Nobility: 1½%
Clergy: ½%

Chart 5-2   Executions during the Reign of Terror

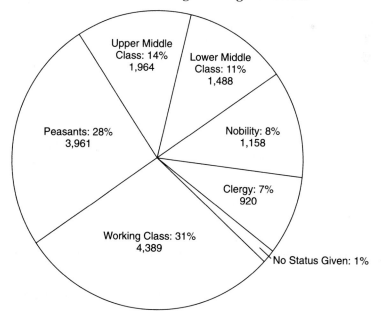

Upper Middle Class: 14%
1,964

Lower Middle Class: 11%
1,488

Peasants: 28%
3,961

Nobility: 8%
1,158

Clergy: 7%
920

Working Class: 31%
4,389

No Status Given: 1%

SECONDARY SOURCES

The Coming
of the
French Revolution
Georges Lefebvre

Probably no event in modern history has been interpreted at greater length and with greater passion than the French Revolution. The historiographic tradition related to this event is so extensive that numerous books and articles have been written on this historiography itself. A central controversy involves the cause or causes of the revolution and is dealt with in the following selection from The Coming of the French Revolution *by Georges Lefebvre. Lefebvre held the prestigious chair of French revolutionary history at the Sorbonne until his death in 1959. His work on the French Revolution continues to be highly respected and accepted among historians, many of whom differ greatly among themselves.*

> **Consider:** *The most important cause of the French Revolution, according to Lefebvre; how this interpretation relates the revolution in France to areas outside of France; how social, economic, and political factors are linked in this interpretation of the French Revolution; how this view is supported by the primary documents.*

The ultimate cause of the French Revolution of 1789 goes deep into the history of France and of the western world. At the end of the eighteenth century, the social structure of France was aristocratic. It showed the traces of having originated at a time when land was almost the only form of wealth, and when the possessors of land were the masters of those who needed it to work and to live. It is true that in the course of age-old struggles (of which the Fronde, the last revolt of the aristocracy, was as recent as the seventeenth century) the king had been able gradually to deprive the lords of their political power and subject nobles and clergy to his authority. But he had left them the first place in the social hierarchy. Still restless at being merely his "subjects," they remained privileged persons.

Meanwhile the growth of commerce and industry had created, step by step, a new form of wealth, mobile or commercial wealth, and a new class, called in France the bourgeoisie, which since the fourteenth century had taken its place as the Third Estate in the General Estates of the kingdom. This class had grown much stronger with the maritime discoveries of the fifteenth and sixteenth centuries and the ensuing exploitation of new worlds, and also because it proved

---

SOURCE: Georges Lefebvre, *The Coming of the French Revolution*, R. R. Palmer, trans. (Princeton, N.J.: Princeton University Press, 1947), pp. 1–3.

highly useful to the monarchical state in supplying it with money and competent officials. In the eighteenth century commerce, industry and finance occupied an increasingly important place in the national economy. It was the bourgeoisie that rescued the royal treasury in moments of crisis. From its ranks were recruited most members of the liberal professions and most public employees. It had developed a new ideology which the "philosophers" and "economists" of the time had simply put into definite form. The role of the nobility had correspondingly declined; and the clergy, as the ideal which it proclaimed lost prestige, found its authority growing weaker. These groups preserved the highest rank in the legal structure of the country, but in reality economic power, personal abilities and confidence in the future had passed largely to the bourgeoisie. Such a discrepancy never lasts forever. The Revolution of 1789 restored the harmony between fact and law. This transformation spread in the nineteenth century throughout the west and then to the whole globe, and in this sense the ideas of 1789 toured the world.

Europe and the French Imperium: Napoleon as Enlightened Despot
Geoffrey Bruun

As with most charismatic figures, it has been difficult to evaluate Napoleon objectively from a historical perspective. Even before his death, a number of myths were developing about him. Since then much of the debate among scholars has dealt with whether Napoleon should be considered a defender or a destroyer of the revolution, whether his rise to power reversed the revolutionary tide or consolidated it. In the following selection Geoffrey Bruun argues that Napoleon should be viewed more as an eighteenth-century enlightened despot than as anything else.

> **Consider:** *Bruun's support for his contention that Napoleon was to a considerable degree a "son of the* philosophes*"; the ways in which Napoleon differed from eighteenth-century monarchs.*

The major misconception which has distorted the epic of Napoleon is the impression that his advent to power was essentially a dramatic reversal, which turned back the tide of democracy and diverted the predestined course of the revolutionary torrent. That this Corsican liberticide could destroy a republic and substitute an empire, seemingly at will, has been seized upon by posterity as the out-

SOURCE: Geoffrey Bruun, *Europe and the French Imperium, 1799–1814.* Reprinted by permission of Harper & Row (New York, 1938), pp. 1–2. Copyright © 1938 by Harper & Row, Publishers, Inc.

standing proof of his arrogant genius. To reduce his career to logical dimensions, to appreciate how largely it was a fulfillment rather than a miscarriage of the reform program, it is necessary to forget the eighteenth century as the seedtime of political democracy and remember it as the golden era of the princely despots, to recall how persistently the thinkers of that age concerned themselves with the idea of enlightened autocracy and how conscientiously they laid down the intellectual foundations of Caesarism. Napoleon was, to a degree perhaps undreamed of in their philosophy, the son of the *philosophes*, and it is difficult to read far in the political writings of the time without feeling how clearly the century prefigured him, how ineluctably in Vandal's phrase *l'idée a précédé l'homme*.

All the reforming despots of the eighteenth century pursued, behind a façade of humanitarian pretexts, the same basic program of administrative consolidation. The success achieved by Frederick the Great in raising the military prestige and stimulating the economic development of Prussia provided the most notable illustration of this policy, but the same ideals inspired the precipitate decrees of Joseph II in Austria, the cautious innovations of Charles III of Spain, the paper projects of Catherine the Great of Russia and the complex program pursued by Gustavus III in Sweden. Military preparedness and economic self-sufficiency were the cardinal principles guiding the royal reformers, but they also shared a common desire to substitute a unified system of law for the juristic chaos inherited from earlier centuries, to eliminate the resistance and confusion offered by guilds, corporations, provincial estates and relics of feudatory institutions, and to transform their inchoate possessions into centralized states dominated by despotic governments of unparalleled efficiency and vigor. In crowning the work of the Revolution by organizing a government of this type in France, Napoleon obeyed the most powerful political tradition of the age, a mandate more general, more widely endorsed, and more pressing than the demand for social equality or democratic institutions. Read in this light, the significance of his career is seen to lie, not in the ten yers of revolutionary turmoil from which he sprang, but in the whole century which produced him. If Europe in the revolutionary age may be thought of as dominated by one nearly universal mood, that mood was an intense aspiration for order. The privileged and the unprivileged classes, philosophers, peasants, democrats, and despots all paid homage to this ideal. Napoleon lent his name to an epoch because he symbolized reason enthroned, because he was the philosopher-prince who gave to the dominant aspiration of the age its most typical, most resolute, and most triumphant expression.

Women and the Napoleonic Code

Bonnie G. Smith

*However they evaluate Napoleon and his rule, most historians point to the set of ration-
ally organized laws—the Napoleonic Code—as one of Napoleon's most important and
lasting legacies. The Code embodied many principles of the Englightenment and French
Revolution, and the Code was modified and adopted outside of France in Europe and the
western hemisphere. While it has been generally considered a progressive legal system,
historians now point out that it may have represented a step back for women. In the
following selection from her recent survey,* Changing Lives: Women in European History
Since 1700, *Bonnie G. Smith analyzes the significance of the Napoleonic Code for women.*

> **Consider:** *Ways the Code made women legally and economically dependent on
> men; what concept of woman's proper role the Code supported; what concept of
> man's proper role the Code supported.*

First, women acquired the nationality of their husbands upon marriage. This made
a woman's relationship to the state an indirect one because it was dependent on
her husband's. Second, a woman had to reside where her husband desired. Women
could not participate in lawsuits or serve as witnesses in court or as witnesses to
civil acts such as births, deaths, and marriages. Such a reduction in woman's civil
status enhanced that of the individual male. Moreover, the code reduced, if not
eliminated, male accountability for sexual acts and thrust it squarely on women.
For example, men were no longer susceptible to paternity suits or legally responsible for the support of illegitimate children. Women were weakened economically
if they bore illegitimate children, whereas men were not so affected if they fa-
thered them. Finally, female adultery was punished by imprisonment and fines
unless the husband relented and took his wife back. Men, however, suffered no
such sanctions unless they brought their sexual partner into the home. The sexual
behavior of women was open to scrutiny and prescribed by law, whereas that of
men, almost without exception, had no criminal aspect attached to it. Thus male
sexuality was accepted with few limitations, but women's was only acceptable if it
remained within strict domestic boundaries. The Napoleonic Code institutional-
ized the republican responsibility of women to generate virtue—a term that began
to acquire sexual overtones to its civic definition.

The Napoleonic Code also defined the space women would occupy in the new
regime as marital, maternal, and domestic—all public matters would be determined by men. This circumscription was made more effective by the way the
property law undercut the possibilities for women's economic independence and

existence in a world beyond the home. In general, a woman had no control over property. Even if she was married under a contract that ensured a separate accounting of her dowry, her husband still had administrative control of funds. This administrative power of the husband and father replaced arbitrary patriarchal rule and was more in tune with modern ideas of government. Instead of serving the king's whim, governmental officials served the best interests of the nation just as the father increased the well-being of the family. This kind of economic control of women held in all classes. Women's wages went to their husbands, and market women and others engaged in business could not do so without permission from their husbands. Once a woman gained permission she did acquire some kind of legal status, in that a business woman could be sued. On the other hand, she had no control of her profits—these always passed to her husband, and court records demonstrate the continuing enforcement of this kind of control. Moreover, the husband's right to a businesswoman's property meant that the property passed to his descendants rather than hers. All of these provisions meant that, in the strictest sense, women could not act freely or independently.

The Napoleonic Code influenced many legal systems in Europe and the New World and set the terms for the treatment of women on a widespread basis. Establishing male power by transferring autonomy and economic goods from women to men, the Code organized gender roles for more than a century. "From the way the Code treats women, you can tell it was written by men," so older women reacted to the new decree. Women's publications protested the sudden repression after a decade of more equitable laws. Even in the 1820s, books explaining the Code to women always recognized their anger. The justification for the Code's provisions involved reminders about men's chivalrous character and women's weakness. Arguments were based on nature both to invoke the equality of all men and to reinforce the consequences of women's supposed physical inferiority. Looking at nature, one writer saw in terms of gender man's "greater strength, his propensity to be active and assertive in comparison to woman's weakness, lack of vigor and natural modesty." At the time the Code was written, the codifiers were looking at nature in two ways. In theorizing about men alone, nature was redolent of abstract rights. As far as women were concerned, however, nature became empirical in that women had less physical stature than men. Although short men were equal to tall men, women were simply smaller than men and thus were unequal.

According to jurists, therefore, women needed protection, and this protection was to be found within the domicile. The law, they maintained, still offered women protection from individual male brutality, in the rare cases when that might occur. Legislators thus used the law officially to carve out a private space for women in which they had no rights. At the same time, law codes were supposed to protect women from the abuses allowed in the first place. The small number of abuses that might result were not seen as significant drawbacks by the jurists. They saw the Code as "insuring the safety of patrimonies and restoring order in families." It mattered little to them that the old regime carried over for women in the form of an "estate"—a term that indicated an unchangeable lifetime situation into which people were born and would always remain. Estates had been abolished for men in favor of mobility, but it continued for women.

By the time the Napoleonic Code went into effect, little remained of liberal revolutionary programs for women except the provision for equal inheritance by sisters and brothers. The Code cleared the way for the rule of property and for individual triumph. It ushered in an age of mobility, marked by the rise of the energetic and heroic. The Code gave women little room for that kind of acquisitiveness or for heroism. Instead, women's realm was to encompass virtue, reproduction, and family.

The Triumph of the Middle Classes: 1848
Charles Morazé

The revolutions of 1848 have been at the center of historical debate for a long time. To some, 1848 represents the end of the system set up by the Congress of Vienna; to others it represents the great battle between the forces of liberalism and conservatism; and to still others, it represents the point at which liberalism, nationalism, socialism, and Romanticism met. Perhaps the most persistent historiographical tradition views 1848 as a point at which history made a "wrong" turn. Some aspects of this historical debate are reflected in the following interpretation of 1848 by the French historian Charles Morazé. Here Morazé views the revolutions from a socioeconomic perspective, emphasizing the revolutions of 1848 as a great victory for middle-class capitalism.

> **Consider:** *According to Morazé, the economic factors that helped cause and end the revolutions of 1848; how Morazé supports his conclusion that this was a victory for middle-class capitalism; in what ways the aristocracy and working classes "lost."*

Thus the revolts of 1848 were an explosion of liberal nationalism which failed, although their effect was to shake the feudal structure so thoroughly that it gave place to a capitalist and bourgeois law, supporting individual ownership, based on a code like that of France. The year 1848 saw the last ineffectual flicker of Romanticism and the first great victory for capitalism.

Eastern Europe then became middle class and shed its tenacious traditions, its feudalism, castes, trade guilds and time-honoured ways of life. It entered the age of codified law, which was kept well up to date by great elected assemblies, and guaranteed the owner his land and the industrialist his credit. In Frankfurt, Rome or Paris there had been little mention of railways, but it was they which had

SOURCE: Charles Morazé, *The Triumph of the Middle Classes* (Cleveland: World Publishing Co., 1966), p. 208.

broken up the rigid framework of credit based on personal estate; and by their demands a new monetary and financial world was created, enabling the railways to expand into new areas. The agricultural crisis activated a revolution in the urban industrial economy. Order was re-established in Europe as in England, for gold from the New World no longer enriched either an antiquated feudalism or a radical socialism, but rather strengthened the financial economy imposed by the railways, which gave its shape to capitalism.

The 1848 revolution saw the definitive failure of socialism. French theorists who had severely criticized the middle-class indifference to poverty as being barely concealed under an affectation of charitable virtue, could not seize power in spite of the vehement eloquence of Proudhon, who dominated the debates in the republican assemblies; they could not even prevent the disastrous failure of the national workshops which were a caricature of the dreams of the first socialist age. Outside France, English chartism collapsed in ridicule, for the worker across the Channel was definitely no revolutionary. In Germany, Marx and his friends had tried to take advantage of the revolutionary movement to win support for their own brand of socialism. After having launched their celebrated manifesto in Paris, they had gone back to Cologne to replace the too liberal *Kölnische Zeitung*, on which Marx had been a collaborator some years earlier, by the *Neue Kölnische Zeitung*. But Marx was expelled in 1849. The crisis of 1846–8 deprived English landlords of the precious Corn Laws and the fedual lords of eastern Germany of the gangs of serf labour and Austria of serfdom itself. Middle-class capitalism was the great victor. From 1850 onwards it was to flourish with extraordinary vigour with the new supplies of American and Australian gold.

Nationalism: Myth and Reality
Boyd Shafer

Although growing nationalism was a general pattern during the nineteenth century, the forms that nationalism took and its actual meaning differed over time and in various areas. Indeed, "nationalism" is a term that historians have usually used quite loosely, adding to problems of understanding its meaning. In the following selection, Boyd Shafer attempts to define nationalism by listing ten characteristics it embodies.

> **Consider:** *What it would mean to be a German or Italian "nationalist" during the second half of the nineteenth century, according to Shafer's definition of national- ism; the political implications of nationalism so defined; the elements of this defini- tion that make nationalism such a historically powerful force.*

SOURCE: Boyd C. Shafer, *Nationalism: Myth and Reality*. Reprinted by permission of Harcourt Brace Jovanovich, Inc. (New York, 1955), pp. 7–8.

1. A certain defined (often vaguely) unit of territory (whether possessed or coveted).
2. Some common cultural characteristics such as language (or widely understood languages), customs, manners, and literature (folk tales and lore are a beginning). If an individual believes he shares these, and wishes to continue sharing them, he is usually said to be a member of the nationality.
3. Some commn dominant social (as Christian) and economic (as capitalistic or recently communistic) institutions.
4. A common independent or sovereign government (type does not matter) or the desire for one. The "principle" that each nationality should be separate and independent is involved here.
5. A belief in a common history (it can be invented) and in a common origin (often mistakenly conceived to be racial in nature).
6. A love or esteem for fellow nationals (not necessarily as individuals).
7. A devotion to the entity (however little comprehended) called the nation, which embodies the common territory, culture, social and economic institutions, government, and the fellow nationals, and which is at the same time (whether organism or not) more than their sum.
8. A common pride in the achievements (often the military more than the cultural) of this nation and a common sorrow in its tragedies (particularly its defeats).
9. A disregard for or hostility to other (not necessarily all) like groups, especially if these prevent or seem to threaten the separate national existence.
10. A hope that the nation will have a great and glorious future (usually in territorial expansion) and become supreme in some way (in world power if the nation is already large).

Chapter Questions

1. Utilizing the material in the sources, what best explains the causes and the general nature of the French Revolution?
2. What possible connections are there between the French Revolution and Napoleon?
3. Analyze liberalism and conservatism as alternative ways of dealing with the issues raised by the French Revolution. What policies would logically follow from each?
4. What connections might there be between nationalism and the French Revolution of 1789? In what ways might both liberals and conservatives have used nationalism to their own advantage during this period?

SIX

Industrialism, Social Change, and Culture in the West, 1700s– 1914

The Industrial Revolution, which transformed economic life in the West during the nineteenth century and throughout the world in the twentieth century, began in England toward the end of the eighteenth century. After the Napoleonic period it spread to western Europe, and by the end of the nineteenth century it had touched most of Western civilization. The Industrial Revolution was characterized by unprecedented economic growth, the factory system of production, and the use of new, artifically powered machines for transportation and mechanical operations. The potential was tremendous; for the first time, human beings had the ability to produce far more than was needed to sustain a large percentage of the population. Whether that potential would be realized, and at what cost, remained to be seen.

In the wake of industrialization came great social changes. The middle and working classes were most affected by industrialization, and both grew in number and social influence as did the urban areas in which they worked and lived. But it was the middle class that benefited most, enjoying a rising standard of living, increased prestige, and growing political influence. Whether the working class benefited from industrialization during the early decades is a matter for debate among historians. Clearly it was this class that bore the burdens of urban social problems: overcrowded slums, poor sanitation, insufficient social services, and a host of related problems. The aristocracy, the peasantry, and the artisans—classes tied to the traditional agricultural economy and older means of production—slowly diminished in numbers and social importance as industrialization spread.

This period of industrialization and social change was also one of great intellectual and cultural ferment. Part of this ferment was the reaction of thinkers, artists, and writers to industrialization itself and accompanying developments such as urbanization. Perhaps an even more important element of the intellectual and cultural ferment was the growth in numbers, wealth, power, and prestige of the urban middle class. This class increasingly asserted its own values and assumptions, which were reflected in the ideas and creative productions that appealed to it. At the same time, this growing influence of the middle class in thought and culture was being challenged on all sides, particularly by those more sensitive to the problems of the working class and those asserting more conservative views.

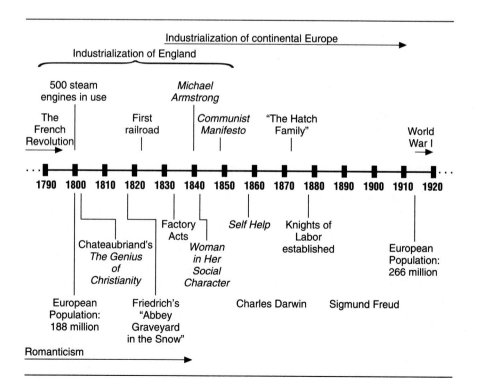

The sources in this chapter deal with these economic, social, and cultural changes. For industrialization, the focus will be on the origins and spread of the Industrial Revolution, particularly in England. For the social changes of the period, the focus will be on those affecting the working and middle classes, who were most tied to industrialization. Here, particular attention is given to women's attitudes and the significance of economic and social changes for women during the period. For cultural changes, emphasis will be on, first, some of the major intellectual and cultural trends of the period such as Darwinism, Marxism, and Freudianism, and second, Romanticism, one of the most important cultural styles during the first half of this period.

The sources in this and the previous chapter provide insights into the nature of European civilization during the nineteenth century, a period in which this civilization was in many ways at its height. The following chapters will focus on the Americas, Asia, and Africa, areas of the world developing according to both their own internal dynamics and the growing impact of European civilization.

PRIMARY SOURCES

Testimony for the Factory Act of 1833: Working Conditions in England

Industrialization carried with it broad social and economic changes that were quickly felt by those involved. The most striking changes were in the working conditions in the new factories and mines. During the first decades of industrialization, there was little government control over working conditions and few effective labor organizations; laborers were thus at the mercy of factory owners who were pursuing profit in a competitive world. Investigations into conditions in factories and mines conducted by the British Parliament in the 1830s and 1840s led eventually to the enactment of legislation, such as the Factory Act of 1833. These parliamentary investigations provide us with extensive information about working conditions and attitudes toward them. The following selection contains three excerpts from a parliamentary commission's investigations into child labor in factories. The first is a summary by the commission of medical examiners from northeastern

SOURCE: Commission for Inquiry into the Employment of Children in Factories, *Second Report, with Minutes of Evidence and Reports by the Medical Commissioners*, vol. V, Session 29 January—20 August, 1833 (London: His Majesty's Printing Office, 1833), pp. 5, 26–28.

England. The second is the testimony of John Wright, a steward in a silk factory. The third is the testimony of William Harter, a silk manufacturer.

> **Consider:** *What these people perceived as the worst abuses of factory labor; the causes of the poor working conditions; how Harter might defend himself against the charges that he was abusing the working class; what biases the witnesses might hold.*

TESTIMONY OF THE COMMISSION OF MEDICAL EXAMINERS

The account of the physical condition of the manufacturing population in the large towns in the North-eastern District of England is less favourable. It is of this district that the Commissioners state, "We have found undoubted instances of children five years old sent to work thirteen hours a day; and frequently of children nine, ten, and eleven consigned to labour for fourteen and fifteen hours." The effects ascertained by the Commissioners in many cases are, "deformity," and in still more "stunted growth, relaxed muscles, and slender conformation:" "twisting of the ends of the long bones, relaxation of the ligaments of the knees, ankles, and the like." "The representation that these effects are so common and universal as to enable some persons invariably to distinguish factory children from other children is, I have no hesitation in saying, an exaggerated and unfaithful picture of their general condition; at the same time it must be said, that the individual instances in which some one or other of those effects of severe labour are discernible are rather frequent than rare. . . .

"Upon the whole, there remains no doubt upon my mind, that under the system pursued in many of the factories, the children of the labouring classes stand in need of, and ought to have, legislative protection against the conspiracy insensibly formed between their masters and parents, to tax them to a degree of toil beyond their strength.

"In conclusion, I think it has been clearly proved that children have been worked a most unreasonable and cruel length of time daily, and that even adults have been expected to do a certain quantity of labour which scarcely any human being is able to endure. I am of opinion no child under fourteen years of age should work in a factory of any description for more than eight hours a day. From fourteen upwards I would recommend that no individual should, under any circumstances, work more than twelve hours a day; although if practicable, as a physician, I would prefer the limitation of ten hours, for all persons who earn their bread by their industry."

TESTIMONY OF JOHN WRIGHT

How long have you been employed in a silk-mill?—More than thirty years.
Did you enter it as a child?—Yes, betwixt five and six.
How many hours a day did you work then?—The same thirty years ago as now.

What are those hours?—Eleven hours per day and two over-hours: over-hours are working after six in the evening till eight. The regular hours are from six in the morning to six in the evening, and two others are two over-hours: about fifty years ago they began working over-hours. . . .

Why, then, are those employed in them said to be in such a wretched condition?—In the first place, the great number of hands congregated together, in some rooms forty, in some fifty, in some sixty, and I have known some as many as 100, which must be injurious to both health and growing. In the second place, the privy is in the factory, which frequently emits an unwholesome smell; and it would be worth while to notice in the future erection of mills, that there be betwixt the privy door and the factory wall a kind of a lobby of cage-work. 3dly, The tediousness and the everlasting sameness in the first process preys much on the spirits, and makes the hands spiritless. 4thly, the extravagant number of hours a child is compelled to labour and confinement, which for one week is seventy-six hours. . . . 5thly, About six months in the year we are obliged to use either gas, candles, or lamps, for the longest portion of that time, nearly six hours a day, being obliged to work amid the smoke and soot of the same; and also a large portion of oil and grease is used in the mills.

What are the effects of the present system of labour?—From my earliest recollections, I have found the effects to be awfully detrimental to the well-being of the operative; I have observed frequently children carried to factories, unable to walk, and that entirely owing to excessive labour and confinement. The degradation of the workpeople baffles all description: frequently have two of my sisters been obliged to be assisted to the factory and home again, until by-and-by they could go no longer, being totally crippled in their legs. And in the next place, I remember some ten or twelve years ago working in one of the largest firms in Macclesfield, (Messrs. Baker and Pearson,) with about twenty-five men, where they were scarce one half fit for His Majesty's service. Those that are straight in their limbs are stunted in their growth; much inferior to their fathers in point of strength. 3dly, Through excessive labour and confinement there is often a total loss of appetite; a kind of langour steals over the whole frame—enters to the very core—saps the foundation of the best constitution—and lays our strength prostrate in the dust. In the 4th place, by protracted labour there is an alarming increase of cripples in various parts of this town, which has come under my own observation and knowledge. . . .

Are all these cripples made in the silk factories?—Yes, they are, I believe. . . .

TESTIMONY OF WILLIAM HARTER

What effect would it have on your manufacture to reduce the hours of labour to ten?—It would instantly much reduce the value of my mill and machinery, and consequently of far prejudice my manufacture.

How so?—They are calculated to produce a certain quantity of work in a given time. Every machine is valuable in proportion to the quantity of work which it will turn off in a given time. It is impossible that the machinery could produce as much work in ten hours as in twelve. If the tending of the machines were a laborious occupation, the difference in the quantity of work might not always be in exact proportion to the difference of working time; but in my mill, and silk-mills in general, the work requires the least imaginable labour; therefore it is perfectly impossible that the machines could produce as much work in ten hours as in twelve. The produce would vary in about the same ratio as the working time.

The Knights of Labor: Unionization

As industrialization spread across Europe and North America, workers found that they were constantly attacked on a number of fronts. Skilled labor in particular found their position eroding as mechanization undermined their ability to control the pace of work and output. Workers, once independent artisans working out of their own homes and workshops, found themselves drawn into factories where they faced long hours, horrid work conditions, and low pay. Although in the United States workers did not organize socialist parties, they did organize unions that sought to protect their position as skilled independent workers. The Knights of Labor was among the first national, cross-industry organizations in the United States that addressed the problems created by industrialization. It was at the center of nationwide strikes and was succeeded by the American Federation of Labor which chose to organize only skilled craftsmen. This selection is the preamble to the Constitution adopted by the Knights of Labor meeting in Pennsylvania, January 3, 1878.

> **Consider:** *The problems facing workers as reflected in this document; how they justify their demands; the goals of the Knights of Labor; how their goals compare with those of labor unions today.*

The recent alarming development and aggression of aggregated wealth, which, unless checked, will inevitably lead to the pauperization and hopeless degradation of the toiling masses, render it imperative, if we desire to enjoy the blessings of life, that a check should be placed upon its power and upon unjust accumulation, and a system adopted which will secure to the laborer the fruits of his toil; and as this much-desired object can only be accomplished by the thorough unification of labor, and the united efforts of those who obey the divine injunction that "In the sweat of thy brow shalt thou eat bread," we have formed the ° ° ° ° ° with a view of securing the organization and direction, by co-operative effort, of the power of the industrial classes; and we submit to the world the objects sought to be accomplished by our organization, calling upon all who believe in securing "the greatest good to the greatest number" to aid and assist us: . . .

SOURCE: Terrence V. Powderly, *Thirty Years of Labor* (Philadelphia, 1890), pp. 128–130.

II. To secure to the toilers a proper share of the wealth that they create; more of the leisure that rightfully belongs to them; more societary advantages; more of the benefits, privileges and emoluments of the world; in a word, all those rights and privileges necessary to make them capable of enjoying, appreciating, defending and perpetuating the blessings of good government. . . .

IV. The establishment of co-operative institutions, productive and distributive.

V. The reserving of the public lands—the heritage of the people—for the actual settler; not another acre for railroads or speculators.

VI. The abrogation of all laws that do not bear equally upon capital and labor, the removal of unjust technicalities, delays and discriminations in the administration of justice, and the adopting of measures providing for the health and safety of those engaged in mining, manufacturing or building pursuits.

VII. The enactment of laws to compel chartered corporations to pay their employes weekly, in full, for labor performed during the preceding week, in the lawful money of the country. . . .

X. The substitution of arbitration for strikes, whenever and wherever employers and employes are willing to meet on equitable grounds.

XI. The prohibition of the employment of children in workshops, mines and factories before attaining their fourteenth year.

XII. To abolish the system of letting out by contract the labor of convicts in our prisons and reformatory institutions.

XIII. To secure for both sexes equal pay for equal work.

XIV. The reduction of the hours of labor to eight per day, so that the laborers may have more time for social enjoyment and intellectual improvement, and be enabled to reap the advantages conferred by the labor-saving machinery which their brains have created.

The Communist Manifesto
Karl Marx and Friedrich Engels

Although initially only one of many radical doctrines, Marxism proved to be the most dynamic and influential challenge to industrial capitalism and middle-class civilization in general. Its most succinct and popular statement is contained in the Communist Manifesto, *written by Karl Marx (1818–1883) and Friedrich Engels (1820–1895) and first published in 1848. Karl Marx was born in Germany, studied history and philosophy, and entered a career as a journalist, writer, and revolutionary. For most of his life he lived in exile in London. His collaborator, Friedrich Engels, was also born in Germany and lived in England, but there he helped manage his family's cotton business in Manchester. Their doctrines directly attacked the middle class and industrial capitalism, presenting commu-*

SOURCE: Karl Marx and Friedrich Engels, *Manifesto of the Communist Party*, 2nd ed. (New York: National Executive Committee of the Socialist Labor Party, 1898), pp. 30–32, 41–43, 60.

nism as a philosophically, historically, and scientifically justified alternative that would inevitably replace capitalism. They saw themselves as revolutionary leaders of the growing proletariat (the working class). The following is a selection from the Communist Manifesto.

> **Consider:** *The appeal of the ideas presented here; the concrete policies advocated by Marx and Engels; the historical and intellectual trends reflected in the Manifesto.*

A specter is haunting Europe–the specter of Communism. All the powers of old Europe have entered into a holy alliance to exorcise this specter; Pope and Czar, Metternich and Guizot, French radicals and German police spies.

Where is the party in opposition that has not been decried as Communistic by its opponents in power? Where the opposition that has not hurled back the branding reproach of Communism, against the more advanced opposition parties, as well as against its reactionary adversaries?

Two things result from this fact.

I. Communism is already acknowledged by all European powers to be in itself a power.

II. It is high time that Communists should openly, in the face of the whole world, publish their views, their aims, their tendencies, and meet this nursery tale of the Specter of Communism with a Manifesto of the party itself.

To this end the Communists of various nationalities have assembled in London, and sketched the following manifesto to be published in the English, French, German, Italian, Flemish and Danish languages.

✧

In what relation do the Communists stand to the proletarians as a whole?

The Communists do not form a separate party opposed to other working class parties.

They have no interests separate and apart from those of the proletariat as a whole.

They do not set up any sectarian principles of their own by which to shape and mould the proletarian movement.

The Communists are distinguished from the other working class parties by this only: 1. In the national struggles of the proletarians of the different countries, they point out and bring to the front the common interests of the entire proletariat, independently of all nationality. 2. In the various stages of development which the struggle of the working class against the bourgeoisie has to pass through, they always and everywhere represent the interests of the movement as a whole.

The Communists, therefore, are on the one hand, practically, the most advanced and resolute section of the working class parties of every country, that section which pushes forward all others; on the other hand, theoretically, they have over the great mass of the proletariat the advantage of clearly understanding the line of march, the conditions, and the ultimate general results of the proletarian movement.

The immediate aim of the Communists is the same as that of all the other proletarian parties: formation of the proletariat into a class, overthrow of the bourgeois supremacy, conquest of political power by the proletariat.

The theoretical conclusions of the Communists are in no way based on ideas or principles that have been invented, or discovered, by this or that would-be universal reformer.

They merely express, in general terms, actual relations springing from an existing class struggle, from a historical movement going on under our very eyes. The abolition of existing property relations is not at all a distinctive feature of Communism.

All property relations in the past have continually been subject to historical change, consequent upon the change in historical conditions.

The French revolution, for example, abolished feudal property in favor of bourgeois property.

The distinguishing feature of Communism is not the abolition of property generally, but the abolition of bourgeois property. But modern bourgeois private property is the final and most complete expression of the system of producing and appropriating products, that is based on class antagonisms, on the exploitation of the many by the few.

In this sense the theory of the Communists may be summed up in the single sentence: Abolition of private property.

We have seen above that the first step in the revolution by the working class is to raise the proletariat to the position of the ruling class; to win the battle of democracy.

The proletariat will use its political supremacy to wrest, by degrees, all capital from the bourgeoisie; to centralize all instruments of production in the hands of the State, *i.e.,* of the proletariat organized as the ruling class; and to increase the total of productive forces as rapidly as possible.

Of course, in the beginning this cannot be effected except by means of despotic inroads on the rights of property and on the conditions of bourgeois production; by means of measures, therefore, which appear economically insufficient and untenable, but which, in the course of the movement, outstrip themselves, necessitate further inroads upon the old social order and are unavoidable as a means of entirely revolutionizing the mode of production.

These measures will, of course, be different in different countries.

Nevertheless in the most advanced countries the following will be pretty generally applicable:

1. Abolition of property in land and application of all rents of land to public purposes.
2. A heavy progressive or graduated income tax.
3. Abolition of all right of inheritance.

4. Confiscation of the property of all emigrants and rebels.
5. Centralization of credit in the hands of the State, by means of a national bank with State capital and an exclusive monopoly.
6. Centralization of the means of communication and transport in the hands of the State.
7. Extension of factories and instruments of production owned by the State; the bringing into cultivation of waste lands, and the improvement of the soil generally in accordance with a common plan.
8. Equal liability of all to labor. Establishment of industrial armies, especially for agriculture.
9. Combination of agriculture with manufacturing industries: gradual abolition of the distinction between town and country, by a more equable distribution of the population over the country.
10. Free education for all children in public schools. Abolition of children's factory labor in its present form. Combination of education with industrial production, etc., etc.

When, in the course of development, class distinctions have disappeared and all production has been concentrated in the hands of a vast association of the whole nation, the public power will lose its political character. Political power, properly so called, is merely the organized power of one class for oppressing another. If the proletariat during its contest with the bourgeoisie is compelled, by the force of circumstances, to organize itself as a class, if, by means of a revolution, it makes itself the ruling class, and, as such, sweeps away by force the old conditions of production, then it will, along with these conditions, have swept away the conditions for the existence of class antagonisms, and of classes generally, and will thereby have abolished its own supremacy as a class.

In place of the old bourgeois society with its classes and class antagonisms we shall have an association in which the free development of each is the condition for the free development of all.

Self-Help: Middle-Class Attitudes
Samuel Smiles

Middle-class liberals were not totally unaware of the consequences of industrialization for society. Doctrines were developed that reflected and appealed to their attitudes. Such doctrines served to justify the position of the middle class, to support policies it usually favored, and to rationalize the poor state of the working class. Many of these doctrines

SOURCE: Samuel Smiles, *Self-Help* (Chicago: Belford, Clarke, 1881), pp. 21–23, 48–49.

appeared in Self-Help, *the popular book by Samuel Smiles, a physician, editor, secretary of two railroads, and author. First published in 1859,* Self-Help *became a best seller in England and was translated into many languages. The following excerpt is a good example of the individualism and moral tone that appear throughout the book.*

> **Consider:** *How Smiles justifies his assertion that self-help is the only answer to problems; how Smiles would analyze the situation of the working class and how he would react to the testimony presented to the parliamentary commission on child labor.*

"Heaven helps those who help themselves" is a well tried maxim, embodying in a small compass the results of vast human experience. The spirit of self-help is the root of all genuine growth in the individual; and, exhibited in the lives of many, it constitutes the true source of national vigor and strength. Help from without is often enfeebling in its effects, but help from within invariably invigorates. Whatever is done *for* men or classes, to a certain extent takes away the stimulus and necessity of doing for themselves; and where men are subjected to over-guidance and over-government, the inevitable tendency is to render them comparatively helpless.

Even the best institutions can give a man no active help. Perhaps the most they can do is, to leave him free to develop himself and improve his individual condition. But in all times men have been prone to believe that their happiness and well-being were to be secured by means of institutions rather than by their own conduct. Hence the value of legislation as an agent in human advancement has usually been much overestimated. To constitute the millionth part of a Legislature, by voting for one or two men once in three or five years, however conscientiously this duty may be performed, can exercise but little active influence upon any man's life and character. Moreover, it is every day becoming more clearly understood, that the function of Government is negative and restrictive, rather than positive and active; being resolvable principally into protection—protection of life, liberty, and property. Laws, wisely administrated, will secure men in the enjoyment of the fruits of their labor, whether of mind or body, at a comparatively small personal sacrifice; but no laws, however stringent, can make the idle industrious, the shiftless provident, or the drunken sober. Such reforms can only be effected by means of individual action, economy, and self-denial; by better habits, rather than by greater rights. . . .

Indeed, all experience serves to prove that the worth and strength of a State depend far less upon the form of its institutions than upon the character of its men. For the nation is only an aggregate of individual conditions, and civilization itself is but a question of the personal improvement of the men, women, and children of whom society is composed.

National progress is the sum of individual industry, energy, and uprightness, as national decay is of individual idleness, selfishness, and vice. What we are accustomed to decry as great social evils, will for the most part be found to be but the outgrowth of man's own perverted life; and though we may endeavor to cut them down and extirpate them by means of Law, they will only spring up again with fresh luxuriance in some other form, unless the conditions of personal life and character are radically improved. If this view be correct, then it follows that the highest patriotism and philanthropy consist, not so much in altering laws and modifying institutions, as in helping and stimulating men to elevate and improve themselves by their own free and independent individual action.

One of the most strongly marked features of the English people is their spirit of industry, standing out prominent and distinct in their past history, and as strikingly characteristic of them now as at any former period. It is this spirit, displayed by the commons of England, which has laid the foundations and built up the industrial greatness of the empire. This vigorous growth of the nation has been mainly the result of the free energy of individuals, and it has been contingent upon the number of hands and minds from time to time actively employed within it, whether as cultivators of the soil, producers of articles of utility, contrivers of tools and machines, writers of books, or creators of works of art. And while this spirit of active industry has been the vital principle of the nation, it has also been its saving and remedial one, counteracting from time to time the effects of errors in our laws and imperfections in our constitution.

The career of industry which the nation has pursued, has also proved its best education. As steady application to work is the healthiest training for every individual, so is it the best discipline of a state. Honorable industry travels the same road with duty; and Providence has closely linked both with happiness. The gods, says the poet, have placed labor and toil on the way leading to the Elysian fields. Certain it is that no bread eaten by man is so sweet as that earned by his own labor, whether bodily or mental. By labor the earth has been subdued, and man redeemed from barbarism; nor has a single step in civilization been made without it. Labor is not only a necessity and a duty, but a blessing: only the idler feels it to be a curse. The duty of work is written on the thews and muscles of the limbs, the mechanism of the hand, the nerves and lobes of the brain—the sum of whose healthy action is satisfaction and enjoyment. In the school of labor is taught the best practical widsom; nor is a life of manual employment, as we shall hereafter find, incompatible with high mental culture.

Woman in Her Social and Domestic Character
Elizabeth Poole Sandford

Industrialization also had its effects on middle-class women. As the wealth and position of these women rose in a changing economic environment, previous models of behavior no longer applied. A variety of books and manuals appeared to counsel middle-class women

SOURCE: Mrs. John Sandford (Elizabeth Poole Sandford), *Woman in Her Social and Domestic Character* (Boston: Otis, Broaders and Co., 1842), pp. 5–7, 15–16.

on their proper role and behavior. The following is an excerpt from one of these, Woman in Her Social and Domestic Character *(1842), written by Mrs. John Sandford.*

> **Consider:** *Woman's ideal function in relation to her husband, according to this document; by implication, the role of the middle-class man in relation to his wife; possible explanations for this view of women.*

The changes wrought by Time are many. It influences the opinions of men as familiarity does their feelings; it has a tendency to do away with superstition, and to reduce every thing to its real worth.

It is thus that the sentiment for woman has undergone a change. The romantic passion which once almost deified her is on the decline; and it is by intrinsic qualities that she must now inspire respect. She is no longer the queen of song and the star of chivalry. But if there is less of enthusiasm entertained for her, the sentiment is more rational, and, perhaps, equally sincere; for it is in relation to happiness that she is chiefly appreciated.

And in this respect it is, we must confess, that she is most useful and most important. Domestic life is the chief source of her influence; and the greatest debt society can owe to her is domestic comfort: for her happiness is almost an element of virtue; and nothing conduces more to improve the character of men than domestic peace. A woman may make a man's home delightful, and may thus increase his motives for virtuous exertion. She may refine and tranquillize his mind—may turn away his anger or allay his grief. Her smile may be the happy influence to gladden his heart, and to disperse the cloud that gathers on his brow. And in proportion to her endeavors to make those around her happy, she will be esteemed and loved. She will secure by her excellence that interest and regard which she might formerly claim as the privilege of her sex, and will really merit the deference which was then conceded to her as a matter of course. . . .

Perhaps one of the first secrets of her influence is adaptation to the tastes, and sympathy in the feelings, of those around her. This holds true in lesser as well as in graver points. It is in the former, indeed, that the absence of interest in a companion is frequently most disappointing. Where want of congeniality impairs domestic comfort, the fault is generally chargeable on the female side. It is for woman, not for man, to make the sacrifice, especially in indifferent matters. She must, in a certain degree, be plastic herself if she would mould others. . . .

To be useful, a woman must have feeling. It is this which suggests the thousand nameless amenities which fix her empire in the heart, and render her so agreeable, and almost so necessary, that she imperceptibly rises in the domestic circle, and becomes at once its cement and its charm.

°

Nothing is so likely to conciliate the affections of the other sex as a feeling that woman looks to them for support and guidance. In proportion as men are themselves superior, they are accessible to this appeal. On the contrary, they never feel interested in one who seems disposed rather to offer than to ask assistance. There is, indeed, something unfeminine in independence. It is contrary to nature, and therefore it offends. We do not like to see a woman affecting tremors, but still less do we like to see her acting the amazon. A really sensible woman feels her dependence. She does what she can; but she is conscious of inferiority, and therefore grateful for support. She knows that she is the weaker vessel, and that as such she should receive honor. In this view, her weakness is an attraction, not a blemish.

In every thing, therefore, that women attempt, they should show their consciousness of dependence. If they are learners, let them evince a teachable spirit; if they give an opinion, let them do it in an unassuming manner. There is something so unpleasant in female self-sufficiency that it not unfrequently deters instead of persuading, and prevents the adoption of advice which the judgment even approves.

The Origin of Species
and
The Descent of Man
Charles Darwin

The nineteenth century was a period of great scientific ideas and discoveries. Perhaps the most important, and certainly the most controversial, was Darwin's theory of evolution. Charles Darwin (1809–1882), a British naturalist, gathered data while on voyages in the southern Pacific. He used that data to develop his theory of evolution by natural selection. This theory of evolution, particularly as applied to human beings, challenged biblical accounts of creation. He argued that all life, including human life, evolved from lower forms. Evolution was slow and extended over a much longer period than had been assumed. Natural selection, or survival of the fittest, determined how species evolved. Darwin first formulated his findings and theory in an 1844 essay. However, it was only after 1859, when he published The Origin of Species by Means of Natural Selection, *that his ideas became well known and widely controversial. The first of two selections below is from that book. The second is from* The Descent of Man, *which he published in 1871.*

> **Consider:** *Why his ideas might be so welcome by some, so disturbing to others; the possible psychological impact of his ideas; how those favoring biblical accounts might respond.*

. . . [C]an we doubt (remembering that many more individuals are born than can possibly survive) that individuals having any advantage, however slight, over others, would have the best chance of surviving and of procreating their kind? On

SOURCE: Charles Darwin, *The Origin of Species by Means of Natural Selection*, 6th ed., London: John Murray, 1872, pp. 63, 85. Charles Darwin, *The Descent of Man*, New York: D. Appleton and Co., 1883, pp. 606–607, 619.

the other hand, we may feel sure that any variation in the least degree injurious would be rigidly destroyed. This preservation of favourable individual differences and variations, and the destruction of those which are injurious, I have called Natural Selection, or the Survival of the Fittest. . . .

Natural selection acts solely through the preservation of variations in some way advantageous, which consequently endure. Owing to the high geometrical rate of increase of all organic beings, each area is already fully stocked with inhabitants; and it follows from this, that as the favored forms increase in number, so, generally, will the less favored decrease and become rare. Rarity, as geology tells us, is the precursor to extinction.

✿

The main conclusion here arrived at, and now held by many naturalists who are well competent to form a sound judgment, is that man is descended from some less highly organized form. The grounds upon which this conclusion rests will never be shaken, for the close similarity between man and the lower animals in embryonic development, as well as in innumerable points of structure and constitution, both of high and of the most trifling importance,—the rudiments which he retains, and the abnormal reversions to which he is occasionally liable,—are facts which cannot be disputed. They have long been known, but until recently they told us nothing with respect to the origin of man. Now when viewed by the light of our knowledge of the whole organic world, their meaning is unmistakable. The great principle of evolution stands up clear and firm, when these groups of facts are considered in connection with others, such as the mutual affinities of the members of the same group, their geographical distribution in past and present times, and their geological succession. It is incredible that all these facts should speak falsely. He who is not content to look, like a savage, at the phenomena of nature as disconnected, cannot any longer believe that man is the work of a separate act of creation. . . .

We have seen that man incessantly presents individual differences in all parts of his body and in his mental faculties. These differences or variations seem to be induced by the same general causes, and to obey the same laws as with the lower animals. In both cases similar laws of inheritance prevail. Man tends to increase at a greater rate than his means of subsistence; consequently he is occasionally subjected to a severe struggle for existence, and natural selection will have effected whatever lies within its scope. A succession of strongly-marked variations of a similar nature is by no means requisite; slight fluctuating differences in the individual suffice for the work of natural selection. . . .

[M]an with all his noble qualities, with sympathy which feels for the most debased, with benevolence which extends not only to other men but to the humblest living creature, with his god-like intellect which has penetrated into the movements and constitution of the solar system—with all these exalted powers—Man still bears in his bodily frame the indelible stamp of his lowly origin.

VISUAL SOURCES

Industrialization and Demographic Change

A comparison of the first two maps, which show the population density of England in 1801 and 1851, reveals the relatively rapid increase in population and urbanization in

Map 6-1   Population Density: England, 1801

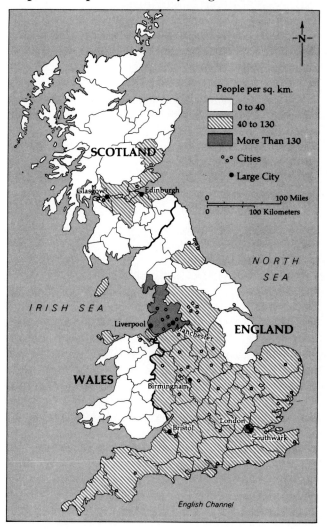

Map 6-2 Population Density: England, 1851

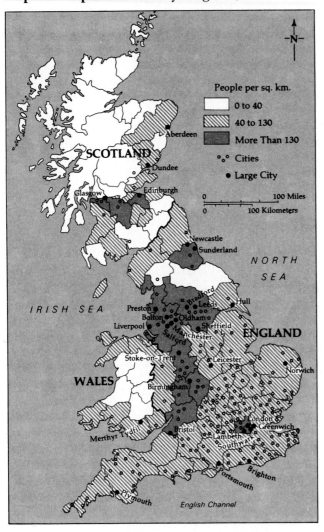

People per sq. km.

- 0 to 40
- 40 to 130
- More Than 130
- Cities
- Large City

0 — 100 Miles
0 — 100 Kilometers

SCOTLAND

Aberdeen
Dundee
Edinburgh
Glasgow

Newcastle
Sunderland

NORTH SEA

IRISH SEA

Preston
Bolton
Liverpool
Salford
Manchester
Oldham
Bradford
Leeds
Hull
Sheffield

ENGLAND

Stoke-on-Trent
Leicester
Norwich

WALES

Birmingham

Merthyr Tydfil
Bristol
Lambeth
Southwark
London
Greenwich

Portsmouth
Brighton

Plymouth

English Channel

Map 6-3   Concentration of Industry in England, 1851

certain areas of England during this period. The third map shows where industry (mainly textiles, metallurgy, and mining) was concentrated in 1851. A comparison of all three maps reveals the connections between shifting population density, urbanization, and industrialization during this period of early, rapid modernization of England's economy.

> **Consider:** *What some of the geopolitical consequences of these connections between demographic and economic changes might be; what some of the social consequences might be.*

Illustration from *Life and Adventures of Michael Armstrong*

This is an illustration from a novel, Life and Adventures of Michael Armstrong *(1840), by the well-known British author, Mrs. Frances Trollope. The illustration depicts several of the main elements of the Industrial Revolution in England. It shows the inside of a textile factory—a factory in the most advanced of the new industries. Thanks to mechanization and artificial power, a few workers can now do the work of many. The workers—men, women, and children—are obviously poor. In the background stands the stern middle-class owner talking with others of his class while in the foreground a child worker embraces his middle-class counterpart for some kindness he has displayed. The scene is reflective of the typical middle-class view of the poor and poverty—as problems of morals, to be treated with pity and philanthropic concern but not yet requiring substantial social or economic change.*

> **Consider:** *The ways in which this illustration reflects aspects of industrialization touched on by other documents in this chapter.*

Photo 6-1

The Bettmann Archive/BBC Hulton

The Hatch Family: The Upper Middle Class
Eastman Johnson

This 1871 portrait of the Hatch family by the American artist Eastman Johnson shows a number of elements of the condition, lifestyle, and values of the upper middle class. Both the quality and quantity of the furnishings and the clothes indicate how materially well-to-do this family is. The clothes and demeanor convey the strong sense of propriety; yet the activities of the children and the position of their toys denote how child-centered this family is. The appropriate sexual roles are suggested: the father at center right in an authoritative pose, with pen in hand sitting at his desk, the grandfather on the left, keeping up on the news by reading a paper, the mother on the right, generally surveying her children, and the grandmother on the left, knitting. The large painting on the left as well as the sculptures on the right show this family to be properly supportive and appreciative of the arts. The large bookcase on the right indicates a respect for literature and learning. Heavy curtains largely block out the outside world; values of domesticity and privacy are evident.

> **Consider:** *What lessons the nineteenth-century viewer might learn from this portrait.*

Photo 6-2

The Metropolitan Museum of Art, Gift of Frederick H. Hatch

The Genius of Christianity:
Literary Romanticism
René de Châteaubriand

The Romantic movement of the late eighteenth century and first half of the nineteenth century was, in part, a rebellion against new trends such as rationalism, industrialism, urbanization, and secularism. Many historians have noted specific connections between Romanticism and conservation, particularly in the longing for a less complex life, the respect for traditional religion, and the sense of unity between rural life and human institutions. This is illustrated in the following selection from The Genius of Christianity *by René de Châteaubriand (1768–1848), a conservative French politician and writer. Published in 1802, it gained considerable popularity and helped Châteaubriand achieve a leading position among French conservatives. Here Châteaubriand describes the Gothic churches of the middle Ages.*

> **Consider:** *Why this description might appeal to members of the aristocracy and the Catholic Church; by implication, the aspects of Châteaubriand's own times that he was attacking.*

You could not enter a Gothic church without feeling a kind of awe and a vague sentiment of the Divinity. You were all at once carried back to those times when a fraternity of cenobites, after having meditated in the woods of their monasteries, met to prostrate themselves before the altar and to chant the praises of the Lord, amid the tranquillity and the silence of night. Ancient France seemed to revive altogether; you beheld all those singular costumes, all that nation so different from what it is at present; you were reminded of its revolutions, its productions, and its arts. The more remote were these times the more magical they appeared, the more they inspired ideas which always end with a reflection on the nothingness of man and the rapidity of life. . . .

The forests of Gaul were, in their turn, introduced into the temples of our ancestors, and those celebrated woods of oaks thus maintained their sacred character. Those ceilings sculptured into foliage of different kinds, those buttresses which prop the walls and terminate abruptly like the broken trunks of trees, the coolness of the vaults, the darkness of the sanctuary, the dim twilight of the aisles, the secret passages, the low doorways,—in a word, every thing in a Gothic church reminds you of the labyrinths of a wood; every thing excites a feeling of religious awe, of mystery, and of the Divinity.

The two lofty towers erected at the entrance of the edifice overtop the elms and yew-trees of the churchyard, and produce the most picturesque effect on the azure of heaven. Sometimes their twin heads are illumined by the first rays of dawn; at others they appear crowned with a capital of clouds or magnified in a

SOURCE: Viscount de Châteaubriand, *The Genius of Christianity,* Charles J. White, trans. (Baltimore, Md.: John Murphy, 1856), pp. 385–387.

foggy atmosphere. The birds themselves seem to make a mistake in regard to them, and to take them for the trees of the forest; they hover over their summits, and perch upon their pinnacles. But, lo! confused noises suddenly issue from the top of these towers and scare away the affrighted birds. The Christian architect, not content with building forests, has been desirous to retain their murmurs; and, by means of the organ and of bells, he has attached to the Gothic temple the very winds and thunders that roar in the recesses of the woods. Past ages, conjured up by these religious sounds, raise their venerable voices from the bosom of the stones, and are heard in every corner of the ancient Sibyl; loud-tongued bells swing over your head, while the vaults of death under your feet are profoundly silent.

Abbey Graveyard in the Snow: Visual Romanticism
Caspar David Friedrich

Abbey Graveyard in the Snow (1819) was painted by the well-known north German artist Caspar David Friedrich. In the center are the ruins of a Gothic choir of a monastic church surrounded by a snow-covered graveyard and leafless winter forest. To the left a procession of monks follows a coffin into the ruins.

This painting exemplifies many elements typical of Romanticism, particularly German Romanticism. The scene, while visually accurate, goes beyond realism: The light is too perfectly placed, the church remains are too majestic, the surrounding forest is too symmetrical a frame, and the funeral procession is out of place (funerals did not take place in ruins). By implication, this painting rejects the limits of Enlightenment rationalism and the reality of nineteenth-century urban life. Instead, a Romantic version of the Middle Ages, the spirituality of nature, and the glories of Christianity are evoked. The Romantic longing to be overwhelmed by eternal nature is suggested particularly by the rendering of small human figures in a large landscape. Romanticism typically exalted the emotional over the rational, even if it was a melancholy sensitivity that was being displayed.

Consider: *The ways in which the Romanticism of this painting is consistent with that of Châteaubriand's description of a Gothic cathedral.*

Photo 6-3

Bildarchiv Preussischer Kulturbesitz

SECONDARY SOURCES

The Making of Economic Society: England, the First to Industrialize

Robert Heilbroner

Although it is clear that industrialization occurred first in England, it is not apparent why this was so. During the eighteenth century, France was prosperous and economically advanced. Other countries such as Belgium and the Netherlands possessed certain economic

SOURCE: Robert L. Heilbroner, *The Making of Economic Society*. Reprinted by permission of Prentice-Hall, Inc. (Englewood Cliffs, N.J., 1980), pp. 76–77, 80–81.

advantages over England and might have industralized earlier but did not. In the follow-
ing selection, Robert Heilbroner, an economist and economic historian, addresses the
question of why England was first.

> **Consider:** *Why Heilbroner stresses the role of the "New Men" over the other fac-*
> *tors he lists; any disadvantages England had to overcome; whether it was simply*
> *the circumstances that gave rise to the "New Men" or whether it was the "New*
> *Men" who took advantage of the circumstances when most men in most other*
> *nations would not have.*

Why did the Industrial Revolution originally take place in England and not on the continent? To answer the question we must look at the background factors which distinguished England from most other European nations in the eighteenth century.

The first of these factors was simply that England was relatively wealthy. In fact, a century of successful exploration, slave-trading, piracy, war, and commerce had made her the richest nation in the world. Even more important, her riches had accrued not merely to a few nobles, but to a large upper-middle stratum of commercial bourgeoisie. England was thus one of the first nations to develop, albeit on a small scale, a prime requisite of an industrial economy: a "mass" consumer market. As a result, a rising pressure of demand inspired a search for new techniques.

Second, England was the scene of the most successful and thoroughgoing transformation of feudal society into commercial society. A succession of strong kings had effectively broken the power of the local nobility and had made England into a single unified state. As part of this process, we also find in England the strongest encouragement to the rising mercantile classes. Then too, as we have seen, the enclosure movement, which gained in tempo in the seventeenth and eighteenth centuries, expelled an army of laborers to man her new industrial establishments.

Third, England was the locus of a unique enthusiasm for science and engineering. The famous Royal Academy, of which Newton was an early president, was founded in 1660 and was the immediate source of much intellectual excitement. Indeed, a popular interest in gadgets, machines, and devices of all sorts soon became a mild national obsession: *Gentlemen's Magazine*, a kind of *New Yorker* of the period, announced in 1729 that it would henceforth keep its readers "abreast of every invention"—a task which the mounting flow of inventions soon rendered quite impossible. No less important was an enthusiasm of the British landed aristocracy for scientific farming: English landlords displayed an interest in matters of crop rotation and fertilizer which their French counterparts would have found quite beneath their dignity.

Then there were a host of other background causes, some as fortuitous as the immense resources of coal and iron ore on which the British sat; others as purposeful as the development of a national patent system which deliberately sought to stimulate and protect the act of invention itself. In many ways, England was "ready" for an Industrial Revolution. But perhaps what finally translated the potentiality into an actuality was the emergence of a group of new men who seized upon the latent opportunities of history as a vehicle for their own rise to fame and fortune. . . .

Pleasant or unpleasant, the personal characteristics fade beside one overriding quality. These were all men interested in expansion, in growth, in investment for investment's sake. All of them were identified with technological progress, and none of them disdained the productive process. An employee of Maudslay's once remarked, "It was a pleasure to see him handle a tool of any kind, but he was *quite splendid* with an 18-inch file." Watt was tireless in experimenting with his machines; Wedgwood stomped about his factory on his wooden leg scrawling, "This won't do for Jos. Wedgwood," wherever he saw evidence of careless work. Richard Arkwright was a bundle of ceaseless energy in promoting his interests, jouncing about England over execrable roads in a post chaise driven by four horses, pursuing his correspondence as he traveled.

"With us," wrote a French visitor to a calico works in 1788, "a man rich enough to set up and run a factory like this would not care to remain in a position which he would deem unworthy of his wealth." This was an attitude entirely foreign to the rising English industrial capitalist. His work was its own dignity and reward; the wealth it brought was quite aside. Boswell, on being shown Watt and Boulton's great engine works at Soho, declared that he never forgot Boulton's expression as the latter declared, "I sell here, sir, what all the world desires to have—Power."

The New Men were first and last *entrepreneurs*—enterprisers. They brought with them a new energy, as restless as it proved to be inexhaustible. In an economic, if not a political, sense, they deserve the epithet "revolutionaries," for the change they ushered in was nothing short of total, sweeping, and irreversible.

The Unfinished Revolution: Marxism Interpreted
Adam B. Ulam

Critical analyses of Marx and Marxism abound and from almost all points of view. From the historian's perspective, one of the most useful ways to approach Marx and Marxism is to place both in their historical context. This is done in the following excerpt from The Unfinished Revolution *by Adam Ulam, a professor of government at Harvard who has written extensively on the history of Marxism and the Soviet Union. Here he attempts to explain aspects of both the content and the appeal of Marxism by pointing to intellectual traditions affecting Marx and social realities conditioning those who accepted it.*

SOURCE: Adam B. Ulam, *The Unfinished Revolution* (New York: Random House, Inc., 1960), pp. 42–44. Reprinted by permission of the author.

Consider: *Why Marxism was most appealing during the early period of industrialization; how Ulam would explain the apparent failure of Marxism to take hold in twentieth-century nations such as the United States; what Ulam means when he calls Marx a child of rationalistic optimism; how a more pro-Marxist scholar might respond to this interpretation.*

Here, then, is a theory attuned ever more closely than other parts of Marxism to the facts and feelings of an early period of industrialization. The class struggle is the salt of Marxism, its most operative revolutionary part. As a historical and psychological concept, it expresses a gross oversimplification, but it is the oversimplification of a genius. The formula of the class struggle seizes the essence of the mood of a great historical moment—a revolution in basic economy—and generalizes it into a historical law. It extracts the grievances of groups of politically conscious workers in Western Europe, then a very small part of the whole proletariat, and sees in it the portent and meaning of the awakening of the whole working class everywhere. The *first* reaction of the worker to industrialization, his feelings of grievance and impotence before the machine, his employer, and the state which stands behind the employer, are assumed by Marx to be typical of the general reactions of the worker to industrialization. What does change in the process of the development of industry is that the worker's feeling of impotence gives way to class consciousness, which in turn leads him to class struggle and socialism. Marx's worker is the historical worker, but he is the historical worker of a specific period of industrial and political development.

Even in interpreting the psychology of the worker of the transitional period, Marx exhibited a rationalistic bias. The worker's opposition to the capitalist order is a total opposition to its laws, its factories, and its government. But this revolutionary consciousness of the worker is to take him next to Marxist socialism, where he will accept the factory system and the state, the *only* difference being the abolition of capitalism. Why shouldn't the revolutionary protest of the worker flow into other channels: into rejection of industrialism as well as capitalism, into rejection of the socialist as well as the capitalist state? It is here that Marx is most definitely the child of his age, the child of rationalistic optimism: the workers will undoubtedly translate their anarchistic protests and grievances into a sophisticated philosophy of history. They will undoubtedly realize that the forces of industrialism and modern life, which strip them of property, status, and economic security, are in themselves benevolent in their ultimate effects and that it is only capitalism and the capitalists which make them into instruments of oppression. The claims felt by the proletariat are the chains of the industrial system. The chains Marx urges them to throw off are those of capitalism. Will the workers understand the difference? And if they do, will they still feel that in destroying capitalism they have a "world to win"?

Europe and the People without History: Labor Migrations

Eric R. Wolf

A large variety of social changes accompanied industrialization. One of the most important was the migration of large numbers of people. Part of this was the movement of people from the countryside to the cities and new industrial centers within Europe. Another part was the wave of labor migration from Europe overseas. In the following selection, Eric Wolf analyzes the waves of labor migrations related to industrialization occurring during the nineteenth and twentieth centuries.

> **Consider:** *The differences between the three waves of migration Wolf describes; the possible economic and social consequences of these labor migrations within and outside of Europe.*

People may move for religious, political, ecological, or other reasons; but the migrations of the nineteenth and twentieth centuries were largely labor migrations, movements of the bearers of labor power. These labor migrations, of course, carried with them newspaper editors to publish papers for Polish miners or German metalworkers, shopkeepers to supply their fellow migrants with pasta or red beans, religious specialists to minister to Catholic or Buddhist souls, and others. Each migration involved the transfer to the new geographical location not only of manpower but also of services and resources. Each migratory wave generated, in turn, supplies of services at the point of arrival, whether these were labor agents, merchants, lawyers, or players of percussion instruments.

In the development of capitalism, three waves of migration stand out, each a response to critical changes in the demand for labor, each creating new working classes. The first of these waves was associated with the initial period of European industrialization. Beginning in England, these initial movements toward capitalist industry covered only short distances, since industrial development was itself still localized and limited. Thus, in the cotton town of Preston in Lancashire, where roughly half the population consisted of immigrants in 1851, over 40 percent had come less than ten miles from their birthplaces and only about 30 percent had come more than thirty miles. Fourteen percent of all immigrants had been born in Ireland, however, and came to Preston as part of the rising tide of Irish immigration in the 1840s. Localized as such movements were, they made Lancashire the most urbanized county in Britain by the middle of the nineteenth century, with more than half the people of the county living in fourteen towns with populations of more than 10,000.

Belgium followed Britain in the movement of workers from the countryside, as

SOURCE: Eric Wolf, *Europe and the People without History*, (Berkeley, California), copyright © 1983 by the Regents of the University of California, University of California Press.

the industrial towns of the Walloon-speaking southern provinces burgeoned in the 1820s. In the 1830s the Prussian provinces of Westphalia, Rhine, Berlin, and Brandenburg initiated their industrial expansion, attracting a large-scale flow of population from Prussia's eastern agricultural regions. This flow intensified greatly in the last quarter of the century, as dependent cultivators were displaced by the consolidation and mechanization of the large Junker estates.

While the first wave of labor migration under capitalism carried people toward the industrial centers within the European peninsula, a second flow sent Europeans overseas. An estimated 50 million people left Europe permanently between 1800 and 1914. The most important destination of this movement was the United States, which between 1820 and 1915 absorbed about 32 million immigrants, most of them of European origins. This influx of people provided the labor power that underwrote the industrialization of the United States.

A third wave of migration carried contract laborers of diverse origins to the expanding mines and plantations of the tropics. This flow represents a number of developments, such as the establishment of a migratory labor force for the South African mines, the growth of the trade in Indian and Chinese contract labor, and the sponsored migration of Italian laborers to the coffee regions of Brazil. These movements not only laid the basis for a large increase in tropical production but also played a major part in creating an infrastructure of transport and communication, prerequisites for a further acceleration of capitalist development.

The Family and Industrialization in Western Europe
Michael Anderson

The tremendous growth of interest in social history over the past twenty years has stimulated scholars from other disciplines to address historical questions. A number of sociologists have applied methods from their discipline to social aspects of nineteenth-century industrialization. In the following selection, Michael Anderson, a sociologist from the University of Edinburgh, discusses the effects of industrialization on the working-class family.

Consider: *The specific ways in which the process of industrialization affected working-class families; how Anderson's interpretation might support the "optimists" or the "pessimists" in their debate over the effects of the Industrial Revolution on the working class; how the effects on middle-class families might differ.*

SOURCE: Michael Anderson, "The Family and Industrialization in Western Europe," *The Forum Series*. Reprinted by permission of Forum Press (St. Louis, Mo., 1978), p. 14. Copyright © 1978 by Forum Press.

In industrial areas, then, the close interdependence of parents and children which was so important in peasant societies gave way, and this was reflected in changes in family relationships. The early stages of industrialization, however, probably changed relationships between husbands and wives much less, though freedom from such close supervision and a more private domestic situation may have allowed rather more affection to develop between them than had been the case in pre-industrial peasant families. Husband and wife were no longer cooperating in the same productive task, but this had never been universal anyway. There was, however, a continued need and possibility for both husbands and wives to work as producers to keep the family above the subsistence line. In a few areas wives actually left the house to work in the factories. More usually, as women had always done, the wives of factory workers worked at home producing small items of clothing, processing some kind of food or drink, taking in the middle class's washing, or running a small shop or lodging house. The manifold needs of an industrial community were thus met in a way which contributed to working class family solidarity while allowing mothers to supervise and care (perhaps rather better than before) for small children during the lengthening period before they were able to enter the labor force themselves.

Initially, then, it was only in a few areas, especially those specializing in mining, machine-making, metal manufacturing, shipbuilding and sawmilling, that a change occurred in the economic status of women and with it in their family situation. In these areas there were not enough openings for female wage employment and, in consequence, many women were forced into the almost totally new situation of full-time housewife. However, as more and more traditional tasks were taken over by the application of factory production methods to clothing and food preparation, the home increasingly became confined to consumption. Only then did the distinction between male productive work outside the home and female consumption-oriented work inside the home become common among the working class.

Though the evidence is patchy, it seems that, at least in some areas, this had an effect on relationships between husbands and wives. Since the husband became the only income producer, the rest of the family became more dependent on him than he was on them. Whatever the husband did, the wife had little power to resist. While the family as a whole relied materially on the father, he needed them only to the extent that he could obtain from them emotional or other rewards which he could not obtain elsewhere or to the extent to which public opinion in the neighbourhood was effective in controlling his behavior (and with the weakened community control of large industrial cities, neighborhood control was often weak). Thus, in the working class, the idea that a woman's place was in the home and that her role was essentially an inferior domestic one is not of great antiquity. Rather it seems only to have developed as a response to a major shift in the power balance between husbands and wives which reflected the new employment situation of late nineteenth and early twentieth century industrial society.

European Women
Eleanor S. Riemer and John C. Fout

In recent years, many historians have pointed out the limitations facing middle-class women between 1850 and 1914. As investigations into women's history have multiplied and deepened, new interpretations have been made. In the following selection, historians Eleanor S. Riemer and John C. Fout argue that middle-class women during this period increasingly questioned their roles and often expanded their activities into new, important areas.

> **Consider:** *How middle-class women's maternal and housewifely roles were justified; ways in which middle-class women expanded their roles; how middle-class women's new roles affected their attitudes.*

Middle-class women, too, faced new situations and challenges in the nineteenth and twentieth centuries. Although some lower-middle-class women continued to work alongside their shopkeeper husbands as they had in the past, most married middle-class women did not, and never expected to have to work for wages. Their lives were centered on caring for their children and homes. But most middle-class women did not lead leisured existences. Indeed, they found that the demands on their time and energy increased as modernization progressed, and middle-class families' standards for cleanliness, food preparation, and physical comfort were upgraded.

Middle-class women's maternal and housewifely roles were justified in the nineteenth century by a twofold conception of women's nature and capabilities. On the one hand, women were considered passive creatures who were physically and intellectually inferior to men. Thus, women needed protection and direction from their fathers and husbands. On the other hand, women, because they were nonaggressive and sexually passive and were removed from the contamination of the competitive workaday world, were deemed morally superior to men and were to be respected for that. A woman's unique capability and greatest responsibility in life was caring for the moral and spiritual needs of her family.

The contradictions within this ideal and women's attempts to reconcile or dispel them are recurring and major themes in the documents. From the middle of the nineteenth century large numbers of middle-class women consciously and methodically expanded their maternal and moral roles—and thus their sphere of competence—outside their homes to society at large. One way they accomplished this was by transforming middle- and upper-class women's traditional, and often haphazard, charitable work into organized movements for social reform. These

---

SOURCE: From *European Women: A Documentary History, 1789–1945*, edited by Eleanor S. Riemer and John C. Fout. Copyright © 1980 by Schocken Books, Inc. Reprinted by permission of Schocken Books, published by Pantheon Books, a division of Random House, Inc.

women became increasingly interested in the problems of poor women and children. They believed they understood and shared many of the concerns of working-
class mothers and considered these women and their children the primary victims
of the economic and social dislocations caused by urbanization and the new
industrial order.

Through their social welfare and reform work, middle-class women gained a
sense of both their own competence and their limitations in a world controlled by
men. Many also realized that although women of their class expected to be dependent wives, economic and social realities were such that there was no guarantee
women would be supported by men throughout their lives. Many came to believe
that their own limited educations and the restrictions placed on them by the law
and the ideals of ladylike conduct left women ill-equipped for the roles they might
have to—or want to—play in life. Thus, the reform of society and reforms for
women became closely identified and often were confronted simultaneously by
organized women all over Europe.

The Freudian Model
of Human Nature
Erich Fromm

*Psychoanalysis became one of the most powerful intellectual influences in the early twen-
tieth century. In part, it was based on the older eighteenth- and nineteenth-century optimism about the power of human rationality and scientific investigation. It assumed that
human behavior could be even more deeply understood than before through scientific
observation and that rational understanding could alleviate pain and problems. In other
ways, however, it reflected the late-nineteenth- and early-twentieth-century attack on rationality: It argued that much of human behavior is irrational, unconscious, and instinc-
tual. Sigmund Freud (1856–1939), the person most responsible for developing psychoanalysis, was a Viennese neurologist who became increasingly interested in psychoanalysis
as a theory of human behavior, as a method of investigation, and as a treatment for
certain illnesses.*

*Freud had many followers and many critics. The German psychoanalyst Erich Fromm
(1900–1980) falls into both categories: He was a neo-Freudian who differed with Freud
on a number of important points. In the following selection from* The Crisis of Psychoanalysis, *Fromm examines the social and historical bases of Freud's thoughts and presents
a brief analysis of the Freudian model of human nature.*

Consider: *The core of Freud's views according to Fromm; why Freud's views have
been so influential.*

Source: Erich Fromm, *The Crisis of Psychoanalysis* (New York: Holt, Rinehart and Winston, 1970), pp. 30–31, 34–35.

As for his concept of man, it is important to point out first that Freud, rooted in the philosophy of humanism and enlightenment, starts out with the assumption of the existence of *man* as such—a universal man, not only man as he manifests himself in various cultures, but someone about whose structure generally valid and empirical statements can be made. Freud, like Spinoza before him, constructed a "model of human nature" on the basis of which not only neuroses, but all fundamental aspects, possibilities, and necessities of man, can be explained and understood.

What is this Freudian model?

Freud saw man as a closed system driven by two forces: the self-preservative and the sexual drives. The latter are rooted in chemophysiological processes moving in a phased pattern. The first phase increases tension and unpleasure; the second reduces the built-up tension and in so doing creates that which subjectively is felt as "pleasure." Man is primarily an isolated being, whose primary interest is the optimal satisfaction of both his ego and his libidinous interest. Freud's man is the physiologically driven and motivated *homme machine*. But, secondarily, man is also a social being, because he needs other people for the satisfaction of his libidinous drives as well as those of self-preservation. The child is in need of mother (and here, according to Freud, libidinous desires follow the path of the physiological needs); the adult needs a sexual partner. Feelings like tenderness or love are looked upon as phenomena that accompany, and result from, libidinous interests. Individuals need each other as means for the satisfaction of their physiologically rooted drives. Man is primarily unrelated to others, and is only secondarily forced—or seduced—into relationships with others.

Freud's *homo sexualis* is a variant of the classic *homo economicus*. It is the isolated, self-sufficient man who has to enter into relations with others in order that they may mutually fulfill their needs. *Homo economicus* has simple economic needs that find their mutual satisfaction in the exchange of goods on the commodity market. The needs of *homo sexualis* are physiological and libidinous, and normally are mutually satisfied by the relations between the sexes. In both variants the persons essentially remain strangers to each other, being related only by the common aim of drive satisfaction.

Chapter Questions

1. Drawing from the sources in the chapter, what social developments might be related to industrialization?
2. How might it be argued that industrialization should be considered a great boon, a mixed blessing, or a disaster for nineteenth-century Europeans?

3. Analyze the social roles of women during this period. In what ways might these roles be connected to the economic and social developments that accompanied industrialization?

4. In what ways was the rise of Marxism connected to industrialization and related social changes?

5. How might the sources be used to analyze Romanticism in art and literature as a reaction to some of the developments occurring in late-eighteenth and early-nineteenth-century Europe?

SEVEN

The Americas, 1700s–1914

In 1700, the enormous land mass that we now call North, Central, and South America was under the colonial control of European powers. By 1914, however, virtually all the countries of this hemisphere were independent republics. Despite the great differences in culture, politics, economies, peoples, and values, they all shared in a common experience of seeking means by which to free themselves of foreign control. Yet, this general process obscures both the enormous price that different peoples paid for gaining liberation as well as the continuing legacies and influences of foreign domination in new and unexpected forms. While the North American nations of the United States and Canada developed urban, industrial economies that were self-sustaining and largely under indigenous control, the economies of Mexico, Central and South America remained largely rural, agricultural and were constantly threatened by dominance from the outside.

The United States, between 1776 and 1914, is a great success story in world history. Initially thirteen colonies of the British Empire, dependent socially and economically on an island three thousand miles away, the United States emerged as the dominant economic power on earth. Furthermore, its

Revolution, built around principles of equality and liberty among men, provided a model of political reform emulated by scores of nations since.

Yet, the tremendous political revolution did not solve all of the problems of inequality that developed during the Colonial Period. Slavery, an institution begun before the revolution, continued for nearly ninety years after and was an underlying cause of one of the bloodiest civil wars in the world's history. Similarly, while the nation was organized to protect the liberty of men, it was not until after the first World War that women were even allowed the vote.

Historians have focused on the nation's important successes. Yet, in these documents, we see that the historical drive toward greater and greater freedom and equality was far from over by the time of the Great War. These documents will deal with three basic issues: First, they will address the apparent goals of equality, liberty, and democracy that were at the heart of the New World's political movements during this time period. The second issue involves the various ways in which resistance to these ideals remained strong and became integral to the economic and political lives of the new nations. Third, these selections look at continuing contradictory impulses, such as slavery and nativism, denial of women's equal rights, and political subjugation of Native American and African American rights.

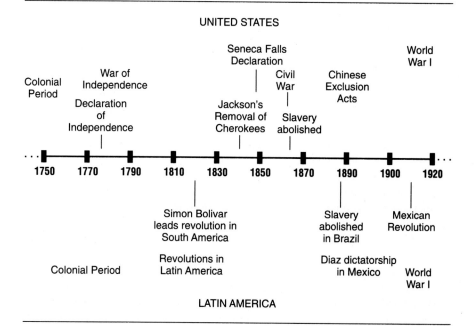

PRIMARY SOURCES

The Declaration of Independence

*By the middle decades of the eighteenth century, relationships between England and the
Colonies had deteriorated. Although the Colonies were divided among themselves over a
host of issues such as slavery, regional interests, and the relative power of a central government over local government, they were united in their belief that they had little to gain
from continuing the traditional colonial relationship. Even so, many colonists, perhaps as
many as one-third, rejected outright rebellion and remained loyal to the Crown. The
Declaration of Independence, written in 1776 at the outset of the Revolutionary War, was
perhaps the most radical statement of the growing Enlightenment philosophies of the era
and would become the model for other revolutionary documents from the French Revolution onward. Written primarily by Thomas Jefferson, it originally contained passages condemning slavery. But, in light of the dependence of the southern states on slavery, anti-
slavery passages were removed.*

> **Consider:** *Who in the Colonies might have been in favor of the Revolution; who
> might have been opposed; how useful this standard is for evaluating the legitimacy
> of a revolution.*

When in the Course of human events, it becomes necessary for one people to
dissolve the political bands which have connected them with another, and to
assume among the Powers of the earth, the separate and equal station to which
the Laws of Nature and of Nature's God entitle them, a decent respect to the
opinions of mankind requires that they should declare the causes which impel
them to the separation.

We hold these truths to be self-evident, that all men are created equal, that
they are endowed by their Creator with certain unalienable Rights, that among
these are Life, Liberty and the pursuit of Happiness. That to secure these rights,
Governments are instituted among Men, deriving their just powers from the
consent of the governed, That whenever any Form of Government becomes
destructive of these ends, it is the Right of the People to alter or to abolish it, and
to institute new Government, laying its foundation on such principles and organizing its powers in such form, as to them shall seem most likely to effect their
Safety and Happiness. Prudence, indeed, will dictate that Governments long
established should not be changed for light and transient causes; and accordingly
all experience hath shown, that mankind are more disposed to suffer, while evils
are sufferable, than to right themselves by abolishing the forms to which they are
accustomed. But when a long train of abuses and usurpations, pursuing invariably
the same Object evinces a design to reduce them under absolute Despotism, it is
their right, it is their duty, to throw off such Government, and to provide new
Guards for their future security.—Such has been the patient sufferance of these
Colonies; and such is now the necessity which constrains them to alter their former
Systems of Government. The history of the present King of Great Britain is a

history of repeated injuries and usurpations, all having in direct object the establishment of an absolute Tyranny over these States. To prove this, let Facts be submitted to a candid world.

He has refused his Assent to Laws, the most wholesome and necessary for the public good.

He has forbidden his Governors to pass Laws of immediate and pressing importance, unless suspended in their operation till his Assent should be obtained; and when so suspended, he has utterly neglected to attend to them.

He has refused to pass other Laws for the accommodation of large districts of people, unless those people would relinquish the right of Representation in the Legislature, a right inestimable to them and formidable to tyrants only.

He has dissolved Representative Houses repeatedly, for opposing with manly firmness his invasions on the rights of the people. . . .

He has endeavoured to prevent the population of these States; . . .

He has obstructed the Administration of Justice, by refusing his Assent to Laws for establishing Judiciary Powers.

He has made Judges dependent on his Will alone, for the tenure of their offices, and the amount and payment of their salaries. . . .

He has kept among us, in times of peace, Standing Armies without the Consent of our legislature.

He has affected to render the Military independent of and superior to the Civil Power. . . .

For quartering large bodies of armed troops among us:

For protecting them, by a mock Trial, from Punishment for any Murders which they should commit on the Inhabitants of these States:

For cutting off our Trade with all parts of the world:

For imposing taxes on us without our Consent:

For depriving us in many cases, of the benefits of Trial by Jury:

For transporting us beyond Seas to be tried for pretended offences: . . .

For taking away our Charters, abolishing our most valuable Laws, and altering fundamentally the Forms of our Governments:

For suspending our own Legislature, and declaring themselves invested with Power to legislate for us in all cases whatsoever.

Independence in South America
Simon Bolivar

Simon Bolivar (1783–1830) was the great liberator of South America. Together with José de San Martin, he led successful revolts against the Spanish crown in South American territories during the first three decades of the nineteenth century. This excerpt is taken

SOURCE: *The Selective Writings of Bolivar* vol. I, Compiled by Vincente Lecuna, edited by Harold A. Bierck, Jr. (Colonial Press, 1951), pp. 175–191.

from Bolivar's "Message to the Congress of Angostura" (1819). It explains his ideas about a new constitution for the newly independent Republic of Venezuela. Bolivar worried about handing power to the uneducated and proposed, instead, to centralize political control in the hands of elite intellectuals and propertied classes.

> **Consider:** *Why Bolivar favors a hereditary senate and a strong executive; why he hesitated at advocating full democracy; how ideas such as Bolivar's may have affected the future political course in Latin America.*

Venezuela had, has, and should have a republican government. Its principles should be the sovereignty of the people, division of powers, civil liberty, proscription of slavery, and the abolition of monarchy and privileges. We need equality to recast, so to speak, into a unified nation, the classes of men, political opinions, and public customs. . . .

A hereditary senate will be the fundamental basis of the legislative power, and therefore the foundation of the entire government. It will also serve as a counterweight to both government and people; and as a neutral power it will weaken the mutual attacks of these two eternally rival powers. In all conflicts the calm reasoning of a third party will serve as the means of reconciliation. Thus the Venezuelan senate will give strength to this delicate political structure, so sensitive to violent repercussions; it will be the mediator that will lull the storms and it will maintain harmony between the head and the other parts of the political body. . . .

Although the authority of the executive power in England may appear to be extreme, it would, perhaps, not be excessive in the Republic of Venezuela. Here the Congress has tied the hands and even the heads of its men of state. This deliberative assembly has assumed a part of the executive functions, contrary to the maxim of Montesquieu, to wit: A representative assembly should exercise no active function. It should only make laws and determine whether or not those laws are enforced. Nothing is as disturbing to harmony among the powers of government as their intermixture. Nothing is more dangerous with respect to the people than a weak executive; and if a kingdom has deemed it necessary to grant the executive so many powers, then in a republic these powers are infinitely more indispensable. . . .

The people of Venezuela already enjoy the rights that they may legitimately and easily exercise. Let us now, therefore, restrain the growth of immoderate pretensions which, perhaps, a form of government unsuited to our people might excite. Let us abandon the federal forms of government unsuited to us; let us put aside the triumvirate which holds the executive power and center it in a president. We must grant him sufficient authority to enable him to continue the struggle against the obstacles inherent in our recent situation, our present state of war, and every variety of foe, foreign and domestic, whom we must battle for some time to come. Let the legislature relinquish the powers that rightly belong to the executive.

Travels in Brazil: Religion and Slavery in Brazil

Henry Koster

Slavery in Brazil was extremely important to the economy and social structure of the country until its abolition in 1889. Slaves accounted for fully one-third of the entire population and worked at most of the productive jobs in the country. In this excerpt, Henry Koster, a British traveler, recounts the important role religion and the church played in establishing control over Africans and ameliorating some of the harsh conditions of plantation life.

> **Consider:** *The biases in Koster's account that make the reader sympathetic to the Church; how an account by an African slave might have differed.*

All slaves in Brazil follow the religion of their masters; and notwithstanding the impure state in which the Christian church exists in that country, still such are the beneficent effects of the Christian religion, that these, its adopted children, are improved by it to an infinite degree; and the slave who attends to the strict observance of religious ceremonies, invariably proves to be a good servant. The Africans, who are imported from Angola, are baptized in lots before they leave their own shores: and on their arrival in Brazil they are to learn the doctrines of the church, and the duties of the religion into which they have entered. These bear the mark of the royal crown upon their breasts, which denotes that they have undergone the ceremony of baptism, and likewise that the king's duty has been paid upon them. The slaves which are imported from other parts of the coast of Africa, arrive in Brazil unbaptized, and before the ceremony of making them Christians can be performed upon them, they must be taught certain prayers, for the acquirement of which one year is allowed to the master, before he is obliged to present the slave at the parish church. The law is not always strictly adhered to as to the time, but it is never evaded altogether. The religion of the master teaches him that it would be extremely sinful to allow his slave to remain a heathen: and indeed the Portuguese and Brazilians have too much religious feeling to let them neglect any of the ordinances of their church. The slave himself likewise wishes to be made a Christian; for his fellow-bondmen will, otherwise, in every squabble or trifling disagreement with him, close their string of opprobrious epithets with the name of *pagão* (pagan). The unbaptized negro feels that he is considered as an inferior being: and although he may not be aware of the value which the whites place upon baptism, still he knows that the stigma for which he is upbraided will be removed by it; and therefore he is desirous of being made equal to his companions. The Africans who have been long imported, imbibe a Catholic feeling;

Source: Henry Koster, *Travels in Brazil* (London: 2 vols., 1816), II, 238–243.

and appear to forget that they were once in the same situation themselves. The slaves are not asked whether they will be baptized or not. Their entrance into the Catholic church is treated as a thing of course: and indeed they are not considered as members of society, but rather as brute animals, until they can lawfully go to mass, confess their sins, and receive the sacrament.

The slaves have their religious brotherhoods as well as the free persons: and the ambition of the slave very generally aims at being admitted into one of these, and at being made one of the officers and directors of the concerns of the brotherhood. Even some of the money which the industrious slave is collecting for the purpose of purchasing his freedom, will oftentimes be brought out of its concealment for the decoration of a saint, that the donor may become of importance in the society to which he belongs. The negroes have one invocation of the Virgin (or I might almost say one virgin) which is peculiarly their own. Our Lady of the Rosary is even sometimes painted with a black face and hands. It is in this manner that the slaves are led to place their attention upon an object in which they soon take an interest, but from which no injury can proceed towards themselves, nor can any through its means be by them inflicted upon their masters. Their ideas are removed from any thought of the customs of their own country; and are guided into a channel of a totally different nature, and completely unconnected with what is practised there. The election of a King of Congo by the individuals who come from that part of Africa, seems indeed as if it would give them a bias towards the customs of their native soil. But the Brazilian Kings of Congo worship Our Lady of the Rosary; and are dressed in the dress of white men. They and their subjects dance, it is true, after the manner of their creole blacks, and mulattos, all of whom dance after the same manner: and these dances are now as much the national dances of Brazil, as they are of Africa. The Portuguese language is spoken by the slaves: and their own dialects are allowed to lie dormant until they are by many of them quite forgotten. No compulsion is resorted to, to make them embrace the habits of their masters: but their ideas are insensibly led to imitate and adopt them. The masters at the same time imbibe some of the customs of their slaves; and thus the superior and his dependent are brought nearer to each other. I doubt not that the system of baptizing the newly imported negroes, proceeded rather from the bigotry of the Portuguese in former times than from any political plan: but it has had the most beneficial effects. The slaves are rendered more tractable. Besides being better men and women, they become more obedient servants. They are brought under the control of the priesthood: and even if this was the only additional hold which was gained by their entrance into the church, it is a great engine of power which is thus brought into action.

The Removal of Native Americans in the United States

Andrew Jackson

Throughout the nineteenth century, the United States expanded westward, displacing Native American populations to reservations. These reservations undermined the health and destroyed the culture of the numerous tribes whose livelihood had depended on open ranges and free migration. In the early part of the century, the Cherokees of Florida and Georgia adopted white agricultural practices and established a written language and even a constitution. Despite these attempts to adapt to white customs, laws, and values, in the winter of 1835–1836 they were forced to abandon their homes and move westward to Oklahoma, then known as the Indian Territory. This trek became known as the Trail of Tears in light of the high death rates and terrible sacrifice. It is estimated that more than 100 Indians per day died from exposure, starvation, and disease. On December 7, 1835, President Andrew Jackson (1828–1836), who gained national renown as an "Indian fighter," presented to Congress his rationale for uprooting thousands of people from their traditional homes and forcing them to march to unfamiliar and unknown territory.

> **Consider:** *How Jackson justifies his policy; what this reveals about attitudes toward Native Americans; alternative resolutions to the conflicts that arose between white and Native American populations.*

. . . The plan of removing the aboriginal people who yet remain within the settled portions of the United States to the country west of the Mississippi River approaches its consummation. . . . All preceding experiments for the improvement of the Indians have failed. It seems now to be an established fact that they can not live in contact with a civilized community and prosper. Ages of fruitless endeavors have at length brought us to a knowledge of this principle of intercommunication with them. The past we can not recall, but the future we can provide for. . . . [N]o one can doubt the moral duty of the Government of the United States to protect and if possible to preserve and perpetuate the scattered remnants of this race which are left within our borders. In the discharge of this duty an extensive region in the West has been assigned for their permanent residence. . . .

The plan for their removal and reëstablishment is founded upon the knowledge we have gained of their character and habits, and has been dictated by a spirit of enlarged liberality. A territory exceeding in extent that relinquished has been granted to each tribe. Of its climate, fertility, and capacity to support an Indian population the representations are highly favorable. To these districts the Indians are removed at the expense of the United States, and with certain supplies of

SOURCE: James D. Richardson, (ed.) *A Compilation of the Messages and Pages of the Presidents 1787–1897* (Washington D.C., Government Printing Office, 1896–1899), vol. 3, pp. 171–172.

clothing, arms, ammunition, and other indispensable articles; they are also furnished gratuitously with provisions for the period of a year after their arrival at their new homes. In that time, from the nature of the country and of the products raised by them, they can subsist themselves by agricultural labor, if they choose to resort to that mode of life; if they do not they are upon the skirts of the great prairies, where countless herds of buffalo roam, and a short time suffices to adapt their own habits to the changes which a change of the animals destined for their food may require. Ample arrangements have also been made for the support of schools; in some instances council houses and churches are to be erected, dwellings constructed for the chiefs, and mills for common use. Funds have been set apart for the maintenance of the poor; the most necessary mechanical arts have been introduced, and blacksmiths, gunsmiths, wheelwrights, millwrights, etc., are supported among them. Steel and iron, and sometimes salt, are purchased for them, and plows and other farming utensils, domestic animals, looms, spinning wheels, cards, etc., are presented to them. And besides these beneficial arrangements, annuities are in all cases paid, amounting in some instances to more than $30 for each individual of the tribe, and in all cases sufficiently great, if justly divided and prudently expended, to enable them, in addition to their own exertions, to live comfortably.

Declaration of Sentiments: Women's Rights in the United States
Seneca Falls Convention

The rhetoric of democracy and freedom that had emerged as a bedrock of American ideology highlighted the innumerable inequities that existed. In addition to the enormous abolitionist movement then overtaking the nation, women began to demand equality. The Seneca Falls Convention of 1848 was the first dedicated to gaining women's rights. More than one hundred men and women gathered in the small upstate New York community and drafted this declaration demanding not only political, but social, religious, and economic quality for the sexes. Self-consciously modeled on the Declaration of Independence, the statement presaged the movement in the early twentieth century that finally gained women the right to vote in 1920.

> **Consider:** *The difficulties, according to this document, facing women at this time; the reasons for the parallels and differences between this statement and the Declaration of Independence; why it took so long for women to gain the vote.*

Source: Elizabeth Cady Stanton, Susan B. Anthony, and Matilda J. Gage, (eds.) *History of Woman Suffrage,* vol. I, pp. 70–71.

We hold these truths to be self-evident: that all men and women are created equal; that they are endowed by their Creator with certain inalienable rights; that among these are life, liberty, and the pursuit of happiness; that to secure these rights governments are instituted, deriving their just powers from the consent of the governed. Whenever any form of government becomes destructive of these ends, it is the right of those who suffer from it to refuse allegiance to it, and to insist upon the institution of a new government, laying its foundation on such principles, and organizing its powers in such form, as to them shall seem most likely to effect their safety and happiness. . . . Such has been the patient sufferance of the women under this government, and such is now the necessity which constrains them to demand the equal station to which they are entitled.

The history of mankind is a history of repeated injuries and usurpations on the part of man toward woman, having in direct object the establishment of an absolute tyranny over her. To prove this, let facts be submitted to a candid world.

He has never permitted her to exercise her inalienable right to the elective franchise. . . .

He has made her, if married, in the eye of the law, civilly dead.

He has taken from her all right in property, even to the wages she earns.

He has made her, morally, an irresponsible being, as she can commit many crimes with impunity, provided they be done in the presence of her husband. In the covenant of marriage, she is compelled to promise obedience to her husband, he becoming, to all intents and purposes, her master—the law giving him power to deprive her of her liberty, and to administer chastisement.

He has so framed the laws of divorce . . . upon a false supposition of the supremacy of man, and giving all power into his hands. . . .

He has monopolized nearly all the profitable employments, and from those she is permitted to follow, she receives but a scanty remuneration. . . .

He has denied her the facilities for obtaining a thorough education, all colleges being closed against her.

He allows her in Church, as well as State, but a subordinate position, claiming Apostolic authority for her exclusion from the ministry, and, with some exceptions, from any public participation in the affairs of the Church.

He has created a false public sentiment by giving to the world a different code of morals for men and women, by which moral delinquencies which exclude women from society, are not only tolerated, but deemed of little account in man. . . .

He has endeavored, in every way that he could, to destroy her confidence in her own powers, to lessen her self-respect, and to make her willing to lead a dependent and abject life.

Now, in view of this entire disfranchisement of one-half the people of this country, their social and religious degradation—in view of the unjust laws above mentioned, and because women do feel themselves aggrieved, oppressed, and fraudulently deprived of their most sacred rights, we insist that they have immediate admission to all the rights and privileges which belong to them as citizens of the United States.

For Land and Liberty
Emiliano Zapata

Throughout the nineteenth century, Latin America struggled first to gain its independence from Spain and Portugal and then to establish popular democracies. The United States had always provided inspiration for these independence and democratic struggles. But, in the wake of the Spanish American War in 1898, the United States assumed an imperialist role for some of the Central American and Caribbean nations. In Mexico, Emiliano Zapata led a popular revolution that culminated in the establishment of an agrarian reform program for Mexico's peasants. He was assassinated in 1919 but remained a symbol of popular resistance to oppression for millions in his country and around the world. In this selection, the plan of Ayala, Emiliano Zapata calls for radical reform of the economic as well as the political system.

> **Consider:** *Why Zapata adopted the slogan "Tierra y Libertad" (land and liberty) rather than simply calling for political democracy; what this reveals about the discontents of the peasantry and urban poor.*

We, the undersigned, constituted as a Revolutionary Junta, in order to maintain and achieve the fulfillment of the promises made by the revolution of November 29, 1910, declare to the civilized world which judges us and before the Nation to which we belong and love, the principles that we have formulated in order to end the tyranny that oppresses us. . . .

1. . . . Considering that the President of the Republic, Señor Don Francisco I. Madero, had made a bloody mockery of Effective Suffrage by . . . entering into an infamous alliance with the *cientificios*, the *haciendos*, the feudalists, and oppressive *caciques*, enemies of the Revolution that he proclaimed, in order to forge the chains of a new dictatorship more hateful and terrible than that of Porfirio Díaz . . . : For these reasons we declare the said Francisco I. Madero unfit to carry out the promises of the Revolution of which he was the author . . . for having betrayed the principles and mocked the faith of the people . . . and from today onward we continue the Revolution begun by him, until we overthrow the dictatorship which exists. . . .

5. The Revolutionary Junta of the State of Morales will not conduct regular business until the dictatorial elements of Porfirio Díaz and Francisco Madero are overthrown. The country is tired of false men and traitors who make promises as liberators but when they get to power, they forget their promises. . . .

6. As an additional part of the plan which we are invoking, we proclaim that the lands, woods, and waters usurped by the *hacendados*, *cientificos*, or *caciques*

SOURCE: Gilberto Magana, *Emiliano Zapata Y El Agrarismo en Mexico* (Mexico: 1934–1937), vol. II, pp. 126–129 (excerpt translated by Andrea Vasquez).

through tyranny and venal justice henceforth belong to the towns or citizens who have corresponding titles to these properties, of which they were despoiled by the bad faith of our oppressors. They shall retain possession of the said properties at all costs, arms in hand. The usurpers who think they have a right to the said lands may state their claims before special tribunals to be established upon the triumph of the Revolution.

7. Since the immense majority of the Mexican towns and citizens own nothing but the ground on which they stand and suffer the horrors of a miserable existence, without the opportunity to improve their social condition or to dedicate themselves to industry or agriculture because a few individuals monopolize the lands, woods, and waters—for these reasons the great estates shall be expropriated, with indemnification to the owners of one third of such monopolies so that the towns and citizens of Mexico may obtain colonies, towns sites and arable lands. Thus the lack of prosperity and welfare of all the Mexican people can improve.

Banning Chinese Immigration to the United States
United States House of Representatives

The American nation contained vast natural resources such as coal, iron, oil, water, and wood. Yet, the relative scarcity of workers raised the costs of labor and forced industrialists to encourage immigration. Vast numbers of Irish, German, Italian, Jewish, and Eastern European immigrants came to the east coast in the last decades of the century. On the west coast, Asians and Mexicans were recruited to provide a ready supply of labor in railroads, mining, fishing, and agriculture. This led to enormous tensions as native-born workers and earlier immigrants competed for jobs at reduced pay. Race and racism were potent issues in defining the conflicts on the west coast and led to political movements to restrict immigration. The Chinese Restriction Act of 1882 was the first measure specifically aimed at a particular ethnic group. It was renewed and broadened in 1892 and was not finally repealed until World War II. This selection is from a report by the United States Congress, House Committee on Immigration and Naturalization in 1892 that strongly recommended the passage of a bill renewing restrictions on Chinese immigration.

> **Consider:** *The attitudes exhibited toward the Chinese in this document; the justifications and motivations for this legislation.*

There is urgent necessity for prompt legislation on the subject of Chinese immigration. The exclusion act approved May 6, 1882, and its supplement expires by limitation of time on May 6, 1892, and after that time there will be no law to

---

SOURCE: U.S. Congress, House of Representatives, *Report #225*, February 10, 1892, pp. 1–4.

prevent the Chinese hordes from invading our country in number so vast, as soon to outnumber the present population of our flourishing States on the Pacific slope. . . .

The popular demand for legislation excluding the Chinese from this country is urgent and imperative and almost universal. Their presence here is inimical to our institutions and is deemed injurious and a source of danger. They are a distinct race, saving from their earnings a few hundred dollars and returning to China. This they succeed in doing in from five to ten years by living in the most miserable manner, when in cities and towns in crowded tenement house, surrounded by dirt, filth, corruption, pollution, and prostitution; and gambling houses and opium joints abound. When used as cooks, farm-hands, servants, and gardeners they are more cleanly in habits and manners. They, as a rule, have no families here; all are men, save a few women, usually prostitutes. They have no attachment to our country, its laws or its institutions, nor are they interested in its prosperity. They never assimilate with our people, our manners, tastes, religion, or ideas. With us they have nothing in common.

Living on the cheapest diet (mostly vegetable), wearing the poorest clothing, with no family to support, they enter the field of labor in competition with the American workman. In San Francisco, and in fact throughout the whole Pacific slope, we learn from the testimony heretofore alluded to, that the Chinamen have invaded almost every branch of industry; manufacturers of cigars, cigar boxes, brooms, tailors, laundrymen, cooks, servants, farm-hands, fishermen, miners and all departments of manual labor, for wages and prices at which white men and women could not support themselves and those dependent upon them. Recently this was a new country, and the Chinese may have been a necessity at one time, but now our own people are fast filling up and developing this rich and highly favored land, and American citizens will not and can not afford to stand idly by and see this undesirable race carry away the fruits of the labor which justly belongs to them. A war of races would soon be inaugurated; several times it has broken out, and bloodshed has followed. The town of Tacoma, in 1887, banished some 3,000 Chinamen on twenty-four hours' notice, and no Chinaman has ever been permitted to return.

Our people are willing, however, that those now here may remain, protected by the laws which they do not appreciate or obey, provided strong provision be made that no more shall be allowed to come.

VISUAL SOURCES

Manifest Destiny
John Gast

This painting, "Manifest Destiny," by John Gast, reveals the idealized myth of westward expansion that prevailed in the United States during the nineteenth century. Moving from the Atlantic coast cities of the east across the plains and mountains toward the Pacific, the goddess of Destiny carries a schoolbook in one hand and a telegraph wire in the other. Below, here come white male hunters and settlers, pushing Indians and buffalo farther west in retreat. In Destiny's wake follows the railroad.

> **Consider:** *The impressions the nineteenth-century viewer might have gotten on viewing this; the meaning and justification of westward expansion according to this image.*

Photo 7-1

The Library of Congress

Photo 7-2

National Palace of Mexico

The Mexican Revolution
Diego Rivera

The Mexican Revolution stands out as the first successful revolt against dictatorship and foreign domination during the twentieth century in Latin America. This illustration is from a vast mural that the great Mexican artist, Diego Rivera (1886–1957), painted in the National Palace, depicting the history of Mexico. Here he depicts the ways that foreigners have dominated and destroyed so much of indigenous Mexican culture over the centuries. The Spanish Conquistadors are shown at the bottom of the mural killing Aztec warriors. In the middle, the Church is shown as a force of oppression, executing heretics. At the top, Rivera shows the widespread support that the Revolution enjoyed among peasants, workers, and the middle class. Note particularly, in the very center, the phrase "Tierra, Libertad y Pan,"—Land, Liberty and Bread—the slogan of the Revolution. At the very top of the painting are the latest foreign interests that were seen as destroying Mexican freedoms: British and United States' oil interests.

> **Consider:** *What the viewer might conclude from this painting; whether Rivera considers this a hopeful view of Mexican history or a warning of the dangers that lie ahead.*

The Western Hemisphere, 1770 and 1830

In 1770 most of the Western Hemisphere was governed by the European powers. The Native American populations of North and South America maintained some autonomy in remote areas, but, for the most part, their populations had been decimated by disease and conquest. Yet, sixty years later, wars of independence by former Spanish, French, English, and Portuguese colonies had virtually ended European colonialism.

These two maps illustrated the rapid decolonization that occurred during this time period. The first map shows the extent of European control in the late eighteenth century, before the wars of independence. The second map illustrates the new independent nation-states that were established at the beginning of the nineteenth century. By 1830, only the Caribbean region, Guinea, Alaska, and Canada were still ruled by the original colonial powers. Together, these maps show the rapid disintegration of the European colonial systems in both North and South America and the rise of independent states that still maintained close economic and political ties to their former colonial masters.

> **Consider:** *How these maps illustrate the anticolonial sentiments of the peoples of the Western Hemisphere; what you might use as indicators of continuing cultural and linguistic ties to the Old World.*

Map 7-1

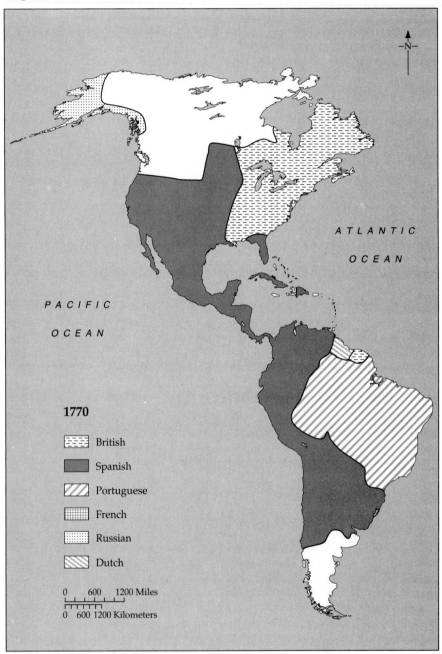

1770

British

Spanish

Portuguese

French

Russian

Dutch

0   600   1200 Miles

0   600 1200 Kilometers

ATLANTIC

OCEAN

PACIFIC

OCEAN

—N—

Map 7-2

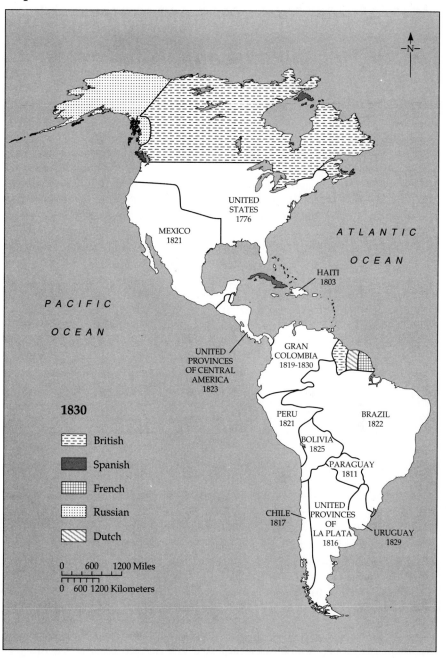

–N–

UNITED
STATES
1776

MEXICO
1821

ATLANTIC

OCEAN

HAITI
1803

PACIFIC

OCEAN

UNITED
PROVINCES
OF CENTRAL
AMERICA
1823

GRAN
COLOMBIA
1819–1830

PERU
1821

BRAZIL
1822

BOLIVIA
1825

PARAGUAY
1811

CHILE
1817

UNITED
PROVINCES
OF
LA PLATA
1816

URUGUAY
1829

1830

British
Spanish
French
Russian
Dutch

0   600   1200 Miles

0   600 1200 Kilometers

SECONDARY SOURCES

Democracy and the American Revolution
Merrill Jensen

The American Revolution is usually viewed as a revolt by the Colonists against England. But historians have also argued that the rhetoric of the revolution led many of the poor farmers and artisans to demand greater social and economic equality as well. In this excerpt, Merrill Jensen, a noted historian of the revolutionary era, argues that the War of Independence in the United States was also an internal revolution that sought a greater degree of democracy and freedom for the less well-to-do segments of American society.

> **Consider:** *The revolutionary changes resulting from the break from Great Britain, according to Jensen; the evidence Jensen uses to support this thesis.*

. . . [B]y 1776 there were people in America demanding the establishment of democratic state governments, by which they meant legislatures controlled by a majority of the voters, and with none of the checks upon their actions such as had existed in the colonies. At the same time there were many Americans who were determined that there should be no changes except those made inevitable by separation from Great Britain. . . .

The significant thing is not the continuity of governmental structure, but the alteration of the balance of power within the structure, and in the political situation resulting from the break away from the supervising power of a central government—that of Great Britain.

The first and most revolutionary change was in the field of basic theory. In May 1776, to help bring about the overthrow of the Pennsylvania assembly, the chief stumbling block in the way of independence, Congress resolved that all governments exercising authority under the crown of Great Britain should be suppressed, and that "all the powers of government [be] exerted under the authority of the people of the colonies. . . ." John Adams described it as "the most important resolution that ever was taken in America." The Declaration of Independence spelled it out in terms of the equality of men, the sovereignty of the people, and the right of a people to change their governments as they pleased.

SOURCE: Merrill Jensen, "Democracy and the American Revolution," *The Huntington Library Quarterly,* 20 (August 1957), 338–341. Reprinted with the permission of the Henry E. Huntington Library.

Second: the Revolution ended the power of a sovereign central government over the colonies. Britain had had the power to appoint and remove governors, members of upper houses of legislatures, judges, and other officials. It had the power to veto colonial legislation, to review cases appealed from colonial supreme courts, and to use armed force. All of this superintending power was wiped out by independence.

Third: the new central government created in America by the Articles of Confederation was, in a negative sense at least, a democratic government. The Congress of the United States had no power over either the states or their citizens. Hence, each state could govern itself as it pleased, and as a result of some of the new state constitutions, this often meant by a majority of the voters within a state.

Fourth: in writing the state constitutions, change was inevitable. The hierarchy of appointed legislative, executive, and judicial officials which had served as a check upon the elective legislatures was gone. The elective legislature became the supreme power in every state, and the lower houses, representing people however inadequately, became the dominant branch. The appointive houses of colonial times were replaced by elective senates, which in theory were supposed to represent property. They were expected to, and sometimes did, act as a check upon the lower houses, but their power was far less than that of pre-war councils.

Fifth: the office of governor underwent a real revolution. The governors of the royal colonies had, in theory at least, vast powers, including an absolute veto. In the new constitutions, most Americans united in shearing the office of governor of virtually all power.

Sixth: state supreme courts underwent a similar revolution. Under the state constitutions they were elected by the legislatures or appointed by governors who were elected officials. And woe betide a supreme court that tried to interfere with the actions of a legislature.

What such changes meant in terms of political realities was that a majority of voters within a state, if agreed upon a program and persistent enough, could do what it wanted, unchecked by governors or courts or appeals to a higher power outside the state. . . .

. . . The American Revolution was a democratic movement, not in origin, but in result. Certainly the political leaders of the eighteenth century thought the results were democratic. Whether they thought the results were good or bad is another story.

By Reasonable Force: Power Politics and International Relations in South America

Robert N. Burr

When the peoples of the New World achieved their independence from the various European powers, some leaders believed that the newly freed states should reject Old World values and ways of relating to each other. But as Robert N. Burr explains in the following selection, most of the elites in South America accepted the prevailing European model of international relations and this led to constant conflict within the continent. Burr also shows how, even though colonialism was defeated in most of Latin America, European powers and nationals found new ways to exert their influence and control during the nineteenth century.

> **Consider:** *Why the European powers were able to exert such a dominant influence in South America after independence; what alternatives there were to the European system of power politics.*

South American nations tended early to focus their political interests on one another, if only because of their confinement to a continent separated from the rest of the world by wide expanses of ocean. Moreover, rivalries and conflicts over elements of national power, and fluctuations in the power structure of the continent, produced interactions among South American nations. . . .

[An] early component of a system of power politics in South America was acceptance by its leaders of the axioms and techniques of power politics. The culture and education of the ruling elite were of European derivation; European values and forms in literature, fashions, and politics tended to be accepted and imitated, along with the European state system. To be sure, some voices in the wilderness cried out against the transplantation to the New World of European-style power politics, damning them as decadent, corrupt, and un-American. But those who gained power did not seriously question the concept of a community of competing sovereign states, each with the duty to defend itself and to expand its interests, preferably by peaceful means but by force if "necessary," even at the expense of other states. The Great Powers of Europe, those leading practitioners of the art of power politics, were the specific models for the international behavior of the South American nations. And because South American culture was largely derivative, and because South Americans suffered from a sense of inferiority bequeathed by their former colonial status and by the relative weakness of their

SOURCE: Robert N. Burr, *By Reason or Force: Chile and the Balancing of Power in South America.* (Berkeley, California, University of California Press) Copyright © 1966 The Regents of the University of California.

respective nations, high prestige was attached to the imitation of European models. . . .

Difficulties in regularization of relations with the Great Powers . . . [diverted] the attention of the new states from intra–South American matters. Upon independence, recognition and expanded commerce had been sought from the Great Powers. South Americans wished, moreover, to borrow funds for both public and private purposes and to import the more highly developed technology and the skillful nationals of Europe and the United States. South America's attraction of money, people, and technology from Europe and the United States was indispensable to its fulfillment of urgent material and cultural aspirations. The more highly developed nations responded with alacrity to such an opportunity to exploit markets and resources, which Spain had so long denied them. But difficulties soon arose concerning the protection of the interests of Great Power nationals. Poverty often prevented South American governments from fulfilling their financial commitments; instability imperiled the persons and the interests of foreign nationals; the attitudes of the parties to resultant disputes made solution difficult. Xenophobia was prevalent among the Spanish-speaking peoples of South America to whom both the Spanish economic system and the Inquisition had for centuries denied contact with and knowledge of the outside world. In turn, immigrants from the Great Powers regarded the "backward" peoples of South America with contempt. They tended to enlist the superior coercive strength of their home governments to resolve conflicts of interest rather than to negotiate upon a basis of theoretical equality.

The Mansions and the Shanties: The Making of Modern Brazil
Gilberto Freyre

During the nineteenth century, urban areas grew in South America. In these new environments, the social classes built their own institutions. In the process, they created new social relationships in which both rich and poor were forced to coexist. In the following selection, Gilberto Freyre, a noted Brazilian historian, analyzes the relationships between elites and the poor in nineteenth-century Brazil. Here he focuses on the changing functions of "the street"—the place where the poor and rich came into direct contact with each other.

SOURCE: Gilberto Freyre, *The Mansions and the Shanties, the Making of Modern Brazil* (Berkeley: University of California Press, 1963, 1986), pp. xxiv–xxix. Reprinted by permission of the Gilberto Freyre Foundation.

Consider: *The different circumstances for the rich and poor in new urban communities; the different ways the street served these two classes and how they viewed its purpose.*

It was when our social environment began to change in the sense that the plantation manors became city mansions more after the European manner, and the slave quarters were reduced practically to servants' rooms, that adjustment disintegrated, and new forms of subordination, new social barriers began to develop between rich and poor, white and colored, between the big house and the little. Settlements of shanties and slums sprang up alongside the mansions, but with almost no communication between them, and African cults, diverging more from Catholicism than had been the case on plantations and ranches. A new distribution of power came about, but still resting for the most part in the hands of white landowners. Sharper antagonisms arose between the rulers and the ruled, between white children brought up in the house and colored children brought up in the street, without the old zone of fraternization between the two that was common on the plantations, and between the mistress of the mansion and the women of the street. There was a greater economic gap between the two extremes.

Only gradually did there begin to emerge moments of fraternization between these social extremes: the religious procession, the church festival, carnival revelries. For the parks, the so-called public promenades, the squares shaded by spreading *gameleira* trees and, for many years, encircled by iron railings similar to those which were taking the place of walls around the most fashionable houses, were limited to the use and enjoyment of the wearers of high shoes, silk hat, cravat, sunshade—insignia of race, but principally of class. They were for the use and enjoyment of the man of a certain social position, but only for the man. The women and children stayed inside the house, or in the grounds to the rear—at most, on the verandah, at the gate, by the hitching rail, by the garden wall. The boy who went out to fly his kite or spin his top in the street was looked upon as a vagabond. A lady who went into the street to shop ran the risk of being taken for a streetwalker. . . .

By the beginning of the nineteenth century the street was ceasing to be the drain for the dirty water of the city houses, through which the well-shod foot of the respectable citizen had to pick its way, and was taking on dignity and social importance. By night it was no longer a dark passage which citizens crossed, preceded by a slave bearing a lantern, but was lighted by street lamps burning fish oil and hung from wires on high posts. This was the beginning of public lighting, the first gleam of dignity of the street, previously so neglected that it depended for its illumination on that of private houses and the candles burning in the saints' niches.

At about this time the municipality began to defend the street against the abuses of the mansion, which had moved into the cities bringing with it the same high-handed ways, almost the same arrogance of its plantation and ranch days, making of the street a place to chop wood, a dump for dead animals, refuse, dirty water, at times even chamber pots. The very architecture of the town mansion developed on the basis of the street as its adjunct: the drain pipes emptying their flood of rain water into the streets; doors and shutters opening on to the street; and windows—when windows came to take the place of jalousies—which made it convenient for men to expectorate into the street.

City ordinances at the beginning of the nineteenth century were for the most part directed toward restraining these abuses and toward establishing the importance, dignity, rights of the street which had been so disregarded and flouted. . . .

The Negro shanty dwellers were forbidden by ordinance to wash clothes at the public fountain in the middle of the city, and were ordered to do this in the streams outside the gates.

Other restrictions on individual liberties followed, such as forbidding the mansion owners to whip their slaves after the church bell, which played such an important role in the domestic and even the public life of Brazilian cities before clocks became common, had solemnly rung nine at night.

Still other ordinances were designed to make the street respected by the backwoodsman who came down from the hills, the backlands, or the plantations, riding high in the saddle or in his oxcart. He was ordered to dismount and lead his animal by bridle or reins, failure to do so carrying a penalty of twenty-four hours in jail; in the case of Negro slaves, two dozen lashes. And nobody was any longer to show such disrespect as to enter the city in shirt and drawers, or cantering or galloping through the streets down which, since the end of the eighteenth century, vehicles had begun to roll, coaches, chaises, buggies, at first, then cabriolets, cabs, tilburies, gigs, all jolting over cobblestones and potholes.

The builders and owners of urban property were also being made to respect the street. They had to build their houses in a straight line along it and not at random or hit-or-miss as before. They had to fill in the holes and mud puddles in front of them. They had to observe a similar alignment in the promenades and sidewalks, doing away with the constant ups-and-downs from one strip of pavement to another, laid when each houseowner followed his own whim and thought only of what suited him best.

Thus the street was becoming emancipated from the absolute dominion of the "villa," the "manor," the mansion. The street urchin—that vivid expression of the Brazilian street—was showing a growing lack of respect for the great house as he defaced walls and fences with scrawls that were often obscene. Not to mention relieving himself on the doorstep of illustrious portals and even on the stair landing in the halls of the mansion itself.

Yet, though losing face to the street and diminished in its patriarchal functions (which it preserved even in the heart of certain cities) by the cathedral, the factory, the school, the hotel, the laboratory, the drugstore, the house of the nineteenth century continued to exert more influence than any other factor on the social formation of the urban Brazilian. The mansion, more European, produced one social type; the shanty, more African or Indian, produced another. And the street, the square, the church festival, the market, the school, the carnival, all contributed to the communication between classes, the intermingling of races, and the working out of a Brazilian solution for coming to terms with different ways of life, different cultural patterns.

The Cult of True Womanhood
Barbara Welter

During the nineteenth century, an ideology was being developed calling for American women to return to the home and family. Femininity was idealized in literature, popular imagery, and professional journals and was linked to leisure and domesticity. Some have suggested that the "cult of true womanhood" was, in fact, an attack on the professional and political ambitions of a rising group of middle-class women. Others have suggested that it was an attempt to distinguish between middle-class and working-class women, thereby splitting a potentially powerful new force in American society and culture. The following article by Barbara Welter was crucial in identifying for historians the subtle ways in which culture was used to create separate spheres for women and men and to relegate women to a position below men.

Consider: *How "putting women on a pedestal" led to their degradation and dependence on men.*

The nineteenth-century American man was a busy builder of bridges and railroads, at work long hours in a materialistic society. The religious values of his forebears were neglected in practice if not in intent, and he occasionally felt some guilt that he had turned this new land, this temple of the chosen people, into one vast countinghouse. But he could salve his conscience by reflecting that he had left behind a hostage, not only to fortune, but to all the values which he held so dear and treated so lightly. Woman, in the cult of True Womanhood presented by the women's magazines, gift annuals and religious literature of the nineteenth century, was the hostage in the home. In a society where values changed frequently, where fortunes rose and fell with frightening rapidity, where social and economic mobility provided instability as well as hope, one thing at least remained the same—a true woman was a true woman, wherever she was found. If anyone, male or female, dared to tamper with the complex of virtues which made up True Womanhood, he was damned immediately as an enemy of God, of civilization and of the Republic. It was a fearful obligation, a solemn responsibility, which the nineteenth-century American woman had—to uphold the pillars of the temple with her frail white hand.

The attributes of True Womanhood, by which a woman judged herself and was

SOURCE: Barbara Welter, "The Cult of True Womanhood: 1820–1860," *American Quarterly*, 18 (Summer 1966), 151–153, 173–174. Copyright © 1966 American Studies Association.

judged by her husband, her neighbors and society could be divided into four cardinal virtues—piety, purity, submissiveness and domesticity. Put them all together and they spelled mother, daughter, sister, wife—woman. Without them, no matter whether there was fame, achievement or wealth, all was ashes. With them she was promised happiness and power. . . .

The American woman had her choice—she could define her rights in the way of the women's magazines and insure them by the practice of the requisite virtues, or she could go outside the home, seeking other rewards than love. It was a decision on which, she was told, everything in her world depended. "Yours it is to determine," the Rev. Mr. Stearns solemnly warned from the pulpit, "whether the beautiful order of society . . . shall continue as it has been" or whether "society shall break up and become a chaos of disjointed and unsightly elements." If she chose to listen to other voices than those of her proper mentors, sought other rooms than those of her home, she lost both her happiness and her power "that almost magic power, which, in her proper sphere, she now wields over the destinies of the world."

But even while the women's magazines and related literature encouraged this ideal of the perfect woman, forces were at work in the nineteenth century which impelled woman herself to change, to play a more creative role in society. The movements for social reform, westward migration, missionary activity, utopian communities, industrialism, the Civil War—all called forth responses from woman which differed from those she was trained to believe were hers by nature and divine decree. The very perfection of True Womanhood, moreover, carried within itself the seeds of its own destruction. For if woman was so very little less than the angels, she should surely take a more active part in running the world, especially since men were making such a hash of things.

Chapter Questions

1. What were some of the common issues behind the revolutions, rebellions, and protests that marked this period of history in the western hemisphere?

2. In what ways were ideals established when nations gained their independence and carried out thereafter, and in what ways were these ideals not firmly established and not carried out?

3. What methods were used by governments and powerful groups to maintain the status quo and hinder others from either joining the mainstream of society or moving to positions of equality with white-, middle-, or upper-class males?

4. Drawing on the sources in this and previous chapters, in what ways should the Americas be most usefully thought of as part of Western civilization during this period? In what ways should the Americas be most usefully thought of as separate from European civilization?

EIGHT

Asia, 1700–1914

Throughout most of Asia, the eighteenth and nineteenth centuries was a period of transition from independence and concern with internal affairs to increasing intervention by Europeans and response to that external threat.

During the eighteenth century, China was at the height of its geographic expansion, ruled by the Manchus since 1644. It maintained its world view of itself as the center of civilization surrounded by lesser civilizations. By the end of that century Europeans were beginning to make inroads into Chinese affairs. By the middle of the nineteenth century, the British and others had forced trade and unequal treaties on the Chinese, seriously weakening the Chinese throne. The Manchus also had to contend with a population explosion (140 million in 1700 to 420 million in 1850) with only a 10 percent increase in arable land, a problem that was to persist to this day. These events contributed to internal problems and revolts, further weakening the throne. However, China remained too large and powerful to entirely lose its independence.

Japan had cut itself off from the West and limited its contact with its neighbors in the early 1600s and enjoyed its isolation until the early 1800s when

British, Russian, and American ships began to probe its shores. Soon the Japanese were facing the same dilemmas as China, but unlike the Chinese, quickly resolved them by launching a social and political revolution from the top down. Borrowing heavily from the European and American models, they created a melding of Western institutions, technology, and Japanese culture. By the end of the nineteenth century, Japan was acquiring an empire and bidding for equality with the Western powers.

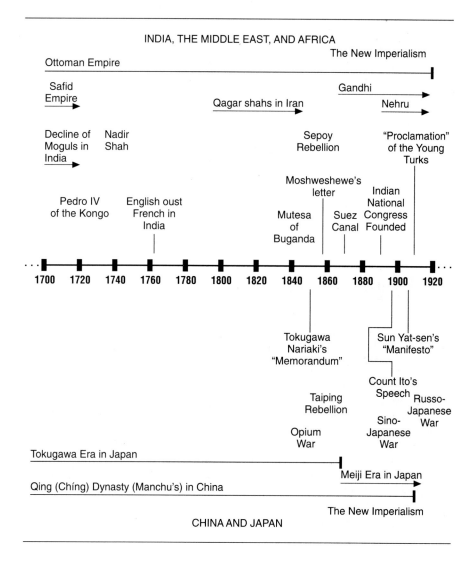

The nations of southeast Asia, weaker and distracted by rivalries of their own, were less able to withstand the Europeans. During the eighteenth and nineteenth centuries, the British (in Burma, Malaya, Singapore) and the French (in Cambodia, Laos, and Vietnam) gained control.

In India, the Moguls were losing power. Europeans quickly stepped into the vacuum, the British winning in their competition with the Portuguese and French. By the nineteenth century, the British had brought together a hodge-podge of princely states, territories, and tribal groups to create the Indian state under British control. British rule resulted in important economic, social, and cultural changes in India as well as development of a growing feeling of anti-British nationalism.

Finally, Islamic powers such as the Ottomans in the Middle East were in decline but still in control of their heartland. This empire increasingly faced internal problems from peoples with conflicting loyalties and external pressure from European powers, particularly Russia, who were well aware of the Empire's weaknesses.

The sources in this chapter focus on changes facing these Asian civilizations and how they responded to the changes. Perhaps the most pressing question was how to deal with Western influence that was growing so dramatically, particularly during the second half of this period. In a later chapter, developments in these areas connected with the rise of the new imperialism at the end of the nineteenth century will be examined.

PRIMARY SOURCES

Confessions of Taiping Rebels: The Chinese People Rebel

The importation of opium, the arrival of Western businesses and the resulting weakening of the Chinese government (including a loss of face due to their inability to repel the foreigners) created in China conditions which severely speeded up the demise of the Qing (Ch'ing) Dynasty. Rebellions broke out widely. One group of rebels in particular, the Taipings, seriously threatened the Manchus when they conquered more than half of the country. Internal squabbles among the Taiping leaders, the ability of the Manchus to regroup their forces, and the aid of a Western mercenary army all led to the demise of the

Source: Patricia Buckley Ebrey (ed.), *Chinese Civilization and Society. A Sourcebook* (New York: The Free Press, 1981), pp. 225–226.

Taipings. This reading is a confession, after their capture sometime in the 1850s, by three Chinese rebels who were associated with the Taipings.

> **Consider:** *Their reasons for joining the rebels; the social, political, and economic problems facing China that are revealed here.*

We were born in a time of prosperity and were good people. We lived in towns and were taught to distinguish right from wrong. But because of continuous flooding in our area, we could not get a grain of rice to eat even if we worked hard in the fields, and we could not engage in business because we lacked the funds. As a result we all joined the bandits.

Not long ago we came to Guangxi (Kwangsi) to try to make a living. We met others who had come from our hometowns. We pitied each other because of our sad situation, and together we began to imitate outlaws in order to relieve our hungry stomachs. In other words, no one forced us to join the outlaws. We were driven to join them because we were desperate. Given the chance, we would have returned gladly to our normal way of life.

We thought constantly of our families, but we could not return to them. Indeed, we were drifting on a hungry, painful sea and knew not when we would reach the other side. We hope Your Excellency will forgive our past sins. We hope you will think of the great benevolence of our imperial house and give us a chance to start a new life. Grass and trees are without feeling, yet they still appreciate the dew and rain that falls upon them to nourish them. Men are conscious beings; therefore how could we forget your great benevolence if you should allow us a new life? We are laying out our situation sincerely to you. We hope you can state clearly your intention. If you are willing to forgive us, please issue a statement of amnesty. If we could again become children of Heaven and return to the kingdom of benevolence and longevity, we will serve you as loyally as your dogs and horses. We will obey all your orders, and we will be willing to serve in your military camp. We have presented our situation to you. Knowing that we have bothered Your Honor with our petty matters, trembling we await our punishment. We sincerely present our case to Your Excellency. . . .

We hate the army runners who recently made heavy demands on us and disturbed our villages. They used the excuse of establishing a local militia to cause trouble for the good and honest people and create opportunities for the wicked ones. The words they used were virtuous-sounding; yet the deeds they actually perpetrated were most wicked. They allied themselves with government officials and formed cliques so that they could oppress our village and make excessive demands whenever they wished. They falsely reported that certain persons were connected with the bandits. This was due to personal grudges against the accused or to the fact that they wanted to obtain rewards. They burned down our houses and took all we had; they robbed us of our property and threatened our lives. Therefore we banded together to insure our own safety. Those who still remain in the village may run away someday while those who have left can hardly come back. Therefore, for each ordinary person who ran away, there was one more bandit, and the numbers of bandits became greater and greater. Since there are so many of us, we could not survive except by pillage, nor could we save our lives if we did not fight against the imperial troops that were sent out to exterminate us. As a consequence, we have offended the court and hurt the merchants.

Manifesto of the United League
Sun Yat-sen

In the end, no rebel movement brought down the Qing (Ch'ing) Dynasty; it fell of its own corruption and ineptitude in 1911. But all the rebellions had the combined effect of pushing the dynasty to its final collapse.

No rebel was more prominent, fought longer and was more determined than Sun Yat-sen (1865–1925). Born near Macao, Sun became a Western-educated medical doctor and convert to Christianity who spoke fluent English. Having lived and traveled in Europe and the United States, Sun dreamed of establishing a modern republican form of government in China. To this end he devoted his last thirty-five years and, as a result, is known as the "Father of Modern China." This reading from Sun's "Manifesto of the Tong Menghui (T'ung-Meng-Hui)" (United League) was written in 1905 and meant to lay out Sun's goals for a new China.

Consider: *Sun's vision of a new China; how that vision fit into traditional Chinese culture; ways in which Sun's vision was influenced by Western ideas.*

"National revolution" means that all people in the nation will have the spirit of freedom, equality, and fraternity; that is, they will all bear the responsibility of revolution. . . . Therefore we proclaim to the world in utmost sincerity the outline of the present revolution and the fundamental plan for the future administration of the nation.

1) *Drive out the Tartars:* The Manchus of today were originally the eastern barbarians beyond the Great Wall. They frequently caused border troubles during the Ming dynasty; then when China was in a disturbed state they came inside Shanhaikuan, conquered China, and enslaved our Chinese people. Those who opposed them were killed by the hundreds of thousands, and our Chinese have been a people without a nation for two hundred and sixty years. The extreme cruelties and tyrannies of the Manchu government have now reached their limit. With the righteous army poised against them, we will overthrow that government, and restore our sovereign rights. . . .

SOURCE: Sun Yat-sen, "Manifesto of the T'ung-Meng-Hui [Tong Menghui]," by Ssu-Yu Teng and John K. Fairbank in *China's Response to the West. A Documentary Survey, 1839–1923* (NY: Atheneum, 1963) pp. 227–229.

2) *Restore China:* China is the China of the Chinese. The government of China should be in the hands of the Chinese. After driving out the Tartars we must restore our national state. . . .

3) *Establish the Republic:* Now our revolution is based on equality, in order to establish a republican government. All our people are equal and all enjoy political rights. The president will be publicly chosen by the people of the country. The parliament will be made up of members publicly chosen by the people of the country. A constitution of the Chinese Republic will be enacted, and every person must abide by it. Whoever dares to make himself a monarch shall be attacked by the whole country.

4) *Equalize land ownership:* The good fortune of civilization is to be shared equally by all the people of the nation. We should improve our social and economic organization, and assess the value of all the land in the country. Its present price shall be received by the owner, but all increases in value resulting from reform and social improvements after the revolution shall belong to the state, to be shared by all the people, in order to create a socialist state, where each family within the empire can be well supported, each person satisfied, and no one fail to secure employment. . . .

The above four points will be carried out in three steps in due order. The first period is government by military law. When the righteous army has arisen, various places will join the cause. . . . Evils like the oppression of the government, the greed and graft of officials, the squeeze of government clerks and runners, the cruelty of tortures and penalties, the tyranny of tax collectors, the humiliation of the queue—shall all be exterminated together with the Manchu rule. Evils in social customs, such as the keeping of slaves, the cruelty of foot-binding, the spread of the poison of opium, the obstructions of geomancy (*feng-shui*), should also all be prohibited. . . .

The second period is that of government by a provisional constitution. When military law is lifted in each xian (*hsien*), the Military Government shall return the right of self-government to the local people. The members of local councils and local officials shall all be elected by the people. All rights and duties of the Military Government toward the people and those of the people toward the government shall be regulated by the provisional constitution, which shall be observed by the Military Government, the local councils, and the people. . . .

The third period will be government under the constitution. Six years after the provisional constitution has been enforced a constitution shall be made. The military and administrative powers of the Military Government shall be annulled; the people shall elect the president, and elect the members of parliament to organize the parliament. The administrative matters of the nation shall proceed according to the provisions of the constitution.

. . . It is hoped that our people will proceed in due order and cultivate their free and equal status; the foundation of the Chinese Republic will be entirely based on this.

Japan, Reject the Westerners
Tokugawa Nariaki

After almost two centuries of self-imposed isolation, Japan suddenly found itself the object of Western curiosity as British, Russian and American ships began to arrive, uninvited and unwanted. The Japanese watched events unfolding in China in the early nineteenth century with tremendous trepidation. Seeing that resistance to the arrival of foreigners was useless due to their superior military technology, Japan's response to the arrival of American ships and its forced opening was relatively calm. However, as we see from the following selection, not everyone was reconciled to it. Written in 1853, this memorandum was from Tokugawa Nariaki, a high official to the Bakufu (the military government led by a Shogun). He urged an immediate and aggressive response to the foreign ships attempting to land on Japanese soil.

Consider: *The reason for rejecting Westerners; what this reveals about Japanese culture and attitudes; similarities and differences between Japanese and Chinese responses to Western imperialism.*

It is my belief that the first and most urgent of our tasks is for the Bakufu to make its choice between peace and war, and having determined its policy to pursue it unwaveringly thereafter. When we consider the respective advantages and disadvantages of war and peace, we find that if we put our trust in war the whole country's morale will be increased and even if we sustain an initial defeat we will in the end expel the foreigner; while if we put our trust in peace, even though things may seem tranquil for a time, the morale of the country will be greatly lowered and we will come in the end to complete collapse. This has been amply demonstrated in the history of China. . . . However, I propose to give here in outline the ten reasons why in my view we must never choose the policy of peace.

1. Although our country's territory is not extensive, foreigners both fear and respect us. . . . Despite this, the Americans who arrived recently, though fully aware of the Bakufu's prohibition, entered Uraga displaying a white flag as a symbol of peace and insisted on presenting their written requests. Moreover they entered Edo Bay, fired heavy guns in salute and even went so far as to conduct surveys without permission. They were arrogant and discourteous, their actions an outrage. Indeed, this was the greatest disgrace we have suffered since the dawn of our history. . . .

2. The prohibition of Christianity is the first rule of the Tokugawa house. . . . Yet if the Americans are allowed to come again this religion will inevitably raise its head once more, however strict the prohibition; and this, I fear, is something we could never justify to the spirits of our ancestors. . . .

3. To exchange our valuable articles like gold, silver, copper, and iron for useless

---

SOURCE: *In*: G. Beasley (trans. and ed.), *Select Documents on Japanese Foreign Policy, 1853–1868*. (London: Oxford University Press, 1960), pp. 102–107.

foreign goods like woollens and satin is to incur great loss while acquiring not the smallest benefit. The best course of all would be for the Bakufu to put a stop to the trade with Holland. . . .

4. For some years Russia, England, and others have sought trade with us, but the Bakufu has not permitted it. Should permission be granted to the Americans, on what grounds would it be possible to refuse if Russia and the others [again] request it? . . .

5. It is widely stated that [apart from trade] the foreigners have no other evil designs and that if only the Bakufu will permit trade there will be no further difficulty. However, it is their practice first to seek a foothold by means of trade and then go on to propagate Christianity and make other unreasonable demands. . . .

6. [Some argue that] Japan . . . clinging to ideas of seclusion in isolation . . . is a constant source of danger to us and that our best course would . . . be to communicate with foreign countries and open an extensive trade; yet, to my mind, if the people of Japan stand firmly united, if we complete our military preparations and return to the state of society that existed before the middle ages, then we will even be able to go out against foreign countries and spread abroad our fame and prestige. . . .

9. I hear that all, even though they be commoners, who have witnessed the recent actions of the foreigners, think them abominable; and if the Bakufu does not expel these insolent foreigners root and branch there may be some who will complain in secret, asking to what purpose have been all the preparations of gun-emplacements. It is inevitable that men should think in this way when they have seen how arrogantly the foreigners acted at Uraga. That, I believe, is because even the humblest are conscious of the debt they owe their country, and it is indeed a promising sign. Since even ignorant commoners are talking in this way, I fear that if the Bakufu does not decide to carry out expulsion, if its handling of the matter shows nothing but excess of leniency and appeasement of the foreigners, then the lower orders may fail to understand its ideas and hence opposition might arise from evil men who had lost their respect for Bakufu authority. It might even be that Bakufu control of the great lords would itself be endangered.

The Japanese Constitution
Count Ito

For over two hundred years Japan lived in self-imposed isolation from the rest of the world. From early in the seventeenth to the middle of the nineteenth century, only a tiny handful of Japanese scholars knew of the scientific and military progress of the European powers.

SOURCE: W. W. McLaren (ed.), *Transactions of the Asiatic Society of Japan*, vol. 92:1 (1914), pp. 614–622.

Eventually Japan would be forced to end its isolation. In the years after Perry's arrival in Japan (1853), the Tokugawa Shogunate collapsed and the Meiji Restoration (1868) began. Japan's leaders abruptly ended the feudal structure of the country, disarmed the samurai, created a modern conscript army, abolished hereditary social classes, introduced universal education, and initiated a modern industrial economic system. This revolution included the substitution of absolute rule with a written Constitution. This exceptional document codified the rights of the Japanese and ended extraterritoriality (the principle whereby foreigners were subject only to the laws of the countries of which they were citizens). The reasoning behind this system (in China as well) was that Europeans and Americans could not understand the local legal system. Constitutional rule in Japan forced foreigners to end extraterritoriality.

In this excerpt from a speech made in 1889, Count Ito, one of Japan's new progressive leaders, comments on the importance of the Constitution to a revitalized Japan.

Consider: *How Ito justifies the changes that Japan made; what Ito hopes the consequences of these changes are or will be; the significance of having a written constitution.*

. . . Now that the Constitution has been promulgated, it will be of interest to discuss it briefly from a historical point of view, with the object of demonstrating that this momentous event is no mere fortuitous occurrence. . . . That great achievement, resulting in the return of power and rule to the proper hands, was due to two causes; namely, loyalty and foreign intercourse. The loyalty found its expression in a strong desire to revert to that system under which power was vested in the Emperor, while foreign intercourse operated through an earnest wish to substitute for the national policy hitherto pursued (that of seclusion) a course aiming at the extension and development of our relations with foreign peoples. . . . As you are no doubt aware, the affairs of the country were, in the simple days of old, administered under the personal direction of the Emperor, by means of the gun and ken systems. As time went on the military classes, however, acquired a hold on the governing power, and eventually the court became a mere ornament; though the people at large, remembering the facts of history, always entertained a hope that sooner or later the Throne should have its own again. . . . This page of our history cannot be sufficiently regretted, but as a matter of fact the failure of the loyalists then operated beneficially by stimulating to greater enthusiasm the minds of later generations. For feudalism long presented to its enemies a firm and impregnable front; but its end was surely though slowly approaching. Towards the close of the Tokugawa regime, the regency found itself face to face with the disagreeable necessity of opening to foreigners the gates which for so long had been closed against them; and of concluding treaties with some of those whom the Japanese people had been accustomed to despise as "barbarians." The unsatisfactory course pursued by the Shōgunate with regard to foreigners speedily evoked disapprobation, and as its policy went from bad to worse, the old loyal sentiment, which had only been slumbering, was at last roused into action, and the Restoration was accomplished. . . . [I]t became evident that further attempts to maintain the seclusion and isolation of the country from the rest of the world would be highly impolitic. Treaties were therefore concluded with our visitors, and intercourse with them was duly initiated. But those who had now been entrusted by the Emperor with the chief share in the conduct of public affairs were not satisfied with the restoration of power to the Throne and the inauguration of treaty relations with foreign powers. They set themselves to the task of introducing Western civilisation into Japan and of eliminating such undesirable features as became apparent by contrast with the conditions of the West. They saw foreign powers actively engaged in the rivalry of cultivating their strength and resources; and they could not help asking themselves how Japan could hope to hold her own in the struggle, or maintain her independence and integrity so that, in common with other countries, she might enjoy the benefits of civilisation and enlightenment. It was plain to them that if the national dignity was to be demonstrated in the face of the world the national resources must be developed and the national power strengthened by some uniform process of government and administration. . . . So much having been accomplished, the next question was, how should these resources be husbanded and encouraged in their development. The answer plainly was, to educate the people with a view to their becoming factors in the progress of the country. . . . If we carefully regard the method in which public education has advanced, from the cultivation of knowledge in connection with political economy, law, and kindred branches, to commerce, trade, and industries, and compare the present state of affairs with that which existed some twenty years ago, we shall not exaggerate if we say that the country has undergone a complete metamorphosis. . . . It is only by the protection of the law that the happiness of the nation can be promoted and the safety of person and property secured, and to attain these ends the people may elect their representatives and empower the latter to deliberate on laws with a view to the promotion of their own happiness and the safeguarding of their rights. This, gentlemen, is enacted by the Constitution, and I think you will agree that it constitutes a concession to the people of a most invaluable right.

China Declares War against Japan

Emperor Guangxu (Kuang-hsü)

For almost two thousand years China and Japan coexisted as friendly neighbors. Japan adapted Chinese Confucian teachings, Buddhism, Chinese script, and other aspects of Chinese culture to its own. This relationship ended late in the nineteenth century.

When Japan emerged from its isolation, its new leaders put it on a course destined for

SOURCE: Dun Jen Li (ed.), *China in Transition: 1517–1911* (New York: Van Nostrand Reinhold Company, 1969), pp. 213–214.

equality with the major European powers of that day. One of the ways in which that goal was to be accomplished was through the possession of foreign lands. This new ideology viewed China as no longer the source of culture to be respected but a weakened land open to conquest and exploitation. By the late 19th century both nations viewed the other as an enemy. The following selection is the official Declaration of War by the Chinese Emperor, Guangxu (Kuang-hsü) against the Japanese on August 1, 1894.

> **Consider:** *How China justifies this declaration of war; how the Japanese might respond; what this reveals about the relative strength of Japan and China at this time.*

It is common knowledge, here and abroad, that Korea has been a tributary state of the Great Ch'ing [Qing] Dynasty for more than 200 years and has sent tribute missions to China, without fail, each and every year. During the past ten years, time and again civil disturbances raged the country and our government, feeling compassionate for the common and the innocent, repeatedly dispatched troops to restore order. A commissioner was sent to that country to reside in its capital and provide protection for all the Korean people whenever it was needed.

In the fourth month of this year once again there were bandits who staged a rebellion. Having received an urgent request from the king of Korea for assistance, I ordered Li Hung-chang [Li Hongzhang] to send a contingent of troops to Korea to restore order. The bandits were scattered as soon as our expeditionary force reached Ya-shan. We did not expect Japan to take the unjustifiable course of sending troops to Korea too, and her troops, which had not been invited by the Korean government, nevertheless occupied its capital Han-ch'eng [Mancheng] [Seoul]. Later, by increasing her military strength to more than 10,000 men, she forced the Korean government to change its policies, foreign as well as domestic, in addition to other unreasonable demands too numerous to mention. Our dynasty has always maintained the most cordial relationship with all of its tributary states and has followed a policy of noninterference in their domestic affairs. Since Korea has concluded a treaty with Japan, she is sovereign as far as Japan is concerned. On what ground can Japan be justified in the employment of military might to intimidate her, thus forcing her to change her existing policies? Regarding the Japanese expedition as unjustifiable and unwarranted, all of the foreign countries have advised Japan to withdraw her troops and to enter into peaceful negotiations with China. Japan ignored this advice in the most arrogant manner, and consequently nothing constructive has come about. Meanwhile she continued to increase her military strength in Korea.

As Korean citizens and Chinese traders in Korea continued to suffer from Japanese harassment, the Chinese government had no choice but to send more men to protect them. On their way towards Korea and on the open seas outside the port of Ya-shan, our transports were suddenly fired upon by Japanese warships. Because of our unpreparedness, we received heavy damages. This treachery on the part of Japan violates not only existing treaties but also international law as commonly recognized by all nations. Her ruthlessness in the conduct of her relations with other countries and her employment of duplicity and deceit to further her ends have thus become clear for all people to see. She opened hostilities against us without the slightest provocation.

It is hoped that through this proclamation all the people in the world will know that this government has done its utmost to avoid conflict and that Japan, by violating treaty obligations and opening hostilities, has committed an unjustifiable act of the greatest extreme which we can no longer tolerate. Let Li Hung-chang [Li Hongzhang] dispatch our armed forces to Korea in the speediest manner possible—they are to crush all resistance in order to save the Korean people from their unbearable sufferings. Meanwhile all the generals, governors, and military commanders who have been charged with the responsibility of coastal and river defense should maintain vigilance and diligently prepare themselves and their men for possible action. If Japanese ships ever sail into the ports under their jurisdiction, they should immediately launch an attack to exterminate them. They will be severely punished if they show cowardliness.

Let this decree be made known to all of our citizens!

Proclamation of the Young Turks

For the Islamic Ottoman Empire, the nineteenth century was part of a long period of decline. One reaction to that decline was an effort to infuse Turkey, the heart of the Empire, with Western-style nationalism, secularism, and political reform. In the 1860s and 1870s a group of modern reformers, called the Young Ottomans, began to press for a constitutional democracy in Turkey. In 1867 they achieved their aim when a constitution was proclaimed. Unfortunately, the new Sultan, Abdul Hamid II, was not in agreement with the reforms and ignored the Constitution while ruling as an absolute monarch.

Nationalists began to organize opposition to the Sultan. One such group was called the Committee of Union and Progress and was established in 1889. These young people, commonly known as the Young Turks, were persecuted, imprisoned, and forced into exile for their attempts to restore the 1867 Constitution.

In 1908 there was an extensive army mutiny. The Young Turks took the opportunity to openly demand a restoration of parliamentary rule and the Sultan, unable to resist, was forced to submit. After the reinstatement of the Constitution, the Young Turks issued this proclamation which outlined their ideas for the "new" Turkey that they envisioned. The state they created was secular, repressive, and oppressive of racial minorities, although it had the trappings of a democracy.

> **Consider:** *The nature of the Young Turks' political demands; the similarities and differences between this vision of the state and the democratic, liberal state of western Europe; who might be in agreement with this program.*

SOURCE: A. Sarrou, *La Jeune-Turquie et al Révolution* "The Young Turks," in Rondo Cameron, ed., CIVILIZATION SINCE WATERLOO, (Paris, 1912), pp. 40–42.

1. The basis for the Constitution will be respect for the predominance of the national will. One of the consequences of this principle will be to require without delay the responsibility of the minister before the Chamber, and, consequently, to consider the minister as having resigned, when he does not have a majority of the votes of the Chamber.

2. . . . [T]he Senate will be named . . . as follows: one third by the Sultan and two thirds by the nation, and the term of senators will be of limited duration.

3. . . . [A]ll Ottoman subjects having completed their twentieth year, regardless of whether they possess property or fortune, shall have the right to vote. . . .

4. It will be demanded that the right freely to constitute political groups be inserted in a precise fashion in the constitutional charter. . . .

7. The Turkish tongue will remain the official state language. . . .

9. Every citizen will enjoy compete liberty and equality, regardless of nationality or religion, and be submitted to the same obligations. All Ottomans, being equal before the law as regards rights and duties relative to the State, are eligible for government posts, according to their individual capacity and their education. Non-Muslims will be equally liable to the military law.

10. The free exercise of the religious privileges which have been accorded to different nationalities will remain intact. . . .

14. Provided that the property rights of landholders are not infringed upon . . . it will be proposed that peasants be permitted to acquire land, and they will be accorded means to borrow money at a moderate rate. . . .

16. Education will be free. . . .

17. All schools will operate under the surveillance of the state. In order to obtain for Ottoman citizens an education of a homogenous and uniform character, the official schools will be open, their instruction will be free, and all nationalities will be admitted. . . .

Secondary and higher education will be given in the public and official schools indicated above. . . . Schools of commerce, agriculture and industry will be opened with the goal of developing the resources of the country. . . .

Steps shall also be taken for the formation of Roads and Canals to increase the facilities of communication and increase the sources of the wealth of the country. Everything that can impede commerce or agriculture shall be abolished.

VISUAL SOURCES

Foreigners at Yokohama
Gountei Sadahide

When the Westerners arrived in Japan in the nineteenth century, the Japanese embraced them to the point of making a passion of things Western. Artists rushed to depict the newcomers so that Japanese outside of the treaty ports could see what these strange visitors were like.

This triptych print is by Gountei Sadahide (1807–1873). It portrays, from left to right, families from Russia, the Netherlands, and Britain. Artists enjoyed depicting Europeans and Americans with very sharp facial features, especially noses. They often wore baggy clothes in these pictures and were always carrying exotic items such as telescopes and concertinas. In these renderings, take note of the women's faces, which are less European than a standard form adopted for Japanese women in the nineteenth century by painters of the Utagawa school.

Consider: *What these pictures reveal about the Japanese vision of Western men, women, and children.*

Photo 8-1

The British Museum

Rauneah, A Village in the Punjab
Ghulam Ali Khan

Through high culture we have been able to preserve a record of the lives of the elite and life in towns and urban areas. This is as true of India as anywhere else. However, the vast majority of Indians have always lived, and still do live, in villages—and there are fewer depictions of the lives of these people.

This painting of a nineteenth-century village, probably by Ghulam 'Ali Khan, is part of a collection of over 100 portrayals of village life commissioned by an eccentric Englishman named William Fraser who lived in India from 1799 until his death in 1835. As Fraser made his rounds among his estates in Harayana Province and elsewhere, he developed the habit of being accompanied by experienced Indian painters trained in the Mogul tradition whose purpose was to record the scenes they encountered as accurately as possible. As a result of these efforts, we have an incomparable record of everyday life in nineteenth-century India. In this example, called "Rauneah, A Village in the Punjab," we see the mixture of English townscapes, probably at Fraser's insistence, and the precision for detail for which miniaturists in the Mogul tradition were known. Notice the peacock on the thatched roof, the array of animals, and the busy life of the village.

Consider: *The conditions of village life in nineteenth-century India; the roles of men and women revealed in this painting.*

Photo 8-2

The British Library

The Weakening of China, 1839–1878

Since the second century B.C. *Chinese imperial rulers strove to maintain strong central rule. Confucian teaching inculcated in the people the belief that a lack of strong central authority and benevolent rule called for the violent overthrow of the dynasty. Indeed, such overthrows occurred over twenty times in Chinese history.*

Although the Qing (Ch'ing) Dynasty had been in power since 1644, beginning in the late eighteenth century, the arrival of Europeans led increasingly to a weakening central authority. This weakening was accelerated after 1839 by the developments shown in this map. First, the Qing Emperors were unable to halt Britain's illegal importation of opium into China and suffered humiliation in the two Opium Wars with Great Britain. This weakening, in turn, pressured the government to grant special privileges to Western powers in "treaty ports," all of which allowed for numerous uprisings around the country. While these internal uprisings were ended by 1873, the cycle toward dissolution had inexorably begun.

> **Consider:** *The sorts of forces that can fundamentally undermine a government; the benefits and detriments of trade and cultural contact with outside powers.*

Map 8-1

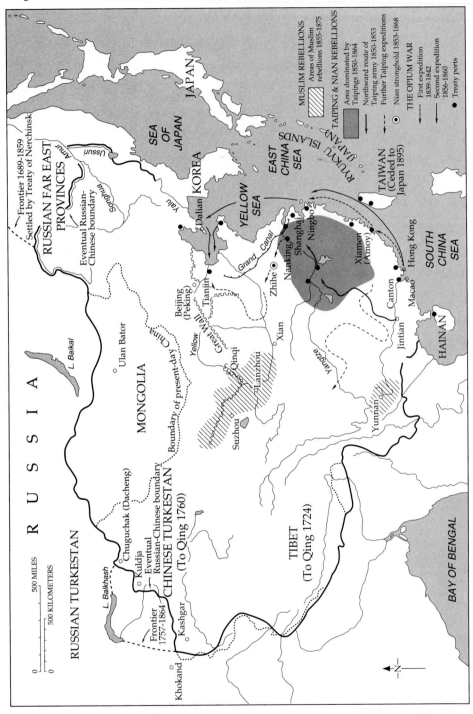

SECONDARY SOURCES

China's Food Revolution
Ping-ti Ho

One consequence of the global encounters after the sixteenth century was the transplant-
ing of seeds from one continent to the next. In China, new crops such as peanut, maize,
"Irish" potato, and sweet potato were especially suited to the soil and weather conditions
there. In part because of this food availability, China's population grew. During the Qing
(Ch'ing) Dynasty (1644–1912) it more than doubled to about 400 million. In this excerpt,
Ping-ti Ho, a noted expert on China's population, describes the introduction of these new
crops.

> **Consider:** *The significance of the introduction of these crops for China; some of*
> *the possible social and political consequences of a greater food supply and larger*
> *population.*

So far as can be ascertained from written records, the peanut was the first American food plant introduced into China, probably by the Portuguese. . . . By the
1530's peanuts were being grown in some lower Yangzi (Yangtze) localities, and
they attracted the attention of some gentry-scholars. Nevertheless, it took more
than one and a half centuries for peanuts to be disseminated extensively in the
sandy loams north and south of the lower Yangzi and in southeastern coastal
provinces. Although before 1700 not a few of the coastal localities had specialized
in extensive peanut and peanut-oil production, sometimes for export to the rest
of China, peanuts were not yet a common and cheap food in the southeast; they
were still regarded as a delicacy and were served at formal banquets. . . .

Throughout the last three centuries peanuts have gradually brought about a
revolution in the utilization of sandy soils along the lower Yangzi, the lower Yellow
River, the southeast coast, particularly Fujian (Fukien) and Guangdong (Kwang-
tung), and numerous inland rivers and streams. Even within the crowded cropping
system of some rice districts, they usually have a place in the rotation [of crops].
. . . Farmers, without knowing the function of the nitrogen-fixing nodules at the
roots of the peanut plant, have learned [by practice] that it helps to preserve soil
fertility. Peanuts, unlike rice and wheat, are necessarily a secondary food crop in
so large a country as China. But China . . . ranks with India as one of the world's
leading peanut-producing countries.

✿

The sweet potato is first recorded in some local histories of Yunnan in the 1560's and 1570's, which suggests an overland introduction from India and Burma. But it was also independently introduced into coastal Fujian two or three decades before it was officially blessed by the governor in the famine year 1594. It then made rapid headway in the southeastern coastal provinces. . . . Its unusually high per-acre yield, its nutritiousness (in terms of calories next only to rice), its pleasant taste, preservability, and value as an auxiliary food, its relative immunity to locusts, its greater resistance to drought as compared with native Chinese yams, and the fact that it can easily adapt itself to poorer soils and hence does not compete with other food crops for good land, are among the many advantages. . . .

In the southeastern coastal provinces, which were always deficient in rice and where the people were long accustomed to Chinese yams and taros as secondary food, the sweet potato suited the dietary habit of the maritimers and was promptly welcomed. It soon became the poor man's staple. In the imperial [edicts] of the Yong-zheng (Yung-cheng) emperor [1723–1735], officials in Fujian and eastern Guandong annually estimated the degree of regional food sufficiency and the quantities of food that had to be imported in terms of rice and sweet-potato harvests. In the eighteenth century the sweet potato gradually spread to all inland Yangzi provinces, among which Sichuan (Szechwan) was a leading producer.

✿

Like the sweet potato, maize was introduced into China through both the overland India-Burma and the maritime routes before the middle of the sixteenth century. The overland introduction probably came slightly before the maritime. Owing to mountainous terrain and relatively backward economic and agricultural conditions, maize scored an early success in Yunnan. . . . From Yunnan maize gradually spread to Guizhou (Kweichow) and Sichuan (Szechwan). . . .

Despite its early appearance in coastal Fujian and Zhejiang (Chekiang), maize remained relatively neglected; the people preferred rice and sweet potatoes and, even more important, maize competed with native cereal plants for good land. Up to 1700, therefore, it was grown mostly in the southwest and in a few scattered districts on the southeast coast. . . . The hills and mountains along other tributaries of the Yangzi were likewise turned into maize fields. In these newly developed mountainous districts maize and sweet potatoes were sometimes complementary and sometimes competitive, depending on the dietary habits of the local people and on the locality's demand for grain cereals. . . .

. . . The ruthless destruction of virgin forests and consecutive intensive maize farming, . . . [with seed frequently planted] in straight rows, resulted in serious soil erosion which in turn led to the silting of river and lake beds and more frequent [flooding] of the Yangzi.

✿

The Irish potato was slower in winning wide acceptance by the people. From northern Fujian it slowly spread to a limited number of localities in the Yangzi interior in the eighteenth century. During the first half of the nineteenth century it became a significant crop in some high mountainous areas. . . . Unlike the sweet potato, it seldom competed with maize because it could be adapted to climatic and soil conditions unsuitable for either maize or the sweet potato. Whether served whole or dried and ground into flour, the Irish potato, as had the sweet potato along the southeast coast, became the poor mountaineer's staple.

The Discovery of India: British Colonization of India Challenged
Jawaharlal Nehru

By the beginning of the eighteenth century the French, Portuguese, and British were all competing in India. But within a few decades the British became predominant, operating out of Bengal in the northeast. As early as 1818 the British East India Company was a leading force in India, eventually becoming its government, for all intents and purposes. The British brought together a hodgepodge of princely states, territories, and tribal groups and created a nation-state of India. In this state they introduced an English education system whose graduates would play increasingly important roles in Indian history. They also brought India into the British economic scheme by using it as a supplier of raw materials and as a vast market for the finished goods of the British Industrial Revolution.

The British, like all their European and American (and even later, Japanese) counterparts, believed that their governance over Asians was to the latter's benefit. It was, the British fervently believed, a selfless sharing of the benefits of their religion, government, social policies, technological know-how and modern military experiences.

Indian nationalists did not quite see the presence of the British in their country in the same benign light. In this selection, Jawaharlal Nehru, one of India's foremost intellectuals and nationalists, and independent India's first Prime Minister, looks at the British role in his country and questions their motives.

> **Consider:** *The impact of Western culture on India according to Nehru; British intentions according to Nehru; how someone from a pro-British perspective might respond.*

"Our writing of India's history is perhaps resented more than anything else we have done"—so writes an Englishman well acquainted with India and her history. It is difficult to say what Indians have resented most in the record of British rule in India; the list is long and varied. But it is true that British accounts of India's history, more especially of what is called the British period, are bitterly resented. . . .

SOURCE: *In*: Jawaharlal Nehru, *The Discovery of India* (New York: John Day, 1946), pp. 287–294.

. . . The British who came to India were not political or social revolutionaries; they were conservatives representing the most reactionary social class in England. [They argued that the] impact of Western culture on India was the impact of a dynamic society, of a "modern" consciousness, on a static society wedded to medieval habits of thought, which, however sophisticated and advanced in its own way, could not progress because of its inherent limitations. . . .They encouraged and consolidated the position of the socially reactionary groups in India, and opposed all those who worked for political and social change. If change came, it was in spite of them or as an incidental and unexpected consequence of their other activities. The introduction of the steam engine and the railway was a big step toward a change of the medieval structure, but it was intended to consolidate their rule and facilitate the exploitation, for their own benefit, of the interior of the country. . . .

The feudal landlords and their kind who came from England to rule over India had the landlord's view of the world. To them India was a vast estate belonging to the East India Company, and the landlord was the best and the natural representative of his estate and his tenants. That view continued even after the East India Company handed over its estate of India to the British crown, being paid very handsome compensation at India's cost. . . . The British government of India then became the landlords. . . . For all practical purposes they considered themselves "India," just as the Duke of Devonshire might be considered "Devonshire" by his peers. The millions of people who lived and functioned in India were just some kind of landlord's tenants who had to pay their rents and cesses and to keep their place in the natural feudal order. For them a challenge to that order was an offense against the very moral basis of the universe and a denial of a divine dispensation. . . .

This sense of identifying India with their own interests was strongest in the higher administrative services, which were entirely British. In later years these developed in that close and well-knit corporation called the Indian Civil Service, "the world's most tenacious trade union," as it has been called by an English writer. They ran India, they were India, and anything that was harmful to their interests must of necessity be injurious to India. From the Indian Civil Service and the kind of history and record of current events that was placed before them, this conception spread in varying degrees to the different strata of the British people. The ruling class naturally shared it in full measure, but even the worker and the farmer were influenced by it to some slight extent and felt, in spite of their own subordinate position in their own country, the pride of possession and empire.

I remember that when I was a boy the British-owned newspapers in India were full of official news and utterances; of service news, transfers, and promotions; of the doings of English society, of polo, races, dances, and amateur theatricals. There was hardly a word about the people of India, about their political, cultural, social, or economic life. Reading them, one would hardly suspect that they existed.

In Bombay there used to be quadrangular cricket matches between four elevens made up respectively of Hindus, Moslems, Parsis, and Europeans. The European eleven was called "Bombay Presidency"; the others were just Hindus, Moslems, Parsis. Bombay was thus essentially represented by the Europeans; the others, one would imagine, were foreign elements who were recognized for this purpose. . . .

English clubs in India usually have territorial names—the Bengal Club, the Allahabad Club, etc. They are confined to Britishers, or rather to Europeans. . . . The exclusion of non-Europeans is . . . a racial affair. . . .

Racialism in India is not so much English versus Indian. It is European as opposed to Asiatic. . . .

In this land of caste the British, and more especially the Indian Civil Service, have built up a caste which is rigid and exclusive. Even the Indian members of the service do not really belong to that caste, though they wear its insignia and conform to its rules. That caste has developed something in the nature of a religious faith in its own paramount importance, and round that faith has grown an appropriate mythology which helps to maintain it. A combination of faith and vested interests is a powerful one, and any challenge to it arouses the deepest passions and fierce indignation.

Mass Culture, Popular Culture, and Social Life in the Middle East
Reinhard Schulze

Islamic culture throughout the Middle East has a long and glorious tradition which it successfully exported through parts of Africa and much of Asia. As European influence spread, however, the notions that all non-European cultures were inferior ("decadent" and "heathen") had a strong influence on the very peoples who were being degraded. This Westernization of the Middle Eastern elites led them to begin to see their own culture in Western terms and to oversee a secularization of their culture. In the following selection, Reinhard Schulze, a professor in the Department of Oriental Studies at the University of Bonn, argues that this process of Europeanization was deleterious to Middle East culture.

Consider: *Ways in which Islamic culture was influenced by the West; possible consequences of such Western influences.*

In the main, Islamic cultural history was determined by the development of a cultural self-understanding on the part of the new colonial élites. In the same manner that patterns of action, behaviour and communication coined by the West

---

SOURCE: Georg Stauth, et al., *Mass Culture, Popular Culture, and Social Life in the Middle East* (New York, 1987) pp. 205–207.

were adopted by the indigenous cultural élite, the process by which it found its own cultural identity was also mediated by Europe. Its self-understanding or self-representation was bound up with "universal categories" postulated in European concepts of culture. The Islamic intellectuals, as a part of the colonial élites, were compelled to rewrite the Islamic cultural tradition to make it fit European patterns of the history of mind and culture. The adoption of the Europeans' categories such as tradition, modernity, decadence and renaissance, was most important. The last category itself represented the colonial élites' striving for a new form of cultural utterance of their own. At first, reevaluation began on the basis of Islamic categories which, however, reflected European concepts. . . .

. . . Modernity serving as a collective notion for forms of social and cultural utterance in colonial society, was joined to the negative counterpart or antinomy tradition identified as the Dark Age. . . . The historical process which gave birth to "modernity" was understood as a renaissance requiring, of course, an antinomy, namely decadence. In analogy with European patterns of cultural history, renaissance had to refer historically to a classical period which the Islamic intellectuals traced to the Golden Age of the revelation and (mostly) the first calife (610–661). And again in analogy to a European historiography of culture, the Golden Age was seen as a timeless universality. This caused no difficulty since in Islamic traditions, Muhammad's community was already regarded as an ideal-type or as an archetype of social organization.

But as the "Islamic classical epoch" also served to legitimate cultural modernity, reevaluation also touched the concept of the ideal-type. Thus, the social reality of modernity (expressed as the cultural self-understanding of the colonial élites) was reflected in the mirror of the ideal-type of the Muhammadan community.

Chapter Questions

1. In what ways did Asian civilizations, and in particular their governments, respond to the increasing presence and demands of Westerners? What do these responses reveal about the politics and culture of their civilizations?

2. Using some of the sources in this chapter, how might it be argued that some Asian societies reaped benefits from contacts with the West? How might some of these same sources and others be used to show the opposite—that Asian societies suffered from contacts with the West?

3. How might sources in this chapter and chapter 3 (Asia, 1500–1700) be used to show the "rise" of Japan and "decline" of China, India, and the Ottoman Empire during this period? How might this "rise" and "decline" be explained?

NINE

Africa, 1500–1880

From the sixteenth century on, Africa would be increasingly affected by trade and contact with Europeans. However, except for the coastal and certain limited areas such as south Africa, much of sub-Saharan Africa would remain dominated by internal developments during the sixteenth and seventeenth centuries. By the end of the seventeenth century, the issue of how the states were to be governed was being worked out. In some cases this led to civil wars (in Benin and Kongo, for example), in others (the Gold Coast, for example) larger and more autocratically governed states evolved; while in others (Senegambia, for example) there was a combination of both processes. In areas such as north Africa and parts of east Africa, changes in the Islamic world were of great consequence. The Ottoman Empire extended its control over large areas of north Africa during the sixteenth century, and during the seventeenth century Islamic Arabs from Oman gained some control in coastal areas of east Africa. Meanwhile, Islam had fused with African religious traditions and a distinctly local variant of Islam had emerged and was spreading.

The eighteenth and nineteenth centuries were crucial both for Africa's relationship to Europe and for the major internal changes which the continent underwent. To outsiders, Africa was a primary supplier of labor and raw materials for European and Muslim markets. European possessions in the Americas alone received some seven million slaves from 1700 to 1810. After 1810, in the period generally referred to as the period of free trade, Africa supplied a variety of raw materials—hardwoods, palm products, ivory, rubber, and the like to the expanding industrial centers of Europe and America. Even more fundamental than this external trade were the major political and economic transformations which were occurring within Africa. In many regions new and strong states were emerging (the Sotho and Asanti, for example) while in other regions (Kongo and Zimbabwe, for example) older state systems were consolidating different kinds of constitutional arrangements. But during the second half of the nineteenth century, and particularly after the 1880s, most of Africa would succumb to colonial conquest by European powers.

The sources in this chapter focus on two main topics. The first topic is the internal developments within Africa during these centuries. What was the political nature of these states? What sorts of societies developed, particularly in west Africa? How did individual states interact with others? The second topic involves the growing presence of foreigners in Africa. How did Africans attempt to deal with Western influence? What were some of the attitudes of African leaders toward Europeans? This second topic will bring us to the last decades of the nineteenth century when Africa would be overwhelmed by a new wave of imperialism—a subject that will be explored in Chapter 10.

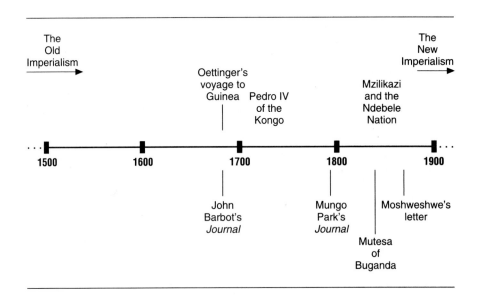

PRIMARY SOURCES

Voyage to Guinea: The European Slave Trade in Africa
Johann Peter Oettinger

Johann Peter Oettinger was a surgeon who took a position with the Brandenburg (Prussia) Africa Company and took the voyage described in this journal in 1692–93. His comments highlight the trading system between Europeans and Africans that had developed on the west African coast since the first European contact in the 1440s. The slaves purchased from this area would be sent to European possessions in the New World, where the sugar boom of the late seventeenth century created a huge demand for labor. Commerce in slaves was fast becoming the most significant aspect of Euro-African relations from this period until the nineteenth century.

> **Consider:** *How international the business on the African coast was, with agents from many different countries involved; the treatment of the slaves as if they were commodities; the author's attitudes toward Africans.*

[A]rrangements were made on that ship for accommodating slaves. Large cauldrons were fitted into the upper deck, to prepare food for seven to eight hundred mouths. Water vats in considerable numbers were taken on board, and on top of the ballast another sort of deck was laid, to accommodate the black cargo in several tiers.

Communication between the ships and the shore was maintained by our own boats or, when the sea was too rough for these to be used, so-called "surf boats"— light vessels of a peculiar design, which were locally built. When occupied on the ships, the Negroes . . . sometimes jumped overboard and swam back to the shore, which was in some circumstances a dangerous undertaking. On one such occasion it happened that a young Negro boy had both his legs torn off up to the knees by a shark, and only the mutilated corpse could be brought back to the miserable parents. . . .

Accra was occupied by the English, Danes and Dutch, and the fortifications formed a belt around the landing place. It is no more favoured with a harbour than any of the other places on the Gold Coast. The land there is even less accessible than elsewhere, as the surfboats must be particularly on their guard against the rocks, against which the rolling waves of the ocean break. To our right,

SOURCE: Adam Jones, ed. and trans., "Johann Peter Oettinger's Account of His Voyage to Guinea", in *Brandenburg Sources For West African History*, 1680–1700 (Stuttgart, Franz Steiner, 1985), pp. 187, 189, 195–6 as excerpted.

half a mile further east, lay Fort Christiansborg, on a high shore covered with beautiful vegetation and shaded by palm trees. In the distance a wooded chain of hills stood out against the horizon. An extremely colourful, picturesquely higgledy-piggledy crowd of naked children and several hundred dirty Negroes, wearing cotton garments which shone in every colour of the rainbow, received us as soon as we had been safely dragged . . . ashore and made our entry. During our stay at Accra a lively, friendly relationship developed between our captain and the Commandant. Our chief factor Hoffmann made use of the time to land silk goods, linen, gunpowder, glass beads etc. and exchange them for gold and slaves. A male slave cost about 25 thaler, a female 20 to 22, a boy 12 to 14 and a girl about 10. . . .

. . . As soon as a sufficient number of the unfortunate victims were collected, they were examined by me: the healthy and strong ones were bought, whereas the *magrones*—those who had fingers or teeth missing or were disabled—were rejected. The slaves who had been bought then had to kneel down, twenty or thirty at a time; their right shoulder was smeared with palm oil and branded with an iron which bore the initials C AB C (*Churfürstlich-Afrikanisch-Brandenbur-gische Compagnie*). Then those who had thus been marked were strictly guarded in the quarters allotted to them. When about fifty or a hundred slaves were present, they were tied together in twos and threes and driven to the coast under escort. The task of guarding the transport was given to me, and for that purpose I was carried in the rear in a hammock, so that I could survey the column. Some of these poor people obeyed their leaders without a will of their own or any resistance, even when they were hurried on with a whip; others, on the other hand, howled and danced. There were also many, especially women, who filled the air with heart-rending cries which could hardly be drowned by the drums or other noisy instruments and often cut me to the quick. But it did not lie in my power to alter the fate of these unfortunates. When we reached the coast, a pre-arranged signal was given and the ship's boats came ashore to take the black cargo on board.

On the way back, the negro escorts, numbering about a hundred, were employed to carry the merchandize landed from the ship. I again had the duty of leading and supervising them, which, given the thievish . . . character of these wretched scoundrels, involved difficulties of many kinds. Not only did the carriers have to be induced by kindness or strictness to walk faster, but often, either on purpose or accidentally, they dropped those barrels which they suspected to contain the dainty little shells, or damaged them in other ways, whereby a portion of the contents which fell out found its way into their large straw hats.

On one of these trips I caught the thieves in the act and wanted to flog them with my sword. But I only made things worse; for the fellows threw the barrel down and fled, so that I had trouble getting it carried to its destination by other carriers.

On 4 April the ship was at last loaded with 738 slaves, male and female, so that we could take our leave of the king and return to the ships. As on our arrival, we were carried back to the beach in palanquins. Then we treated our carriers and attendants with brandy and climbed into the boat.

Government, Taxes, and War in Benin

John Barbot

During the seventeenth century, Benin, on the coast of west Africa, became one of the most powerful and wealthy states in the region. In the last quarter of the seventeenth century, John Barbot, a private trader, traveled to west Africa. The following are excerpts from a combination of two journals, including material by others, containing information collected between the 1630s and 1700. Here he describes Benin's political system, its taxation policies, and its conflicts with neighboring states.

> **Consider:** *The nature of this political system and its complexity; how the social system is reflected in the system of taxation; how power is maintained by military means.*

The government of *Benin* is principally vested in the king, and three chief ministers, call'd great *Veadors*; that is, intendants, or overseers; besides the great marshall of the crown, who is intrusted with the affairs relating to war, as the three others are with the administration of justice, and the management of the revenue; and all four are obliged to take their circuits throughout the several provinces, from time to time, to inspect into the condition of the country, and the administration of the governors and justices in each district, that peace and good order may be kept as much as possible. Those chief ministers of state have under them each his own particular officers and assistants in the discharge of their posts and places. They call the first of the three aforemention'd ministers of state, the *Onegwa*, and second *Ossade*, and the third *Arribon*.

They reside constantly at court, as being the king's privy council, to advise him on all emergencies and affairs of the nation; and any person that wants to apply to the prince, must address himself first to them, and they acquaint the king with the petitioner's business, and return his answer accordingly: but commonly, as in other countries, they will only inform the king with what they please themselves; and so in his name, act very arbitrarily over the subjects. Whence it may well be inferr'd, that the government is intirely in their hands; for it is very seldom they will favour a person so far as to admit him to the king's presence, to represent his own affairs to that prince: and every body knowing their great authority, indeavours on all occasions to gain their favour as much as possible, by large gratifications and presents, in order to succeed in their affairs at court, for which reason their offices and posts are of very great profit to them.

Besides these four chief ministers of state, there are two other inferior ranks about the king: the first is composed of those they call *Reis de Ruas*, signifying in

---

Source: G. M. Theal, (ed.) *Records of South-East African History*, vol. II (London/Capetown: Government of Capetown, 1898–1903), pp. 384–388.

Portuguese, kings of streets, some of whom preside over the commonalty, and others over the slaves; some again over military affairs; others over affairs relating to cattle and the fruits of the earth, &c. there being supervisors or intendants over every thing that can be thought of, in order to keep all things in a due regular way.

✿　　✿　　✿

The king's income is very great, his dominions being so large, and having such a number of governors, and other inferior officers, each of whom is obliged, according to his post, to pay into the king's treasury so many bags of *Boejies*, some more some less, which all together amount to a prodigious sum; and other officers of inferior rank are to pay in their taxes in cattle, chicken, fruits, roots and cloths, or any other things that can be useful to the king's household; which is so great a quantity, that it doth not cost the king a penny throughout the year to maintain and subsist his family; so that there is yearly a considerable increase of money in his treasury. Add to all this, the duties and tolls on imported or exported goods, paid in all trading places, to the respective *Veadors* and other officers, which are also partly convey'd to the treasury; and were the collectors thereof just and honest, so as not to defraud the prince of a considerable part, these would amount to an incredible sum.

✿　　✿　　✿

This prince is perpetually at war with one nation or other that borders on the northern part of his dominions, and sometimes with another north-west of his kingdom, which are all potent people, but little or not at all known to *Europeans*, over whom he obtains from time to time considerable advantages, subduing large portions of those unknown countries, and raising great contributions, which are partly paid him in jasper, and other valuable goods of the product of those countries. Wherewith, together with his own plentiful revenue, he is able, upon occasion, to maintain an army of an hundred thousand horse and foot; but, for the most part, he doth not keep above thirty thousand men, which renders him more formidable to his neighbours than any other *Guinea* king: nor is there any other throughout all *Guinea*, that has so many vassals and tributary kings under him; as for instance, those of *Istanna, Forcado, Jaboe, Issabo* and *Oedoba*, from whom he receives considerable yearly tributes, except from him of *Issabo*, who, though much more potent than all the others, yet pays the least.

Travels in the Interior Districts of Africa: Urban Life and Women in West Africa

Mungo Park

Beginning in the eleventh century, some Arabs had established themselves in urban and commercial centers of west Africa. But it was not until the late eighteenth and early nineteenth century that many Europeans penetrated beyond the coast into the interior of west Africa. Mungo Park, a Scottish doctor, was one of the earliest of these. He reached the long-sought Niger River at Segu (Sego), the capital of Bambarra, in 1796. In the following excerpts from his journal he describes Sego, where the King of Bambarra resided, then his interactions with women in a nearby village.

Consider: *The qualities of the urban areas Mungo Park describes; the significance of the presence of Moorish mosques; the involvement of the king in the slave trade; the role and independence of women.*

Sego, the capital of Bambarra, at which I had now arrived, consists, properly speaking, of four distinct towns; two on the northern bank of the Niger, called Sego Korro, and Sego Boo; and two on the southern bank, called Sego Soo Korro, and Sego See Korro. They are all surrounded with high mud-walls; the houses are built of clay, of a square form, with flat roofs; some of them have two stories, and many of them are whitewashed. Besides these buildings, Moorish mosques are seen in every quarter; and the streets, though narrow, are broad enough for every useful purpose, in a country where wheel carriages are entirely unknown. From the best inquiries I could make, I have reason to believe that Sego contains altogether about thirty thousand inhabitants. The King of Bambarra constantly resides at Sego See Korro; he employs a great many slaves in conveying people over the river, and the money they receive (though the fare is only ten Kowrie shells for each individual) furnishes a considerable revenue to the king, in the course of a year. . . .

. . . The view of this extensive city; the numerous canoes upon the river; the crowded population, and the cultivated state of the surrounding country, formed altogether a prospect of civilization and magnificence, which I little expected to find in the bosom of Africa.

I waited more than two hours, without having an opportunity of crossing the river; during which time the people who had crossed, carried information to Mansong the King, that a white man was waiting for a passage, and was coming to see him. He immediately sent over one of his chief men, who informed me that the king could not possibly see me, until he knew what had brought me into

---

Source: Mungo Park, *Travels in the Interior Districts of Africa* (London, 1799), pp. 195–198.

his country; and that I must not presume to cross the river without the king's permission. He therefore advised me to lodge at a distant village, to which he pointed, for the night; and said that in the morning he would give me further instructions how to conduct myself. This was very discouraging. However, as there was no remedy, I set off for the village; where I found, to my great mortification, that no person would admit me into his house. I was regarded with astonishment and fear, and was obliged to sit all day without victuals, in the shade of a tree; and the night threatened to be very uncomfortable, for the wind rose, and there was great appearance of a heavy rain; and the wild beasts are so very numerous in the neighbourhood, that I should have been under the necessity of climbing up the tree, and resting amongst the branches. About sunset, however, as I was preparing to pass the night in this manner, and had turned my horse loose, that he might graze at liberty, a woman, returning from the labours of the field, stopped to observe me, and perceiving that I was weary and dejected, inquired into my situation, which I briefly explained to her; whereupon, with looks of great compassion, she took up my saddle and bridle, and told me to follow her. Having conducted me into her hut, she lighted up a lamp, spread a mat on the floor, and told me I might remain there for the night. Finding that I was very hungry, she said she would procure me something to eat. She accordingly went out, and returned in a short time with a very fine fish; which, having caused to be half boiled upon some embers, she gave me for supper. The rites of hospitality being thus performed towards a stranger in distress; my worthy benefactress (pointing to the mat, and telling me I might sleep there without apprehension) called to the female part of her family, who had stood gazing on me all the while in fixed astonishment, to resume their task of spinning cotton; in which they continued to employ themselves great part of the night. They lightened their labour by songs, one of which was composed extempore; for I was myself the subject of it. It was sung by one of the young women, the rest joining in a sort of chorus. The air was sweet and plaintive, and the words, literally translated, were these. "The winds roared, and the rains fell. The poor white man, faint and weary, came and sat under our tree. He has no mother to bring him milk; no wife to grind his corn. *Chorus.* Let us pity the white man; no mother has he, &c. &c." Trifling as this recital may appear to the reader, to a person in my situation, the circumstance was affecting in the highest degree. I was oppressed by such unexpected kindness; and sleep fled from my eyes. In the morning I presented my compassionate landlady with two of the four brass buttons which remained on my waistcoat; the only recompence I could make her.

The Ndebele Nation in Central Africa

Robert Moffat

The Ndebele nation was a military state that rose to power in central Africa after the 1820s when their ruler, Mzilikazi, broke away from Shaka, the founder of the great Zulu military state in south Africa. The autocratic Mzilikazi enjoyed success in wars against various central and south African peoples but was defeated by a combination of Boer (Afrikaner) and African allies in 1837–1838. He moved north with his followers to the Rhodesian uplands where he ruled, supported by a strong army and centralized political control, until 1868. The following selection is by Robert Moffat, a British missionary who developed a close relationship with Mzilikazi. Here Moffat records the trial and judgment of a noble warrior accused of a crime and brought before Mzilikazi.

> **Consider:** *Factors involved in this system of justice; the importance of class and rank in Ndebele society.*

He [the accused] was a man of rank, and what was called an Entuna, (an officer,) who wore on his head the usual badge of dignity. He was brought to head-quarters. His arm bore no shield, nor his hand a spear; he had been divested of these, which had been his glory. He was brought into the presence of the king, and his chief council, charged with a crime, for which it was in vain to expect pardon, even at the hands of a more humane government. He bowed his fine elastic figure, and kneeled before the judge. The case was investigated silently, which gave solemnity to the scene. Not a whisper was heard among the listening audience, and the voices of the council were only audible to each other, and the nearest spectators. The prisoner, though on his knees, had something dignified and noble in his mien. Not a muscle of his countenance moved, but his bright black eyes indicated a feeling of intense interest, which the moving balance between life and death only could produce. The case required little investigation; the charges were clearly substantiated, and the culprit pleaded guilty. But, alas! he knew it was at a bar where none ever heard the heartreviving sound of pardon, even for offences small compared with his. A pause ensued, during which the silence of death pervaded the assembly. At length the monarch spoke, and, addressing the prisoner, said, "You are a dead man, but I shall do to-day what I never did before; I spare your life for the sake of my friend and father"—pointing to the spot where I . . . stood. "I know his heart weeps at the shedding of blood; for his sake I spare your life; he has travelled from a far country to see me, and he has made my heart white; but he tells me that to take away life is an awful thing, and never can be undone again. He has pleaded with me not to go to war, nor destroy life. I wish him, when

---

SOURCE: Robert Moffat, *Missionary Labours and Scenes in Southern Africa* (London: J. Snow, 1842), pp. 539–541.

he returns to his own home again, to return with a heart as white as he has made mine. I spare you for his sake, for I love him, and he has saved the lives of my people. But," continued the king, "you must be degraded for life; you must no more associate with the nobles of the land, nor enter the towns of the princes of the people; nor ever again mingle in the dance of the mighty. Go to the poor of the field, and let your companions be the inhabitants of the desert." The sentence passed, the pardoned man was expected to bow in grateful adoration to him whom he was wont to look upon and exalt in songs applicable only to One to whom belongs universal sway and the destinies of man. But, no! holding his hands clasped on his bosom, he replied, "O king, afflict not my heart! I have merited thy displeasure; let me be slain like the warrior; I cannot live with the poor." And, raising his hand to the ring he wore on his brow, he continued, "How can I live among the dogs of the king, and disgrace these badges of honour which I won among the spears and shields of the mighty? No, I cannot live! Let me die, O Pezoolu!" His request was granted.

Letter To Sir George Grey: Conflict and Diplomacy in South Africa
Moshweshewe

In the interior regions of south Africa, Africans had effectively blocked European expansion from the Cape Coast and Natal settlements for most of the eighteenth century. However, from the early 1800's onward, the original Dutch settlers (now known as Afrikaners) moved inward to avoid exactions from the new British overlords. There were increasing clashes between the newcomers and the African populations as they attempted to protect their land from being expropriated by the Afrikaners. The Sothos [Basutos], led by their king Moshweshewe, used skillful diplomacy to exploit the conflicts between the British and the Afrikaners. They were among the few African peoples in south Africa to maintain some territorial integrity in the wake of later European takeover. The lands eventually became the independent state of Lesotho in 1966. The following letter from Moshweshewe to Sir George Grey, written in 1858, is an excellent demonstration of Moshweshewe's diplomatic skill.

Consider: *How much the letter reveals about black-white relations in south Africa at the time; how the king achieved his aim of preserving his people's independence against European aggression; how much the letter reveals about internal African political organization at the time.*

SOURCE: G. M. Theal, (ed.) *Records of South/Eastern Africa* (London/Capetown: Government of Capetown, 1898–1903).

Thaba Bosigo, June, 1858.

Your Excellency,—it may scarcely appear necessary to lay before Your Excellency any lengthened details of what has taken place between the Orange Free State and myself. I know that you have followed with interest the transactions which have led to the commencement of hostilities, and you have heard with pain of the horrors occasioned by the war, at present suspended in the hopes that peace may be restored by Your Excellency's mediation.

Allow me, however, to bring to your remembrance the following circumstances:—About twenty-five years ago my knowledge of the White men and their laws was very limited. I knew merely that mighty nations existed, and among them was the English. These, the blacks who were acquainted with them, praised for their justice. Unfortunately it was not with the English Government that my first intercourse with the whites commenced. People who had come from the Colony first presented themselves to us, they called themselves Boers. I thought all white men were honest. Some of these Boers asked permission to live upon our borders. I was led to believe they would live with me as my own people lived, that is, looking to me as to a father and a friend.

About sixteen years since, one of the Governors of the Colony, Sir George Napier, marked down my limits on a treaty he made with me. I was to be ruler within those limits. A short time after, another Governor came, it was Sir P. Maitland. The Boers then began to talk of *their right* to places I had then lent to them. Sir P. Maitland told me those people were subjects of the Queen, and should be kept under proper control; he did not tell me that he recognised any right they had to land within my country, but as it was difficult to take them away, it was proposed that all desiring to be under the British rule should live in that part near the meeting of the Orange and Caledon rivers.

Then came Sir Harry Smith, and he told me not to deprive any chief of their lands or their rights, he would see justice done to all, but in order to do so, he would make the Queen's Laws extend over every white man. He said the Whites and Blacks were to live together in peace. I could not understand what he would do. I thought it would be something very just, and that he was to keep the Boers in my land under proper control, and that I should hear no more of their claiming the places they lived on as their exclusive property. But instead of this, I now heard that the Boers consider all those farms as their own, and were buying and selling them one to the other, and driving out by one means or another my own people.

In vain I remonstrated. Sir Harry Smith had sent Warden to govern in the Sovereignty. He listened to the Boers, and he proposed that all the land in which those Boers' farms were should be taken from me. I was at that time in trouble, for Sikonyela and the Korannas were tormenting me and my people by stealing and killing; they said openly the Major gave them orders to do so, and I have proof he did so. One day he sent me a map and said, sign that, and I will tell those people (Mantatis and Korannas) to leave off fighting: if you do not sign the map, I cannot help you in any way. I thought the Major was doing very improperly and unjustly. I was told to appeal to the Queen to put an end to this injustice. I did not wish to grieve Her Majesty by causing a war with her people. I was told if I did not sign the map, it would be the beginning of a great war. I signed, but soon after I sent my cry to the Queen. I begged Her to investigate my case and remove 'the line,' as it was called, by which my land was ruined. I thought justice would soon be done, and Warden put to rights. . . .

I tried my utmost to satisfy them and avert war. I punished thieves, and sent my son Nehemiah and others to watch the part of the country near the Boers, and thus check stealing. In this he was successful, thieving did cease. We were at peace for a time. In the commencement of the present year (1858) my people living near farmers received orders to remove from their places. This again caused the fire to burn, still we tried to keep all quiet, but the Boers went further and further day by day in troubling the Basutos and threatening war. The President (Boshof) spoke of Warden's line, this was as though he had really fired upon us with his guns. Still I tried to avert war.

It was not possible, it was commenced by the Boers in massacreing my people of Beersheba, and ruining that station, against the people of which there was not a shadow of a complaint ever brought forward. Poor people, they thought their honesty and love for Christianity would be a shield for them, and that the white people would attack in the first place, if they attacked at all, those who they said were thieves. I ordered my people then all to retreat towards my residence, and let the fury of the Boers be spent upon an empty land; unfortunately some skirmishes took place, some Boers were killed, some of my people also. We need not wonder at this, such is war! But I will speak of many Basutos who were taken prisoners by the Whites and then killed, most cruelly. If you require me to bring forward these cases, I will do so. I will however speak of the horrible doings of the Boers at Morija, they there burnt down the Missionary's house, carried off much goods belonging to the Mission, and pillaged and shamefully defiled the Church Buildings.

I had given orders that no farms should be burnt, and my orders were obeyed till my people saw village after village burnt off, and the corn destroyed, they then carried destruction among the enemy's homes.

On coming to my mountain, the Boers found I was prepared to check their progress, and they consequently retired. My intention was then to have followed them up, and to have shewn them that my people could also carry on offensive operations, believing that having once experienced the horrors of war in their midst, I should not soon be troubled by them again.

My bands were getting ready to make a descent upon them, when the Boers thought proper to make request for a cessation of hostilities. I knew what misery I should bring upon the country by leaving the Basutos to ravage the Boer places, and therefore I have agreed to the proposal of Mr. J. P. Hoffman. I cannot say that I do so with the consent of my people, for many of those who suffered by the enemy were anxious to recover their losses.

If they have remained quiet, it has been owing to my persuasions and my promises that they might have good hope of justice,—Your Excellency having consented to act as arbitrator between the Boers and Basutos. With the expectation of soon meeting you, I remain, etc.,

Mark × of Moshesh. Chief of the Basutos.

Culture and Imperialism in East Africa
Ernest Linant de Fellefonds

From the 1830s to 1885, European missionaries reopened the cultural and religious exchanges that the Portuguese and Africans had initiated in the sixteenth century. These new openings were happening at a time when in many parts of Africa rulers were increasingly willing to welcome European trade as well as ideas.

Kabaka Mutesa (M'Tesa) of Buganda in the interior of east Africa was one such ruler. Born ca. 1838, Mutesa made Buganda a major power in east Africa through wars against neighboring states. He entertained both Christians and Muslims, seeking to play off each against the other to preserve his kingdom's independence in an era of growing imperialism. His meetings with European missionaries illustrate his attempts to come to terms with the new knowledge, which he realized was necessary in order to maintain his country's independence. Ernest Linant de Fellefonds, a Roman Catholic missionary of French ancestry, wrote the following observation of Kabaka Mutesa (M'Tesa) I in 1875.

> **Consider:** *Fellefonds' perspective of the European as teacher, his disdain for both African and Islamic knowledge, and his reaction to Mutesa's intelligence; the king's concern that his closest advisers be exposed to the new knowledge; the existence of a group of Africans already literate in European languages.*

21, 22, 23 April—I have had many different discussions with M'Tesa during the last three days. Our conversation had dwelled on all the different powerful forces of the world in turn: America, England, France, Germany, Russia, the Ottoman Empire, constitutions, government, military might, production, industry and religion.

The King's sister was present at these sessions. The daughters and sisters of the King never go on foot; they are always carried by their slaves.

25th April—M'Tesa summoned me at eleven o'clock at the same time as the Fakir of the Xoderia.[1] Our talk therefore was exclusively about the Koran. The poor Fakir was at a loss as to how to answer all the King's questions. I had to give him some help.

I informed the King of the system of trade by means of money. The value of

---

SOURCE: D. A. Low, *Mind of Buganda: Documents of the Modern History of an African Kingdom*, (Berkeley, Calif., University of California Press), pp. 2–3.

[1] A Muslim cleric from the upper Nile region.

all goods is based on the tallari. This system makes trade and transactions easier. 27th April—In answer to all M'Tesa's questions concerning the earth, the sun, the moon, the stars and the sky and in order to make him understand the movements of the heavenly bodies. I had to make shapes on a board, the heavenly bodies being represented by little glass balls. The lecture took place today. The gathering was not very large. The two viziers Katikiro and Chambarango, four leading officers, the two scribes and a few favourites. The four cardinal points, the rotation of the earth, its movement round the sun, night and day, the seasons, the movement of the moon round the earth and its phases (which I did by means of a mirror) and the general movement of our system in space.

M'Tesa grasped everything perfectly. We were seated on the ground in a circle and there was a very friendly atmosphere. I have never seen M'Tesa so happy. It was the first time that we had spoken to each other directly without using interpreters, and this is against all the laws of etiquette. M'Tesa himself explained afterwards to the wonder-struck gathering. What was so surprising was that M'Tesa was able to inspire in his associates and in many of his people this quest for understanding, for self-instruction and for knowledge. There is great rivalry among them and they are very eager to improve. They are an inquiring, observant, intelligent people with minds longing for the learning of white people whose superiority they recognize; and with the help of a mission having farmers, carpenters and smiths amongst them, these Gandas will soon become an industrial people. This being so, Ganda would be the centre of civilization of all this part of Africa. . . .

I left the King at two o'clock after we had arranged to meet again at four. The same people were there as in the morning. The talk was of Genesis. M'Tesa had the story of Genesis from the Creation to the Flood taken down on a writing-tablet. We parted at nightfall. M'Tesa is spellbound and I shall be able to obtain all I want from him. . . .

VISUAL SOURCES

The Oba of Bein

The west Africans were skilled sculptors and carvers of metal, terra-cotta, and ivory. Perhaps the most famous of their metalworks were the elaborate Benin bronzes, of which this is a striking example. Probably dating from the sixteenth, seventeenth, or eighteenth centuries, when Benin was at its height of wealth and power, this shows the Oba (king) of

Benin mounted on a horse and surrounded protectively by his subordinates. The cords or necklaces around his neck as well as his size and position reveal his status as monarch.

Consider: *The possible meanings of this image to contemporary viewers; the qualities of the society that produced this.*

Photo 9-1

The Metropolitan Museum of Art, The Michael C. Rockefeller Memorial Collection, Gift of Nelson A. Rockefeller, 1978

Indigenous States in Sub-Saharan Africa to the Nineteenth Century

This map shows some of the major states of sub-Saharan Africa to the nineteenth century. While what is shown is far from complete, it indicates the long and varied history of civilizations throughout Africa. (The presence of many small political units precludes in-

Map 9-1

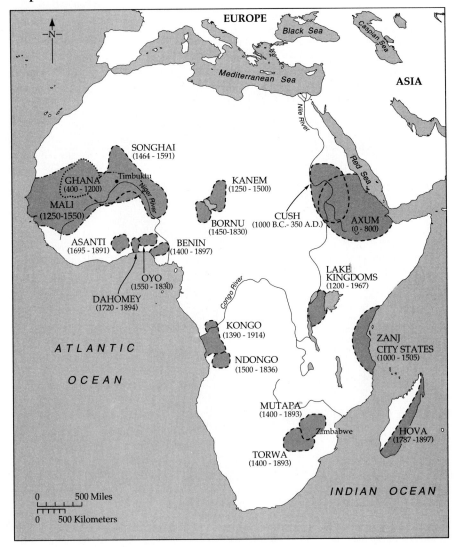

cluding them on the map.) It also reveals how dynamic the political history of some areas, such as west Africa, was, with various states competing with and succeeding each other over time. When viewed with the maps in Chapter 10 on the New Imperialism, it allows a fuller understanding of the significance of the late-nineteenth-century conquests and partitions of Africa by Europeans.

> **Consider:** *The relationship between states and their location near rivers; the size of states and changing political boundaries over time.*

SECONDARY SOURCES

Africa and Africans in the Making of the Atlantic World, 1400–1680: the Atlantic Slave Trade

John K. Thornton

Europeans began arriving along the Atlantic coast of Africa in the fifteenth and sixteenth centuries. They were drawn there mainly for the trade in gold, spices and other products, among them slaves. However, Europeans had no military success against African states as they were later to achieve against various American peoples. In the following excerpt, John Thornton shows why African leaders and merchants were willing and able to sell as many as 15 million people to European and American merchants over the next four centuries.

> **Consider:** *How the political and economic situation in Atlantic Africa was both conducive to entry by European slave merchants and averted possible conquest; what factors made African decision makers continue the trade for so long.*

Africans were not under any direct commercial or economic pressure to deal in slaves. Furthermore, we have seen not only that Africans accepted the institution of slavery in their own societies, but that the special place of slaves as private productive property made slavery widespread. At the beginning, at least, Europeans were only tapping existing slave markets. Nevertheless, one need not accept that these factors alone can explain the slave trade. There are scholars who contend

SOURCE: John K. Thornton, *Africa and Africans in the Making of the Atlantic World, 1400–1680* (New York: Cambridge University Press, 1992), pp. 98, 99, 125, as excerpted.

that although Europeans did not invade the continent and take slaves themselves, they did nevertheless promote the slave trade through indirect military pressure created by European control of important military technology, such as horses and guns. In this scenario—the "gun–slave cycle" or "horse–slave cycle"—Africans were compelled to trade in slaves, because without this commerce they could not obtain the necessary military technology (guns and horses) to defend themselves from any enemy. Furthermore, possession of the technology made them more capable of obtaining slaves, because successful war guaranteed large supplies of slaves. . . .

The contemporary evidence strongly supports the idea that there was a direct connection between wars and slavery, both for domestic work and for export. This did not mean that there was no nonmilitary enslavement, of course. Judicial enslavement was one common way of obtaining slaves, and judges, moreover, were not above distorting the law to provide more captives or enslaving distant relatives of guilty parties. Jesuit observers believed that this was common in Ndongo as early as 1600, and missionary travelers often commented on it in the seventeenth-century Upper Guinea region. But however scandalous this may have been, it is unlikely that judicial enslavement accounted for more than a few percent of the total exports from Africa.

Thus the fact that military enslavement was by far the most significant method is important, for it means that rulers were not, for the most part, selling their own subjects but people whom they, at least, regarded as aliens. The fact that many exported slaves were recent captives means that they were drawn from those captured in the course of warfare who had not yet been given an alternative employment within Africa. In these cases, rulers were deciding to forgo the potential future use of these slaves. Some of the exports were slaves whom local masters wished to dispose of for one reason or another and those who had been captured locally by brigands or judicially enslaved. . . .

In conclusion, then, we must accept that African participation in the slave trade was voluntary and under the control of African decision makers. This was not just at the surface level of daily exchange but even at deeper levels. Europeans possessed no means, either economic or military, to compel African leaders to sell slaves.

The willingness of Africa's commercial and political elite to supply slaves should be sought in their own internal dynamics and history. Institutional factors predisposed African societies to hold slaves, and the development of Africa's domestic economy encouraged large-scale trading and possession of slaves long before Europeans visited African shores. The increase in warfare and political instability in some regions may well have contributed to the growth of the slave trade from those regions, but one cannot easily assign the demand for slaves as the cause of the instability, especially as our knowledge of African politics provides many more internal causes. Given the commercial interests of African states and the existing slave market in private hands in Africa, it is not surprising that Africans were able to respond to European demands for slaves, as long as the prices attracted them.

The Yoruba Kingdom of Oyo and the Kingdom of Benin in the Sixteenth, Seventeenth, and Eighteenth Centuries
Robert O. Collins

The Yoruba Kingdom of Oyo and the Kingdom of Benin in west Africa rose to consider-able power and prosperity during the sixteenth, seventeenth, and eighteenth centuries. By the nineteenth century both kingdoms were in decline. In this selection from his African History: Text and Readings, *Robert O. Collins compares these two states, emphasizing the cycle of their rise and decline and the competition for wealth and power among states in this area of Africa.*

> **Consider:** *The economic factors underlying the power of these states; the differ-ences in their political and administrative systems; the causes for their decline.*

THE YORUBA KINGDOM OF OYO

Oyo rose to predominance among the forest kingdoms of Nigeria during the seventeenth century, when its armies subordinated the peoples of Yorubaland in western Nigeria to the rule of the Alafin of Oyo. The expansion of Oyo, spear-headed by its famous cavalry, continued during the eighteenth century until the suzerainty of the alafin extended from Benin to the borders of Togo. Like the other forest states, Oyo relied on the slave trade to provide an economic base for expansion, selling prisoners of war to European merchants in return for guns to equip its armies, but the ability to utilize this economic and military power clearly arose from the political and social organization of the state. The origins of Oyo are obscure, but Ife appears to have been its spiritual progenitor, as it was for Benin. The development of Oyo north and west of Ife near the present city of Ilorin took place under Alafin Shango, the fourth alafin after the traditional foun-der, Oranmiyan. Thereafter Oyo's armies sallied forth during every dry season to exact tribute from surrounding states. The alafin himself was elected by a council of local officials, or *obas*, who acknowedged, in theory at least, the spiritual au-thority of Ife. In theory the alafin possessed both absolute political and spiritual power in Oyo, but in fact his authority was circumscribed by numerous secular institutions, the paramount one being the council of obas, which could, and on occasion did, rid itself of an unpopular or tyrannical alafin.

As Oyo reached the height of its power in the eighteenth century, Yoruba

---

SOURCE: Robert O. Collins, *African History: Text and Readings* (New York: Random House, 1971), pp. 133–134.

colonies were established to the west, perhaps as a by-product of military expe-ditions, advancing the network of Yoruba trade. By 1800, however, the alafins of Oyo could no longer hold the state together. A disparity in power appeared between the southern regions, which had grown wealthy as a result of the slave trade, and the north, which remained the supplier. The Fon of Dahomey and the *Egba* were the first to break away, followed by Ilorin, who, with Fulani assistance, prevented horses and slaves from reaching Oyo and precipitated the long and destructive Yoruba wars that preoccupied Oyo until the coming of the British.

THE KINGDOM OF BENIN

Although the founding of Oyo may have been contemporary with that of Benin, the verifiable history of Benin has given that state a primacy in the history of the south Nigerian kingdoms. The origins of Benin, like those of Oyo, are tied to Ife, from which came the spiritual authority of the Oba, the ruler of Benin. Under a series of warrior obas, Benin experienced a steady stream of Portuguese mission-aries and merchants who traded in pepper and slaves, which were exchanged on the Gold Coast for gold. Trade brought increasing prosperity—pepper, slaves, and ivory in return for firearms, copper, and beads—and emissaries from Benin were sent to Lisbon while Catholic missionaries built churches and proselytized among the people of Benin.

The strength of both Oyo and Benin was attributable as much to political organization as to economic prosperity. The title of Oba of Benin was hereditary, however; that of Alafin of Oyo was not. A difference of even greater importance was that the chiefs of Oyo retained great power from the lineages that supported them, whereas the chiefs of Benin were not necessarily heads of lineages and consequently owed their position and power to the ruler more than to relatives or subjects. The emergence in Benin of a bureaucracy of nonhereditary, title-holding groups permitted a strong and able oba greater freedom that his coun-terpart, the Alafin of Oyo.

Beginning in the eighteenth century, Benin slipped into a long period of decline. Rivalries among the nobles were exacerbated by a century of warfare and the rise of Oyo. Moreover, the traders of Benin could no longer compete on favorable terms with the slave merchants of Dahomey or Oyo. Economically depressed and politically confused, Benin could no longer exert a paramount influence over its vassal states, and one by one they obtained their freedom. By the nineteenth century, both the size and influence of the kingdom had shrunk to that of a petty city-state.

Beyond Decline: The Kingdom of the Kongo in the Eighteenth and Nineteenth Centuries

Susan Herlin Broadhead

The kingdom of the Kongo, located on the west coast of central Africa, had been a relatively strong, centralized state by the time the Portuguese arrived in the fifteenth century. Despite periods of difficulties, both with the Portuguese and internally, the kingdom remained powerful until its collapse during the second part of the seventeenth century. In 1718, when the kingdom was restored under king Pedro IV after more than half a century of civil war, it was much less centralized and the major ruling families continued to compete. Over the following century and a half, no ruler was able to assert control over all parts of the country or to completely defeat the rival families. It was this weakness in the political system that laid the foundations for the Portuguese takeover at the end of the nineteenth century. In the following selection, Susan Broadhead analyzes the political beliefs of the Bakongo (Kongo) people and the structure of the Kongo state that help explain Portuguese conquest.

> **Consider:** *The Kongo conception of political order and social hierarchy; the effects of this political ideology on the integrity of the state; how this political perspective compares to those in non-African societies during the same period.*

Before we can proceed with their history, it is necessary to consider something of what the Bakongo people believed about politics and right government. What were the basic elements of the political system from the point of view of those principles of political theory and action generally accepted by the public? By what models did they form their organizations, judge their leaders and settle their quarrels? The outline of these principles can be inferred by carefully reading historical data in the light of modern political theory.

The first principle, understood by all, was (and is) that politics—the exercise of power in this world—is not a purely secular activity. On the contrary, it is intrinsically sacred, and sacred power can be controlled only by the appropriate ritual means. This is clearly demonstrated by the overlapping functions and insignia of the major spiritual specialists of the Bakongo—chief, magician, witch and prophet—all of whom share the ability to see things supernaturally and to participate in the power of darkness, that is, of death.

Building on this fundamental premise, two sets of organizing principles can be identified—one hierarchical and ideal, the other egalitarian and pragmatic. There were two kinds of hierarchical structures: one based in the ritually powerful

---

SOURCE: Susan Herlin Broadhead, "Beyond Decline: The Kingdom of the Kongo in the Eighteenth and Nineteenth Centuries," in *International Journal of African Historical Studies*, 1980, pp. 623–27, as excerpted.

institution of sacred chief and the other on the more generalized idea of hierarchical relationships between elder and junior (fathers-sons, patrons-clients, masters-slaves) which operated at all levels of society. In the kingdom hierarchy was, of course, associated with the activities of a political elite. In practice, however, these groups did not always have the resources to impose their authority; they had to attract followers through patronage, prestige or purchase.

The apex of the Bakongo political hierarchy was occupied in theory by the king at Mbanza Kongo, who embodied the ideal combination of sacred power and secular authority. Conceptually this was paralleled in the role of all invested chiefs, that is, political leaders whose investiture confirmed in them the sacred power of life and death. Investiture required not only personal qualification, but also hierarchy. Investment was performed by a superior on an inferior. It further required wealth since regalia were only conferred on those who could pay the required fees and who might reasonably be expected to contribute periodic tribute and military assistance. In the centralized structure of the seventeenth century, the king was elected by a committee, but subordinate titles were appointed from the center. The structure of investiture remained in the eighteenth and nineteenth centuries, although the power to select officials devolved upon the localities. . . .

However, invested chiefs, of whom the king at Mbanza Kongo was the senior, had ritual powers. . . . The supernatural powers of the invested chiefs in eighteenth and nineteenth century Kongo derived from at least two sources: the ritual strength of the ancient cult of the local priests of the land and the powers of the Christian cult built up as a counterweight by the ruling aristocrats in their earlier struggles for control with the local officials. Both elements were represented in the installation of titleholders or chiefs. With the disappearance of the strong concentration of economic, military and ritual power represented by mid-seventeenth century San Salvador, the nobility faced a problem. How could they maintain their preeminence in society and the kingdom without giving up too much to any central authority? Their answer appears to have been to continue their campaign to strengthen the Christian cult, which was already closely associated with the aristocracy. Thus their introduction of a Christian founding hero into the traditions of Kongo, the emphasis on a central Christian ancestor cult dedicated to that hero, Afonso I, and the consequent continuation of their interest—and especially that of a king—in Catholic priests, practices and artifacts.

Chapter Questions

1. Drawing on the materials in this chapter, what were some of the most important sources of political power of African states during these centuries?
2. Using sources from this and previous chapters on European history, in what

ways might it be argued that African societies were similar to European societies during the sixteenth, seventeenth, and eighteenth centuries? In what ways might it be argued that they differed?

3. In what ways did African civilizations respond to the increasing presence and demands of Westerners? What do these responses reveal about the politics and cultures of these civilizations? How are these responses similar or different from the responses to the West by other non-Western civilizations?

TEN

The New Imperialism, 1880–1914

Between the fifteenth and the eighteenth centuries, European nations gained control over most of the Western Hemisphere, the west coast of Africa, and southern Asia. Then, from the 1760s to the 1870s, there was a relative lull in expansion and indeed several imperial powers lost many of their overseas holdings. In the period between 1880 and 1914, however, there was a new burst of imperial expansion, the "new imperialism." The impetus came from Europe, where the powers engaged in a sudden quest for control over new territories in Asia, Africa, and the Pacific. Explorers, missionaries, traders, troops, and government officials quickly followed one another into these lands and established direct and indirect political control. Other lands already partially controlled, such as in India and southeast Asia, were brought under tighter reign. In this process Europe greatly increased its dominance over much of the rest of the world, bringing Western culture and institutions to the indigenous societies whether they wanted it or not. While the impact of the new imperialism varied in different lands, it was intensely felt and inspired resistance that would grow over the course of the twentieth century.

As the United States, long the strongest nation in the Americas, emerged as a dominant economic power in the world, it assumed some of the roles held by European imperial powers. Following the Spanish-American War in 1898, the United States acquired Puerto Rico and the Philippines. It also established a protectorate over Cuba. While opposing European imperialism and expansionism elsewhere in the world, the United States often assumed that it could act as if Latin American countries were only semiautonomous. And as with the European powers, the United States would have to face the consequences of this new imperialism throughout the twentieth century.

Certainly imperialism has been a topic of considerable debate among historians, as the questions addressed in this chapter indicate. What were the nationalistic, economic, and political motives for imperialism? What were some of the attitudes toward imperialism, particularly as reflected in materials glorifying it as a Christian and humanitarian movement? How is imperialism understood from a Marxist perspective? In what ways was imperialism opposed as nations struggled for independence from imperial powers? What were some of the consequences of imperialism?

Here our focus on the competitive struggle between imperial powers leads us toward the outbreak of World War I, which will be examined in Chapter 11. Subsequent chapters will deal with the worldwide impact of imperialism throughout the twentieth century.

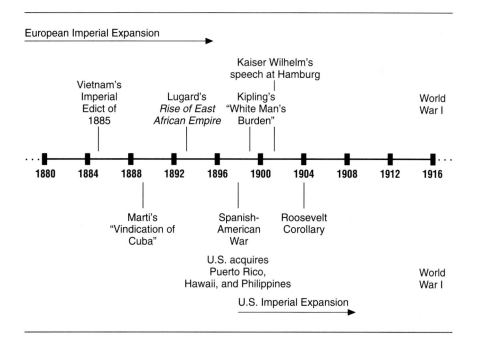

PRIMARY SOURCES

Speech at Hamburg, 1901: Imperialism
Kaiser Wilhelm II

Imperialism swept through Europe with extraordinary force in the late nineteenth century. For many the step between the increasingly assertive nationalism of the time and the new imperialism was a short one. This view is illustrated in the following speech given at Hamburg in 1901 by Kaiser Wilhelm II (1888–1919) of Germany. Addressing an audience with strong commercial interests, he refers to a recent intervention by European powers in China.

> **Consider:** *How Wilhelm II connects nationalism and imperialism; by what means he hopes to spread German influence throughout the world; the ways in which this speech might appeal to both liberals and conservatives.*

In spite of the fact that we have no such fleet as we should have, we have conquered for ourselves a place in the sun. It will now be my task to see to it that this place in the sun shall remain our undisputed possession, in order that the sun's rays may fall fruitfully upon our activity and trade in foreign parts, that our industry and agriculture may develop within the state and our sailing sports upon the water, for our future lies upon the water. The more Germans go out upon the waters, whether it be in the races of regattas, whether it be in journeys across the ocean, or in the service of the battle-flag, so much the better will it be for us. For when the German has once learned to direct his glance upon what is distant and great, the pettiness which surrounds him in daily life on all sides will disappear. Whoever wishes to have this larger and freer outlook can find no better place than one of the Hanseatic cities.[1] What we have learned out of the previous history of our development amounts really to what I already pointed out when I sent my brother to the East Asiatic station (Dec. 15, 1897). We have merely drawn the logical conclusions from the work which was left us by Emperor William the Great, my memorable grandfather, and the great man whose monument we have recently unveiled. These consequences lie in the fact that we are now making our efforts to do what, in the old time, the Hanseatic cities could not accomplish, because they lacked the vivifying and protecting power of the empire. May it be the function of my Hansa during many years of peace to protect and advance commerce and trade!

SOURCE: C. Gauss, *The German Kaiser as Shown in His Public Utterances* (New York: Charles Scribner's Sons, 1915), pp. 181–183.

[1] The Hanseatic cities formed a league in the Late Middle Ages to facilitate trade.

In the events which have taken place in China I see the indication that European peace is assured for many years to come; for the achievements of the particular contingents have brought about a mutual respect and feeling of comradeship that can only serve the furtherance of peace. But in this period of peace I hope that our Hanseatic cities will flourish. Our new Hansa will open new paths and create and conquer new markets for them.

As head of the empire I therefore rejoice over every citizen, whether from Hamburg, Bremen, or Lübeck, who goes forth with this large outlook and seeks new points where we can drive in the nail on which to hang our armour. Therefore, I believe that I express the feeling of all your hearts when I recognize gratefully that the director of this company who has placed at our disposal the wonderful ship which bears my daughter's name has gone forth as a courageous servant of the Hansa, in order to make for us friendly conquests whose fruits will be gathered by our descendants.

In the joyful hope that this enterprising Hanseatic spirit may be spread even further, I raise my glass and ask all of those who are my comrades upon the water to join with me in a cheer for sailing and the Hanseatic spirit!

The Rise of Our East African Empire
Lord Lugard

Probably the most apparent motive for the new imperialism was economic. With new conquests made, people expected to develop new commerce and particularly new markets for manufactured goods. This attitude is reflected by Lord Lugard in his Rise of Our East African Empire *(1893), largely an account of his experiences in colonial service. Lugard, as a British soldier and administrator, helped bring large parts of Africa into the British empire. Here he analyzes the "scramble" for Africa.*

> **Consider:** *How Lugard connects nationalistic and economic motives for imperialism; some of the main arguments presented against imperialism and how Lugard responds to them; Lugard's perceptions of Africans and how such perceptions might facilitate the new imperialism.*

The Chambers of Commerce of the United Kingdom have unanimously urged the retention of East Africa on the grounds of commercial advantage. The Presidents of the London and Liverpool chambers attended a deputation to her Majesty's Minister for Foreign Affairs to urge "the absolute necessity, for the prosperity of this country, that new avenues for commerce such as that in East Equatorial Africa should be opened up, in view of the hostile tariffs with which

SOURCE: Captain F. D. Lugard, *The Rise of Our East African Empire*, vol. I (London: William Blackwood and Sons, 1893), pp. 379–382, 473.

British manufacturers are being everywhere confronted." Manchester followed with a similar declaration; Glasgow, Birmingham, Edinburgh, and other commercial centres gave it as their opinion that "there is practically no middle course for this country, between a reversal of the free-trade policy to which it is pledged, on the one hand, and a prudent but continuous territorial extension for the creation of new markets, on the other hand." Such is the view of the Chambers of Commerce, and I might quote endless paragraphs from their resolutions and reports in the same sense.

This view has been strongly endorsed by some of our leading statesmen. Space forbids me to quote extracts from speeches by our greatest politicians, which I might else adduce as proof that they held the opinions of the Chambers of Commerce, which I have quoted, to be sound and weighty. . . .

The "Scramble for Africa" by the nations of Europe—an incident without parallel in the history of the world—was due to the growing commercial rivalry, which brought home to civilised nations the vital necessity of securing the only remaining fields for industrial enterprise and expansion. It is well, then, to realise that it is for our *advantage*—and not alone at the dictates of duty—that we have undertaken responsibilities in East Africa. It is in order to foster the growth of the trade of this country, and to find an outlet for our manufactures and our surplus energy, that our far-seeing statesmen and our commercial men advocate colonial expansion. . . .

There are some who say we have no *right* in Africa at all, that "it belongs to the natives." I hold that our right is the necessity that is upon us to provide for our ever-growing population—either by opening new fields for emigration, or by providing work and employment which the development of over-sea extension entails—and to stimulate trade by finding new markets, since we know what misery trade depression brings at home.

While thus serving our own interests as a nation, we may, by selecting men of the right stamp for the control of new territories, bring at the same time many advantages to Africa. Nor do we deprive the natives of their birthright of freedom, to place them under a foreign yoke. It has ever been the key-note of British colonial method to rule through and by the natives, and it is this method, in contrast to the arbitrary and uncompromising rule of Germany, France, Portugal, and Spain, which has been the secret of our success as a colonising nation, and has made us welcomed by tribes and peoples in Africa, who ever rose in revolt against the other nations named. In Africa, moreover, there is among the people a natural inclination to submit to a higher authority. That intense detestation of control which animates our Teutonic races does not exist among the tribes of Africa, and if there is any authority that we replace, it is the authority of the Slavers and Arabs, or the intolerable tyranny of the "dominant tribe." . . .

°

So far, therefore, as my personal experience goes, I have formed the following estimate: (1) No kind of men I have ever met with—including British soldiers, Afghans, Burmese, and many tribes of India—are more amenable to discipline, more ready to fall into the prescribed groove willingly and quickly, more easy to handle, or require so little compulsion as the African. (2) To obtain satisfactory results a great deal of system, division of labour, supervision, etc., is required. (3) On the whole, the African is very quick at learning, and those who prove themselves good at the superior class of work take a pride in the results, and are very amenable to a word of praise, blame, or sarcasm.

The White Man's Burden
Rudyard Kipling

Imperialism was often glorified both by those actively involved in it and by the public at home. Part of this glorification involved perceiving imperialism as a Christian and nationalistic venture. More broadly it involved portraying imperialism as a heroic deed carried out by idealistic leaders of Western civilization in an effort to spread the "benefits" of "true civilization" to "less advanced" peoples of the world. One of the most popular expressions of this is found in the writings of Rudyard Kipling (1865–1936), particularly in his poem "The White Man's Burden," written in 1899 to celebrate the American annexation of the Philippines.

> **Consider:** *What Kipling means by "the White Man's burden"; how Kipling justifies imperialism; why such a justification might be so appealing.*

Take up the White Man's burden—
    Send forth the best ye breed—
Go, bind your sons to exile
    To serve your captives' need;
To wait, in heavy harness,
    On fluttered folk and wild—
Your new-caught sullen peoples,
    Half devil and half child.

Take up the White Man's burden—
    In patience to abide,
To veil the threat of terror
    And check the show of pride;
By open speech and simple,
    An hundred times made plain,
To seek another's profit
    And work another's gain.

Take up the White Man's burden—
    The savage wars of peace—

SOURCE: Rudyard Kipling, "The White Man's Burden," *McClure's Magazine*, vol. XII, no. 4 (February 1899), pp. 290–291.

Fill full the mouth of Famine,
    And bid the sickness cease;
And when your goal is nearest
    (The end for others sought)
Watch sloth and heathen folly
    Bring all your hope to nought.

Take up the White Man's burden—
    No iron rule of kings,
But toil of serf and sweeper—
    The tale of common things.
The ports ye shall not enter,
    The roads ye shall not tread,
Go, make them with your living
    And mark them with your dead.

Take up the White Man's burden,
    And reap his old reward—
The blame of those ye better
    The hate of those ye guard—
The cry of hosts ye humour
    (Ah, slowly!) toward the light:—
"Why brought ye us from bondage,
    Our loved Egyptian night?"

Take up the White Man's burden—
    Ye dare not stoop to less—
Nor call too loud on Freedom
    To cloke your weariness.
By all ye will or whisper,
    By all ye leave or do,
The silent sullen peoples
    Shall weigh your God and you.

Take up the White Man's burden!
    Have done with childish days—
The lightly-proffered laurel,
    The easy ungrudged praise:
Comes now, to search your manhood
    Through all the thankless years,
Cold, edged with dear-bought wisdom,
    The judgment of your peers.

Nationalism and Colonialism in Vietnam
Imperial Edict, 1885

Traditionally in mainland southeast Asia, rivalries between Thailand, Laos, Cambodia, and Vietnam led to shifting patterns of control. The eighteenth and nineteenth centuries added the British (in Burma, Malaya, and Singapore) and the French (in Cambodia, Laos, and Vietnam) to the equation. Nationalism was a constant theme throughout the histories of southeast Asia during the eighteenth and nineteenth centuries. Yet no nation was more militant in its nationalism than Vietnam. The reasons are easy to discern. Before the French arrived, the Vietnamese had suffered through a thousand years of Chinese colonialism, Mongol invasions, encroachment from Cambodia, and more. Militant nationalism became a central theme of their cultural identity.

From the very beginning of their hundred-year colonization of Vietnam, the French had to deal with nationalistic resistance. This reading is from the Loyalty to the King (Can Vuong) Edict promulgated in 1885, which calls on all Vietnamese to resist the French.

Consider: *Imperial Vietnamese attitudes toward the advancing French colonialists; sources of Vietnamese strength.*

The Emperor proclaims:

From time immemorial there have been only three strategies for opposing the enemy: attack, defense, negotiation. Opportunities for attack were lacking. It was difficult to gather required strength for defense. And in negotiations the enemy demanded everything. In this situation of infinite trouble we have unwillingly been forced to resort to expedients. . . .

Our country recently has faced many critical events. . . . Nevertheless, with every passing day the Western envoys got more and more overbearing. Recently they brought in troops and naval reinforcements, trying to force on Us conditions We could never accept. We received them with normal ceremony, but they refused to accept a single thing. People in the capital became very afraid that trouble was approaching. The high ministers sought ways to retain peace in the country and protect the court. It was decided, rather than bow heads in obedience, sitting around and losing chances, better to appreciate what the enemy was up to and move first. If this did not succeed, then we could still follow the present course to make better plans, acting according to the situation. . . .

Court figures had best follow the righteous path, seeking to live and die for righteousness. . . . Our virtue being insufficient, amidst these events We did not have the strength to hold out and allowed the royal capital to fall, forcing the Empresses to flee for their lives. The fault is Ours entirely, a matter of great

SOURCE: David Marr, *Vietnamese Anticolonialism 1885–1925* (Berkeley, Calif. University of California Press, copyright © 1971), The Regents of the University of California.

shame. But traditional loyalties are strong. Hundreds of mandarins and commanders of all levels, perhaps not having the heart to abandon Me, unite as never before, those with intellect helping to plan, those with strength willing to fight, those with riches contributing for supplies—all of one mind and body in seeking a way out of danger, a solution to all difficulties.

On the other hand, those who fear death more than they love their king, who put concerns of household above concerns of country, mandarins who find excuses to be far away, soldiers who desert, citizens who do not fulfill public duties eagerly for a righteous cause, officers who take the easy way and leave brightness for darkness—all may continue to live in this world, but they will be like animals disguised in clothes and hats. Who can accept such behavior? With rewards generous, punishments will also be severe. The court retains normal usages, so that repentance should not be postponed. All should follow this Edict strictly.

The Roosevelt Corollary: American Imperialism
Theodore Roosevelt

The successful revolutions in Latin America during the early nineteenth century, combined with the United States' belief in the inevitability of expansion from the Atlantic to the Pacific Oceans, led United States' President James Monroe to declare in 1823 that European powers should avoid future intrusion into North and South America. This statement, known as the Monroe Doctrine, was little noticed at the time, yet, by the early 1900s, it became a part of a much larger rationale for extending American power throughout Central and South America. The Roosevelt Corollary to the Monroe Doctrine was actually a part of President Theodore Roosevelt's (1901–1909) message to Congress in 1904. It stated the new assumptions regarding the conditions under which the United States had the right to intervene in Latin America. This became the rationale for American interventions in Santo Domingo, Haiti, Nicaragua, and Cuba in subsequent years.

> **Consider:** *How Roosevelt justifies intervention; what Roosevelt meant by the term "civilized"; how Latin Americans might react to such a policy.*

. . . It is not true that the United States feels any land hunger or entertains any projects as regards the other nations of the Western Hemisphere save such as are for their welfare. All that this country desires is to see the neighboring countries stable, orderly, and prosperous. Any country whose people conduct themselves well can count upon our hearty friendship. If a nation shows that it knows how to act with reasonable efficiency and decency in social and political matters, if it

---

SOURCE: Theodore Roosevelt, Annual Message, Dec. 6, 1904, *Messages and Papers of the Presidents*, vol. XIV, pp. 6923ff.

keeps order and pays its obligations, it need fear no interference from the United States. Chronic wrongdoing, or an impotence which results in a general loosening of the ties of civilized society, may in America, as elsewhere, ultimately require intervention by some civilized nation, and in the Western Hemisphere the adherence of the United States to the Monroe Doctrine may force the United States, however reluctantly, in flagrant cases of such wrongdoing or impotence, to the exercise of an international police power. . . . It is a mere truism to say that every nation, whether in America or anywhere else, which desires to maintain its freedom, its independence, must ultimately realize that the right of such independence can not be separated from the responsibility of making good use of it.

In asserting the Monroe Doctrine, in taking such steps as we have taken in regard to Cuba, Venezuela, and Panama, and in endeavoring to circumscribe the theater of war in the Far East, and to secure the open door in China, we have acted in our own interest as well as in the interest of humanity at large. There are, however, cases in which, while our own interests are not greatly involved, strong appeal is made to our sympathies. . . . But in extreme cases action may be justifiable and proper. What form the action shall take must depend upon the circumstances of the case; that is, upon the degree of the atrocity and upon our power to remedy it. The cases in which we could interfere by force of arms as we interfered to put a stop to intolerable conditions in Cuba are necessarily very few.

A Vindication of Cuba
Jose Marti

Before the Spanish-American War in 1898, Cuba had been engaged in a ten-year struggle of liberation from Spain. Jose Marti (1853–1895) was one of the island's most vocal patriots. He was also one of Cuba's great nationalist poets. In this selection, Marti defends his people and rejects the paternalism of United States' leaders who, under the guise of "aiding" the anti-Spanish forces, actually sought to impose a new form of external rule.

> **Consider:** *Marti's view of the United States; his view of Cubans and their character; the nature and importance of nationalism for this Latin American poet.*

There are some Cubans who, from honorable motives, from an ardent admiration for progress and liberty, from a prescience of their own powers under better political conditions, from an unhappy ignorance of the history and tendency of annexation, would like to see the island annexed to the United States. But those who have fought in war and learned in exile, who have built, by the work of hands and mind, a virtuous home in the heart of an unfriendly community; who by their

SOURCE: Jose Marti, *Our America, Writings on Latin America and the Struggle for Cuban Independence* (New York, Monthly Review Press, 1977), pp. 234–237, as excepted.

successful efforts as scientists and merchants, as railroad builders and engineers, as teachers, artists, lawyers, journalists, orators, and poets, as men of alert intelligence and uncommon activity, are honored wherever their powers have been called into action and the people are just enough to understand them; those who have raised, with their less prepared elements, a town of workingmen where the United States had previously a few huts in a barren cliff; those, more numerous than the others, do not desire the annexation of Cuba to the United States. They do not need it [or] . . . believe that excessive individualism, reverence for wealth, and the protracted exultation of a terrible victory are preparing the United States to be the typical nation of liberty, where no opinion is to be based in greed, and no triumph or acquisition reached against charity and justice. . . .

We have suffered impatiently under tyranny; we have fought like men, sometimes like giants, to be freemen; we are passing that period of stormy repose, full of germs of revolt, that naturally follows a period of excessive and unsuccessful action. . . .

But because our government has systematically allowed after the war the triumph of criminals, the occupation of the cities by the scum of the people, the ostentation of ill-gotten riches by the myriad Spanish officeholders and their Cuban accomplices, the conversion of the capital into a gambling den, where the hero and the philosopher walk hungry by the lordly thief of the metropolis; because the healthier farmer, ruined by a war seemingly useless, turns in silence to the plough that he knew well how to exchange for the *machete;* because thousands of exiles, profiting by a period of calm that no human power can quicken until it is naturally exhausted, are practicing in the battle of life in the free countries the art of governing themselves and of building a nation; because our halfbreeds and city-bred young men are generally of delicate physique, of suave courtesy, and ready words, hiding under the glove that polishes the poem the hand that fells the foe— are we to be considered . . . an "effeminate" people?; These city-bred young men and poorly built halfbreeds knew in one day how to rise against a cruel government, to pay their passages to the seat of war with the pawning of their watches and trinkets, to work their way in exile while their vessels were being kept from them by the country of the free in the interest of the foes of freedom, to obey as soldiers, sleep in the mud, eat roots, fight ten years without salary, conquer foes with the branch of a tree, die—these men of eighteen, these heirs of wealthy estates, these dusky striplings—a death not to be spoken of without uncovering the head. They died like those other men of ours who, with a stroke of the *machete,* can send a head flying, or by a turn of the hands bring a bull to their feet.

VISUAL SOURCES

Imperialism Glorified
George Harcourt

This 1900 painting by George Harcourt conveys some of the meaning of imperialism to Europeans. First displayed at the Royal Academy in 1900, it shows British soldiers leaving by train for the Boer War in south Africa. The soldiers are clearly cast in the role of masculine heroes, both in their own eyes as well as in the eyes of civilians, young and old. This is further evidenced by the couple in the center, representing the epitome of sentimentalized British masculinity and femininity. For many, imperialism enabled Europeans to have a sense of adventure and to prove their superiority to themselves and the rest of the world. Avoided in this picture is the reality of the bloodshed and exploitation to be experienced by these same soldiers and the populations of the colonized lands.

Consider: *How this painting fits with Kipling's description of "the White Man's burden."*

Imperialism in Africa

The first of these two maps shows the approximate divisions among indigenous peoples in the centuries prior to European colonization. There were also extremely important cultural and political divisions throughout Africa at this time. The second map shows areas of Africa under European control prior to 1880 and the colonial partition of Africa by European nations by 1914.

Together these maps indicate a number of things about imperialism in Africa. First, the manner and speed with which Africa was divided demonstrate the intense competition involved in this late-nineteenth-century imperial expansion. Second, the European partition of Africa did not take account of the already established social, political, cultural, and ethnic divisions among Africans. From this geopolitical perspective alone, one can imagine some of the disruption to native societies and cultures caused by imperialism. Third, these maps help explain problems experienced by Africans after decolonization occurred. The new African nations were generally formed on the basis of the arbitrary political lines established by European colonizers. Thus, many African countries had to deal with persisting divisions and rivalries among their populations, stemming from the nineteenth-century partition of Africa.

Consider: *How these maps help explain the effects of imperialism on Africans.*

Photo 10-1

The Bettmann Archive/BBC Hulton

Map 10-1

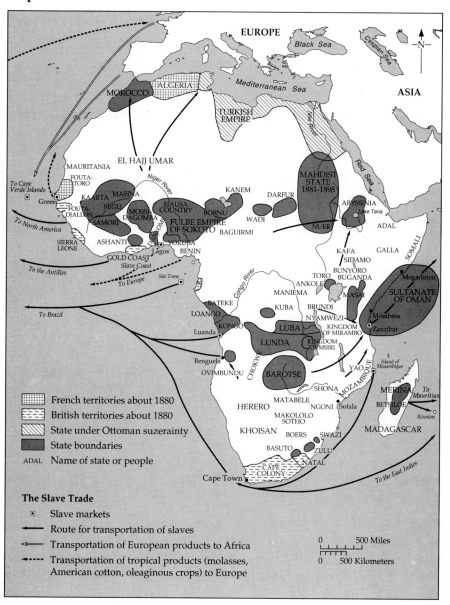

EUROPE

Black Sea

ASIA

Mediterranean Sea

MOROCCO   ALGERIA

TURKISH
EMPIRE

Nile River

Caspian Sea

EL HAJJ UMAR

MAURITANIA

To Cape
Verde Islands

FOUTA-
TORO

Goree

KAARTA   MASINA

FOUTA-
DJALLON   SEGU

SAMORI   MOSSI
DAGOMBA

To North America

SIERRA
LEONE   ASHANTI

GOLD COAST
Slave Coast

To the Antilles

To Europe

Niger River

HAUSA
COUNTRY

FULBE EMPIRE
OF SOKOTO

YORUBA
Lagos   BENIN

São Tomé

KANEM

BORNU

WADI

BAGUIRMI

DARFUR

MAHDIST
STATE
1881-1898

Red Sea

ABYSSINIA
Lake Tana

NUER

ADAL

SOMALI

KAFA
SIDAMO

GALLA

To Brazil

Congo River

LOANGO

Luanda

KONGO

BATEKE

LUBA

LUNDA

KUBA

BRUNDI
NYAMWEZI

KINGDOM
OF MIRAMBO

KINGDOM
OF MSIRI

TORO
ANKOLE

MANIEMA

BUNYORO
BUGANDA

MASAI

SULTANATE
OF OMAN

Mogadisico

Mombasa
Zanzibar

Benguela

OVIMBUNDU

CHOKWE

BAROTSE

YAO

Island of
Mozambique

SHONA

MOZAMBIQUE

MERINA

To
Mauritius

Réunion

MATABELE

HERERO

MAKOLOLO
SOTHO

NGONI (Sofala)

BETSILEO

KHOISAN   BOERS   SWAZI

BASUTO

ZULU

MADAGASCAR

Cape Town

CAPE
COLONY

NATAL

To the East Indies

▦	French territories about 1880
▨	British territories about 1880
▧	State under Ottoman suzerainty
■	State boundaries
ADAL	Name of state or people

The Slave Trade

▫   Slave markets

←   Route for transportation of slaves

⇐   Transportation of European products to Africa

----◄   Transportation of tropical products (molasses,
        American cotton, oleaginous crops) to Europe

0   500 Miles

0   500 Kilometers

Map 10-2   European Control of Africa

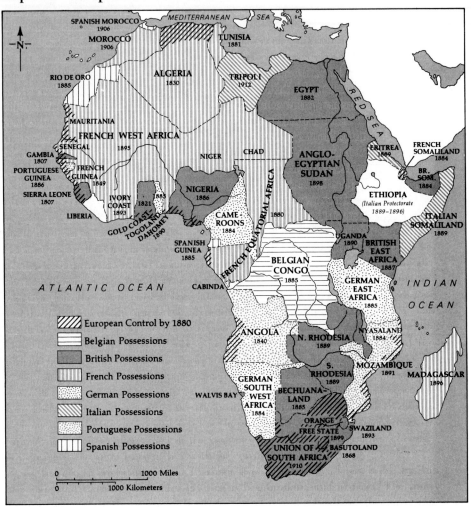

SPANISH MOROCCO
1906

MEDITERRANEAN   SEA

MOROCCO
1906

TUNISIA
1881

RIO DE ORO
1885

ALGERIA
1830

TRIPOLI
1912

EGYPT
1882

RED SEA

MAURITANIA

FRENCH WEST AFRICA   1895

NIGER   CHAD

ANGLO-
EGYPTIAN
SUDAN
1898

ERITREA
1889

FRENCH
SOMALILAND
1884

GAMBIA
1807

SENEGAL

PORTUGUESE
GUINEA
1886

FRENCH
GUINEA   1849

SIERRA LEONE
1807

LIBERIA

IVORY
COAST   1821
1893

GOLD COAST
TOGOLAND
DAHOMEY
1890

NIGERIA
1886

1885

CAME-
ROONS
1884

SPANISH
GUINEA
1885

FRENCH EQUATORIAL AFRICA

1880

BR.
SOM.
1884

ETHIOPIA
(Italian Protectorate
1889–1896)

ITALIAN
SOMALILAND
1889

UGANDA
1890

BRITISH
EAST
AFRICA
1887

ATLANTIC   OCEAN

CABINDA

BELGIAN
CONGO
1885

GERMAN
EAST
AFRICA
1885

INDIAN

OCEAN

⬛ European Control by 1880	
⬛ Belgian Possessions	
⬛ British Possessions	
⬛ French Possessions	
⬛ German Possessions	
⬛ Italian Possessions	
⬛ Portuguese Possessions	
⬛ Spanish Possessions	

ANGOLA
1840

N. RHODESIA
1889

NYASALAND
1884

WALVIS BAY

GERMAN
SOUTH
WEST
AFRICA
1884

BECHUANA-
LAND
1885

S.
RHODESIA
1889

MOZAMBIQUE
1891

MADAGASCAR
1896

ORANGE
FREE STATE
1899

SWAZILAND
1893

UNION OF
SOUTH AFRICA
1910

BASUTOLAND
1868

0   1000 Miles

0   1000 Kilometers

SECONDARY SOURCES

Imperialism as a Nationalistic Phenomenon
Carlton Hayes

Although the economic interpretation of imperialism has not lost its strength, other views have been offered recently as supplements and sometimes as direct alternatives to an economic interpretation. A direct alternative appears in the following selection by Carlton J. H. Hayes. One of the earliest historians to develop a sophisticated understanding of nationalism, Hayes argues that economic motives were at best secondary; on the whole, imperialism was a nationalistic phenomenon.

> **Consider:** *The evidence Hayes uses to reject economic interpretations of nationalism; the ways in which this view fits with the documents on imperialism.*

The founding of new colonial empires and the fortifying of old ones antedated the establishment of neo-mercantilism, and that the economic arguments adduced in support of imperialism seem to have been a rationalization *ex post facto*. In the main, it was not Liberal parties, with their super abundance of industrials and bankers, who sponsored the outward imperialistic thrusts of the '70's and early '80's. Instead, it was Conservative parties, with a preponderantly agricultural clientele notoriously suspicious of moneylenders and big business, and, above all, it was patriotic professors and publicists regardless of political affiliation and unmindful of personal economic interest. These put forth the economic arguments which eventually drew bankers and traders and industrialists into the imperialist camp.

Basically the new imperialism was a nationalistic phenomenon. It followed hard upon the national wars which created an all-powerful Germany and a united Italy, which carried Russia within sight of Constantinople, and which left England fearful and France eclipsed. It expressed a resulting psychological reaction, an ardent desire to maintain or recover national prestige. France sought compensation for European loss in oversea gain. England would offset her European isolation by enlarging and glorifying the British Empire. Russia, halted in the Balkans, would turn anew to Asia, and before long Germany and Italy would show the world that the prestige they had won by might inside Europe they were entitled to enhance by imperial exploits outside. The lesser powers, with no great prestige at stake,

SOURCE: Carlton J. H. Hayes, *A Generation of Materialism: 1871–1900*. Reprinted by permission of Harper & Row (New York, 1941), pp. 223–224. Copyright © 1941 by Harper & Row, Publishers, Inc., renewed 1969 by Mary Evelyn Hayes.

managed to get on without any new imperialism, though Portugal and Holland displayed a revived pride in the empires they already possessed and the latter's was administered with renewed vigor. . . .

Most simply, the sequence of imperialism after 1870 appears to have been, first, pleas for colonies on the ground of national prestige; second, getting them; third, disarming critics by economic argument; and fourth, carrying this into effect and relating the results to the neo-mercantilism of tariff protection and social legislation at home.

The Scramble for Africa
M. E. Chamberlain

The era of European imperialism in Africa (1884–1914) witnessed the military conquest of Africa by different European powers and resulted in the replacement of the various African ruling elites by Europeans. This period has generated significant interest by scholars seeking to explain imperialism by locating it squarely within the realm of European political, economic, and cultural developments. British imperialist expansion has perhaps been subject to more scholarly debates than the actions of any other imperialist power in Africa. In the following selection, Chamberlain, a noted British historian, argues that economic competition was responsible for British actions in west Africa.

> **Consider:** *The relationship between a restricted group of industrialists and the general public in the democratic politics of Great Britain; the reasons historians would regard the British actions as defensive, not offensive; how unimportant developments in Africa seem to be in this assessment.*

British participation in the Scramble in West Africa was largely defensive, to protect existing interests against new competition. But both the new challenge from the continental powers and the strength of the British response may have had their roots in more general economic factors. Whereas during the greater part of the nineteenth century there had only been one highly industrialised power, Britain, which had supplied a large part of the world with its manufacturing requirements, there were now a number of competing industrial powers. The United States was getting into its stride again after the Civil War. Germany, united in 1871, and helped by the huge indemnity exacted from the defeated French, was industrialising at a rate that left Britain standing still. Even the France of the Third Republic, although slower off the mark than Germany, was modernising quickly. As a natural result of competitive conditions, nations were once again turning to protective tariff policies. Only Britain had committed herself completely to a free trade policy in the middle of the century. For many Britons free trade had indeed become almost a religious doctrine, a necessary precondition of peace,

---

Source: M. E. Chamberlain, *The Scramble For Africa* (New York, Longman, 1974), pp. 60–62.

prosperity and international cooperation. In these circumstances Britain could hardly abandon it as an obsolete economic theory, but other nations had no such inhibitions. The United States never really relaxed the high tariffs they had put on during the abnormal circumstances of the Civil War. Germany introduced a protectionist tariff in 1879—partly, it is true, for domestic and revenue reasons. France, which had never been a whole-hearted convert to free trade, reverted to traditional protectionist duties in 1882. British traders protested time and time again that their real objection to foreign protectorates was that they meant damage to British trade arising from discriminatory duties.

A shrill note was added to the complaints of the traders, German and French, as well as British, by the background fact of the 'Great Depression.' This depression, about which economic historians still argue vigorously, was marked by low prices, low profits, low interest rates, over production of certain commodities and, irregularly, high unemployment. It affected most of western Europe. It began with a financial crisis in 1873 and lasted, with varying degrees of intensity, until 1896. Germany and Britain were badly affected in the 1870s. In France the main effect was not felt until the 1880s. In Germany the French indemnity had proved a two-edged weapon. After an initial boom hundreds of companies had gone bankrupt in 1873. By 1879 both British and German economists were seriously alarmed. The depression had already lasted longer than was normal and there seemed no way out of it. Some men in both countries began to think in terms of colonial solutions. A few bold men in Britain began to ask for 'Fair Trade,' a euphemism for the taboo word 'Protection.' They also began to ask for a parliamentary enquiry. This was eventually set up in 1885 and issued a massive report at the end of 1886. It was one of the most thorough enquiries ever conducted into the state of British industry in the nineteenth century. The Commission called for evidence, not only from government experts but also from chambers of commerce and employers' and working men's asociations. The evidence revealed deep and widespread anxieties. There was a great division of opinion as to how the crisis should be met but many spoke of the need for new markets and a few spoke specifically of the existing colonies and of the new possibilities of Africa.

It would be wrong to see a massive or articulate public demand for imperial expansion in the mid-1880s, but the climate of opinion had undoubtedly changed. Britain's industrial position was now challenged and with it the prosperity of all classes of her population, Lancashire cotton workers as much as city businessmen, and this was widely realised. There was a distinct disposition to hang on to everything Britain had and not to shrink fom new acquisitions, if this kept them out of the hands of a rival. The government was affected by this as well as the public. There was little logic about Britain's large acquisitions of territory in tropical Africa in the mid-1880s. They were essentially an anxious, even panicky, reaction to new challenges in an already worrying situation.

Imperialism in the Americas
Manuel Maldonado-Denis

While United States' historians generally present United States' involvement in Latin America as being a product of mistakes or good intentions gone awry, Latin Americans see these political and economic manipulations through a very different lens. Maldonado-Denis, a Puerto Rican historian, uses much starker Marxist concepts of imperialism to explain the subjugation of an island that is ostensibly part of the United States.

> **Consider:** *How Maldonado-Denis thinks the expansion of the United States should be viewed and understood; how U.S. interests in Puerto Rico should be understood according to Maldonado-Denis; how one might disagree with Maldonado-Denis' interpretation.*

The expansion of the United States must . . . be seen in its proper perspective as a movement destined to gain commercial, industrial, and financial hegemony in the Western Hemisphere, and, as a necessary corollary to that, naval and military bases indispensable to maintaining this hegemony. Nor can this expansionist movement to the south be seen apart from U.S. expansion to the Orient—in search of new markets in the Philippines, Hawaii, China, and other countries for its surplus products. Acquiring influence in all of these geographical areas fell within the great master plan of this empire which, according to its most fervent apologists, sought to extend to "savage and backward" people the immense benefits of its civilization. The rhetoric of the period—stripped of all pretense about the sensibilities and rights of colonized peoples—reveals that . . . North American capitalism had as its motivating force the pressing need to expand its influence beyond its borders or face crises . . . as, for example, the depression of 1893—which shook the system to its roots.

Imperialism is inherently a global system of domination. Therefore, with successful North American expansion at the end of the nineteenth century there arose a curious mixture of colonialism in the classic sense (Puerto Rico, Hawaii, the Philippines) and what we today know of as neocolonialism (as, for example, in the case of Cuba, and later Santo Domingo, Haiti, etc.) Viewed in perspective, neocolonialism did not first develop in the postwar period; at the time of the War of 1898 it was already germinating in North American foreign policy. The Monroe Doctrine, with its particular corollaries (Olney, T. Roosevelt), and "manifest destiny" are more or less comprehensive examples of the phenomenon referred to. When Olney, because of the dispute between England and Venezuela over British Guiana, issued his famous corollary—"The United States is today practically sovereign in America, and her fiat is the law in those matters in which she inter-

---

SOURCE: M. Madonado Denis, *Puerto Rico: A Socio-Historic Interpretation*, trans., E. Vialo. Translation Copyright © 1972 by Random House, Inc. Reprinted by permission of the publisher.

venes"—he unabashedly admitted that the North American hegemony was already so deeply entrenched that no other power had sufficient strength to oppose its will. . . .

Seen from this point of view, U.S. interest in Puerto Rico can be more clearly understood. First of all, . . . [f]or a system that, as we have seen, needed markets for its surplus products, the smallest of the Antilles could not be unimportant. In the second place, once the United States became a great naval power, it found it necessary to construct coaling stations, provision centers, and so forth, to enable the U.S. Navy to cross the seas with as few stops as possible. In 1891 Blaine wrote to Benjamin Harrison, "I believe that there are only three places of sufficient value to be taken: one is Hawaii and the others are Puerto Rico and Cuba." In addition, Harrison's administration considered acquiring the Dutch West Indies, the Bay of Samaná in Santo Domingo, and the St. Nicholas Mole in Haiti. This preoccupation with the acquisition of strategic areas continued to manifest itself as a major characteristic of U.S. foreign policy with the opening of the Panama Canal some years later. . . .

Therefore, to convert the Caribbean into a "North American Mediterranean" was not something alien to the concerns of the ruling North Americans. Because of her strategic position, Puerto Rico had her importance to the new empire. The same could be said for Cuba, Hawaii, and the Philippines.

The Effects of Imperialism
David Landes

Earlier in the twentieth century, historians, even those quite critical of imperialism, saw its impact mainly in European terms. In recent decades, the effects of imperialism have been viewed more from the perspective of native populations subject to imperial control. This has led to a more subtle understanding of imperialism and helps explain some of the persisting problems between the West and many "underdeveloped" or "third world" countries. This perspective is illustrated in the following selection by David Landes, an economic historian from Harvard. Here he focuses on Egypt.

> **Consider:** *The nature of the double standard described by Landes; how this double standard affected people's and nations' attitudes; whether this view fits best with a nationalistic or an economic interpretation of imperialism.*

While most Europeans in Egypt lived according to principles, they had two sets of principles: the same rules did not apply in dealing with the in-group of Westerners and the out-group of natives. Some Europeans drew the line between the two societies more sharply than others. There were those for whom the Turk was

SOURCE: David S. Landes, *Bankers and Pashas.* Reprinted by permission of Harvard University Press (Cambridge, Mass., 1958), pp. 322–323. Copyright © by David S. Landes.

of his nature treacherous, Moslem justice hopelessly corrupt, the native population mean and despicable. There were others who found the Turk not deliberately false, but lazy and neglectful; who recognized the validity of Moslem law within the framework of Egyptian society, but felt that it offered little protection to foreigners habituated to other codes and that the native tribunals were excessively submissive to government pressure; who had more sympathy than scorn for the Arab, and deplored his inadaptability to the discipline and precision implicit in modern industry and trade. Some saw in every Egyptian a potential enemy whose ill faith required constant vigilance and strong remedies; others looked upon the natives as children whose fumblings and misconduct were best handled by the paternal chastisement of their European friends and protectors. All, however, were agreed that Egyptian society was backward and Egyptian civilization inferior; that the European could not afford to submit to the customs of the country, but that the Egyptian would have to learn the ways and accept the justice of the European; that the standards of behaviour accepted in Europe, the values of honesty, fair play, reasonableness, and so on that shaped—at least in principle—the social and business relations of the West, had to be modified to fit the circumstances of a strange environment. . . .

More than anything, more even than the enormous material costs of imperialism, it was the imposition of inferior social and moral status that shaped the reaction of the Egyptian to the European. Actually, the one implies the other: material exploitation is difficult if not impossible without the sanction of a double set of values and a corresponding double code of behaviour; if they were not there to begin with, the exploiter would have to create them. The fact remains, however, that in the many-sided impact of imperialism, it is the injury to self-respect that hurts most. It is the resentment aroused by spiritual humiliation that gives rise to an irrational response to rational exploitation. The apparently unreasonable, and certainly unprofitable, resistance of many of the world's underdeveloped countries today to Western business enterprise makes sense only in this context.

Chapter Questions

1. How might you use the sources in this chapter to explain the rise of the new imperialism in the late nineteenth century?
2. In what ways was imperialism justified by Westerners? Take care to distinguish between justifications and causes.
3. What do you think were the most important consequences of imperialism during this period, for the imperialized areas of the world as well as for the imperial nations themselves?
4. Using sources from this chapter as well as from Chapter 1, compare the new imperialism with the imperial expansion of the fifteenth and sixteenth centuries. What were the similarities? What were the differences?

ELEVEN

War, Revolution, and Authoritarianism in the West, 1914–1945

Western historians usually mark the end of the nineteenth century not at the turn of the century but with the outbreak of World War I in 1914. At first, few expected the war to be so widespread or long-lasting. In the end, the destruction was so unprecedented and the fighting so brutal that one had to question whether Western civilization had progressed at all.

War strains contributed to revolutions occurring during and after the war in a number of areas, most notably in Germany, the Austro-Hungarian Empire, and Russia. The revolutions in Russia were the most important. In March 1917 the tsarist government was swept from power by relatively moderate, liberal groups. In November of that year the new Provisional Government was toppled by the Bolsheviks, who initiated a communist regime that proved surprisingly resilient. Under this government, the Soviet Union was to become a significant force in world politics.

The two decades following World War I were marked by instability and uncertainty. Except in the Soviet Union, where the Bolsheviks had taken power, it appeared that liberal democracy had been established throughout much of the West. But soon a trend toward authoritarianism appeared. The economic problems left from World War I did not disappear, despite a brief period of fragile prosperity in the mid-1920s. In 1929 the stock market crash in New York initiated the Great Depression in the United States, which quickly spread to Europe. Huge numbers of people suffered economically, and governments were pressured to effect radical solutions to the problems. Swept by uncertainty about the present and the future, societies seemed to polarize into opposing classes and around opposing ideologies.

While Communist parties spread throughout the West and were perceived as a great threat, they did not come to power outside of the Soviet Union. Authoritarian movements of the right became the most immediate danger to parliamentary democracies. The first of these movements was Mussolini's fascism, which became dominant in Italy in 1922. By the end of the decade, regimes in eastern and southern Europe were becoming more authoritarian. This trend became stronger during the Depression of the 1930s, both in Europe and Latin America. The most extreme of rightist ideologies was Hitler's Nazism, which became dominant in Germany in 1933 and spawned a totalitarian form of government there. By the end of that decade, Europe, and soon thereafter most of the West, was embroiled in a new World War even greater than World War I.

The sources in this chapter focus on four topics. The first concerns the two world wars of the period, particularly the causes and consequences of World War I. The second concerns the causes and nature of the revolutions in Russia, which eventually brought the Bolsheviks to power and transformed

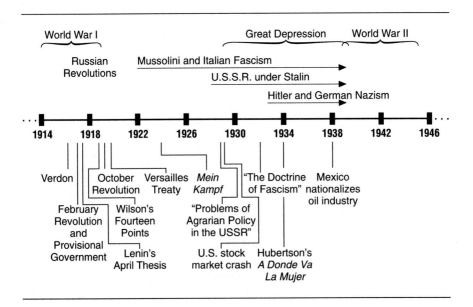

the country into the Soviet Union. The third involves some of the social and economic problems of the period, including those stemming from World War I and the Great Depression; particular attention is paid to the extent to which changes affected women. The fourth is the rise of authoritarianism and totalitarianism, with emphasis on Fascism in Italy, Nazism in Germany, and Communism under Stalin in the Soviet Union.

As the sources indicate, the period between 1914 and 1945 was traumatic for European nations in particular and of related significance for the West (including the Americas) as a whole. In following chapters we will see that this period and developments stemming from it marked a turning point in world history.

PRIMARY SOURCES

Reports from the Front: The Battle for Verdun, 1916

The widely anticipated short war typified by heroic offensive thrusts failed to materialize. Instead, it turned into a long, extraordinarily brutal struggle. On the Western front, opposing armies slaughtered each other from their trenches. There are numerous reports of life at the front, such as the following account by a French Army officer of the battle for Verdun in 1916.

> **Consider:** *Why the defense was at such an advantage; why there was a willingness to sacrifice so much for such small advances.*

The Germans attacked in massed formation, by big columns of five or six hundred men, preceded by two waves of sharpshooters. We had only our rifles and our machine guns, because the 75's could not get to work.

Fortunately the flank batteries succeeded in catching the Boches on the right. It is absolutely impossible to convey what losses the Germans must suffer in these attacks. Nothing can give the idea of it. Whole ranks are mowed down, and those that follow them suffer the same fate. Under the storm of machine gun, rifle and 75 fire, the German columns were plowed into furrows of death. Imagine if you can what it would be like to rake water. Those gaps filled up again at once. That

---

SOURCE: From *Source Records of the Great War*, vol. IV, Charles F. Horne, ed. (New York: National Alumni, 1923), pp. 222–223.

is enough to show with what disdain of human life the German attacks are planned and carried out.

In these circumstances German advances are sure. They startle the public, but at the front nobody attaches any importance to them. As a matter of fact, our trenches are so near those of the Germans that once the barbed wire is destroyed the distance between them can be covered in a few minutes. Thus, if one is willing to suffer a loss of life corresponding to the number of men necessary to cover the space between the lines, the other trench can always be reached. By sacrificing thousands of men, after a formidable bombardment, an enemy trench can always be taken.

There are slopes on Hill 304 where the level of the ground is raised several meters by mounds of German corpses. Sometimes it happens that the third German wave uses the dead of the second wave as ramparts and shelters. It was behind ramparts of the dead left by the first five attacks, on May 24th, that we saw the Boches take shelter while they organized their next rush.

We make prisoners among these dead during our counterattacks. They are men who have received no hurt, but have been knocked down by the falling of the human wall of their killed and wounded neighbors. They say very little. They are for the most part dazed with fear and alcohol, and it is several days before they recover.

The Fourteen Points
Woodrow Wilson

Each nation entered World War I for its own mixture of pragmatic and idealistic reasons. In considering their war aims and a possible peace settlement, governments did not antic- ipate the changes that would occur in this unexpectedly long and costly war. By 1918 various governments had fallen and the United States had entered the conflict. On Janu- ary 8, 1918, in an address to a joint session of the U. S. Congress, President Woodrow Wilson (1856–1924) presented his Fourteen Points, a delineation of American war aims and proposals for a peace settlement. The Fourteen Points served as a basis for debate at the Paris Peace Conference in 1919 and represented the most idealistic statement of what might be gained in a final peace settlement.

> **Consider:** *The ideals that hold these points together; the grievances recognized and unrecognized in these points; the assumptions about what measures would pre- serve peace in the postwar world.*

We entered this war because violations of right had occurred which touched us to the quick and made the life of our own people impossible unless they were

Source: Woodrow Wilson, "Fourteen Points," *Congressional Record*, vol. LVI, part I (1918), Washington, D.C.: U. S. Government Printing Office, pp. 680–681.

corrected and the world secured once for all against their recurrence. What we demand in this war, therefore, is nothing peculiar to ourselves. It is that the world be made fit and safe to live in; and particularly that it be made safe for every peace-loving nation which, like our own, wishes to live its own life, determine its own institutions, be assured of justice and fair dealing by the other peoples of the world as against force and selfish aggression. All the peoples of the world are in effect partners in this interest, and for our own part we see very clearly that unless justice be done to others it will not be done to us. The program of the world's peace, therefore, is our program; and that program, the only possible program, as we see it, is this:

I. Open covenants of peace, openly arrived at, after which there shall be no private international understandings of any kind but diplomacy shall proceed always frankly and in the public view.

II. Absolute freedom of navigation upon the seas, outside territorial waters, alike in peace and in war, except as the seas may be closed in whole or in part by international action. . . .

III. The removal, so far as possible, of all economic barriers and the establishment of an equality of trade conditions among all the nations consenting to the peace and associating themselves for its maintenance.

IV. Adequate guarantees given and taken that national armaments will be reduced to the lowest point consistent with domestic safety.

V. A free, open-minded, and absolutely impartial adjustment of all colonial claims, based upon a strict observance of the principle that in determining all such questions of sovereignty the interests of the populations concerned must have equal weight with the equitable claims of the government whose title is to be determined.

VI. The evacuation of all Russian territory and such a settlement of all questions affecting Russia as will secure the best and freest cooperation of the other nations of the world in obtaining for her an unhampered and unembarrassed opportunity for the independent determination of her own political development and national policy and assure her of a sincere welcome into the society of free nations under institutions of her own choosing; and, more than a welcome, assistance also of every kind that she may need and may herself desire.

VII. Belgium, the whole world will agree, must be evacuated and restored, without any attempt to limit the sovereignty which she enjoys in common with all other free nations. . . .

VIII. All French territory should be freed and the invaded portions restored, and the wrong done to France by Prussia in 1871 in the matter of Alsace-Lorraine, which has unsettled the peace of the world for nearly fifty years, should be righted, in order that peace may once more be made secure in the interest of all.

IX. A readjustment of the frontiers of Italy should be effected along clearly recognizable lines of nationality.

X. The peoples of Austria-Hungary, whose place among the nations we wish to see safeguarded and assured, should be accorded the freest opportunity of autonomous development. . . .

XII. The Turkish portions of the present Ottoman Empire should be assured a secure sovereignty, but the other nationalities which are now under Turkish rule should be assured an undoubted security of life and an absolutely unmolested opportunity of autonomous development. . . .

XIII. An independent Polish state should be erected which should include the territories inhabited by indisputably Polish populations. . . .

XIV. A general association of nations must be formed under specific covenants for the purpose of affording mutual guarantees of political independence and territorial integrity to great and small states alike.

In regard to these essential rectifications of wrong and assertions of right we feel ourselves to be intimate partners of all the governments and peoples associated together against the Imperialists. We cannot be separated in interest or divided in purpose. We stand together until the end.

. . . We have no jealousy of German greatness, and there is nothing in this program that impairs it. We grudge her no achievement or distinction of learning or of pacific enterprise such as have made her record very bright and very enviable. We do not wish to injure her or to block in any way her legitimate influence or power. . . .

Neither do we presume to suggest to her any alteration or modification of her institutions. But it is necessary . . . that we should know whom her spokesmen speak for when they speak to us, whether for the Reichstag majority or for the military party and the men whose creed is imperial domination.

. . . An evident principle runs through the whole program I have outlined. It is the principle of justice to all peoples and nationalities, and their right to live on equal terms of liberty and safety with one another, whether they be strong or weak. . . . The people of the United States could act upon no other principle; and to the vindication of this principle they are ready to devote their lives, their honor, and everything that they possess. The moral climax of this the culminating and final war for human liberty has come and they are ready to put their own strength, their own highest purpose, their own integrity and devotion to the test.

April Theses: The Bolshevik Strategy
V. I. Lenin

In the spring of 1917 a revolution finally toppled the disintegrating tsarist government in Russia. A relatively moderate, liberal Provisional Government was formed under the leadership of men such as Prince Lvov and Paul Miliukov. While the provisional government had to share and even compete for power with the more radical workers' political organi-

SOURCE: From V. I. Lenin, *Collected Works*, vol. XXIV (Moscow: Progress Publishers, 1964), pp. 21–24. Reprinted by permission of the Copyright Agency of the U.S.S.R.

zations—the soviets—it initially acted with speed to make important changes. However, faced with a continuing war and deep discontent, the Provisional Government soon came under attack by those such as Vladimir Ilyich Lenin (1870–1924), who called for more radical changes. Lenin, who spent much of his life as a revolutionary—often in exile—had risen to the leadership of the Bolshevik faction of the Russian Marxists. He combined the skills of a superb Marxist theoretician and a revolutionary organizer. In April 1917 the Germans aided his return to Russia in an effort to weaken the new government there. On his arrival, Lenin presented his April Theses, *at first criticized by Russian Marxists but eventually accepted by the Bolshevik Central Committee.*

> **Consider:** *Why Lenin rejects support for the Provisional Government; to whom this program might be appealing and why; the ways in which this program is particularly Marxist.*

1. In our attitude towards the war, which under the new government of Lvov and Co. unquestionably remains on Russia's part a predatory imperialist war owing to the capital nature of that government, not the slightest concession to a "revolutionary defencism" is permissible. . . .

2. The specific feature of the present situation in Russia is that the country is *passing* from the first stage of the revolution—which, owing to the insufficient class-consciousness and organisation of the proletariat, placed power in the hands of the bourgeoisie—to its *second* stage, which must place power in the hands of the proletariat and the poorest sections of the peasants. . . .

3. No support for the Provisional Government; . . .

5. Not a parliamentary republic—to return to a parliamentary republic from the Soviets of Workers' Deputies would be a retrograde step—but a republic of Soviets of Workers', Agricultural Labourers' and Peasants' Deputies throughout the country, from top to bottom. Abolition of the police, the army and the bureaucracy. The salaries of all officials, all of whom are elective and displaceable at any time, not to exceed the average wage of a competent worker.

6. The weight of emphasis in the agrarian programme to be shifted to the Soviets of Agricultural Labourers' Deputies.
Confiscation of all landed estates.
Nationalisation of *all* lands in the country, the land to be disposed of by the local Soviets of Agricultural Labourers' and Peasants' Deputies. The organisation of separate Soviets of Deputies of Poor Peasants. The setting up of a model farm on each of the large estates (ranging in size from 100 to 300 dessiatines, according to local and other conditions, and to the decisions of the local bodies under the control of the Soviets of Agricultural Labourers' Deputies and for the public account.

7. The immediate amalgamation of all banks in the country into a single national bank, and the institution of control over it by the Soviet of Workers' Deputies.

8. It is not our *immediate* task to "introduce" socialism, but only to bring social production and the distribution of products at once under the *control* of the Soviets of Workers' Deputies.

The Doctrine of Fascism
Benito Mussolini

Italy was the first European power to turn to fascism. She was one of the victors in World War I, but the war was costly and Italy did not gain much. After the war the country was marked by instability, weak governments, and an apparent threat from the left. Benito Mussolini (1883–1945), a former leader of the Socialist party and a veteran of the war, organized the Italian Fascist Party in 1919. Strongly nationalistic, the party stood against the Versailles Treaty, left-wing radicalism, and the established government. After leading his Blackshirts in a march on Rome in 1922, Mussolini was invited by King Victor Emmanuel III to form a government. Over the next few years Mussolini effectively eliminated any opposition and installed his fascist state system, which would last some twenty years. The following document contains excerpts from "The Political and Social Doctrine of Fascism," an article signed by Mussolini and written with the philosopher Giovanni Gentile that originally appeared in the Enciclopedia Italiana *in 1932. It describes the ideological foundations of Italian fascism. These excerpts emphasize the rejection of traditional democracy, liberalism, and socialism as well as faith in the authoritarian, fascist state.*

> **Consider:** *The greatest sources of appeal in the doctrine according to Mussolini; the ways in which this doctrine can be considered a rejection of major historical trends that had been developing over the previous century; the government policies that would logically flow from such a doctrine.*

Fascism, the more it considers and observes the future and the development of humanity quite apart from political considerations of the moment, believes neither in the possibility nor the utility of perpetual peace. It thus repudiates the doctrine of Pacifism—born of a renunciation of the struggle and an act of cowardice in the face of sacrifice. War alone brings up to its highest tension all human energy and puts the stamp of nobility upon the peoples who have the courage to meet it. . . .

The Fascist accepts life and loves it, knowing nothing of and depising suicide; he rather conceives of life as duty and struggle and conquest, life which should be high and full, lived for oneself, but above all for others—those who are at hand and those who are far distant, contemporaries, and those who will come after. . . .

Source: Benito Mussolini, "The Political and Social Doctrine of Fascism," *International Conciliation*, No. 306 (January 1935), pp. 7–17. Originally published by the Carnegie Endowment for International Peace, as part of the *International Counciliation Series*.

Such a conception of life makes Fascism the complete opposite of that doctrine, the base of so-called scientific and Marxian Socialism, the materialist conception of history. . . . Fascism, now and always, believes in holiness and in heroism; that is to say, in actions influenced by no economic motive, direct or indirect. . . .

Fascism repudiates the conception of "economic" happiness, to be realized by Socialism and, as it were, at a given moment in economic evolution to assure to everyone the maximum of well-being. Fascism denies the materialist conception of happiness as a possibility, and abandons it to its inventors, the economists of the first half of the nineteenth century. . . .

After Socialism, Fascism combats the whole complex system of democratic ideology, and repudiates it, whether in its theoretical premises or in its practical application. Fascism denies that the majority, by the simple fact that it is a majority, can direct human society; it denies that numbers alone can govern by means of a periodical consultation, and it affirms the immutable, beneficial, and fruitful inequality of mankind, which can be permanently leveled through the mere operation of a mechanical process such as universal suffrage. . . .

Fascism denies, in democracy, the absurd conventional untruth of political equality dressed out in the garb of collective irresponsibility, and the myth of "happiness" and indefinite progress. But, if democracy may be conceived in diverse forms—that is to say, taking democracy to mean a state of society in which the populace are not reduced to impotence in the State—Fascism may write itself down as "an organized, centralized, and authoritative democracy."

Fascism has taken up an attitude of complete opposition to the doctrines of Liberalism, both in the political field and the field of economics. . . . For if the nineteenth century was a century of individualism (Liberalism always signifying individualism) it may be expected that this will be the century of collectivism, and hence the century of the State. It is a perfectly logical deduction that a new doctrine can utilize all the still vital elements of previous doctrines. . . .

The foundation of Fascism is the conception of the State, its character, its duty, and its aim. Fascism conceives of the State as an absolute, in comparison with which all individuals or groups are relative, only to be conceived of in their relation to the State. The conception of the Liberal State is not that of a directing force, guiding the play and development, both material and spiritual, of a collective body, but merely a force limited to the function of recording results: on the other hand, the Fascist State is itself conscious, and has itself a will and a personality—thus it may be called the "ethic" State. . . .

If every age has its own characteristic doctrine, there are a thousand signs which point to Fascism as the characteristic doctrine of our time. For if a doctrine must be a living thing, this is proved by the fact that Fascism has created a living faith; and that this faith is very powerful in the minds of men, is demonstrated by those who have suffered and died for it.

Fascism has henceforth in the world the universality of all those doctrines which, in realizing themselves, have represented a stage in the history of the human spirit.

The German Woman and National Socialism [Nazism]
Guida Diehl

From the beginning, the Nazi party stood against any expansion of women's political or economic roles. Indeed the Nazi policy was to keep women in their own separate sphere as mothers and wives and remove them from jobs and politics—the man's sphere. Nevertheless, many women supported the Nazi party and joined Nazi women's organizations. The following selection is from a book published in 1933 by Guida Diehl, a leader of pro-Nazi women's organizations.

> **Consider:** *The ways this might appeal to German women; how this fits with other ideals of Nazism.*

This tumultuous age with all its difficulties and challenges must create a new type of woman capable of partaking in the achievement of the Third Reich and of fulfilling the womanly task that awaits her.

Let us not forget that this new woman holds her honor high above all else. A man's honor rests on fulfilling the tasks of public life entrusted to him. He safeguards his honor by doing his work honorably and with firmness of character and pride. A woman's honor rests on the province specifically entrusted to her, for which she is responsible, the province where new life is to grow: love, marriage, family, motherhood. A woman who does not accept this responsibility, who misuses this province for mere enjoyment, who will not let herself be proudly wooed before she surrenders—which is nature's way—who does not in marriage provide a new generation with the basis of a family—such a woman desecrates her honor. For we live in a time when womanly worth and dignity, womanly honor and pride, are of the utmost importance for the future of the nation, for the next generation. Therefore, the proud safeguarding of her honor must be an essential characteristic of this new type of woman. The German man wants to look up again to the German maid, the German woman. He wants to admire in her this dignity, this pride, this safeguarding of her honor and her heroic fighting spirit along with her native, cheerful simplicity. He wants to know again that German women and German fidelity go hand in hand, and that it is worthwhile to live and die for such German womanhood.

SOURCE: Guida Diehl, *The German Woman and National Socialism* (Eisenach, 1933), pp. 111–113, in Eleanor S. Riemer and John C. Fout, eds., *European Women: A Documentary History. 1789–1945.* New York: Schocken Books, 1980, pp. 108–109. Copyright © by Schocken Books, Inc. Reprinted by permission of Pantheon Books, a division of Random House, Inc.

The Informed Heart: Nazi Concentration Camps
Bruno Bettelheim

Organized, official racial persecution was a direct consequence of Nazi theories, attitudes, and practices. During the 1920s and early 1930s, however, the extent of the persecution was unanticipated. The most extreme form of this occurred in the late 1930s, with the introduction of forced labor and concentration camps, later to be followed by camps in which a policy of literal extermination was pursued. In the following selection, Bruno Bettelheim, a psychoanalyst in Austria at the time and later a leading psychoanalyst in the United States, describes his experiences in the concentration camps at Dachau and Buchenwald. He focuses on the dehumanizing processes involved and some of the ways prisoners adapted in an effort to survive.

> **Consider:** *The methods used to gain control over the prisoners; the psychological means developed by Bettelheim and other prisoners to cope with and survive this experience; how the existence, nature, and functioning of these camps reflect the theory and practice of Nazi totalitarianism.*

Usually the standard initiation of prisoners took place during transit from the local prison to the camp. If the distance was short, the transport was often slowed down to allow enough time to break the prisoners. During their initial transport to the camp, prisoners were exposed to nearly constant torture. The nature of the abuse depended on the fantasy of the particular SS man in charge of a group of prisoners. Still, they all had a definite pattern. Physical punishment consisted of whipping, frequent kicking (abdomen or groin), slaps in the face, shooting, or wounding with the bayonet. These alternated with attempts to produce extreme exhaustion. For instance, prisoners were forced to stare for hours into glaring lights, to kneel for hours, and so on.

From time to time a prisoner got killed, but no prisoner was allowed to care for his or another's wounds. The guards also forced prisoners to hit one another and to defile what the SS considered the prisoners' most cherished values. They were forced to curse their God, to accuse themselves and one another of vile actions, and their wives of adultery and prostitution. . . .

The purpose of this massive initial abuse was to traumatize the prisoners and break their resistance; to change at least their behavior if not yet their personalities. This could be seen from the fact that tortures became less and less violent to the degree that prisoners stopped resisting and complied immediately with any SS order, even the most outrageous. . . .

It is hard to say just how much the process of personality change was speeded

SOURCE: Bruno Bettelheim, *The Informed Heart: Autonomy in a Mass Age.* Reprinted by permission of Macmillan Publishing Co., Inc. Copyright © 1960 by The Free Press, a corporation.

up by what prisoners experienced during the initiation. Most of them were soon totally exhausted; physically from abuse, loss of blood, thirst, etc.; psychologically from the need to control their anger and desperation before it could lead to a suicidal resistance. . . .

If I should try to sum up in one sentence what my main problem was during the whole time I spent in the camps, it would be: to protect my inner self in such a way that if, by any good fortune, I should regain liberty, I would be approximately the same person I was when deprived of liberty. So it seems that a split was soon forced upon me, the split between the inner self that might be able to retain its integrity, and the rest of the personality that would have to submit and adjust for survival. . . .

I have no doubt that I was able to endure the horrors of the transport and all that followed, because right from the beginning I became convinced that these dreadful and degrading experiences were somehow not happening to "me" as a subject, but only "me" as an object. . . .

All thoughts and feelings I had during the transport were extremely detached. It was as if I watched things happening in which I took part only vaguely. . . .

This was taught me by a German political prisoner, a communist worker who by then had been at Dachau for four years. I arrived there in a sorry condition because of experiences on the transport. I think that this man, by then an "old" prisoner, decided that, given my condition, the chances of my surviving without help were slim. So when he noticed that I could not swallow food because of physical pain and psychological revulsion, he spoke to me out of his rich experience: "Listen you, make up your mind: do you want to live or do you want to die? If you don't care, don't eat the stuff. But if you want to live, there's only one way: make up your mind to eat whenever and whatever you can, never mind how disgusting. Whenever you have a chance, defecate, so you'll be sure your body works. And whenever you have a minute, don't blabber, read by yourself, or flop down and sleep."

Problems of Agrarian Policy in the U.S.S.R.: Soviet Collectivization

Joseph Stalin

Joseph Stalin (1879–1953) rose from his working-class origins to become a leading member of the Bolsheviks before the 1917 revolution, the general secretary of the Russian Communist party in 1922, and the unchallenged dictator of the U.S.S.R. by 1929. In 1927

SOURCE: J. V. Stalin, "Problems of Agrarian Policy in the U.S.S.R.," in *Problems of Leninism*, J. V. Stalin, ed. (Moscow: Foreign Languages, 1940), pp. 303–305, 318–321. Reprinted by permission of the Copyright Agency of the U.S.S.R.

Stalin and the leadership of the Russian Communist party decided on a policy for the planned industrialization of the U.S.S.R.—the First Five-Year Plan. At the same time they decided on a policy favoring the collectivization of agriculture. By 1929 Stalin made that policy more drastic, using massive coercion against the kulaks (relatively rich independent peasants). Kulaks resisted this enforced collectivization and widespread death and destruction resulted. Nevertheless, by 1932 much of Russian agriculture was collectivized. The following is an excerpt from a 1929 speech delivered by Stalin at the Conference of Marxist Students of the Agrarian Question. In it he explains and justifies the policy of collectivization and the need to eliminate the kulaks as a class.

> **Consider:** *The relations of this policy toward the kulaks to the policy for the planned industrialization of the U.S.S.R.; how Stalin justifies this policy as "socialist" as opposed to "capitalist"; the differences between Stalin's attitudes and ideas toward the kulaks and Hitler's toward the Jews.*

Can we advance our socialized industry at an accelerated rate while having to rely on an agricultural base, such as is provided by small peasant farming, which is incapable of expanded reproduction, and which, in addition, is the predominant force in our national economy? No, we cannot. Can the Soviet government and the work of Socialist construction be, for any length of time, based on two *different* foundations; on the foundation of the most large-scale and concentrated Socialist industry and on the foundation of the most scattered and backward, small-commodity peasant farming? No, they cannot. Sooner or later this would be bound to end in the complete collapse of the whole national economy. What, then, is the solution? The solution lies in enlarging the agricultural units, in making agriculture capable of accumulation, of expanded reproduction, and in thus changing the agricultural base of our national economy. But how are the agricultural units to be enlarged? There are two ways of doing this. There is the *capitalist* way, which is to enlarge the agricultural units by introducing capitalism in agriculture—a way which leads to the impoverishment of the peasantry and to the development of capitalist enterprises in agriculture. We reject this way as incompatible with the Soviet economic system. There is a second way: the *Socialist* way, which is to set up collective farms and state farms, the way which leads to the amalgamation of the small peasant farms into large collective farms, technically and scientifically equipped, and to the squeezing out of the capitalist elements from agriculture. We are in favour of this second way.

And so, the question stands as follows: either one way or the other, either *back*—to capitalism or *forward*—to Socialism. There is no third way, nor can there be. The "equilibrium" theory makes an attempt to indicate a third way. And precisely because it is based on a third (non-existent) way, it is Utopian and anti-Marxian. . . .

Now, as you see, we have the material base which enables us to *substitute* for kulak output the output of the collective farms and state farms. That is why our offensive against the kulaks is now meeting with undeniable success. That is how the offensive against the kulaks must be carried on, if we mean a real offensive and not futile declamations against the kulaks.

That is why we have recently passed from the policy of *restricting* the exploiting proclivities of the kulaks to the policy of *eliminating the kulaks as a class*.

Well, what about the policy of expropriating the kulaks? Can we permit the expropriation of kulaks in the regions of solid collectivization? This question is asked in various quarters. A ridiculous question! We could not permit the expropriation of the kulaks as long as we were pursuing the policy of restricting the exploiting proclivities of the kulaks, as long as we were unable to launch a determined offensive against the kulaks, as long as we were unable to substitute for kulak output the output of the collective farms and state farms. At that time the policy of not permitting the expropriation of the kulaks was necessry and correct. But now? Now the situation is different. Now we are able to carry on a determined offensive against the kulaks, to break their resistance, to eliminate them as a class and substitute for their output the output of the collective farms and state farms. Now, the kulaks are being expropriated by the masses of poor and middle peasants themselves, by the masses who are putting solid collectivization into practice. Now, the expropriation of the kulaks in the regions of solid collectivization is no longer just an administrative measure. Now, the expropriation of the kulaks is an integral part of the formation and development of the collective farms. That is why it is ridiculous and fatuous to expatiate today on the expropriation of the kulaks. You do not lament the loss of the hair of one who has been beheaded.

There is another question which seems no less ridiculous: whether the kulak should be permitted to join the collective farms. Of course not, for he is a sworn enemy of the collective-farm movement. Clear, one would think.

Mexico Nationalizes Its Oil Industry
Lazlo Cardenas

During the early part of the twentieth century, European and United States' companies bought up large sections of Latin American countries in search of natural resources such as copper and other heavy metals and, more significantly, oil. In the midst of the world-wide economic depression, and in an environment of growing nationalism, many Latin American countries tried to regain control over companies that controlled valued resources and enormous political power. In this excerpt, Lazlo Cardenas, the President of Mexico from 1934 to 1940, announced the reasons for the nationalization of Mexico's oil industry. Until this point, North American and British companies controlled the oil industry of this poverty-stricken nation.

> **Consider:** *How Cardenas justifies the nationalization; the effects of the foreign companies on Mexico's social, economic, and political life; how this reflects a turning inward typical of many nations during this period.*

Source: *In*: Benjamin Keane, ed. *Readings in Latin American Civilization, 1942–Present* (Houghton-Mifflin, 1967), 362–364. Used by permission.

For additional justification of the measure herein announced, let us trace briefly the history of the oil companies' growth in Mexico and of the resources with which they have developed their activities.

It has been repeated *ad nauseam* that the oil industry has brought additional capital for the development and progress of the country. This assertion is an exaggeration. For many years, throughout the major period of their existence, the oil companies have enjoyed great privileges for development and expansion, including customs and tax exemptions and innumerable prerogatives; it is these factors of special privilege, together with the prodigious productivity of the oil deposits granted them by the Nation often against public will and law, that represent almost the total amount of this so-called capital.

Potential wealth of the Nation; miserably underpaid native labor; tax exemptions; economic privileges; governmental tolerance—these are the factors of the boom of the Mexican oil industry.

Let us now examine the social contributions of the companies. In how many of the villages bordering on the oil fields is there a hospital, or school or social center, or a sanitary water supply, or an athletic field, or even an electric plant fed by the millions of cubic meters of natural gas allowed to go to waste?

What center of oil production, on the other hand, does not have its company police force for the protection of private, selfish, and often illegal interests? These organizations, whether authorized by the Government or not, are charged with innumerable outrages, abuses, and murders, always on behalf of the companies that employ them.

Who is not aware of the irritating discrimination governing construction of the company camps? Comfort for the foreign personnel; misery, drabness, and insalubrity for the Mexicans. Refrigeration and protection against tropical insects for the former; indifference and neglect, medical service and supplies always grudgingly provided, for the latter; lower wages and harder, more exhausting labor for our people. . . .

Another inevitable consequence of the presence of the oil companies, strongly characterized by their anti-social tendencies, and even more harmful than all those already mentioned, has been their persistent and improper intervention in national affairs.

The oil companies' support to strong rebel factions against the constituted government in the Huasteca region of Veracruz and in the Isthmus of Tehuantepec during the years 1917 to 1920 is no longer a matter for discussion by anyone. Nor is anyone ignorant of the fact that in later periods and even at the present time, the oil companies have almost openly encouraged the ambitions of elements discontented with the country's government, every time their interests were affected either by taxation or by the modification of their privileges or the withdrawal of the customary tolerance. They have had money, arms, and munitions for rebellion, money for the anti-patriotic press which defends them, money with which to enrich their unconditional defenders. But for the progress of the country, for establishing an economic equilibrium with their workers through a just compensation of labor, for maintaining hygenic conditions in the districts where they themselves operate, or for conserving the vast riches of the natural petroleum gases from destruction, they have neither money, nor financial possibilities, nor the desire to subtract the necessary funds from the volume of their profits.

Nor is there money with which to meet a responsibility imposed upon them by judicial verdict, for they rely on their pride and their economic power to shield them from the dignity and sovereignty of a Nation which has generously placed in their hands its vast natural resources and now finds itself unable to obtain the satisfaction of the most elementary obligations by ordinary legal means.

As a logical consequence of this brief analysis, it was therefore necessary to adopt a definite and legal measure to end this permanent state of affairs in which the country sees its industrial progress held back by those who hold in their hands the power to erect obstacles as well as the motive power of all activity and who, instead of using it to high and worthy purposes, abuse their economic strength to the point of jeopardizing the very life of a Nation endeavoring to bring about the elevation of its people through its own laws, its own resources, and the free management of its own destinies.

VISUAL SOURCES

World War I: The Home Front and Women

This picture of a British war plant gives an idea of how industrialization and technology have helped turn any extended war into a massive strain. Large factories had to be built or converted to the production of war munitions, here heavy artillery shells. A new labor force had to be trained, often involving a change of values. Here women and older men predominate to make up for the drain on manpower caused by the armed services. Finally, this picture suggests the enormous logistical organization and government cooperation with capitalist enterprises necessary to keep a modern war effort going.

The need for labor on the home front resulted in large numbers of women entering the labor force or changing jobs. The following two charts indicate the changing employment of women in Great Britain between 1914 and 1918, the first chart for all employment, the second chart for industrial employment.

> **Consider:** *The ways in which a modern war effort affects a nation's people and economy even though the war is being fought on foreign soil; the potential significance for women of these changes in employment.*

Photo 11-1

Courtesy, The Trustees of the Imperial War Museum

Chart 11-1   Women in the Labor Force, Great Britain, 1914–1918

Numbers of Women Working	In July, 1914	In July, 1918	In July, 1918, over (+) or under (−) numbers in July, 1914
On their own account or as employers	430,000	470,000	+ 40,000
In industry	2,178,600	2,970,000	+ 792,000
In domestic service	1,658,000	1,258,000	− 400,000
In commerce, etc.	505,500	934,500	+ 429,000
In national and local government, including education	262,200	460,200	+ 198,000
In agriculture	190,000	228,000	+ 38,000
In employment of hotels, public houses, theatres, etc.	181,000	220,000	+ 39,000
In transport	18,200	117,200	+ 99,000
In other, including professional employment and as home workers	542,500	652,500	+ 110,000
Altogether in occupations	5,966,000	7,311,000	+ 1,345,000
Not in occupations but over 10	12,946,000	12,496,000	− 450,000
Under 10	4,809,000	4,731,000	− 78,000
Total females	23,721,000	24,538,000	+ 817,000

Chart 11-2   Women in Industry, Great Britain, 1914–1918

Trades	Estimated number of Females employed in July, 1914	Estimated number of Females employed in July, 1918	Difference between numbers of Females employed in July, 1914, and July, 1918	Percentage of Females to total number of Workpeople employed		Estimated number of Females directly replacing Males in Jan., 1918
				July, 1914	July, 1918	
Metal	170,000	594,000	+ 424,000	9	25	195,000
Chemical	40,000	104,000	+ 64,000	20	39	35,000
Textile	863,000	827,000	− 36,000	58	67	64,000
Clothing	612,000	568,000	− 44,000	68	76	43,000
Food, drink, and tobacco	196,000	235,000	+ 39,000	35	49	60,000
Paper and printing	147,500	141,500	− 6,000	36	48	21,000
Wood	44,000	79,000	+ 35,000	15	32	23,000
China and earthenware	32,000					
Leather	23,100	197,100	+ 93,000	4	10	62,000
Other	49,000					
Government establishments	2,000	225,000	+ 223,000	3	47	197,000
Total	2,178,600	2,970,600	+ 792,000	26	37	704,000

SOURCE: *Women in Industry: Report of the War Cabinet Committee on Women in Industry.* London: His Majesty's Stationery Office, 1919.

Nazi Mythology
Richard Spitz

This is an example of Nazi propaganda art, with its characteristic blend of realistic style and romantic vision. It shows Nazi soldiers and civilian folk marching in brotherly comradeship toward Valhalla, the final resting place of Aryan heroes. Above them, Nazi flags and wounded soldiers are being lifted together toward the same heavens. Stereotypes, rather than distinct individuals, are shown. The soldiers all look almost the same, and on the right there are representatives of civilian youth, middle-aged and elderly people, farmers, and workers. Those being glorified are all males and almost all soldiers. Viewers of this picture are supposed to feel proud, to feel that sacrifices for the state will be rewarded and that the greatest glory comes from military service. In subject and style, this picture represents a rejection of the major twentieth-century artistic trends.

Consider: *How this picture fits the image and ideals of Nazism and Fascism.*

Photo 11-2

U.S. Army Photo by Garner

Socialist Realism
K. I. Finogenov

This example of socialist realism has great similarities to Nazi art: its realistic style, its romantic vision, its propagandistic purpose. In this case, however, the emphasis on economic themes is greater than that on military themes. Painted in 1935 by K. I. Finogenov, it shows Communist party and government leaders, led by Stalin, on a modern Soviet farm. On the right, an expert checks the soil. In the background a new tractor is displayed. All the figures are relatively well dressed; no one looks like a peasant farmer.

> **Consider:** *How this picture relates to the role of the government in the Soviet Union and to Stalin's place in it; what insight into the agricultural policy during the 1930s the picture is supposed to convey; how the image presented here fits with Stalin's explanation of collectivization.*

Photo 11-3

Tass from Sovfoto

Authoritarianism and Totalitarianism, 1919–1937

This map shows the spread of authoritarian and totalitarian governments in Europe between 1919 and 1937. Although no firm rules apply here, those countries retaining parliamentary democratic forms of government generally had a longer tradition of democratic institutions, were more satisfied winners in World War I, and were located in more advanced industrialized areas in northwestern Europe.

> **Consider:** *Taking account of the relevant geography, historical background, and experience of World War I, the commonalities of two or more countries that became dictatorships or changed to right-wing authoritarian regimes.*

Map 11-1   The Spread of Authoritarian Governments

Parliamentary Democracies

Communist Governments, 1917

Parliamentary Governments that became, at least temporarily, totalitarian or right-wing authoritarian regimes (with dates of change).

SECONDARY SOURCES

The Origins of World War I: Militant Patriotism
Roland Stromberg

Many observers were struck by the almost universal enthusiasm with which people greeted the news that war had been declared in August 1914. This has led some scholars to reevaluate traditional interpretations of the causes for World War I and emphasize the underlying social forces that led people to welcome its outbreak. In the following selection, Roland Stromberg, a historian of modern Europe at the University of Wisconsin, examines various attempts to explain the outbreak of war and suggests that the willingness of European peoples to go to war may have been more important than "the system of sovereign states" or any other cause for World War I.

Consider: *The explanations that Stromberg rejects and why he rejects them; how militant patriotism played a role in the outbreak of the war.*

No wonder the sudden outbreak of a major international war at the beginning of August caught everyone by surprise. Th sobering lesson was that war could happen without anybody seeming to want it or to will it. All kinds of myths grew up later, as bewildered people attempted to explain the outbreak of war. As usual, conspiracy theories flourished. In particular it was alleged that the Germans plotted war; Wilhelm II, the unhappy German monarch, was depicted in the Allied countries as a monster with tentacles reaching out to ensnare small countries. That "Prussian militarism" was the canker in the olive branch became an article of faith in France and England and later, after she had joined the war, in the United States. For their part, the Germans believed that jealous neighbors plotted to encircle and destroy a country whose only crime was her economic success.

Then, too, the theory arose that the capitalistic economic system, far from being a force for peace, had engineered the war because war was profitable or because there was competition for markets and raw materials. Although they may contain germs of truth, all such simple-minded "devil theories" must be dismissed as inadequate to the serious study of events, more interesting as folklore than as history.

Though it is tempting to look for it, no single all-embracing cause can successfully explain the war or any other major historical event. . . .

The states of Europe were like individuals living in a primeval state of nature

SOURCE: Roland N. Stromberg, *Europe in the Twentieth Century* (Englewood Cliffs, N.J.: Prentice-Hall, Inc., 1980), pp. 43–44, 74.

marked by incessant strife between one and another. They acknowledged no higher authority that might have forced them to keep the peace. What was called "international law" was not in fact binding on them, being backed by no more than a moral or customary sanction. . . .

More and more people had acquired a larger stake in defending the state. This was the natural result of democratization and increase in wealth. However imperfectly or inequitably these had come about, the large majority of citizens had some interest in defending the political community of which they were a part. All over Europe, 1914 was to prove that the masses as well as the classes were militantly patriotic when they thought their country was being attacked. . . .

Virtually no one had expected war; it came with dramatic suddenness. When it did come, . . . a sense of joy rather than of gloom prevailed. Huge cheering crowds surrounded the kaiser, stood outside Buckingham Palace, saluted departing French troops at the railroad stations, made love publicly in St. Petersburg. A Parisian observer on August 2 described a "human torrent, swelling at every corner" screaming, shouting, singing the "Marseillaise." In Berlin, crowds passed through the streets incessantly for two days singing "Deutschland über alles" and "Wacht am Rhein." A mob attacked the German embassy in St. Petersburg. An "indescribable crowd" blocked the streets around government offices in London a few minutes after midnight August 4–5, and continued to fill the streets for days. It was with exultation, not sorrow, that the peoples of Europe greeted the war, a fact that in the last analysis may go farther to explain its coming than all the details of diplomacy. . . .

Women, Work, and World War I

Bonnie S. Anderson and Judith P. Zinsser

As men were drawn into the armed forces during World War I and there were new demands for arms and other goods to support the war effort, the demand for women workers grew. Women entered the work force in great numbers, often taking jobs previously only offered to men. Historians have pointed to this as a crucial change for women, but recently other historians question how much women, in the long run, benefited from their experiences as workers during World War I. In the following excerpt from A History of Their Own, *Bonnie S. Anderson and Judith P. Zinsser argue that the changes for women were fewer and less permanent than generally assumed.*

SOURCE: Excerpts from *A History of Their Own*, vol. II, by Bonnie Anderson and Judith Zinsser. Copyright © 1988 by Harper & Row, Publishers, Inc. Reprinted by permission of Harper & Row, Publishers, Inc.

Consider: Why, according to Anderson and Zinsser, changes for women were more apparent than real, more short-term than long-lasting; how employers, governments, and the mass media undermined changes for women; how this document relates to the visual sources on the home front and women.

The improved standard of living, smaller family size, maternity benefits, protective legislation, union, and new jobs comprised the most important changes in the lives of urban working-class women between the 1870s and the 1920s. Compared to these changes, the impact of World War I (1914–1918) on these women's lives was relatively minor. While middle- and upper-class women often reported that the war freed them from nineteenth-century attitudes limiting both work and personal life, working-class women's lives changed relatively little. Unlike more privileged women, working-class women were used to earning income outside the home, and their entry into war work was more likely to be exploitative than liberating. Unlike more privileged women, working-class women and girls had rarely been shielded by a "double standard" of sexual behavior for women and men; rather, working-class women made the maintenance of the double standard possible for men of property. For working-class women in the cities, the growth of the new white-collar jobs was the one new trend fostered by the war which was not reversed afterward. Otherwise, World War I brought only a temporary suspension of the normal conditions of work outside the home, and traditional patterns returned in the postwar era.

As soon as the war broke out, European governments moved to suspend protective legislation for women for the duration. Just as nations expected working-class men to serve in the military, so they exhorted working-class women to serve in the factories, taking the places of the men who had joined the armed forces. Drawn by high wages as well as patriotism, women thronged into these new, previously male jobs. . . .

Governments initially insisted that women receive equal pay for doing a job formerly done by a man, but this policy was largely ineffective: factories tended to divide up jobs into smaller operations and pay women at a lesser rate. Women's industrial wages rose during the war, both relative to men's and absolutely, but they still remained measurable as a percentage of male earnings. In Paris, women in metallurgy earned only 45 percent of what men earned before the war; by 1918, the women earned 84 percent of what men earned. In Germany, women's industrial earnings relative to men's rose by about 5 percent. Both women and men seemed to view the changes brought by the war as temporary. After the war, the men would return to their jobs, the women would leave men's work, and all would return to normal. . . .

As soon as the war was over, all belligerent governments acted quickly to remove women from "men's" jobs. In England, these women were made "redundant" and let go; in France, they were offered a bonus payment if they left factory work; and in Germany, the government issued regulations calling for women to be dismissed before men if necessary. These policies were effective: by 1921, fewer

French and English women worked in industry than had before the war. Women's earnings decreased to return to lower percentages of men's, and the promise of "equal remuneration for work of equal value" made in the Versailles Treaty of 1919 remained a dead letter. Mass media concentrated on the relatively superficial changes in women's clothing, hair styles, and use of cosmetics and ignored the deeper continuities which structured most women's lives.

Women in Latin America
Amanda LaBarca Hubertson

The struggle for equality between the sexes was fought on many levels throughout the Western Hemisphere. In the United States, women confronted sexism in the political and economic arenas. In Latin America, machismo, the cultural glorification of male domination, was important in holding back the progress of women throughout the nineteenth and twentieth centuries. In this excerpt, from her 1934 book, A Donde Va la Mujer?, *Amanda LaBarca Hubertson, a well-known Chilean educational reformer and feminist, analyzes the progress of Latin American women and the difficulties of overcoming entrenched opposition in the larger culture.*

> **Consider:** *The "gains" and "losses" of women in Latin America; the causes for these gains and losses; how this analysis compares with that of Anderson and Zinsser.*

. . . Has feminism brought gains or losses to the Latin-American middle-class girl of today?

Gains. First of all, the consciousness of her own worth in the totality of human progress. Today's girl knows that there are no insurmountable obstacles to the flight of her intelligence; that the question of whether her entire sex is intelligent will not be raised before she is permitted to engage in any intellectual activity; that in the eyes of the majority her womanhood does not mark her with the stigma of irremediable inferiority, and that if she has talent she will be allowed to display it.

The law codes have returned to her, in large part, control over her life and property. She has well-founded hopes of seeing abolished within her lifetime the laws that still relegate her, in certain aspects, to the position of a second-class citizen, and that accord her unequal legal treatment.

She has made progress in economic liberty, basis of all independence, whether it be a question of a simple individual or one of nations. Today she is gaining admission into fields of labor forbidden to her mother. . . .

SOURCE: *In:* Benjamin Keane, ed. *Readings in Latin American Civilization, 1942–Present* (Houghton-Mifflin, 1967). Used by permission.

She has lost, in the first place, the respect of the male majority. One might say that formerly consideration for women formed part of good breeding, and it was denied only to one who by her conduct showed that she did not merit it. Today it is the only way around. In general, woman receives no tribute, and she must prove convincingly that she is a distinguished personage before receiving the homage that once was common.

Which has diminished—the respect or the quality of respectability?

It is worth one's while to analyze the point.

Men used to expect of women a stainless virtue, perfect submission—after God, thy husband, orders the epistle of St. Paul—and a life-long devotion to the orbit in which her man revolved. A saint in the vaulted niche of her home, saint to the world, mistress of her four walls, and slave to her man. In exchange for this—respect and devotion. . . .

It is unnecessary to refer again to the upheavals that the invention of machinery brought to the world, the sharp rise in the cost of living, and the pauperization of the household, which from producer was reduced to being a simple consumer. It became impossible for a man of average means to satisfy the needs of all his womenfolk, and women had to enter offices, the professions, and other remunerative employment that had been men's traditional source of income. Woman has gone out into the world, and although this fact in itself is an economic imperative and does not essentially imply the abandonment of any virtue, the ordinary man has denied her his respect. As if it were not much more difficult, and consequently more meritorious, to preserve one's purity, sweetness, and delicacy amid the turmoil of the world than in the secluded garden of the old-time home!

On entering the economic struggle she rubs shoulders with misery. Yesterday she only knew of it by hearsay. Today it bespatters her. The rawness of life surrounds her. Often she must solve the problem of staying in the path of rectitude without the help of, or even defending herself from, the man who is ready to exploit any of her weaknesses. For the ordinary man, woman's freedom is license; her equality, the right to treat her without courtesy.

She has lost in opportunities for marriage, for establishing a household, and for satisfying that yearning for maternity that is her fundamental instinct. The more cultured a woman, the more difficult for her to find a husband, because it is normal for her to seek refuge, understanding, and guidance in a person superior to herself. And the latter do not always prefer cultured women. They imagine that knowledge makes them unfeeling—an absurd notion—that it makes them domineering—which concerns not acquired knowledge but character—or that it makes them insufferably pedantic. I regret to say that here they have a little justice on their side. Knowledge is such a recent attainment of women that the majority make an excessive show of it. We play the role of the *nouveaux-riches* of the world of culture. For their wives men prefer the "old-fashioned" girl.

That is the pathos of the tragedy of middle-class women in the Latin countries. Evolution has taken place in opposition to the fundamental convictions of men, who only tolerate it—in the case of their daughters, for example—because imperious necessity dictates it, and only with profound chagrin. Men—I repeat that I speak of the majority—continue to judge women from the viewpoint of fifty years ago, and if they retain some respect and esteem in their inner beings, they tender it to the woman who remained faithful to the classic type—the woman who has progressed they place very close to those for whom they have no respect.

Red October: The Bolshevik Revolution of 1917
Robert V. Daniels

How one interprets the Russian Revolution has much to do with how one views Marxism in general and the Russian application of Marxism during the twentieth century in particular. As with the French Revolution, a body of highly ideological historiography has grown up that is difficult to separate from the times in which it was written. In the following selection, Robert Daniels, professor of Russian history at the University of Vermont, describes different schools of interpretation and emphasizes the difficulty of the task facing the Bolsheviks.

> **Consider:** *The relative strengths and weaknesses of both the official Communist and anti-Communist interpretations; how historians from each side might utilize the primary documents in this chapter to support their own views.*

The official Communist history of the revolution has held rigidly to an orthodox Marxist interpretation of the event: it was an uprising of thousands upon thousands of workers and peasants, the inevitable consequence of the international class struggle of proletariat against bourgeoisie, brought to a head first in Russia because it was "the weakest link in the chain of capitalism." At the same time it is asserted, though the contradiction is patent, that the revolution could not have succeeded without the ever-present genius leadership of Lenin. This attempt to have it both ways has been ingrained in Communist thinking ever since Lenin himself campaigned in the name of Marx for the "art of insurrection."

Anti-Communist interpretations, however they may deplore the October Revolution, are almost as heavily inclined to view it as the inescapable outcome of overwhelming circumstances or of long and diabolical planning. The impasse of the war was to blame, or Russia's inexperience in democracy, or the feverish laws of revolution. If not these factors, it was Lenin's genius and trickery in propaganda, or the party organization as his trusty and invincible instrument. Of course, all of these considerations played a part, but when they are weighed against the day by

---

SOURCE: Robert V. Daniels, *Red October: The Bolshevik Revolution of 1917* (New York: Charles Scribner's Sons, 1967), p. 215.

day record of the revolution, it is hard to argue that any combination of them made Bolshevik power inevitable or even likely.

The stark truth about the Bolshevik Revolution is that it succeeded against incredible odds in defiance of any rational calculation that could have been made in the fall of 1917. The shrewdest politicians of every political coloration knew that while the Bolsheviks were an undeniable force in Petrograd and Moscow, they had against them the overwhelming majority of the peasants, the army in the field, and the trained personnel without which no government could function. Everyone from the right-wing military to the Zinoviev-Kamenev Bolsheviks judged a military dictatorship to be the most likely alternative if peaceful evolution failed. They all thought—whether they hoped or feared—that a Bolshevik attempt to seize power would only hasten or assure the rightist alternative.

The Great Depression in Europe
James Laux

Most scholars agree that the Great Depression was very important, but they disagree over its precise significance. For Marxists, it was the greatest in a series of periodic economic crises inevitably flowing from the capitalist system and an indication that this system would soon collapse. For liberal economic historians, it was an indictment of conservative, nationalistic economic policies that would be forced to give way to modern Keynesian policies characterized by greater government activity and planning. For others, it was a crucial cause of the rise of Nazism and World War II itself. In the following selection, James Laux of the University of Cincinnati analyzes the impact of the Great Depression, emphasizing various changes in attitude that stemmed from it.

> **Consider:** *Whether, as some scholars argue, the Great Depression forced governments to modify* laissez-faire *just enough to save capitalism as a whole; why economic planning appeared more attractive after the experience of the Depression.*

The Depression, perhaps, had the most serious impact in Europe on people's thinking about economic matters. Looking back on the experience, most Europeans agreed that the orthodoxy of laissez-faire no longer held. They would not again accept the view that a government must interfere as little as possible in the operation of the economic system. Governments must accept wider responsibilities than balancing their own budgets. The value of the currency in terms of gold must give way to economic expansion if the two appear to conflict. Laissez-faire already was wheezing and laboring in the 1920s; after the decade of the 1930s it

SOURCE: James M. Laux, from "The Great Depression in Europe" (*The Forum Series*). Reprinted by permission of Forum Press (St. Louis, Mo., 1974), pp. 13–14. Copyright © 1974 by Forum Press.

was nearly prostrate. As so often happens, a philosophy came along to justify this changed attitude, a new approach to theoretical economics worked out by the Englishman John Maynard Keynes. The most influential economist of the twentieth century, Keynes published his classic work in 1936, *The General Theory of Employment, Interest and Money*. He argued that governments can and should manipulate capitalist economies, by running surpluses or deficits, by investing heavily in public works, by changing the size of the money and credit supply, and by altering rates of interest. In his analysis he emphasized the total economy, the relations among savings, investment, production, and consumption, what is called macroeconomics, rather than an investigation of a single firm or sector. A critic of socialism, Keynes scorned the significance of government ownership of production facilities, but promoted government intervention in an economy to make capitalism work better.

Bolstering this view were the remarkable production achievements of many European industrial states during the two world wars. In these crises national economies expanded military production enormously under government direction. Many asked why such techniques could not be applied in peacetime also, but to make consumer products rather than tools of destruction.

The upshot was that by 1945 if not 1939 most Europeans abandoned the idea that they lived at the mercy of an impersonal economic system whose rules could not be changed and accepted the proposition that the economy could operate the way people wanted it to. From this it was a short step to the concept of planning the future development of the economy—both the whole and particular segments of it. Economic planning became an acceptable posture for capitalist societies and enjoyed a considerable reputation. Some of those who supported it perhaps underestimated the possible merits of free markets as guiding production decisions and did seem to assume that planners somehow possess more wisdom than ordinary human beings.

Economic nationalism was a more immediate result of the Depression—the policy that short-run national economic interests have highest priority and that international economic cooperation and trade must give way before narrowly conceived national interests. Economic nationalism showed its sharpest teeth in those European states where political nationalism reached a peak—Germany, Italy, and the Soviet Union. Its strength declined in western Europe after the Second World War as people saw once again that economic prosperity among one's neighbors could bring great benefits to oneself. In an expanding continental or world economy everyone can get richer. But one wonders if economic nationalism may not revive in western Europe, especially if it seems a popular policy in a crisis.

The Great Depression had important political repercussions too. In Germany, the Depression's tragic gloom made the dynamism of the Nazi movement seem more attractive. It is difficult to imagine the Nazis achieving power without the Depression and its pervasive unemployment in the background. In France, the Depression convinced many that the regime of the Third Republic had lost its élan and relevance to twentieth-century problems, but the lack of a widely popular alternative meant that the Republic could limp along until a disastrous military defeat brought it down. In Britain, the Depression was less serious and no fundamental challenge to the political regime developed. The Conservatives held power for most of the interwar period and their failure to work actively to absorb the large unemployment that continued there until late in the 1930s brought widespread rancor and bitterness against them. Doubts as to the Conservatives' ability to manage a peacetime economy led to the first majority Labour government in the 1945 election. More profoundly, the years of heavy unemployment bred a very strong anticapitalist sentiment in much of British labor, a sentiment that led them after the war to demand moves toward socialism, such as nationalization of major industries.

The Depression helped convince Europeans that their governments must try to manage their economies. Most agreed that full employment and expanding output should be the goals. They did not agree on the means to achieve these ends.

Fascism in Western Europe
H. R. Kedward

Both fascism and communism, as they were practiced during the first half of the twentieth century, are traditionally categorized as totalitarian systems. Yet fascism is typically placed on the extreme right of the political spectrum, communism on the extreme left. Indeed, the two usually consider each other archenemies. In the following selection, H. R. Kedward, a British historian at the University of Sussex, takes account of these facts in developing and diagraming a working political definition of fascism.

> **Consider:** *Why the extreme left should be placed next to the extreme right on the political spectrum even though they consider each other enemies; the historical developments that justify using the second diagram for the twentieth century and the first for the nineteenth century; the characteristics of fascism according to Kedward.*

It could be argued that the best way to define fascism is not in a positive but in a negative way, by references to its opposites, but this too presents difficulties. At one time its opposite was naturally assumed to be communism, since fascism was said to be on the extreme Right of politics and communism on the extreme Left. This appeared self-evident when the traditional semicircle of political parties was drawn, i.e.:

Source: H. R. Kedward, *Fascism in Western Europe: 1900–1945*. Reproduced by kind permission of Blackie and Son Ltd. (Bishopbriggs, Glasgow, 1971), pp. 240–241.

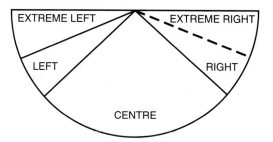

Such a diagram served the political scene of the 19th century when socialism was on the extreme Left and autocratic conservatism on the extreme Right, but in the 20th century a new diagram is needed in the form of a circle, i.e.:

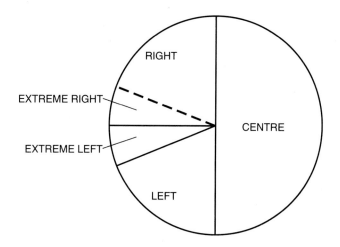

This circular image does greater justice to the realities of 20th-century politics by recognizing that extreme Left and extreme Right, communism and fascism, converge at many points and are in some cases indistinguishable. Doriot, for example, moved with ease from French communism to his Fascist P.P.F. without changing his attitudes or methods, and most of the conclusions on Nazi culture . . . could be applied to Stalinism. The circle, however, does not minimize the differences which kept the two systems apart. Travelling the longest route round the circle, it is a very long way indeed from extreme Left to extreme Right. Thus communism and fascism are as distinct in some respects as they are similar in others.

This was most clearly apparent in the Spanish Civil War. If one looked at methods, the Communists were as violent, as authoritarian and as tightly organized as the Fascists; they were both supported by dictators, Stalin on the one hand and

Hitler and Mussolini on the other, and they were both as intolerant of any deviation from the party line. They were next to each other on the circle. But if one looked at their history and their ideology the two had little in common: the Communists stood in the Marxist tradition and aimed at proletarian revolution, while the Fascists had their national values and a vision of an organic society. They were quite distinct.

Fascism therefore will only be partly defined by its opposition to communism. It is perhaps more profitable to look for its political opposites across the circle in the centre, where one finds progressive conservatism.

The Origins of World War II
Keith Eubank

The issues involved with appeasement, which have so often been a focus for analysis, lead to the broader questions of why war broke out in 1939 and whether it could have been prevented. Keith Eubank, a diplomatic historian from the City University of New York, takes a balanced approach in attempting to answer these questions.

> **Consider:** *Whether anything might have prevented war; the extent to which World War II was a direct consequence of the ideas and doctrines of Nazism rather than of political and diplomatic developments of the 1930s.*

The war that came to Europe in 1939 came because the only alternative for Hitler—when faced with a country that would not succumb to threats—was war. Hitler had promised to restore Germany to its rightful place in the world. Poland had received German territory through the Treaty of Versailles. Therefore, Hitler could not back down from Poland; he had to proceed with his objectives, and the only thing that would be able to alter his course would be war.

Many political commentators since 1939 have claimed that, if nations had acted earlier, there would have been no war. If the League had fought Japan over Manchuria, they claim, or if the League had defended Ethiopia, in 1935, or if France and Britain had invaded the Rhineland in 1936, then Hitler could not have attacked Poland. But it would have been impossible for Britain and France to have entered any kind of war—offensive or defensive, small-scale or large-scale—before 1939, because neither the people nor the governments of the two countries were conditioned to the idea of war. The only way they could accept war after 1918 was for it to be thrust upon them by a series of crises, such as those that finally culminated in the German invasion of Poland. Arguments over when and where Hitler should have been halted, then, are purely academic, because before

SOURCE: Keith Eubank, *The Origins of World War II* (Arlington Heights, IL: Harlan Davidson, Inc., 1969), pp. 166–167. Copyright © 1969 by Keith Eubank.

September 1, 1939 Hitler had done nothing that any major power considered dangerous enough to warrant precipitating a major European war.

Nor was there any existing coalition that could have opposed Hitler's massive forces. For Britain sought to appease Hitler, the French feared a repetition of the bloody sacrifices of 1914–1918, Stalin wanted an agreement with Hitler on partitioning Europe, and the United States rejected all responsibility for Europe. Peace would have been possible in 1939 only if there had existed a great military alliance, including both France and Britain, but headed by the United States and the Soviet Union, that was prepared to defend the governments of eastern Europe. But, until Hitler would force them into an alliance, capitalism and communism were prevented from cooperating to oppose nazism by their ideological differences, jealousies, suspicions, and power politics.

Chapter Questions

1. Utilizing the sources, what were some of the social, economic, and political effects of World War I?

2. In light of the evidence and interpretations presented in this chapter about the nature of authoritarianism and totalitarianism, how would you explain its appeal or relative success in the first half of the twentieth century? In what ways should Italian fascism, German nazism, and Russian communism be distinguished here?

3. In what ways do developments between 1914 and 1945 support the argument that Western civilization reached its apogee between 1789 and 1914, and that starting with World War I it was relatively on the decline? What factors might be pointed out to mitigate or counter this interpretation?

TWELVE

Asia and Africa between World Wars I and II

In Asia and Africa, the period between World War I and World War II was marked by the struggle with Western influence, by rising nationalism, and, particularly in China, by revolutionary turmoil.

The struggle with Western influence differed in various areas. In some places, such as India, southeast Asia, and Africa, both accommodation and resistance to Western colonialism were common. In Africa in particular, these were the years that produced the prototype of European colonial rule. As colonial masters, Europeans found willing collaborators amongst the African elite and the population at large. They thus no longer needed to pursue guerrilla campaigns against resisting or rebellious Africans (in west, central, and east Africa). European officials and their African agents now collected taxes and advised Africans on what to produce to meet the demands of European industrial centers. In other places, such as parts of the Middle East, the struggle was against Western imperialism. In still other places, such as Iran and Japan, the struggle was with the extent to which Western models and ideas should be copied.

The growth of nationalism was widespread throughout Asia and Africa.

West Africa, with its modern elites whose roots went back to the nineteenth century, led the way in presenting organized challenges to European hegemony. In south Africa, Kenya, and southern Rhodesia, transplanted European settlers' regimes sought to maintain control of the state, at times by opposing metropolitan plans for the colonies or by seeking metropolitan support for their interests. And throughout Africa, as people recovered from the trauma of conquest, they also presented major challenges to the colonial system which had displaced African states of the nineteenth century. In Asia, like Africa, nationalism was harnessed into the struggle with Western influence. In some places, above all Japan, nationalism was a force for political authoritarianism and foreign expansionism. Paradoxically, it was Japan that

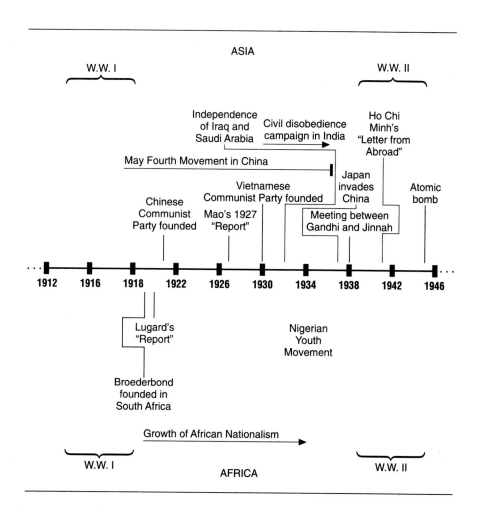

fueled nationalism and the struggle against Western colonialism by promising "liberation" while at the same time creating fear of her own empire and military strength.

Revolutionary turmoil was most prominent and of greatest significance in China, Asia's largest and most populated nation. The overthrow of the Qing (Ch'ing) dynasty in 1911 initiated a period of social, political, and military conflict that did not end until the Communists gained control in 1949. For much of that period the internal struggle was between the Kuomintang, headed by General Chiang Kai-shek, and the Chinese Communist Party, under the leadership of Mao Zedong.

The sources in this chapter focus on each of these three developments—the struggle with Western influence, the growth of nationalism, and China's revolutionary turmoil—that affected the peoples of these regions so deeply in the period between World Wars I and II. In the process, the sources will also provide insights into some of this period's social, cultural, and military developments. This sets the stage for the end of colonial rule and the realignments of power that would occur throughout the world in the years following 1945.

PRIMARY SOURCES

Japanese Nationalism and Expansionism
Hashimoto Kingoro

Japan leaped from existing in self-imposed exile until the 1850s to being one of the most militarily powerful nations in the world by the 1930s. In the course of this transformation, Japan defeated China and, more importantly, Russia in 1905, and acquired an Asian empire in its quest for equality with the colonial powers of the world. During the 1920s and 1930s, nationalist groups gained influence in Japan and elements of the military became increasingly involved in politics. Overseas, Japan followed a policy of growing adventurism and expansion.

Whatever the non-Japanese thought of Japan's territorial expansion, the vast majority of Japanese agreed with it. First, there was the attempt to be equal with the major mili-

SOURCE: Ryusaku Tsuneda, et al., eds., *Sources of Japanese Tradition* (New York and London: Columbia University Press, 1961), pp. 796–798.

tary and economic powers (Britain, the United States, France); one of the ways to accomplish that goal was to have colonies as they did. Second, there was the feeling that Japanese civilization was superior, and the rest of Asia should appreciate the exporting of it.

These sentiments are reflected in the following selection by Hashimoto Kingoro, an ultranationalist. Here he justifies Japan's foreign policy of colonial acquisition.

> **Consider:** *The appeal of this argument; Hashimoto's attitudes toward the west; why, according to Hashimoto, policies based on nationalism and expansion are justified for Japan.*

We have already said that there are only three ways left to Japan to escape from the pressure of surplus population. We are like a great crowd of people packed into a small and narrow room, and there are only three doors through which we might escape, namely emigration, advance into world markets, and expansion of territory. The first door, emigration, has been barred to us by the anti-Japanese immigration policies of other countries. The second door, advance into world markets, is being pushed shut by tariff barriers and the abrogation of commercial treaties. What should Japan do when two of the three doors have been closed against her?

It is quite natural that Japan should rush upon the last remaining door.

It may sound dangerous when we speak of territorial expansion, but the territorial expansion of which we speak does not in any sense of the word involve the occupation of the possessions of other countries, the planting of the Japanese flag thereon, and the declaration of their annexation to Japan. It is just that since the Powers have suppressed the circulation of Japanese materials and merchandise abroad, we are looking for some place overseas where Japanese capital, Japanese skills and Japanese labor can have free play, free from the oppression of the white race.

We would be satisfied with just this much. What moral right do the world powers who have themselves closed to us the two doors of emigration and advance into world markets have to criticize Japan's attempt to rush out of the third and last door?

If they do not approve of this, they should open the doors which they have closed against us and permit the free movement overseas of Japanese emigrants and merchandise. . . .

At the time of the Manchurian incident, the entire world joined in criticism of Japan. They said that Japan was an untrustworthy nation. They said that she had recklessly brought cannon and machine guns into Manchuria, which was the territory of another country, flown airplanes over it, and finally occupied it. But the military action taken by Japan was not in the least a selfish one. Moreover, we do not recall ever having taken so much as an inch of territory belonging to another nation. The result of this incident was the establishment of the splendid new nation of Manchuria. The Powers are still discussing whether or not to recognize this new nation, but regardless of whether or not other nations recognize her, the Manchurian empire has already been established, and now, seven years after its creation, the empire is further consolidating its foundations with the aid of its friend, Japan.

And if it is still protested that our actions in Manchuria were excessively violent, we may wish to ask the white race just which country it was that sent warships and troops to India, South Africa, and Australia and slaughtered innocent natives, bound their hands and feet with iron chains, lashed their backs with iron whips, proclaimed these territories as their own, and still continues to hold them to this very day?

They will invariably reply, these were all lands inhabited by untamed savages. These people did not know how to develop the abundant resources of their land for the benefit of mankind. Therefore it was the wish of God, who created heaven and earth for mankind, for us to develop these undeveloped lands and to promote the happiness of mankind in their stead. God wills it.

This is quite a convenient argument for them. Let us take it at face value. Then there is another question that we must ask them.

Suppose that there is still on this earth land endowed with abundant natural resources that have not been developed at all by the white race. Would it not then be God's will and the will of Providence that Japan go there and develop those resources for the benefit of mankind?

And there still remain many such lands on this earth.

The Chinese Communist Party Mobilizes the Masses

Mao Zedong (Mao Tse-tung)

During the decades between World War I and World War II, China experienced great instability. This environment fostered new political and social movements, one of which was Chinese Communism. The Chinese Communist Party grew after 1927, especially after 1935 under the leadership of Mao Zedong (Mao Tse-tung, 1893–1976). Though its fortunes ebbed and flowed, eventually it would achieve victory. One of the reasons the Chinese Communist Party was able to achieve victory was its recognition, very early in its history, that the Chinese farmer (peasant) would be a major revolutionary force. This was in direct opposition to the orthodox teachings of Karl Marx and Vladimir Lenin, which argued that only an industrial proletariat could be the vanguard of any socialist revolution. The problem in China, however, was that in the 1920s the urban proletariat represented a minute fraction of the workforce where the rural population accounted for over 80 percent of the people. More problematic than the numbers, though, was the Marxist-Leninist view that rural people were not sufficiently politicized or capable of being a revolutionary force.

SOURCE: Mao Tse-tung, *Selected Works of Mao Tse-tung*, vol. I (Peking: Foreign Languages Press, 1965), pp. 23–28.

Although not the first to recognize this, Mao Zedong came to realize the potential of these farmers after visiting his home province of Hunan in 1927. The first selection is from Mao's report of that trip.

Consider: *The concerns of Chinese peasants; why it might be difficult to see poor farmers as a political force; what kinds of persuasion had to be utilized to get the farmers to see themselves as a revolutionary force.*

During my recent visit to Hunan I made a first-hand investigation of conditions. . . . [T]he present upsurge of the peasant movement is a colossal event. In a very short time, . . . several hundred million peasants will rise like a mighty storm, like a hurricane, a force so swift and violent that no power, however great, will be able to hold it back. They will smash all the trammels that bind them and rush forward along the road to liberation. They will sweep all the imperialists, warlords, corrupt officials, local tyrants and evil gentry into their graves. Every revolutionary party and every revolutionary comrade will be put to the test, to be accepted or rejected as they decide. There are three alternatives. To march at their head and lead them? To trail behind them, gesticulating and criticizing? Or to stand in their way and oppose them? Every Chinese is free to choose, but events will force you to make the choice quickly. . . .

The main targets of attack by the peasants are the local tyrants, the evil gentry and the lawless landlords, but in passing they also hit out against patriarchal ideas and institutions, against the corrupt officials in the cities and against bad practices and customs in the rural areas. In force and momentum the attack is tempestuous; those who bow before it survive and those who resist perish. . . . With the collapse of the power of the landlords, the peasant associations have now become the sole organs of authority and the popular slogan "All power to the peasant associations" has become a reality. Even trifles such as a quarrel between husband and wife are brought to the peasant association. . . .

. . . [T]he great peasant masses have risen to fulfil their historic mission and that the forces of rural democracy have risen to overthrow the forces of rural feudalism. The patriarchal-feudal class of local tyrants, evil gentry and lawless landlords has formed the basis of autocratic government for thousands of years and is the cornerstone of imperialism, warlordism and corrupt officialdom. To overthrow these feudal forces is the real objective of the national revolution. In a few months the peasants have accomplished what Dr. Sun Yat-sen wanted, but failed, to accomplish in the forty years he devoted to the national revolution. . . .

. . . The peasants are clear-sighted. Who is bad and who is not, who is the worst and who is not quite so vicious, who deserves severe punishment and who deserves to be let off lightly—the peasants keep clear accounts, and very seldom has the punishment exceeded the crime. Secondly, a revolution is not a dinner party, or writing an essay, or painting a picture, or doing embroidery; it cannot be so refined, so leisurely and gentle, so temperate, kind, courteous, restrained and magnanimous. A revolution is an insurrection, an act of violence by which one class overthrows another. A rural revolution is a revolution by which the peasantry overthrows the power of the feudal landlord class. Without using the greatest force, the peasants cannot possibly overthrow the deep-rooted authority of the landlords which has lasted for thousands of years. The rural areas need a mighty revolutionary upsurge, for it alone can rouse the people in their millions to become a powerful force.

Women and Chinese Communism
Shan-fei and Agnes Smedley

When dynastic rule in China collapsed in 1911, a cultural, social, and political vacuum was created because no new societal forms were available to replace what had just been discredited.

One of the newest ideas was the equality of women and no one supported that idea more than the Chinese Communist Party. While it was largely urban women that initially joined this movement, some rural women did as well; but only in cases where male family members were absent or were extraordinarily progressive. Even for the women who joined the communist party, total equality was never to be achieved. Nevertheless, the status of these women increased dramatically, if for no other reason than because their original status was so low. Women connected to the party were given positions, responsibilities, and had some power, however limited.

This selection was written by American journalist Agnes Smedley who spent many years in China recording the stories of the people she met. Although somewhat romanticized—because Smedley herself tended to see communist women in a romantic fashion—it nonetheless portrays the changes that some women were able to make in the 1920s and 1930s.

Consider: *The consequences to a society when one of its major tenets is radically altered.*

This is the story of Shan-fei, daughter of a rich landowner of Hunan, China. Once she went to school and wore silk dresses and had a fountain pen. But then she became a Communist and married a peasant leader. In the years that followed she—but I will begin from the beginning—

Her mother is the beginning. A strange woman. She was old-fashioned, had bound feet, and appeared to bow her head to every wish of her husband who held by all that was old and feudal. Yet she must have been rebellious. She watched her sons grow up, go to school, and return with new ideas. Some of these new ideas were about women—women with natural feet, who studied as men did, who married only when and whom they wished.

When her sons talked the mother would sit listening, her eyes on her little

SOURCE: Agnes Smedley, *Chinese Destinies. Sketches of Present Day China* (New York: The Vanguard Press, 1933), pp. 35–42.

daughter, Shan-fei, . . . we know that at last she died for the freedom of her daughter.

This battle was waged behind the high stone walls that surrounded her home. The enemy was her husband and his brothers. And the mother's weapons were the ancient weapons of subjected women: tears, entreaties, intrigue, cunning. At first she won but one point: her husband consented to Shan-fei's education, provided the teacher was an old-fashioned man who came to the home and taught only the Chinese characters. But Shan-fei's feet must be bound, and she must be betrothed in marriage according to ancient custom. . . .

Until Shan-fei was eleven years old, her father ruled as tyrants rule. But then he suddenly died. Yet the funeral was not finished before the bandages were taken off the feet of the little girl, and the earth on the grave was still damp when Shan-fei was put in a school one hundred *li* away. . . .

. . . [T]he news came that Shan-fei had led a students' strike against the corrupt administration of her school. She was nearing sixteen at the time, the proper age for marriage. Yet she was expelled in disgrace from the school, and returned home with her head high and proud. And her mother, instead of subduing her, whispered with her alone, then merely transferred her to a still more modern school in far-away Wuchang on the Yangzi (Yangtze) where rumor further had it that she was becoming notorious as a leader in the students' movement. Moreover, men and women students studied together in Wuchang.

. . . [In] the late summer of 1926, . . . China was swept by winds of revolution. . . . Shan-fei gave up her studies and . . . became a member of the Communist Youth, and in this work she met a peasant leader whom she loved and who was loved by the peasants. She defied the old customs . . . and announced her free marriage to the man she loved. . . .

In those days the Guomindang (Kuomintang) and the Communist Parties still worked together, and, as one of the most active woman revolutionaries, Shan-fei was sent back to her ancestral home as head of the Woman's Department of the Guomindang. There she was made a member of the Revolutionary Tribunal that tried the enemies of the revolution, confiscated the lands of the rich landlords and distributed them among the poor peasants. She helped confiscate all the lands of her own family and of the family of her former fiancé.

When the revolution became a social revolution, the Communists and the Guomindang split, and the dread White Terror began. . . . Shan-fei worked openly as the head of the Woman's Department of the Guomindang; secretly, she carried on propaganda amongst the troops and the workers. Then in this city the chief of the judicial department met her and fell in love with her. He was a rich militarist, but she listened carefully to his lovemaking and did not forget to ask him about the plans to crush the peasants. He told her—and she sent the news to the peasant army beyond. One of the leaders of this army beyond was her husband.

Letter from Abroad: Revolutionary Nationalism in Vietnam

Ho Chi Minh

With the Japanese, French, and Chinese all busy warring amongst themselves, the Viet-namese nationalists saw an opportunity to aggressively pursue their struggle for inde-pendence. Moreover, the ease with which the Japanese overcame the French forces early in World War II demonstrated the latter's severe vulnerability. Nationalists used this to rally to their cause more people—particularly those who believed that the Vietnamese would never possess the capabilities to overcome French colonial rule.

Ho Chi Minh (1892–1969), who founded the Indochinese Communist Party in 1930, understood that now was the time to strike. Consequently, in May, 1941, the Viet Nam Doc Lap Dong Minh Hoi (Vietnamese Independence League)—or Viet Minh—was estab-lished. On June 6th, Ho Chi Minh, then in southern China, issued this "Letter from Abroad" as a clarion call to his countrymen and women to combine nationalism with revolutionary goals as the only means to achieve independence.

Consider: *The force of Ho's appeal; how this must have sounded to those looking for leadership in the struggle against colonialism.*

Venerable elders!
Patriotic personalities!
Intellectuals, peasants, workers, traders and soldiers!
Dear fellow-countrymen!

Since France was defeated by Germany, its power has completely collapsed. Nevertheless, with regard to our people, the French rulers have become even more ruthless in carrying out their policy of exploitation, repression and massacre. They bleed us white and carry out a barbarous policy of all-out terrorism and massacre. In the foreign field, bowing their heads and bending their knees, they resign themselves to ceding part of our land to Siam and shamelessly surrendering our country to Japan. As a result our people are writhing under a double yoke of oppression. They serve not only as beasts of burden to the French bandits but also as slaves to the Japanese robbers. Alas! What sin have our people committed to be doomed to such a wretched fate? Plunging into such tragic suffering, are we to await death with folded arms?

No! Certainly not! The twenty-odd million descendants of the Lac and the Hong are resolved not to let themselves be kept in servitude. For nearly eighty years under the French pirates' iron heels we have unceasingly and selflessly

---

SOURCE: Ho Chi Minh, *Ho Chi Minh. Selected Writings, 1920-1969,* "Letter From Abroad," June 6, 1941 (Hanoi: Foreign Languages Publishing House, 1977), pp. 44–46.

struggled for national independence and freedom. . . . The recent uprisings in the South and at Do Luong and Bac Son testify to the determination of our compatriots to follow the glorious example of their ancestors and to annihilate the enemy. If we were not successful, it was not because the French bandits were strong, but only because the situation was not yet ripe and our people throughout the country were not yet of one mind.

Now, the opportunity has come for our liberation. France itself is unable to help the French colonialists rule over our country. As for the Japanese, on the one hand, bogged down in China, on the other, hampered by the British and American forces, they certainly cannot use all their strength against us. If our entire people are solidly united we can certainly get the better of the best-trained armies of the French and the Japanese. . . .

Dear fellow-countrymen! A few hundred years ago, in the reign of the Tran, when our country faced the great danger of invasion by Yuan armies the elders ardently called on their sons and daughters throughout the country to stand up as one man to kill the enemy. Finally they saved their people and their glorious memory will live for ever. Let our elders and patriotic personalities follow the illustrious example set by our forefathers. . . .

The hour has struck! Raise aloft the banner of insurrection and lead the people throughout the country to overthrow the Japanese and the French! The sacred call of the Fatherland is resounding in our ears; the ardent blood of our heroic predecessors is seething in our hearts! The fighting spirit of the people is mounting before our eyes! Let us unite and unify our action to overthrow the Japanese and the French.

The Vietnamese revolution will certainly triumph!

The world revolution will certainly triumph!

Hindus, Muslims, and Nationalism in India
Mohandas K. Gandhi

While the European colonial nations were recovering from the First World War and, shortly thereafter, trying to avoid a second world war, Indian nationalists were trying to develop their movement for independence. During these two decades, the nationalist movement was shaken by a split in the ranks between Hindus and Muslims. Muslims felt that they would be a minority in an Indian state that encompassed all of British India. To protect their rights, they wanted a separate Muslim state, Pakistan.

Hindus objected, fearing that two countries would be weaker than a single, large nation. Additionally, the split caused growing concern about the possibility of communal violence. Perhaps no one was more concerned about the possibilities of violence than Mo-

SOURCE: M. K. Gandhi, *Communal Unity* (Ahmedabad: Navajivan Publishing House, 1949), pp. 217–218.

handas K. Gandhi (1869–1948), the most important Indian leader of the period. The following is a statement made by Gandhi in 1938 just prior to a meeting with Mohammed Ali Jinnah, leader of India's Muslim League.

> **Consider:** *Why Gandhi's views might be appealing; how Gandhi tries to gain credibility for his views; the problems this statement reflects.*

My Hinduism is not sectarian. It includes all that I know to be best in Islam, Christianity, Buddhism, and Zoroastrianism. I approach politics as everything else in a religious spirit. Truth is my religion and *ahimsa* is the only way of its realization. I have rejected once and for all the doctrine of the sword. The secret stabbings of innocent persons, and the speeches I read in the papers are hardly the thing leading to peace or an honourable settlement.

Again I am not approaching the forthcoming interview in any representative capacity. I have purposely divested myself of any such. If there are to be any formal negotiations, they will be between the President of the Congress and the President of the Muslim League. I go as a lifelong worker in the cause of Hindu-Muslim unity. It has been my passion from early youth. I count some of the noblest of Muslims as my friends. I have a devout daughter of Islam as more than a daughter to me. She lives for that unity and would cheerfully die for it. I had the son of the late Muazzin of the Juma Masjid of Bombay as a staunch inmate of the Ashram. I have not met a nobler man. His morning *Azan* in the Ashram rings in my ears as I write these lines during midnight. It is for such reasons that I wait on Shree Jinnah.

I may not leave a single stone unturned to achieve Hindu-Muslim unity. God fulfils Himself in strange ways. He may, in a manner least known to us, both fulfil Himself through the interview and open a way to an honourable understanding between the two communities. It is in that hope that I am looking forward to the forthcoming talk. We are friends, not strangers. It does not matter to me that we see things from different angles of vision. I ask the public not to attach any exaggerated importance to the interview. But I ask all lovers of communal peace to pray that the God of truth and love may give us both the right spirit and the right word and use us for the good of the dumb millions of India.

Indirect Rule in Nigeria
Lord Frederik Lugard

The early literature on the colonial period in Africa focused almost exclusively on the effectiveness of and differences between those colonial governments that practiced direct rule (Portuguese and French) and those run by indirect rule (British). Recent historiography notwithstanding, in the 1930s and 1940s, British intellectuals and colonial adminis-

---

SOURCE: Frederick John D. Baron. *The Dual Mandate in British Tropical Africa* (London: F. Cass, 1965).

trators generally supported a system that relied on traditional African rulers to act as intermediaries between colonial administrators and the mass of African producers and workers. In the following excerpt from a 1920 report, Lord Lugard, the architect of the indirect rule system in Nigeria, describes the system of "Native Administration" which was to be implemented in Nigeria during the interwar years.

> **Consider:** *Why Lord Lugard thought the system would succeed; the responses Africans might have had to the system; European visions of their role in Africa.*

The system of Native Administration in the separate Government of Northern Nigeria had been based on the authority of the Native Chiefs. The policy of the Government was that these Chiefs should govern their people, not as independent but as dependent Rulers. The orders of Government are not conveyed to the people through them, but emanate from them in accordance, where necessary, with instructions received through the Resident. While they themselves are controlled by Government in matters of policy and of importance, their people are controlled in accordance with that policy by themselves. A political Officer would consider it as irregular to issue direct orders to an individual native, or even to a village head, as a General commanding a division would to a private soldier, except through his commanding officers. The courts administer native law, and are presided over by Native Judges (417 in all). Their punishments do not conform to the Criminal Code, but, on the other hand, native law must not be in opposition to the Ordinances of Government, which are operative everywhere, and the courts . . . are under the close supervision of the District Staff. Their rules of evidence and their procedure are not based on British standards, but their sentences, if manifestly faulty, are subject to revision. Their prisoners are confined in their own gaols, which are under the supervision of the British Staff. The taxes are raised in the name of the native ruler and by his agents, but he surrenders the fixed proportion to Government, and the expenditure of the portion assigned to the Native Administration, from which fixed salaries to all native officials are paid, is subject to the advice of the Resident, and the ultimate control of the Governor. The attitude of the Resident is that of a watchful adviser not of an interfering ruler, but he is ever jealous of the rights of the peasantry, and of any injustice to them.

Resentment in Colonial Nigeria
Obafemi Awolowo

The interwar period was a time when Africans in all the colonial regions were facing the realities of European colonial occupation. For the majority of Africans, colonialism meant forced cultivation of agricultural products and migrant labor in mines and plantations

---

SOURCE: Obafemi Awolowo, AWO: *The Autobiography of Chief Obafemi Awolowo* (Cambridge, Cambridge University Press, 1960), pp. 113, 115–116.

owned and operated by Europeans. There were restrictions in all areas of occupational specialization. Moreover, legal codes enforced residential segregation and second-class citizenship for the few Africans who survived the array of examinations required from early childhood onward. As a result of their frustration with the colonial system, Africans began to organize to challenge colonialism. The following selection from Chief Awolowo's autobiography reveals some of the contending aspects of African resentment in colonial Nigeria during the 1930s.

> **Consider:** *What Awolowo's recollections suggest about the strategies Africans adopted; what this illustrates about African perceptions of colonial rule; the role of the educated elite in the emergence of anticolonial sentiments.*

The Nigerian Youth Movement was the first nationalist organisation ever to make real efforts to bring within its fold all the nationalists and politically conscious elements in Nigeria. . . .

In 1934, the Nigerian Government inaugurated the Yaba Higher College. This institution, which was not affiliated to any British university, was to award its own Nigerian diplomas in a number of faculties, including medicine, arts, agriculture, economics and engineering. This institution was assailed by Nigerian nationalists. In the first place, it was inferior in status to a British university; and under no circumstance would an institution of higher learning which bore the stamp of inferiority be tolerated by Nigerians. In the second place, the diplomas to be awarded by the institution were also inferior, since the holders of these diplomas were only expected, in various government departments and institutions, to occupy posts which were permanently subordinate to those filled by the holders of British university degrees (mostly expatriates) in the same faculties and professions. Africanisation of the civil service had been in the air for some time, and it was believed that the Yaba Higher College was an infernal device by British imperialism to foil this legitimate aspiration. This view was further strengthened by the fact that, only five years previously, the Nigerian government had planned to introduce a Nigerian School Certificate in place and to the exclusion of the then Cambridge and Oxford School Certificates. The plan was dropped as a result of the undivided opposition to it by all the political leaders in Lagos, irrespective of their party leanings, . . . In the third place, the diplomas to be awarded by the college would only enjoy an inferior recognition in Nigeria and would not command any respect, much less recognition, outside the country. In the fourth place, though the diplomas were in all respects to be inferior to university degrees, the time required to do a course was longer than was the case for a university degree in the same subject. There was, therefore, widespread resentment in political circles in Lagos, and in some circles in Southern Nigeria. It was in order to canalise this resentment, and to present a united front to the Nigerian government in representing the feelings of the people, that the Lagos Youth Movement was founded by Dr. J. C. Vaughan, Mr. Ernest Ikoli, Oba Samuel Akisanya, and others. I remember the memorandum submitted by the Lagos Youth Movement, the

Movement's rejoinder to the government's reply, and Oba Samuel Akisanya's open letter to Duse Mohammed Ali Effendi, who in his paper *Comet* had criticised the leaders of the Movement and had described them as "half-baked critics." All these remonstrances were analytical, constructive, scathing and crushing. In them, the Movement elaborated its reasons for opposing the establishment of the college as it was then constituted, and made suggestions for its improvement. The Nigerian government, however, persisted in going on with its scheme as originally conceived. The Lagos Youth Movement, on the other hand, continued in existence to initiate and conduct agitations against other unjust manifestations of British rule in Nigeria. In 1936, as a result of clamour from different parts of the country, the name "Lagos Youth Movement" was changed to "Nigerian Youth Movement."

VISUAL SOURCES

The Foolish Old Man Removes the Mountain
Xiu Beihong (Hsu Pei-hung)

The cultural vacuum created in China after the 1911 revolution also extended to art. For the first time, Chinese artists began to seriously study European art and some went to study in Europe. Soon schools were established in China—the most famous being the Tian Han (T'ien Han) Academie du Midi in Nanjing (Nanking)—that bridged the two traditions.

In 1927 this school invited artist Xu Beihong (Hsu Pei-hung) to establish a fine arts department. Xu had studied in Paris and Berlin and soon after his return had began painting Chinese historical subjects in oils in the European tradition. His paintings reflected the dilemma of modernization for modern Chinese artists. Before too long he returned to some of the traditional Chinese methods and eventually developed a style which combined European realism with Chinese brushwork.

The selection below is a good example of this syncretic method. Painted in the late 1930s, this scroll depicts the old Daoist (Taoist) tale whose moral is that everything is possible. The story was also a favorite of Mao Zedong (Mao tse-tung) who liked to tell it when he was trying to empower the peasantry of China.

Consider: *Why Mao may have found these paintings appealing; the difficulties of finding new cultural patterns when the traditional ones have been discarded.*

Photo 12-1

From: Michael Sullivan, *The Meeting of Eastern and Western Art* (Berkeley: UCLA Press, 1982).

Western Technology and Christianity in Colonial Africa

During the period of conquest and early colonial years, western nations brought not only their troops and administrators but their technology, religion, and attitudes to Africa. Europeans usually assumed that their own institutions were superior to African institutions. These European institutions were often spread by apparently well-meaning individ-

Photo 12-2

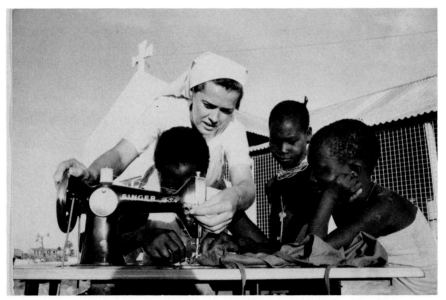

Marc & Evelyne Bernheim/Woodfin Camp & Associates.

uals who believed they were improving the lot of the colonized Africans. This is reflected in this photograph of a Christian missionary showing young Africans how to use a sewing machine.

> **Consider:** *The effects of this introduction of Christianity and technology on African society; the importance of the connection between Christianity, technology, and the role this missionary is playing.*

The Expansion of Japan

Ever since Japan emerged from its self-imposed isolation in the middle of the nineteenth century, one of its major goals was to achieve equality with the major powers in the world. Given that period in history, one key way to achieve that was to acquire a colonial

Map 12-1

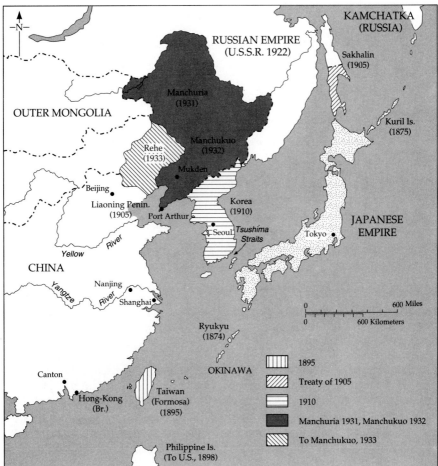

Map 12-2

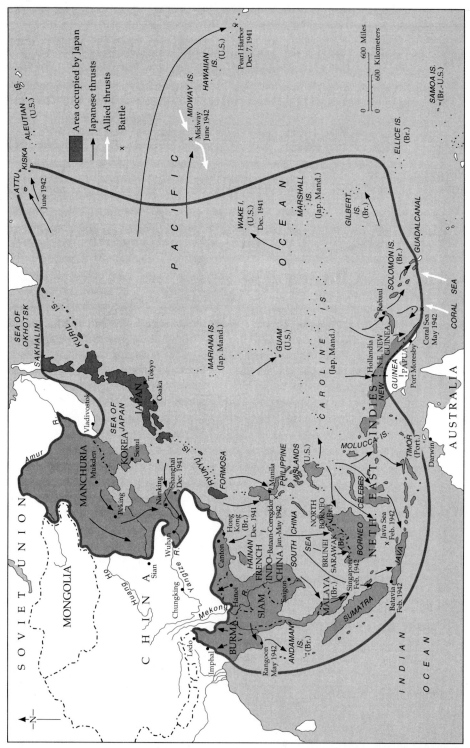

empire. As revealed by the first map, Japan initiated its expansion in the last quarter of the nineteenth century, continued during the first decade of the twentieth century after its successes in the Sino-Japanese War of 1894–1895 and the Russo-Japanese War of 1904–1905, and pushed on during the early 1930s with acquisitions in Manchuria and northern China. As indicated by the second map, by 1942 Japan was in control of a vast empire and was involved in World War II. Japan's defeat in that war would spell the end of its empire and reduce Japan almost to its mid-nineteenth-century boundaries.

> **Consider:** *The possible reasons the Japanese might have used to justify the expansion shown by these maps; ways this expansion may have made Japan increasingly vulnerable.*

SECONDARY SOURCES

Asia in World War I
L. M. Panikkar

Although the war of 1914–1918, otherwise known as World War I, did not take place in Asia, Asia was not unaffected. The colonized nations of Asia were forced to join their colonial masters in the war, while China and Siam allied themselves with what they believed would be the winning side. Japan had treaty obligations. The Asian war effort consisted of dispatching soldiers from the colonized nations or labor brigades from nations such as China. Japan sent neither, but helped protect British interests in Asia, took over German interests, and economically replaced European businesses unable to continue in east Asia.

The war had considerable consequences for Asia and in the selection below, L. M. Panikkar, the well-known Indian scholar and diplomat, describes them.

> **Consider:** *The Asian perception of this war according to Panikkar; the effects on Asians of the ending of the myth of European supremacy.*

The Great War of 1914–18 was from the Asian point of view a civil war within the European community of nations. The direct participation of Asian countries, during some stages of this conflict, was at the invitation and by the encouragement of one of the parties, the *entente* Powers, and was greatly resented by the Germans. . . . [A]t the beginning of the twentieth century . . . European nations . . . remained

---

SOURCE: L. M. Panikkar, *Asia and Western Dominance* (New York, Unwin Hyman, an imprint of HarperCollins Publishers Limited).

unshakably convinced that they had inherited the earth, . . . It was the age of Kipling and the white man's burden, and it seemed the manifest destiny of the white race to hold the East in fee.

In 1914, when the German invaders had reached the Marne, divisions of the Indian Army under British officers had been rushed to France. . . . Later, they were extensively used in the defence of the Suez Canal and the Middle East and in campaigns elsewhere in Africa. In 1917, Siam declared war on Germany. An Indo-Chinese labour force had been recruited and was working in France. On August 14, 1917, China also joined the Allies. . . . However, opinion in India, China and even in Japan was at the time more pro-German than pro-Ally. In India, . . . public opinion rejoiced at every report of German victory and felt depressed when the Allies were winning. . . . [P]ublic opinion in the East looked upon the conflict as a civil war in which neither party had a claim to the friendship of the peoples of Asia, and if any party could appeal to the sympathy of Asians it was the Germanic alliance which had no tradition of Asian conquest and was allied with the chief Muslim Power, Turkey.

But the participation of Asian people in the war had far-reaching consequences. The Indian soldier who fought on the Marne came back to India with other ideas of the *Sahib* than those he was taught to believe by decades of official propaganda. Indo-Chinese Labour Corps in the South of France returned to Annam with notions of democracy and republicanism which they had not entertained before. Among the Chinese who went to France at the time was a young man named Chou En-lai [Zhou Enlai], who stayed on to become a Communist and had to be expelled for activities among the members of the Chinese Labour Corps. . . .

Politically, a further weakening of the colonial and imperialist position came about as a result of President Wilson's declaration of fourteen points. In 1917, the doctrine of the "self-determination of peoples" had the ring of a new revelation. . . . [I]n Asia it was acclaimed as a doctrine of liberation. . . .

Apart from these political considerations economic forces generated by the war were also helping to undermine the supremacy of the West. Japan utilized the four years of war for a planned expansion of her trade in the East. India gained her first major start on the industrial road and, with the strain on British economy, Indian national capital was placed in a position of some advantage. . . .

[T]he growth of a powerful left-wing movement in the countries of Western Europe had a direct effect on shaping events in the Eastern Empire. The Labour Party in England during the days of its growth had been closely associated with the nationalist movement in India. . . . Annamite nationalism had worked hand in hand with left-wing parties in France. . . . [T]he influence of the Russian Revolution. Imperialism meant something totally different after Lenin's definition of it as the last phase of capitalism and his insistence that the liberation of subject peoples from colonial domination was a part of the struggle against capitalism. Also, Russia's call for and practice of racial equality, abolition of the special privileges that Tsarist Russia had acquired in Persia and China, . . . made it difficult for Western nations which had so long claimed to stand for liberty and progress to deny the claims of Eastern nations. . . .

One fact which stands out clear and illustrates this chasm in thought is the lack of faith in imperialist ideals in the period that followed the war. With the solitary exception of Churchill, there was not one major figure in any of the British parties who confessed to a faith in the white man's mission to rule. Successive Viceroys of India, Liberal, Conservative and non-party, professed publicly their adherence to the cause of Indian freedom. . . . There was no conviction left of the European's superiority or sense of vision.

The May Fourth Movement
Chow Tse-tung

When the Qing (Ch'ing) Dynasty collapsed in 1911 it left an enormous vacuum in the political, educational, social, and literary life of China. Before that time all these aspects of Chinese society were tied into Confucianism. The collapse of the dynastic cycle in the face of Western imperialism made this a bankrupt philosophy since it had been unable to withstand the massive onslaught.

This vacuum was filled by a variety of philosophies and China enjoyed a range of debate and literary renaissance that it had rarely seen before. This movement, which began late in the 1910s and lasted until the Japanese invasion of 1937, is called the May Fourth Movement. The name comes from an incident on May 4th, 1919 when the Chinese learned that German concessions in China were being given to the Japanese rather than being restored to China even though China had been on the winning side during World War I. That day produced strikes and demonstrations in Beijing (Peking) and sparked a nationwide anti-Japanese movement. Because of the complexity of this period there has always been some debate as to exactly what this movement was about. In this selection, Chow Tse-tung, the first major historian of the movement, addresses the nature of these activities and offers an interpretation.

> **Consider:** *The ways in which this was an important intellectual movement; the social and economic changes stemming from this movement; what happens to a society that loses trust in its institutions.*

The May Fourth Movement was actually a combined intellectual and sociopolitical movement to achieve national independence, the emancipation of the individual, and a just society by the modernization of China. Essentially, it was an intellectual revolution in the broad sense, intellectual because it was based on the assumption that intellectual changes were a prerequisite for such a task of modernization, because it precipitated a mainly intellectual awakening and transformation, and because it was led by intellectuals. This also accelerated numerous social and political and cultural changes. The most important purpose of the movement was to maintain the existence and independence of the nation, a goal which had actually

SOURCE: Chow Tse-Tsung, *The May Fourth Movement: Intellectual Revolution in Modern China*, (Cambridge, Mass.: Harvard University Press) Copyright © 1960 by the President and Fellows of Harvard College. Reprinted by permission.

generated all of the major reforms and revolutions in China since the latter half of the nineteenth century.

In order to do this, the intellectual reformers, unlike the previous generations, advocated the modernization or Westernization of China in all important aspects of her culture, from literature, philosophy, and ethics to social, political, and economic institutions and customs. They started by attacking tradition and by re-evaluating attitudes and practices in the light of modern Western civilization, the essence of which they thought to be science and democracy. The basic spirit of the movement, therefore, was to jettison tradition and create a new, modern civilization to "save China." . . .

In this process of social transformation fundamental ideological changes among the people and among young intellectuals in particular were most striking. Traditional ethical principles and dogmas were effectively shattered. Idols and authorities trembled before the movement. The prestige of tradition has not since been restored, despite the efforts of later traditionalists and conservatives. The worship of the old was replaced by enthusiasm for the new. Eagerness for new learning among the youth of this period has never been surpassed. New standards began to take form. Among the literati, views of life and the world were broadened and changed.

These ideological changes were accompanied and helped by the adoption of the vernacular as a medium for writing, by the creation of a new literature variously based on humanitarianism, romanticism, realism, and naturalism, and by the rapid development of the press and of popular education. . . .

Along with these ideological changes and intellectual developments there occurred social transformations. After the movement the traditional family system gradually declined. Marriage based on love was more frequently demanded. Against the old family and clan systems, Chinese youth strove to assert their personalities and rights in society. A tendency toward a larger social cohesion as a substitute for the family and clan bonds made itself felt during and after the period. The social status of women began to rise. Coeducation was established. Women began to be emancipated from traditional ethical, social, and political shackles. The movement nurtured a more active woman's suffrage movement and brought women into political and social activities. Truly, the movement started and propelled a "revolution of the family."

China's economic structure also underwent notable changes during the period. These were accompanied by the progressive decline of the landlords' position, unrest among the peasantry, an increase of political activities on the part of urban dwellers, and the increasing significance of the labor problem. . . .

By and large, the tendencies of the May Fourth Movement almost determined China's intellectual, social, and political development in the following decades. The deep social and national consciousness, which had started to take shape in this intellectual fermentation, persisted. After the May Fourth period, the demands of the new intellectuals for a modern "scientific culture" and for an effective government to guarantee the independence and equality of the nation in the family of nation-states were continued and intensified. History proved that political leaders and groups who acted against these trends, such as the traditionalists and conservatives, brought their own downfall, whereas those "boys who played and rode with the tide," even with distortion and manipulation, gained advantages.

Propaganda and Racism in the Pacific War
John W. Dower

In time of war, or in preparation for war, all countries use propaganda as a means to instill in their people a willingness to fight and die for their country. One of the many ways to accomplish this goal is to depict the enemy as vicious, cruel and savage.

Leading up to and immediately after Pearl Harbor, the U.S. government was engaged in just such efforts, depicting Japanese as subhuman lemmings with a cultlike dedication to the Emperor. One of the most influential ways in which this was done was through a series of films by famed movie director Frank Capra entitled "Know Your Enemy—Japan." The Japanese in turn invoked images of Americans as inhuman and barbaric. In this excerpt from a prize-winning book entitled War without Mercy: Race and Power in the Pacific War, *American Japanologist John Dower examines Japanese propaganda to that end and comments on the use of racial stereotypes by both sides.*

Consider: *The arguments used by the Japanese against their Anglo-American opponents; why such propaganda might have been effective.*

. . . [I]n August 1941, the [Japanese] Ministry of Education issued a major ideological manifesto entitled *The Way of the Subject* . . . [which] told the Japanese who they were—or should aspire to be—as a people, nation, and race. At the same time, it offered a critical analysis of modern Western history and culture. In Japanese eyes, it was the non-Axis West that aimed at world domination and had been engaged in that quest, with conspicuous success, for centuries, and it was the value system of the modern West, rooted in acquisitiveness and self-gratification, that explained a large part of its bloody history of war and repression, culminating in the current world crisis. The Japanese thus read Western history in much the same way that Westerners were reading the history of Japan: as a chronicle of destructive values, exploitative practices, and brutal wars. The picture of the Anglo-American enemy presented here and in the Army pamphlet persisted through the war. . . . The early Western defeats and quick surrenders revealed the flabbiness of Western society, Japanese at home were told. Later, the American bombing of Japanese cities was offered as proof beyond any conceivable question of the bestial nature of the enemy.

SOURCE: John Dower, *War Without Mercy*, (New York, 1986). Copyright © 1986 by John W. Dower. Reprinted by permission of Pantheon Books, a division of Random House, Inc.

The southern region, embarking troops were informed in *Read This and the War Is Won,* was the treasure house of the Far East and a land of everlasting summer. It was also a place where a half million British ruled 350 million Indians, and another few score thousands of Englishmen ruled 6 million Malayans; where two hundred thousand Dutchmen governed a native population of 60 million in the East Indies; where twenty thousand Frenchmen controlled 23 million Indochinese, and a few tens of thousands of Americans ruled over 13 million Filipinos. Eight hundred thousand whites, the tally went, controlled 450 million Asians; if India was excluded, the count was 100 million oppressed by three hundred thousand. "Money squeezed from the blood of Asians maintains these small white minorities in their luxurious mode of life—or disappears to the respective home-countries," the Japanese soldiers were told. The white men were described as arrogant colonials who dwelled in splendid houses on mountainsides and hilltops, from which they looked down on the tiny thatched huts of the natives. They took it as their birthright to be allotted a score or so natives as personal slaves. Ties of blood and color linked the Japanese to these oppressed peoples of Asia. And because the latter had been all but emasculated by generations of colonial subjugation, it was left to Japan "to make men of them again" and lead them along the path of liberation—in short, to "liberate East Asia from white invasion and oppression." In the final analysis, this was "a struggle between races."

. . . The Japanese were informed that Western expansion was inspired partly by love of adventure, but more by desire for local resources as well as markets. And they were reminded that the heavy hand of the Occidental expansionists did not fall on Asians alone. Here the Ministry of Education posed two rhetorical questions that would remain effective propaganda to the end of the war: "How were American Indians treated? What about African Negroes?" . . .

Each of these exercises in ideology and propaganda can be seen as a tapestry of truths, half-truths, and empty spaces. When the American and Japanese examples are set side by side, the points each neglected to cover become clearer; and it becomes plain that both sides reveal more about themselves than about the enemy they are portraying. . . . Whether as film, radio broadcast, or written text, such discourse was ideological and overt, calculated and carefully edited, explicitly designed for public consumption. More refined than visceral expressions of race hate, it was also less frank and densely detailed than the calculations of power and interest made in secret at high levels. Yet it was not simply a tissue of lies or purely cynical manipulation of emotional rhetoric. Speakers, viewers, listeners alike (so long as they were all on the same side) generally took these statements seriously, and there is much to be learned here in retrospect about language, stereotyping, and the making of modern myths. Because World War Two is the context, the consequences of such seemingly abstract concerns emerge with special harshness. To people at war, after all, the major purpose in knowing one's enemies is to be better able to control or kill them.

The Politics of Race, Class, and Nationalism in Twentieth-Century South Africa

Shula Marks and Stanley Trapido

Between World War I and II, Afrikaners (Boers—white settlers, primarily of Dutch rather than English origin) became increasingly assertive in south Africa. Not only did they struggle to maintain a separation of white and nonwhite peoples there, they attempted to wrestle power from the British who were still in control. One part of these efforts was the further development of Afrikaner nationalism in south Africa. It was an avowedly racist philosophy, drawing on a Christian heritage and racial ideologies emanating from Europe at the time. Its focus was to institutionalize apartheid (racial segregation) by exploiting British democratic institutions. In the following excerpt, Shula Marks and Stanley Trapido trace the roots of Afrikaner nationalism and particularly the role played by the Afrikaner intelligentsia of the period.

> **Consider:** *Why Afrikaners felt the need to formulate their own ideology; how the elements of Afrikaner nationalism served Afrikaner needs; connections made between ethnicity, religion, economics, and the state.*

To meet the challenge of cheaply purveyed British culture, daily life had to be redefined and an alien world transformed into one in which Afrikaner sensibilities ruled. . . . [N]o artefact was too substantial or too small not to have its Afrikaans version, no occupation too eminent or too humble, not to have its Afrikaans mutation. This coincided with the creation and re-creation of Afrikaner history, fiction, the language and cultural institutions, as well as with the increasingly successful economic movement in the Cape, based on the first Afrikaner insurance company, SANLAM. The activities of both cultural and economic nationalists were further developed through the Christian National ideology adopted by the Broederbond, a secret society founded in 1919 and devoted to mobilising Afrikaners for the nationalist programme. . . .

Much of what they wrote was confused and contradictory, but the general directions were clear. Nations and cultures were divine creations, each was sovereign and had its own calling and destiny. Service to the nation was service to God. Not only was the Almighty best served by worshipping Him in the language He had created; without maintaining this language, the culture and nation He had created would not survive. Language, culture and nation were endangered by an alien capitalism and an equally alien communism. . . .

It was not capitalism *per se* which was the enemy of the Afrikaner people, according to the leading Bond member, L. J. du Plessis, but the control of the

SOURCE: Marks & Trapido, *The Politics of Race, Class, and Nationalism in Twentieth Century South Africa*, (Essex, United Kingdom). Longman Group Publishers.

capitalist system by non-Afrikaners. Afrikaners had to take control of what was their rightful share, through *Volkskapitalisme,* the mobilisation of ethnic resources to foster Afrikaner accumulation. To do this, the northern Broederbond, with its weak financial resources, turned to the Cape-based SANLAM in the calling of the 1939 Ekonomiese Volkskongress (People's Economic Congress). . . .

At the Volkskongress, SANLAM launched the first Afrikaner-owned financial house, the Federale Volksbelegging, which by 1981 had become the second-largest single conglomerate in South Africa. The embryonic entrepreneurs of the north were largely excluded from this, and could only look forward to the small business of the one-man firm also advocated by the Kongress. For the Afrikaner poor, the "solution" offered was employment in the Afrikaner enterprises they were ex-horted to patronise. There was a symbiotic relationship between Afrikaner capital and the growing Afrikaner petty bourgeoisie, but it was not a relationship without tension and conflict.

African Women and the Law
Martin Chanock

The period between the wars also witnessed the creation of social systems in the African colonies that had tremendous impact on the lives of ordinary men and women. Besides having to deal with taxation, forced labor, and the like, Africans were also subject to an array of new legal codes, changing customs relating to division of labor, marriage, divorce, inheritance, and every aspect of household management. Most of the new statutes were a combination of "traditional" legal norms interpreted according to European legal codes. For African women especially, the institutionalization of "customary laws" deprived them of much of their former independence and imposed a system of patriarchy which had no precedent in African society. Moreover, these laws were being imposed on African women at a time when European women had openly challenged the Victorian underpinning of male dominance. In the following excerpt, Martin Chanock describes some of the contradictions inherent in any such social engineering.

> **Consider:** *The argument that these policies lessened the status of women; the likelihood that such social engineering could be successful; the arguments that the women might have made against the new laws.*

The Marriage and Divorce Ordinances of 1902 and 1905 in Malawi made female consent (which could be given by the father, who would not normally have been the guardian) necessary for a valid marriage and lack of consent grounds for annulment. These gave legal backing to the early ambition to establish the free status of women. In the mind of early administrators the status of a 'free woman'

SOURCE: Martin Chanock, *Law, Custom and Social Order: The Colonial Experience in Malawi and Zambia* (Cambridge, Cambridge University Press, 1985), pp. 186–187.

was something to be defended against the institutions of African marriage, with its apparent ignoring of female consent, and with the 'inheriting' of widows by the husband's heirs. There are however relatively few cases reported in which women specifically complained about the kind of restraints which the administration would interpret as absence of consent. As women, usually through their matrikin, appeared to have brought all other kinds of matrimonial cases to the courts, the few consent cases that did come to court must have been those which involved the special perception of status of the newly converted Christian women who were complainants or reflected the spread of bridewealth marriage. The mission churches, and the early administrators, did put an emphasis on the autonomy of female consent to marriage and regarded many of the rights and duties existing in all forms of African marriage as conflicting with this. Emily Maliwa has written that the deepest conflict between Malawian and British ideas about law was over marriage and she emphasises a total conflict between the missions' idea of marriage and the "traditional" one. Women, she writes, looked to the missionaries as protectors and to the missions as a ladder to great equality of status. Chiefs and male adults generally much resented, she says, the erosion of their authority inherent in the way the missions treated women. But Christian marriage and mission influence affected only a small minority, as Maliwa herself notes. While the Churches may have improved the marital position of a small number of women, this was not the main thrust of "western" influence.

In February 1931, as a consequence of the interest being taken in Britain and at the League of Nations in the position of women in tropical Africa, district officers were circulated with a questionnaire on the rights of women. It seemed clear to them that women were free. In the eyes of the chief secretary it was precisely the establishment of the jural status of women at the Boma which had given them this freedom. "One of the strongest arguments in support of the claim that native women have much independence," he wrote, "is the way in which they bring cases, and often win them, before administrative officers or in the Courts." There was general satisfaction that there were no forced marriages or inheritance of widows; that women could own property; and that "where complaint is made of slavery it is usually the insult that is objected to and not the fact of slavery." Some of the answers commented on the advantages women enjoyed in predominantly "matrilineal" areas. The Blantyre district officer reported that the lot of Yao women, who lived with their *nkhoswe* in their own villages, was far happier than that of Ngoni women, and others emphasised that Ngoni women, unlike others in the protectorate, could not hold property independently, could not inherit, and were normally inherited. In "matrilineal" areas, the Mlanje report said, the mother took the children after divorce even where she had been "entirely to blame . . . exceptions to this are very rare: and almost always due to European influence." This gives the essential clue to British attitudes. While they saw themselves as having established the free status of women, they were not at all enamoured by what they appeared to do with it. From Cholo the district officer wrote:

In my opinion Native women in Nyasaland have much, in fact too much, independence. Husbands find it increasingly difficult to maintain order and good behaviour in their households. Women often attend beer drinks, dances, and similar functions against their husbands' wishes and neglect their wifely duties. At the slightest remonstrance or correction they are apt to fly into a rage, become abusive, cause a breach of the peace, and then fly to the Headman or the Boma and complain of cruelty.

In the face of such an attitude jural status was not going to be particularly useful.

Chapter Questions

1. How did nationalism play a role in Asian and African political developments during the decades spanned by World Wars I and II?
2. In what ways did Japan constitute a force against imperialism, and in what ways was Japan a force propagating imperialism?
3. In what ways did Western ideas have an impact on Chinese developments in particular and Asian and African developments in general during this period?
4. Drawing on materials from this and the previous chapter, compare developments in the Western and the non-Western worlds. What sorts of forces in the nonwestern world are being created or unleashed by developments in the Western world? What might be the long-term significance of these developments?

THIRTEEN

The World in the Post-World War II Era

The year 1945 marked the end of World War II and the decades of turmoil that had begun with the outbreak of World War I in 1914. It also marked the beginning of an age of rapidly growing global interdependence brought on by expanding communications, economic dependence, international organizations, systems of alliances, ideological competition, and cultural exchanges. In this chapter we will examine the three decades following World War II by focusing on five developments.

First, Europe emerged from World War II facing an overwhelming task of recovery. She was losing her position of dominance in the world, reflected in the successful independence movements among her colonies and the rise of the two new superpowers: the United States and the Soviet Union. In these postwar decades, European nations adopted new policies which would alter her political, social, and economic institutions in fundamental ways.

Second, almost immediately following the war, the United States and the Soviet Union became engaged in a bitter ideological and political battle of global proportions—the "Cold War." It seemed as if no political development, whether occurring in Europe, Latin America, Asia, Africa, or elsewhere was free of Cold War connotations.

In the Americas, the United States was now the world's leading military and economic power and Latin America had been spared most of the losses from World War II that others suffered. Yet these decades witnessed some important political and social instability. In Latin America, the struggle was usually between the elites, supported by authoritarian governments, and the rural and urban poor, supported by revolutionary movements. In the United States, the Civil Rights Movement and the war in Vietnam spawned major social and political conflicts.

In Asia and Africa, the devastation of two world wars and the rising movements for independence were too much for Western imperial powers to handle. Sometimes gracefully and sometimes only after protracted violence, Europe and the United States relinquished almost all their colonies during these decades.

However, the successful struggles for independence throughout Asia and Africa more often than not carried in their wakes ethnic, political, religious,

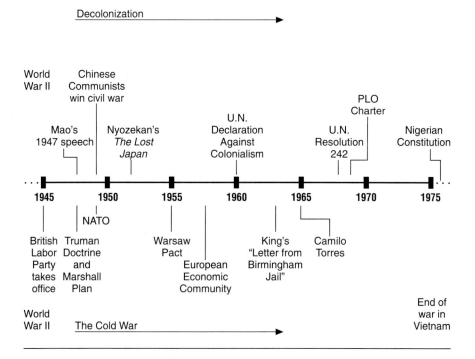

communal, and economic woes. In some cases, such as Japan, South Korea, Hong Kong, Taiwan, Singapore, Israel, and oil-rich areas of the Middle East, nations would come to enjoy relative prosperity. In other cases, such as Vietnam, Cambodia, Laos, India, Bangladesh, and Afghanistan, peace and prosperity would remain elusive. In China, the communists were victorious and set about creating a "new China" not only economically, socially, and politically, but also philosophically. Along the way their policies also produced innumerable deaths and chaos during the Great Leap Forward (1959–1962) and the Great Proletarian Cultural Revolution (1966–1976). In Africa, the nationalistic struggles for independence were often more protracted. As African nations achieved independence, the overriding concern became how to devise state systems that would bring not only stability but economic prosperity as well.

The sources in this chapter deal with each of these five developments, which were of such global importance, as well as some of the connections between these developments. In Chapter 14 the story of some of these developments will be carried forward in an attempt to analyze the present from a historical perspective.

PRIMARY SOURCES

British Labor's Rise to Power
Harry Laidler

During World War II, governments became involved in social and economic activities to an unprecedented degree. Although with the end of the war, this changed to some degree, there was still significant acceptance of government involvement in society. In Great Britain this was combined with an increasing acceptance of the Labor party, whose strength had been growing since the end of World War I. In the elections of 1945, this party, made up of a combination of Socialist and trade-union groups, gained a majority and took office, replacing the Conservatives led by Winston Churchill. The new government initiated policies that substantially changed the relationship between the government and the people during the period following World War II. Excerpts from the Labor party platform set forth shortly before the 1945 elections are presented here.

SOURCE: Harry W. Laidler, "British Labor's Rise to Power," in *League for Industrial Democracy Pamphlet Series* (New York: League for Industrial Democracy, 1945), pp. 24–25. Reprinted by permission of the publisher.

Consider: *The ways in which this platform constituted a major assault on capitalism and "laissez-faire"; how this platform might reflect the experience of the Great Depression and the world wars; how a Conservative might argue against this platform.*

The Labor party is a socialist party, and proud of it. Its ultimate purpose at home is the establishment of the socialist commonwealth of Great Britain—free, democratic, efficient, progressive, public-spirited, its material resources organized in the service of the British people.

But socialism cannot come overnight, as the product of a week-end revolution. The members of the Labor party, like the British people, are practical-minded men and women.

There are basic industries ripe and over-ripe for public ownership and management in the direct service of the nation. There are many smaller businesses rendering good service which can be left to go on with their useful work.

There are big industries not yet ripe for public ownership which must nevertheless be required by constructive supervision to further the nation's needs and not to prejudice national interests by restrictive antisocial monopoly or cartel agreements—caring for their own capital structures and profits at the cost of a lower standard of living for all.

In the light of these considerations, the Labor party submits to the nation the following industrial program:

1. *Public Ownership of the Fuel and Power Industries.* For a quarter of a century the coal industry, producing Britain's most precious national raw material, has been floundering chaotically under the ownership of many hundreds of independent companies. Amalgamation under public ownership will bring great economies in operation and make it possible to modernize production methods and to raise safety standards in every colliery in the country. Public ownership of gas and electricity undertakings will lower charges, prevent competitive waste, open the way for co-ordinated research and development, and lead to the reforming of uneconomic areas of distribution. Other industries will benefit.

2. *Public Ownership of Inland Transport.* Co-ordination of transport services by rail, road, air and canal cannot be achieved without unification. And unification without public ownership means a steady struggle with sectional interests or the entrenchment of a private monopoly, which would be a menace to the rest of industry.

3. *Public Ownership of Iron and Steel.* Private monopoly has maintained high prices and kept inefficient high-cost plants in existence. Only if public ownership replaces private monopoly can the industry become efficient.

   These socialized industries, taken over on a basis of fair compensation, to be conducted efficiently in the interests of consumers, coupled with proper status and conditions for the workers employed in them.

4. *Public Supervision of Monopolies and Cartels* with the aim of advancing industrial efficiency in the service of the nation. Anti-social restrictive practices will be prohibited.

5. *A First and Clear-cut Program for the Export Trade.* We would give State help in any necessary form to get our export trade on its feet and enable it to pay for the food and raw materials without which Britain must decay and die. But State help on conditions—conditions that industry is efficient and go-ahead. Laggards and obstructionists must be led or directed into a better way. Here we dare not fail.

6. *The Shaping of Suitable Economic and Price Controls* to secure that first things shall come first in the transition from war to peace and that every citizen (including the demobilized Service men and women) shall get fair play. There must be priorities in the use of raw materials, food prices must be held, homes for the people must come before mansions, necessities for all before luxuries for the few. We do not want a short boom followed by collapse as after the last war; we do not want a wild rise in prices and inflation, followed by a smash and widespread unemployment. It is either sound economic controls—or smash.

The Truman Doctrine and the Marshall Plan

During World War II the Soviet Union and the United States were allied against their common enemies, the Axis powers. Shortly after the end of the war, animosity began to reappear between the former allies. By 1947 that animosity had risen to the point where it was formalized in government programs and international policies; the "Cold War" had broken out. In the United States this was most clearly announced in two policy decisions excerpted here. The first is a speech delivered by President Truman on March 12, 1947, to Congress, concerning proposed aid to Greece and Turkey, which appeared in danger of falling under the influence of the Soviet Union. The principles contained in this speech became known as the Truman Doctrine. The second is a statement made by Secretary of State George C. Marshall on November 10, 1947, to Senate and House Committees on Foreign Relations, proposing massive aid to Europe. This proposal became known as the Marshall Plan.

Consider: *The American perception of the Soviet Union and its allies; the purposes of this foreign policy; how the Soviet Union would probably perceive and react to this foreign policy.*

SOURCE: U. S. Congress, *Congressional Record*, 80th Congress, 1st Session (Washington, D.C.: U.S. Government Printing Office, 1947), vol. 93, p. 1981.

SOURCE: U.S. Congress, Senate Committee on Foreign Relations, *A Decade of American Foreign Policy: Basic Documents, 1941–1949* (Washington, D.C.: U. S. Government Printing Office, 1950), pp. 1270–1271.

The peoples of a number of countries of the world have recently had totalitarian regimes forced upon them against their will. The Government of the United States has made frequent protests against coercion and intimidation, in violation of the Yalta agreement, in Poland, Rumania, and Bulgaria. I must also state that in a number of other countries there have been similar developments.

At the present moment in world history nearly every nation must choose between alternative ways of life. The choice is too often not a free one.

One way of life is based upon the will of the majority, and is distinguished by free institutions, representative government, free elections, guarantees of individual liberty, freedom of speech and religion, and freedom from political oppression.

The second way of life is based upon the will of a minority forcibly imposed upon the majority. It relies upon terror and oppression, a controlled press and radio, fixed elections, and the suppression of personal freedoms.

I believe that it must be the policy of the United States to support free peoples who are resisting attempted subjugation by armed minorities or by outside pressures.

I believe that we must assist free peoples to work out their own destinies in their own way.

I believe that our help should be primarily through economic and financial aid, which is essential to economic stability and orderly political processes.

✲

As a result of the war, the European community which for centuries had been one of the most productive and indeed creative portions of the inhabited world was left prostrate. This area, despite its diversity of national cultures and its series of internecine conflicts and wars, nonetheless enjoys a common heritage and a common civilization.

The war ended with the armies of the major Allies meeting in the heart of this community. The policies of three of them have been directed to the restoration of that European community. It is now clear that only one power, the Soviet Union, does not for its own reasons share this aim.

We have become involved in two wars which have had their origins in the European continent. The free peoples of Europe have fought two wars to prevent the forcible domination of their community by a single great power. Such domination would have inevitably menaced the stability and security of the world. To deny today our interest in their ability to defend their own heritage would be to disclaim the efforts and sacrifices of two generations of Americans. We wish to see this community restored as one of the pillars of world security; in a position to renew its contribution to the advancement of mankind and to the development of a world order based on law and respect for the individual.

The record of the endeavors of the United States Government to bring about a restoration of the whole of that European community is clear for all who wish to see. We must face the fact, however, that despite our efforts, not all of the European nations have been left free to take their place in the community of which they form a natural part.

Thus the geographic scope of our recovery program is limited to those nations which are free to act in accordance with their national traditions and their own estimates of their national interests. If there is any doubt as to this situation, a glance at the present map of the European continent will provide the answer.

The present line of division in Europe is roughly the line upon which the Anglo-American armies coming from the west met those of the Soviet Union coming from the east. To the west of that line the nations of the continental European community have been grappling with the vast and difficult problem resulting from the war in conformity with their own national traditions without pressure or menace from the United States or Great Britain. Developments in the European countries to the east of that line bear the unmistakable imprint of an alien hand.

Communism in China
Mao Zedong (Mao Tse-tung)

When the Chinese Communist Party achieved victory in the civil war in 1949, they set about immediately to create a new and completely different China. The tasks were enormous, especially since many of the attitudes that the communists wanted to change (the role of women, for example) had been ingrained in Chinese culture for almost four thousand years. Undaunted, the communists launched a series of mass political and social campaigns from 1949 to the present.

The following reading is from a speech on China's future given in 1947 by Mao Zedong (Mao Tse-tung) to the party's leadership. Here the emphasis is on land reform and rewarding the rural population whose sacrifices and aid made victory possible for the communists.

> **Consider:** *How Mao proposes to reward his supporters; who he identifies as his enemies and why; the policies he recommends and the changes that would flow from such policies.*

The Chinese people's revolutionary war has now reached a turning point. That is, the Chinese People's Liberation Army has beaten back the offensive of several million reactionary troops of Chiang Kai-shek, the running dog of the United States of America, and gone over to the offensive. . . .

After the Japanese surrender, the peasants urgently demanded land, and we made a timely decision to change our land policy from reducing rent and interest to confiscating the land of the landlord class for distribution among the peasants. The directive issued by the Central Committee of our party on May 4, 1946, marked this change. In September 1947 our party called the National Land Conference and drew up the Outline Land Law of China, which was promptly carried out in all areas. . . . The Outline Land Law provides for equal distribution

---

SOURCE: Mao Tse-tung, *Selected Works of Mao Tse-tung,* vol. 4 (Peking: Foreign Languages Press, 1961), pp. 170–174.

of land per head, based on the principle of abolishing the land system of feudal and semifeudal exploitation and putting into effect the system of land to the tillers. This is a method which most thoroughly abolishes the feudal system and fully meets the demands of the broad masses of China's peasants. To carry out the land reform resolutely and thoroughly, it is necessary to organize in the villages, as lawful bodies for carrying out the reform, not only peasant associations on the broadest mass basis, including farm laborers, poor peasants, and middle peasants and their elected committees, but first of all poor peasant leagues composed of poor peasants and farm laborers and their elected committees; and these poor peasants' leagues should be the backbone of leadership in all rural struggles. Our policy is to rely on the poor peasants and unite solidly with the middle peasants to abolish the feudal and semifeudal system of exploitation by the landlord class and by the old-type rich peasants. Landlords or rich peasants must not be allotted more land and property than the peasant masses. . . . Although the proportion of landlords and rich peasants in the rural population varies from place to place, it is generally only about 8 percent (in terms of households), while their holdings usually amount to 70 to 80 percent of all the land. . . .

Confiscate the land of the feudal class and turn it over to the peasants. Confiscate monopoly capital, . . . and turn it over to the new democratic state. Protect the industry and commerce of the national bourgeoisie. These are the three major economic policies of the new democratic revolution. . . . The new democratic revolution aims at wiping out only feudalism and monopoly capitalism, only the landlord class and the bureaucrat-capitalist class (the big bourgeoisie), and not at wiping out capitalism in general, the upper petty bourgeoisie or the middle bourgeoisie. In view of China's economic backwardness, even after the country-wide victory of the revolution, it will still be necessary to permit the existence for a long time of a capitalist sector of the economy represented by the extensive petty bourgeoisie and middle bourgeoisie. In accordance with the division of labor in the national economy, a certain development of all parts of this capitalist sector which are beneficial to the national economy will still be needed.

China's Marriage Law: New Rules for the Women of China

From their earliest days in 1921, the Chinese Communist Party supported the notion that women were equal to men. This concept was particularly revolutionary in a society that bound women's feet, thereby restricting their mobility; that practiced the sale of young girls into marriage, concubinage or prostitution; that sanctioned female infanticide; and that generally considered women as almost subhuman.

SOURCE: *The Marriage Law of the People's Republic of China* (Peking: Foreign Languages Press, 1959).

In putting their theories into practice, the Communist Party did offer women a higher status than they had previously. Some women achieved positions of responsibility, some women fought alongside men, and the worst abuses against women, such as child betrothal and foot binding, were indeed eliminated in areas controlled by the communists.

However, women never achieved equality. Even within the ranks of party officials, the men could not bring themselves to share power completely. Nevertheless, the communists were committed to an ideal and when they came to power in 1949 one of their first acts was to pass the following "Marriage Law" which, in legal terms at least, afforded Chinese women the equality they were striving for.

> **Consider:** *The significance of these changes for Chinese raised according to the old traditions; how these principles, rights, and duties reflect an effort to enact communism in China.*

CHAPTER I. GENERAL PRINCIPLES

Article 1. The arbitrary and compulsory feudal marriage system, which is based on the superiority of man over woman and which ignores the children's interests, shall be abolished.

The new democratic marriage system, which is based on free choice of partners, on monogamy, on equal rights for both sexes, and on protection of the lawful interests of women and children, shall be put into effect.

Article 2. Bigamy, concubinage, child betrothal, interference with the remarriage of widows, and the exaction of money or gifts in connection with marriage shall be prohibited. . . .

CHAPTER III. RIGHTS AND DUTIES OF HUSBAND AND WIFE

Article 7. Husband and wife are companions living together and shall enjoy equal status in the home.

Article 8. Husband and wife are in duty bound to love, respect, assist, and look after each other, to live in harmony, to engage in production, to care for the children, and to strive jointly for the welfare of the family and for the building up of a new society.

Article 9. Both husband and wife shall have the right to free choice of occupation and free participation in work or in social activities.

Article 10. Both husband and wife shall have equal right in the possession and management of family property.

Article 11. Both husband and wife shall have the right to use his or her own family name.

Article 12. Both husband and wife shall have the right to inherit each other's property.

The Balfour Declaration, U.N. Resolution 242, and the Palestinian National Charter: Israel, Palestine, and the Middle East

Since World War II, the Middle East has been a center of violent conflict as well as a source of great concern for the world. One of the main sources of conflict has been the struggle over the creation of Israel and the Palestinian problem that resulted. The roots of this Israeli-Palestinian struggle stretch back at least as far as the late nineteenth century when the Zionist movement—a movement to make Palestine the national home of the Jews—began. The struggle over the creation of Israel came to a head in 1948 when the British, who controlled Palestine, left it in the hands of the United Nations. A United Nations resolution and the first Arab-Israeli war resulted in the creation of Israel, a massive number of Palestinian refugees, and decades of conflict between Arabs and Israelis.

The first of the following three documents on this topic is the Balfour Declaration, a 1917 letter from British Foreign Secretary Balfour to Walter Rothschild, the representative of British Jewry. The letter was used by Zionists to support immigration to Palestine and to obligate the British to create a Jewish homeland there. The second document is Resolution 242, passed by the United Nations in 1967, which recognized Israel's existence and its need for security but at the same time called on Israel to withdraw from the territories captured in the 1967 Arab-Israeli war. The third document contains excerpts from the 1968 Palestinian National Charter enunciating the goals of the newly formed Palestine Liberation Organization.

> **Consider:** *Why the Balfour Declaration was so important and why the Palestinians rejected it; why Israel has been reluctant to accept U.N. Resolution 242; the goals and justifications of the Palestine Liberation Organization and how Israelis might respond.*

THE BALFOUR DECLARATION

Dear Lord Rothschild,

I have much pleasure in conveying to you, on behalf of His Majesty's Government, the following declaration of sympathy with Jewish Zionist aspirations which has been submitted to, and approved by, the Cabinet.

"His Majesty's Government view with favour the establishment in Palestine of a national home for the Jewish people, and will use their best endeavours to facilitate the achievement of this object, it being clearly understood that nothing shall be done which may prejudice the civil and religious rights of existing non-

---

SOURCE: *International Documents on Palestine, 1968* edited by Zuhair Diab, (New York, 1971). Excerpts from the Palestine National Charter, document #360.

Jewish communities in Palestine, or the rights and political status enjoyed by Jews in any other country."

I should be grateful if you would bring this declaration to the knowledge of the Zionist Federation.

Yours sincerely,

Arthur James Balfour

U.N. RESOLUTION 242

The Security Council, . . .

1. *Affirms* that the fulfilment of Charter principles requires the establishment of a just and lasting peace in the Middle East which should include the application of both the following principles:
   (i) Withdrawal of Israel armed forces from territories occupied in the recent conflict;
   (ii) Termination of all claims or states of belligerency and respect for and acknowledgement of the sovereignty, territorial integrity and political independence of every State in the area and their right to live in peace within secure and recognized boundaries free from threats or acts of force;
2. *Affirms further* the necessity
   (a) For guaranteeing freedom of navigation through international waterways in the area;
   (b) For achieving a just settlement of the refugee problem;
   (c) For guaranteeing the territorial inviolability and political independence of every State in the area, through measures including the establishment of demilitarized zones.

THE PALESTINIAN NATIONAL CHARTER

1. Palestine, the homeland of the Palestinian Arab people, is an inseparable part of the greater Arab homeland, and the Palestinian people are a part of the Arab Nation. . . .

3. The Palestinian Arab people alone have legitimate rights to their homeland, and shall exercise the right of self-determination after the liberation of their homeland, . . .

4. The Palestinian identity is an authentic, intrinsic and indissoluble quality. . . . Neither the Zionist occupation nor the dispersal of the Palestinian Arab people as a result of the afflictions they have suffered can efface this Palestinian identity.

5. Palestinians are Arab citizens who were normally resident in Palestine until 1947. . . .

6. Jews who were normally resident in Palestine up to the beginning of the Zionist invasion are Palestinians. . . .

8. The Palestinian people is at the stage of national struggle for the liberation of its homeland. . . .

9. Armed struggle is the only way of liberating Palestine. . . .

10. Commando action constitutes the nucleus of the Palestinian popular war of liberation. . . .

12. The Palestinian Arab people believe in Arab unity. To fulfill their role in the achievement of that objective, they must, at the present stage in their national struggle, retain their Palestinian identity. . . .

15. The liberation of Palestine is a national obligation for the Arabs. It is their duty to repel the Zionist and imperialist invasion of the greater Arab homeland and to liquidate the Zionist presence in Palestine. . . .

16. On the spiritual plane, the liberation of Palestine will establish in the Holy Land an atmosphere of peace and tranquility in which all religious institutions will be safeguarded and freedom of worship and the right of visit guaranteed to all without discrimination or distinction of race, color, language or creed.

17. On the human plane, the liberation of Palestine will restore to the Palestinians their dignity, integrity and freedom. . . .

18. On the international plane, the liberation of Palestine is a defensive measure dictated by the requirements of self-defense. . . .

19. The partition of Palestine, which took place in 1947, and the establishment of Israel, are fundamentally invalid, . . . they contravene the will of the people of Palestine and . . . the principles of the United Nations Charter, foremost among which is the right of self-determination.

20. The Balfour Declaration, the Mandate Instrument, and all their consequences, are hereby declared null and void. The claim of historical or spiritual links between the Jews and Palestine is neither in conformity with historical fact nor does it satisfy the requirements for statehood. Judaism is a revealed religion; it is not a separate nationality, nor are the Jews a single people with a separate identity; they are citizens of their respective countries. . . .

22. Zionism is a political movement that is organically linked with world imperialism and is opposed to all liberation movements or movements for progress in the world. The Zionist movement is essentially fanatical and racialist; its objectives involve aggression, expansion and the establishment of colonial settlements, and its methods are those of the Fascists and the Nazis. . . . Israel is a constant threat to peace in the Middle East and the whole world. . . .

26. The Palestine Liberation Organization, as the representative of the forces of the Palestinian revolution, is responsible for the struggle of the Palestinian Arab people to regain, liberate and return to their homeland and to exercise the right of self-determination in that homeland.

Declaration Against Colonialism

The General Assembly of the United Nations

Most colonized peoples gained their independence from Western powers during the twenty years that followed World War II. This reflected both the weakness of Europe after the war and the strength of anti-imperialist sentiments around the world. Yet the process of decolonization was difficult in itself and was complicated by the ideological differences that divided nations. In 1960, after a bitter debate, the United Nations adopted the following "Declaration against Colonialism." Although no nation voted against the resolution, Australia, Belgium, the Dominican Republic, France, Great Britain, Portugal, South Africa, Spain, and the United States abstained.

> **Consider:** *Possible reasons why these nations abstained; justifications used by nations for not giving up their colonial possessions; what this declaration reveals about the strengths and weaknesses of the United Nations.*

THE GENERAL ASSEMBLY

Mindful of the determination proclaimed by the peoples of the world in the Charter of the United Nations to reaffirm faith in fundamental human rights, in the dignity and worth of the human person, in the equal rights of men and women and of nations large and small and to promote social progress and better standards of life in larger freedom,

Conscious of the need for the creation of conditions of stability and well-being and peaceful and friendly relations based on respect for the principles of equal rights and self-determination of all peoples, and of universal respect for, and observance of, human rights and fundamental freedoms for all without distinction as to race, sex, language or religion,

Recognizing the passionate yearning for freedom in all dependent peoples and the decisive role of such peoples in the attainment of their independence,

Aware of the increasing conflicts resulting from the denial of or impediments in the way of the freedom of such peoples, which constitute a serious threat to world peace,

Considering the important role of the United Nations in assisting the movement for independence in Trust and Non-Self-Governing Territories,

Recognizing that the people of the world ardently desire the end of colonialism in all its manifestations,

Convinced that the continued existence of colonialism prevents the develop-

---

SOURCE: General Assembly of the United Nations, "Declaration Against Colonialism," *Official Records of the General Assembly*, Fifteenth Session, Resolution 1514, December 14, 1960.

ment of international economic co-operation, impedes the social, cultural, and economic development of dependent peoples and militates against the United Nations ideal of universal peace,

Affirming that peoples may, for their own ends, freely dispose of their natural wealth and resources without prejudice to any obligations arising out of international economic co-operation, based upon the principle of mutual benefit, and the international law,

Believing that the process of liberation is irresistible and irreversible and that, in order to avoid serious crises, an end must be put to colonialism and all practices of segregation and discrimination associated therewith,

Welcoming the emergence in recent years of a large number of dependent territories into freedom and independence, and recognizing the increasingly powerful trends toward freedom in such territories which have not yet attained independence,

Convinced that all peoples have an inalienable right to complete freedom, the exercise of their sovereignty and the integrity of their national territory,

Solemnly proclaims the necessity of bringing to a speedy and unconditional end colonialism in all its forms and manifestations;

And to this end

Declares that:

1. The subjection of peoples to alien subjugation, domination and exploitation constitutes a denial of fundamental human rights, is contrary to the Charter of the United Nations and is an impediment to the promotion of world peace and co-operation.
2. All peoples have the right to self-determination; by virtue of that right they freely determine their political status and freely pursue their economic, social and cultural development.
3. Inadequacy of political, economic, social or educational preparedness should never serve as a pretext for delaying independence.
4. All armed action or repressive measures of all kinds directed against dependent peoples shall cease in order to enable them to exercise peacefully and freely their right to complete independence, and the integrity of their national territory shall be respected.
5. Immediate steps shall be taken, in Trust and Non-Self-Governing Territories or all other territories which have not yet attained independence, to transfer all powers to the peoples of those territories, without any conditions or reservations, in accordance with their freely expressed will and desire, without any distinction as to race, creed or color, in order to enable them to enjoy complete independence and freedom.
6. Any attempt aimed at the partial or total disruption of the national unity and the territorial integrity of a country is incompatible with the purposes and principles of the Charter of the United Nations.

7. All States shall observe faithfully and strictly the provisions of the Charter of the United Nations, the Universal Declaration of Human Rights and the present Declaration on the basis of equality, noninterference in the internal affairs of all States, and respect for the sovereign rights of all peoples and their territorial integrity.

From Independence to Statehood: Ethnic Conflict in Nigeria

The years between 1957 and the 1980s witnessed the end of European colonial rule in Africa. In some regions, the new leaders hoped to maintain colonial boundaries while changing the system of rewards to benefit Africans, while in other regions, the nationalist leaders wished to depart radically from the former colonial economic and political systems. In the three decades since independence, however, African countries have been ravaged by numerous civil wars, ethnic conflicts, economic collapse and military dictatorships that have contributed to weak postcolonial states. Despite these problems, some African leaders have continued to take the steps to bring about national cohesion. Nigeria, one of the earliest independent countries to overcome a civil war, has been in the forefront of these attempts. The following selection concerning Nigeria's 1979 Constitution details some of the problems in nation building.

Consider: *The role the state seeks to play in controlling regionalism and ethnicity; how these principles compare with the rise of democracy in other areas of the world.*

In augurating the drafting committee on 18 October 1975, the Military Head of State suggested these basic approaches to the problems of national cohesion:

> The major political parties of the past emerged with regional and ethnic support.
>
> The main political parts of the past were in fact little more than (regional or ethnic) armies organised for fighting elections in the regions for the regional and federal legislatures.
>
> So vile was the abuse of the electoral process in the past that this has raised the question as to whether we need continue to accept simple majorities as a basis for political selection especially at the centre.
>
> Given our commitment to a Federal System of Government; to a free democratic and lawful system which guarantees fundamental human rights; and to the emergence of a stable system through constitutional law, the creation of viable political consensus and orderly succession to political power. We should:

SOURCE: Robert B. Goldmann and A. J. Wilson (eds.), *From Independence to Statehood: Managing Ethnic Conflict in Five African and Asian States* (New York, St. Martin's Press, 1984), p. 6.

seek to eliminate cut-throat competition in the political process; discourage institutionalised opposition to the government in power, and instead develop consensus politics and government based on a community of all interests rather than interest of sections of the country;

eliminate over-centralisation of power and as a matter of principle decentralise power wherever possible as a means of diffusing tensions;

evolve an electoral system which is free and fair and ensures adequate representation of our peoples;

evolve a system from which will emerge genuine and truly national political parties;

recommend the establishment of an executive presidential system of government in which the president and vice-president are assigned clearly defined powers and made accountable directly to the people, and in which the making of the president, the vice-president and the members of the executive council deliberately reflect the federal character of the country.

Finally, the Head of the Military Government advised the CDC[1] and the country:

Past events have shown that we cannot build a future for this country on a rigid political ideology. Such an approach would be unrealistic. The evolution of a doctrinal concept is usually predicated upon the general acceptance by the people of a national political philosophy . . . consequently, until all of our people, or a large majority of them, have acknowledged a common ideological motivation, it would be fruitless to proclaim any particular philosophy or ideology in our Constitution.

These fundamental elements of Nigeria's origins, growth and development provide the framework for analysing how this vast, complex system has survived and intends to continue its cohesion in the future.

Chapter II of the Constitution re-states the country's commitment to the principles of federalism, republicanism, democracy and social justice; the fostering of "national integration" together with the directive that the Nigerian State should "promote or encourage the formation of associations that cut across ethnic, linguistic, religious or other sectional barriers . . . foster a feeling of belonging and of involvement among the various peoples of the Federation, to the end that loyalty to the (Nigerian) nation shall override sectional loyalties." Having acknowledged the cultural pluralism of Nigeria, Section 20 of the Constitution directs that "The State shall protect and enhance Nigerian culture."

Section 14 (3) and (4) is even more compelling:

The composition of the Government of the Federation or any of its agencies and the conduct of its affairs shall be carried out in such a manner as to reflect the federal character of Nigeria and the need to promote national unity, and also to command national loyalty, thereby ensuring that there shall be no predominance of persons from

---

[1](The Constitution Drafting Committee)

a few states or from a few ethnic or other sectional groups in that government or in any of its agencies.

The composition of the Government of a State, a local government council, or any of the agencies of such government or council, and the conduct of the affairs of the government or council shall be carried out in such manner as to recognise the diversity of the peoples within its area of authority and the need to promote a sense of belonging and loyalty among all the peoples of the Federation.

The preceding citations from the provisions of the 1979 Constitution illustrate the many objectives and intentions in the Constitution designed to relate constitutional structures to the problems of national cohesion.

Christianity, Communism, and Revolution in Latin America
Camilo Torres

Camilo Torres was a Colombian priest who became a leading revolutionary in the years following the Cuban Revolution in the mid-1960s. In this excerpt he explains to the Colombian people why he refused to join the Catholic hierarchy in opposing the goals of communist insurgents. Although he refused to join the Communist Party, Torres believed that attacks on communists only served to keep the poor and dispossessed from gaining their own political freedom. He felt so strongly that the reigning oligarchies should be overthrown that he joined with the revolutionaries as a guerilla fighter in 1965.

> **Consider:** *What Torres saw as the "common objectives" that could unite Catholic and revolutionary; what arguments Torres used in rejecting anticommunism.*

Because of the traditional relations between Christians and Marxists, and between the Church and the Communist Party, it is quite likely that erroneous suspicions and suppositions will arise regarding the relations of Christians and Marxists within the United Front, and of a priest and the Communist Party.

This is why I want to clarify to the Colombian people my relations with the Communist Party and its position within the United Front.

I have said that I am a revolutionary as a Colombian, as a sociologist, as a Christian, and as a priest. I believe that there are elements within the Communist Party which are genuinely revolutionary. Consequently, I cannot be anti-Communist either as a Colombian, as a sociologist, as a Christian, or as a priest.

I am not anti-Communist as a Colombian because anti-Communism in my country is best on persecuting the dissatisfied, whether they be Communists or not, who in the main are poor people.

SOURCE: John Alvarez Garcia and Christian Restrepo Calle, eds., *Camilo Torres: His Life and His Message* (Springfield, Il. Templegate, 1968), pp. 74–78.

I am not anti-Communist as a sociologist because the Communist proposals to combat poverty, hunger, illiteracy, and lack of housing and public services are effective and scientific.

I am not anti-Communist as a Christian, because I believe that anti-Communism condemns the whole of Communism, without acknowledging that there is some justice in its cause, as well as injustice. By condemning the whole we condemn the just and the unjust, and this is anti-Christian.

I am not anti-Communist as a priest because, whether the Communists realize it or not, there are within their ranks some authentic Christians. If they are working in good faith, they might well be the recipients of sanctifying grace. Should this be true, and should they love their neighbor, they would be saved. My role as a priest, even though I am not exercising its prerogatives externally, is to lead all men to God. The most effective way to do this is to get men to serve the people in keeping with their conscience.

I do not intend to proselytize among the Communists and to try to get them to accept the dogma and teachings of the Catholic Church. I do want all men to act in accordance with their conscience, to look in earnest for the truth, and to love their neighbor effectively.

The Communists must be fully aware of the fact that I will not join their ranks, that I am not nor will I ever be a Communist, either as a Colombian, as a sociologist, as a Christian, or as a priest.

Yet I am disposed to fight with them for common objectives: against the oligarchy and the domination of the United States, and for the takeover of power by the popular class.

I do not want public opinion to identify me with the Communists. This is why in all my public appearances I have wanted to be surrounded not only by the Communists but by all revolutionaries, be they independent or followers of other movements. . . .

Once the popular class assumes power, with the help of all revolutionaries, then our people will be ready to discuss the religious orientation they should give their lives.

Poland is an example of how socialism can be established without destroying what is essential in Christianity. As a Polish priest once said: "As Christians we have the obligation of contributing to the construction of a socialist state so long as we are allowed to adore God as we wish."

Letter from Birmingham Jail: The Civil Rights Movement in the United States

Martin Luther King, Jr.

The late 1950s and early 1960s witnessed one of the greatest social movements in American history. African Americans and whites joined in an effort to overcome the lasting legacy of slavery and racial oppression, organizing the Civil Rights Movement. Using legal challenges, civil disobedience, passive resistance and mass demonstrations, they toppled legal segregation. Martin Luther King, Jr. (1929–1968) was unquestionably the moral leader of the Civil Rights Movement. Like Gandhi, he went to jail dozens of times to bear personal witness against the segregation system that he considered immoral and unconstitutional. In this excerpt, written by King while in jail in Birmingham, Alabama, he explains to his fellow clergymen why he was willing, and they should be willing, to break immoral laws and go to jail.

Consider: *King's distinction between a just and an unjust law.*

You express a great deal of anxiety over our willingness to break laws. This is certainly a legitimate concern. Since we so diligently urge people to obey the Supreme Court's decision of 1954 outlawing segregation in the public schools, at first glance it may seem rather paradoxical for us consciously to break laws. One may well ask: "How can you advocate breaking some laws and obeying others?" The answer lies in the fact that there are two types of laws: just and unjust. I would be the first to advocate obeying just laws. One has not only a legal but a moral responsibility to obey just laws. Conversely, one has a moral responsibility to disobey unjust laws. I would agree with St. Augustine that "an unjust law is no law at all."

Now, what is the difference between the two? How does one determine whether a law is just or unjust? A just law is a man-made code that squares with the moral law or the law of God. An unjust law is a code that is out of harmony with the moral law. . . . All segregation statutes are unjust because segregation distorts the soul and damages the personality. It gives the segregator a false sense of superiority and the segregated a false sense of inferiority. . . . Hence segregation is not only politically, economically and sociologically unsound, it is morally wrong and sinful. . . . Thus it is that I can urge men to obey the 1954 decision of the Supreme Court, for it is morally right; and I can urge them to disobey segregation ordinances, for they are morally wrong. . . .

Let me give another explanation. A law is unjust if it is inflicted on a minority that, as a result of being denied the right to vote, had no part in enacting or devising the law. Who can say that the legislature of Alabama which set up that state's segregation laws was democratically elected? Throughout Alabama all sorts of devious methods are used to prevent Negroes from becoming registered voters, and there are some counties in which, even though Negroes constitute a majority of the population, not a single Negro is registered. Can any law enacted under such circumstances be considered democratically structured?

Sometimes a law is just on its face and unjust in its application. For instance, I have been arrested on a charge of parading without a permit. Now, there is nothing wrong in having an ordinance which requires a permit for a parade. But such an ordinance becomes unjust when it is used to maintain segregation and to deny citizens the First-Amendment privilege of peaceful assembly and protest.

I hope you are able to see the distinction I am trying to point out. In no sense do I advocate evading or defying the law, as would the rabid segregationist. That would lead to anarchy. One who breaks an unjust law must do so openly, lovingly, and with a willingness to accept the penalty. I submit that an individual who breaks a law that conscience tells him is unjust, and who willingly accepts the penalty of imprisonment in order to arouse the conscience of the community over its injustice, is in reality expressing the highest respect for law. . . .

I must make two honest confessions to you, my Christian and Jewish brothers. First, I must confess that over the past few years I have been gravely disappointed with the white moderate. I have almost reached the regrettable conclusion that the Negro's great stumbling block in his stride toward freedom is not the White Citizen's Counciler or the Ku Klux Klanner, but the white moderate, who is more devoted to "order" than to justice; who prefers a negative peace which is the absence of tension to a positive peace which is the presence of justice; who constantly says: "I agree with you in the goal you seek, but I cannot agree with your methods of direct action"; who paternalistically believes he can set the timetable for another man's freedom; who lives by a mythical concept of time and who constantly advises the Negro to wait for a "more convenient season." Shallow understanding from people of good will is more frustrating than absolute misunderstanding from people of ill will. Lukewarm acceptance is much more bewildering than outright rejection.

VISUAL SOURCES

The Cold War and European Integration

This map gives some idea of the movements toward the Cold War and toward European integration in the two decades following World War II. Militarily, west and east divided into NATO, led by the United States, and the Warsaw Pact Organization, led by the U.S.S.R. Economically, western European nations became increasingly tied together through organizations such as the Benelux Customs Union, the European Coal and Steel Community, the European Economic Community (Common Market), and the European Free Trade Association; the East joined in the Council for Mutual Economic Assistance (Comecon). Although military cooperation and economic cooperation were not always linked together, such linkage often did take place.

>   **Consider:** *The geographic logic, if any, of the political and economic decisions that were made by the various countries; how maps of the world indicating regional economic cooperation, military alliances, political upheavals, and international "hotspots" might show the extent and intensity of the Cold War and regional cooperation even more fully than this map of Europe.*

Decolonization in Asia and Africa

Weakened by World War II and faced with growing movements for national liberation, Western imperial powers were forced to start giving up their colonial holdings in the late 1940s. As indicated by this map, the process of decolonization was in some ways rapid— witness the large areas that gained independence in the few years around 1960—and in some ways delayed—it took some three decades for the process to be almost complete with some areas (e.g., Namibia, Hong Kong) still under external control into the 1990s.

>   **Consider:** *Possible explanations for some areas gaining independence sooner, others later; possible problems new countries faced following independence.*

Map 13-1   The Economic and Military Division of Postwar Europe

Map 13-2 Decolonization in Asia and Africa

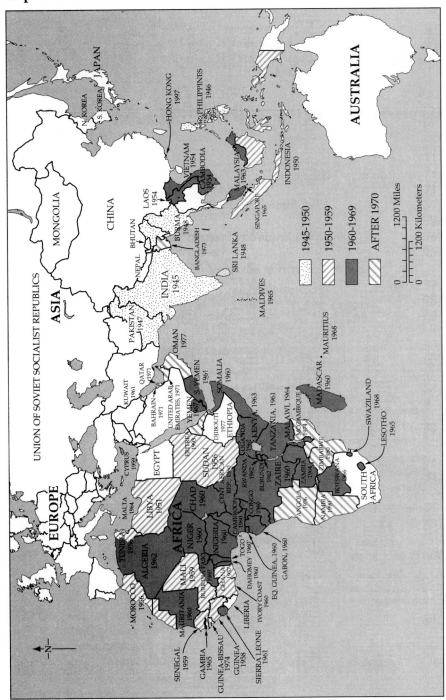

Photo 13-1

From: Ellen Johnston Laing, *The Winking Owl: Art in the Peoples' Republic of China* (Berkeley: UCLA Press, 1988).

Rent Collection Courtyard:
Art and Politics in China

One of the most important aspects of Chinese Communist belief was that art should serve politics. Art should, Mao Zedong (Mao Tse-tung) argued, show people how to act; who their enemies were; who their friends were; and how they should view their own society. Art for art's sake was considered bourgeois and against the interests of the majority of China's population. These notions were taken to an extreme during the period known as the Cultural Revolution (1966–1976) when art was confined to a handful of acceptable works. Moreover, it was deemed appropriate for the subjects of the art to participation in its creation.

Although "Rent Collection Courtyard" was originally done in 1965, just prior to the Cultural Revolution, it was to serve as a model for that period. The original work consisted of 114 life-sized figures created by sculptors at the Sichuan (Szechwan) Institute of Fine Arts. They were aided by provincial Communist Party officials and by local peasants who followed the creations closely, describing their experiences and guiding the sculptors artistically as well as politically. For example, it was the peasants who suggested the use of glass eyes for more realism.

These stark, gripping, and very obvious figures were meant to portray the bitterness of the past which people were then to compare to the much better present realities. The message is very clear. Photographs and copies were later distributed widely throughout the country.

> **Consider:** *What the viewer was to understand about pre-Communist China in looking at this scene; how art is used for political purposes.*

SECONDARY SOURCES

Origins of the Cold War
Arthur Schlesinger, Jr.

The period between the end of World War II and the mid-1960s was marked by the Cold War between the two superpowers emerging from World War II, the United States and the U.S.S.R. Initially, American historians analyzed the Cold War with assumptions not too different from policymakers: The United States was only responding defensively to an aggressive Soviet Union intent on spreading its control and communist ideology over the world. But by the 1960s other interpretations were being offered, most notably a revisionist position holding the Cold War to be at least in part a result of an aggressive, provocative American foreign policy. The following is a selection from one of the most influential interpretations of the Cold War, presented in 1967 by Arthur M. Schlesinger, Jr., a modern American historian from the City University of New York and former adviser to President Kennedy. Here Schlesinger combines elements of both the orthodox and revisionist interpretations.

> **Consider:** *Whether the Cold War was inevitable or could have been avoided; how the speeches by Truman and Marshall support this position.*

The Cold War had now begun. It was the product not of a decision but of a dilemma. Each side felt compelled to adopt policies which the other could not but regard as a threat to the principles of the peace. Each then felt compelled to undertake defensive measures. Thus the Russians saw no choice but to consolidate their security in Eastern Europe. The Americans, regarding Eastern Europe as the first step toward Western Europe, responded by asserting their interest in the zone the Russians deemed vital to their security. The Russians concluded that the West was resuming its old course of capitalist encirclement; that it was purposefully laying the foundation for anti-Soviet régimes in the area defined by the blood of centuries as crucial to Russian survival. Each side believed with passion that future international stability depended on the success of its own conception of world order. Each side, in pursuing its own clearly indicated and deeply cherished principles, was only confirming the fear of the other that it was bent on aggression.

Very soon the process began to acquire a cumulative momentum. The impending collapse of Germany thus provoked new troubles: The Russians, for example, sincerely feared that the West was planning a separate surrender of the German armies in Italy in a way which would release troops for Hitler's eastern front, as

SOURCE: Arthur Schlesinger, Jr., "Origins of the Cold War," *Foreign Affairs*, vol. 46, no. 1 (October 1967), pp. 45–46. Reprinted by permission of Foreign Affairs, (Fall, 1992). Copyright © (1967) by the Council on Foreign Relations, Inc.

they subsequently feared that the Nazis might succeed in surrendering Berlin to the West. This was the context in which the atomic bomb now appeared. Though the revisionist argument that Truman dropped the bomb less to defeat Japan than to intimidate Russia is not convincing, this thought unquestionably appealed to some in Washington as at least an advantageous side-effect of Hiroshima.

So the machinery of suspicion and counter-suspicion, action and counteraction, was set in motion.

The Last Japan
Hasegawa Nyozekan

Perhaps no country has gone through so many cataclysmic changes in such a short span of years as Japan. In one hundred years (1850s–1950s), Japan went from a feudal, prein-dustrial, hermit nation to major industrial and military power, to conqueror and colonial master, to ignominious defeat, and finally to a democratic economic power with a pacifist foreign policy.

Hasegawa Nyozekan was a leading radical journalist, novelist, and critic who, having been born in 1875, lived through many of those events. This selection is from The Last Japan, *written in 1952 when he was seventy-seven years old. He reflects on the changes in Japan over his lifetime and wonders if traditional Japanese culture is conducive to demo-cratic institutions. Hasegawa also raises the issue of the historical tendency for Japan to adopt cultural values from other peoples and wonders if the time has not come to work harder on developing indigenous forms of science and culture.*

> **Consider:** *What modernization in the post-World War II decades meant for Ja-pan; the problems facing Japan in trying to modernize and democratize; the possi-ble effects of modernization on Japanese culture and character.*

The American decrees issued with respect to freedom and democratization in the internal administration of Japan resulted in five major changes: the enfranchise-ment of Japanese women (through granting of the vote); the encouragement given to the formation of labor unions; the liberalization of school instruction; the abolition of institutions which tended to cause the people to live in fear; and the democratization of the economic structure.

These five great changes in the government of the nation followed a course which the history of the modernization of Japan and of the Japanese themselves would have taken anyway if left to its natural tendency; they were, in fact, the direction towards which Japanese history was pointed. The history of Japan since the early '30s was distorted by the mistaken designs of the men in power, but the

---

SOURCE: Ryusaku Tsunoda, et al. (eds.) *Sources of Japanese Tradition* (New York: Columbia University Press, 1961), pp. 891–900.

process of modernization itself was uncompromisingly carried out. We must, therefore, examine whether or not the culture of the Japanese people today is of a nature capable of turning Japan into a truly and completely modern nation. We must also make ourselves aware of those elements in both our strong points and our shortcomings which must be changed.

During the Meiji Era the nation and people advanced boldly in the historical process of modernization which permitted Japan to break out of her isolation and stand among the nations of the world. When we reached the '30s, however, Japan was carried away by the tide of an age of world reaction, and there ensued a revival of feudalistic Japanese institutions. That our nation should have been plunged into destruction by the coercive force of a union of the military and civil proves that there had been no break in the "feudalistic" nature of the forms of our characteristic racial, political and social activities. This factor lent a special quality to our national culture, a quality destined to determine Japanese national and racial characteristics and to lead Japan to its tragic fate. Thus, as a basic condition for the reconstruction of Japan as a free and democratic nation, a change in our cultural nature itself must be planned and executed. . . .

. . . [T]he discovery of a new means of freeing ourselves from attitude of subordination and of developing cultural characteristics of independence which can be shared by the entire people is a prerequisite to the reconstruction of the nation.

The first essential to achieve is an educational and cultural program which will permit the free development of the feelings and intellect of the Japanese. We must restore the cultural attitude held by the Japan of ancient times with respect to all aspects of life: that is, to maintain a receptivity which is free, unbiased, and diverse.

Second, there must be a switch from imitativeness to creativity. Japanese culture, now as in former days, has been said to be imitative in character. This is because Japan during the period from the earliest days to the Middle Ages was always in the position of being obliged to take in the cultural nourishment of China. In modern times she has been in the same position with respect to the West. However, the Japanese have invariably digested and absorbed these cultural influences once they had passed the stage of imitation, and thereby succeeded in creating a new and purely Japanese culture. . . .

. . . The real reason why Japanese politics, philosophy, literature, and art from the Meiji Period to the present have always been engaged in such a frantic pursuit of Western trends is that we have not been able to display sufficient creativity in the development of our own cultural nature.

This failing was not in the least compensated for by the pretended "discovery" or "creation" of "truly Japanese" things, stemming from the cultural commands of the military clique during the war. Such activities were no more than a kind of "cultural self-consolation." . . . The "truly Japanese" things are not things which can be "discovered" or "created" in this manner; they must be a natural product obtained from a nationwide ability and means to create. Education and research must be for the sake of fostering such an ability throughout the country and for the promotion of a structure, organization, form, and content which would permit such a process to take place throughout the country. . . .

We must change the world of the daily life of the Japanese into an environment for living in which we, who up to now have led most unscientific lives, will be given a scientific purpose and form. We will thus be enabled to breathe in a scientific atmosphere, just as a newborn babe drinks its mother's milk. . . .

It is impossible to deny that most of the better educated classes of Japanese society were unhappy over the blind acts of the military clique and sought to prevent them. That their strength was inadequate to the task was due not so much to a deficiency of intellect as to a weakness of the will.

This will power can be strengthened by cultural education or by means quite outside the realm of culture. . . .

Viewed in this light, the difficult conditions under which the Japanese have lived since the defeat may be said to contain hope if we think of them as the environment for strengthening our will power and for molding us.

Economic Decolonization and Arrested Development in Africa
D. K. Fieldhouse

The political instability that independent Africa experienced was not only evident in the political sphere, but in the economy as well. Many supporters of African independence became disillusioned with the steady economic decline that formerly rich colonial regions experienced and sought to identify the causes. Although some scholars and loan agencies have linked the economic disasters to the unstable political climate, more recent analyses have sought the causes in the economic policies of the colonial period. According to this view, African independent leaders inherited from the Europeans an economy with an intrusive state system which they have been unable to alter. According to critics of colonialism, the structure inherited from the period of colonialism has limited the economic choices of Africans and is responsible for Africa's relative economic backwardness. In the following discussion, D. K. Fieldhouse, a noted British historian of imperialism, adds another dimension to the debate.

> **Consider:** *Where the author lays the blame for the "arrested development" of African states; the possible reaction of African nationalists to the deterioration of the economy; why this question of the economy is so important.*

SOURCE: D. K. Fieldhouse, *Black Africa 1945–1980: Economic Decolonization and Arrested Development* (London: Allen & Unwin, 1986) 244–245.

[W]hile the seeds of Africa's dependence on foreign concessionary loans and grants were sown in the late-colonial period, the most important single consequence of decolonization was its grotesque flowering into unmanageable overspending and indebtedness. Colonialism, for most of its course, had kept colonial public expenditure, investment and borrowing in line with a colony's capacity to pay; and this capacity was closely related to the health of the international economy, since this determined a colony's balance of payments position and the size of government revenues. After independence these constraints were gradually thrown off: need and ambition rather than ability to meet the costs became the criteria of policy-making. During the first decade and a half after 1960 international conditions generally concealed the dangers. Commodity prices remained generally good, interest rates and repayment terms on foreign borrowing low, the flow of foreign equity capital high. By the later 1970s most of this had changed. Black Africa found itself in a position no colonial government would ever have permitted, heavily indebted, deeply committed to continuing large expenditure, but facing greatly increased interest charges, lower commodity prices and a virtual stoppage of fresh equity capital as a consequence of the compulsory indigenization of foreign private capital.

It is at this point that the economic consequences of decolonization became for the first time really obvious. Colonial economic policy had been cautious to the point of inertia; but caution had at least provided insurance against disaster. Most new African states preferred to gamble. The superficially impressive achievements of the first two decades after independence, which had made colonialism appear to have achieved so little, were built on sand. Growth resulted from booming exports, unexploited domestic tax potential and huge injections of foreign capital; it did not reflect structural development in Black Africa. When it was no longer possible to extract so large a surplus from the peasants and foreign borrowing became prohibitively expensive at a time when the commodity markets were depressed, most African states found themselves virtually bankrupt.

This, then, is the main link between decolonization and economic failure in Black Africa. Colonial rulers, afraid of the political and social consequences of economic recession, were probably too reluctant to innovate at the cost of indebtedness. Their successors, impelled rather by the political need to demonstrate progress, to reward supporters and to employ growing urban populations, went to the other extreme. Because the development they planned was, in many cases, ill-conceived and based on wildly over-optimistic assessments of what was possible, it was bound sooner or later to slow up or be checked. But that is not to say that it was "arrested" and therefore could not be resumed: merely that development in Black Africa was at all times bound to be slow and that it could only be sustained when governments tackled the underlying weaknesses which neither colonial nor postcolonial regimes had been able to remove by the mid-1980s.

Social and Economic Divisions in Latin America

Oscar Delgado

Throughout Latin American history, the vast majority of people have lived off of the land. Agricultural production and subsistence farming have been basic to the economy and cultures of the region. Yet, the extraordinary concentration of land in the hands of a very few owners has caused continual hardship and, at various times, led to massive social unrest. In this excerpt, Oscar Delgado analyzes the continued maldistribution of land and wealth in Latin America during the post-World War II decades.

> **Consider:** *The sources of economic and social divisions in Latin America; why the call for land reform has had such power throughout Latin American history.*

Latin America had a population of 199 million in 1960, according to a United Nations estimate. Of this total, 108 million or 54 per cent live in rural areas, and of these 28 1/2 million are economically active.

All rural dwellers who are economically active have family and social responsibilities, but almost all of them are underemployed and many are victims of seasonal unemployment. Their income is extremely low, and considerable numbers of them live only on the margin of money economy. Generally speaking, they work the soil in a primitive or almost primitive fashion. The average percentage of literacy in rural Latin America is around 80; but vast areas have no schools at all and an illiteracy rate of 100 per cent. . . .

These 28 1/2 million have to produce food not only for themselves but also directly for their 70 1/2 million dependents and, more indirectly, for the 91 million urban dwellers. Moreover, in terms of the national economy, they have to produce a surplus for economic development. And yet, 63 percent of them—18 million adult farmers—have no land at all. Some 5 1/2 million have an insufficient amount of land; 1.9 million have enough land, and 100,000—mostly absentee landlords—have too much land.

One out of every 185,000 Latin Americans—or one out of every 100,000 rural Latin Americans—owns over 1,000 hectares. For 107,955 landlords, or 1.5 per cent of all landholders, own 471 hectares, or 65 per cent of all land in private hands. Each of them owns an average of 4,300 hectares; but many have more than 10,000, and some have hundreds of thousands—even millions.

So much for individuals. But properties belonging to several members of a family can be registered under the name of its head. There are Latin American families who own more land than is occupied by a number of sovereign nations. In fact, there are families or groups of interrelated families in the Argentine,

---

SOURCE: Oscar Delgado, "Revolution, Reform, Conservatism: Three Types of Agrarian Structure," *Dissent*, IX (Autumn, 1962), 351–353.

Brazil, Chile and Venezuela, of which each has more land than several countries put together. This is a situation with no parallel elsewhere. Statistically speaking, Latin America has the highest index of concentrated accumulation of rural property in the world.

Latin America is now beginning to develop, however slowly. Its indices of urbanization and industrialization are progressively rising. However, this progress is generally unnoticeable because the population rapidly increases at one of the highest rates of growth in the world. Internal migration to the cities is constant and growing, but it does not absorb the rural population explosion caused by the rising birth rate and the falling death rate. This migration, a product of urbanization and industrialization, makes the rural population decrease relatively, in proportion to urban population; but it does not decrease it absolutely. . . .

. . . There can be no question that the rural—and agricultural—population of Latin America is increasing today in a geometrical progression. Every year, every month and every day there are new mouths to feed and new hands to be provided with work, land, tools, and money. Given an annual rate of increase of 3 percent, this means about 6 million new mouths and new pairs of hands every year in all Latin America, and 3.8 million in the rural sector.

The War in Vietnam

The United States became involved in the wars of Indochina in 1947 in support of the French efforts to regain colonial rule. American officials wanted a strong France in Europe and believed that continued colonial possessions would add to that strength. By 1954 the United States was paying for over 80 percent of the French war effort and was unhappy about France's decision to end its involvement after the defeat at Dien Bien Phu.

The United States saw Vietnam as a potential battleground in the Cold War and viewed it as a surrogate of the Chinese, if not the Russians. So Washington subverted the planned elections in 1956, created a new government in the south of Vietnam, importing a leader handpicked by U.S. officials in Washington. Those decisions led only to disaster and the defeat of the Americans in 1973. A civil war between the two governments of Vietnam finally ended in 1975 after the southern forces were defeated.

After the enormous amount of human life which was expended to fight this Indochina War, most Americans (unlike the Vietnamese who knew they were fighting for an end to foreign involvement in their country) still didn't understand what the war was about. This confusion is evident in an editorial which appeared in The New Yorker *on May 5, 1975, excerpted below.*

> **Consider:** *How Americans could fight for so long and know so little about the Vietnamese people and culture, considered their "enemy."*

SOURCE: "Notes and Comment" from the May 5, 1975 issue of *The New Yorker.*

Last week, the war in Vietnam seemed to be moving toward its end, but something stranger than the victory of one side over the other was going on. Not only was the side supported by the United States collapsing; the world view that had given the war its importance in the eyes of American officialdom was collapsing, too. The system of friendships and enmities that had provided the policy with what Secretary of State Henry Kissinger calls its "coherence" was in disarray. The confusion was visible in microcosm in the positions taken on the issue of the Americans who remained in Saigon. The threats to these Americans came from some unexpected quarters. The principal threat, it seemed, came not from the North Vietnamese but from the South Vietnamese, America's ally. Drew Middleton, the military-affairs analyst for the *Times,* wrote of the mood of the South Vietnamese soldiers who had retreated from Danang to Saigon, "Ironically, these forces, who fought better than any other Government troops in the five-week campaign, are now regarded as the most serious danger to Americans in Saigon, as well as to politicians seeking an accommodation with the Communists infiltrating into the city." There was even fear that the South Vietnamese might hold the Americans hostage. Stranger still were reports that Mr. Graham Martin, the American Ambassador to South Vietnam, was slowing the evacuation—that *he* was holding the Americans hostage, in the hope of getting more aid for the South from Congress. Meanwhile, the "enemy"—the North Vietnamese—were promising a safe withdrawal for the Americans. The North Vietnamese, of course, have been trying to get Westerners out of Vietnam for some thirty years now.

The enmity of the South Vietnamese against the Americans was fast becoming the predominant emotion in Saigon. President Thieu, in his speech of resignation, put the blame for his government's plight not on the North Vietnamese but on the United States. The North Vietnamese may have had a supporting role, he seemed to be suggesting, but it was the United States that had "led the South Vietnamese people to death." He sounded as though the United States had been at war with South Vietnam, not North Vietnam, these last fifteen years. Thieu's opinion was apparently shared by the Ford Administration. In Washington, not long before, Mr. Kissinger—whom Thieu bitterly attacked in his resignation speech—had said that the United States must give Thieu more aid if it did not want to "destroy an ally." But while Thieu was blaming Kissinger for the collapse of the Saigon regime, Kissinger was blaming Congress. He contended that it was Congress that had not lived up to the American "commitment" to South Vietnam (Congress, meanwhile, was learning of the "commitment" for the first time, and was surprised at being accused of not having upheld a promise it did not know that the United States had made.) Moreover, as Kissinger was blaming Congress for its failures in the past, another member of the Administration, Vice-President Rockefeller, was looking to the future failures of Congress. Speculating that some thousands of Americans might be killed or captured in Saigon, he said that such an eventuality would make a campaign issue in the Presidential race of 1976; he also said that if Congress did not vote funds "and the Communists take over and there are a million people liquidated, we know where the responsibility will lie."

Then, shortly afterward, President Ford said that Vietnam should not be a campaign issue in 1976.

Oddly, amid all this recrimination and talk of prospective massacres and campaign issues, there was very little mention of Russia, China, and North Vietnam—the nations whose influence the United States had supposedly been opposing in South Vietnam. Indeed, President Ford, in his recent State of the World address, said that America's wounds were "self-inflicted." The foe had apparently been read out of the picture. We had been battling ourselves, it seemed, and had lost. What mention there was of the Communist powers tended to be cordial and understanding. Secretary of Defense James Schlesinger set the tone when he said, a few weeks back, during a discussion of the American presence in Asia, that the Chinese and the Russians sometimes found their Asian allies prone to "exuberance" and welcomed having the United States step in as a restraining influence. President Ford struck the same note in some remarks not long afterward. Speaking of the collapse of the Saigon forces in the northern part of South Vietnam, he said, "I don't think we can blame the Soviet Union and the People's Republic of China in this case. If we had done with our allies what we promised, I think this whole tragedy could have been eliminated." Instead, we could blame the members of our own Congress, who had voted down the extra military aid.

The remarks of the President and the Secretary of Defense seemed to evoke nothing less than a vision of a new world order. At one time, the government had told the public that the United States was fighting against Moscow and Peking in Vietnam, but now it seemed to be saying that these countries were our partners in the war. In the new world order, the great powers had apparently agreed that each would support its own allies in whatever wars were going on. Thus, a balance had been struck in which the Americans and the Russians and the Chinese were to live in peace while the Vietnamese would go on killing each other forever. The name of this order was "détente." But if the United States was in Asia to protect Chinese and Russian interests, as Mr. Schlesinger had said, Mr. Kissinger had not been told, for the day after the President had said we could not blame Russia and China for what was happening in Vietnam, Kissinger did blame them. "We shall not forget who supplied the arms which North Vietnam used to make a mockery of its signature on the Paris accords," he said.

The regime in Saigon was falling, but official Washington seemed at a loss to explain why. Some people were pointing the finger of blame at Russia and China, but others were saying that those countries were innocent. Some were saying that the fault was President Thieu's (while he was saying that the fault was ours). Some were saying that Congress was to blame, but then they were saying that there was enough blame for all Americans to share. The longest war in our history was at last coming to an end, and we did not know who the enemy had been.

Chapter Questions

1. What argument could be made for the assertion that the fundamental historical shift in the last two hundred years did not come with World War I, as some historians argue, but with World War II, as indicated by the consequences of that war and the developments of the postwar period?

2. What were some of the alternatives available to societies trying to deal with modernization during this period? What role might the Cold War have played in choosing among these alternatives? What role might the experience of colonization and decolonization have played in this choice?

3. Drawing from the sources in this chapter, in what ways was the period one of struggle between the elites in power and those below them demanding recognition? What are some of the similarities and differences in these struggles in various parts of the world?

FOURTEEN

The Present in Perspective

The most recent years in World history are particularly difficult to evaluate. They are so much a part of the present that it is almost impossible to gain a historical perspective on them.

While many of the basic trends of the postwar era examined in the previous two chapters have continued, some important changes have become apparent—particularly in the last few years. The Cold War between the United States and the Soviet Union waned during the late 1980s, and in recent years revolutionary changes have been taking place in what was the Soviet Union and in eastern Europe. At least for the West, these changes may be so far-reaching as to constitute a historical watershed—a marking of the end of the twentieth century and the beginning of the twenty-first century. The rest of Europe, and indeed much of the world, has pursued an increasingly independent course from the two superpowers. The strife-ridden, oil-rich Middle East has become an area of great concern and importance to the world community. Certain areas in Asia, such as Japan, South Korea, Taiwan, and Singapore have developed strong economies, helping to shift the economic balance of power in the world. New technological accomplishments, ranging from space exploration to the production of computers, affect our civilizations in many ways. Numerous other recent trends and events could be added to this necessarily brief list.

This chapter is not organized in the usual way, for the sources are so much a part of the present that the usual distinctions between primary and secondary sources are no longer useful. The selections deal with three kinds of developments. The first concerns changes in the communist world, particularly the former Soviet Union and China. The second has to do with social, cultural, and ecological trends that have been of particular significance and still affect us today. The third involves interpreting the present era as a whole and predicting the future.

There is much ambivalence about recent developments. Our own involvement makes evaluation of the present particularly difficult. At best, the selections in this chapter can help put elements of the present into perspective.

Modernization: The Western and Non-Western Worlds

Although almost all areas of the world that were once colonies of the Western powers gained independence during the quarter century following World War II, the penetration of the rest of the world by Western ideas, values, institutions, and products has been extremely widespread. This is illustrated in this photograph showing a citizen of Kuwait, an oil-rich sheikdom of the Persian Gulf, carrying a Western television set across a road. He is wearing Western-style tennis shoes that were probably manufactured in the far east. In the background are a bilingual store sign and Western automobiles. Reflected in the glass of the television set is a modern building probably designed by a Western architect and built under the direction of an international construction firm using both foreign and domestic labor and materials. This photograph suggests that some of the formerly colonized areas are taking economic, political, and social steps in the same direction as Western industrialized states.

> **Consider:** *The effects of westernization on non-Western culture as illustrated by this photo.*

Photo 14-1

Bruno Barbey/Magnum

Communist China: The Four Modernizations

Communique of the Central Committee, December 1978

Over the past two decades, there have been some striking changes within the communist world. One of the most important was initiated in China in 1978. Since the 1950s, under the leadership of Mao Zedong (Mao Tse-tung), China had pursued a policy of economic development similar to the Five-Year Plans in the Soviet Union emphasizing centralized planning, heavy industry, and agricultural collectivization. After a power struggle follow-

SOURCE: *The Peking Review,* July 28, 1978.

ing Mao's death in 1976, more moderate officials, led by Deng Xiaoping (Teng Hsiao-p'ing), came to power. In 1978 they initiated the policy of the "Four Modernizations." As indicated in the following official statement of this policy, China would be abandoning many elements of its old program of economic development in favor of more pragmatic methods.

> **Consider:** *By implication, what sorts of economic problems China was having; ways in which the old policy of centralized planning is being attacked; the significance of changes in agricultural policy.*

[N]ow is an appropriate time . . . to shift the emphasis of our Party's work and the attention of the people of the whole country to socialist modernization. This is of major significance for fulfilment of the three-year and eight-year programmes for the development of the national economy and the outline for 23 years, for the modernization of agriculture, industry, national defence and science and technology and for the consolidation of the dictatorship of the proletariat in our country. The general task put forward by our Party for the new period reflects the demands of history and the people's aspirations and represents their fundamental interests. Whether or not we can carry this general task to completion, speed socialist modernization and on the basis of a rapid growth in production improve the people's living standards significantly and strengthen national defence—this is a major issue which is of paramount concern to all our people and of great significance to the cause of world peace and progress. Carrying out the four modernizations requires great growth in the productive forces, which in turn requires diverse changes in those aspects of the relations of production and the superstructure not in harmony with the growth of the productive forces, and requires changes in all methods of management, actions and thinking which stand in the way of such growth. Socialist modernization is therefore a profound and extensive revolution. . . .

. . . [W]e are now, in the light of the new historical conditions and practical experience, adopting a number of major new economic measures, conscientiously transforming the system and methods of economic management, actively expanding economic co-operation on terms of equality and mutual benefit with other countries on the basis of self-reliance, striving to adopt the world's advanced technologies and equipment and greatly strengthening scientific and educational work to meet the needs of modernization. . . .

The session points out that one of the serious shortcomings in the structure of economic management in our country is the overconcentration of authority, and it is necessary boldly to shift it under guidance from the leadership to lower levels so that the local authorities and industrial and agricultural enterprises will have greater power of decision in management under the guidance of unified state planning; big efforts should be made to simplify bodies at various levels charged with economic administration and transfer most of their functions to such enterprises as specialized companies or complexes; it is necessary to act firmly in line with economic law, attach importance to the role of the law of value, consciously combine ideological and political work with economic methods and give full play to the enthusiasm of cadres and workers for production; it is necessary, under the centralized leadership of the Party, to tackle conscientiously the failure to make a distinction between the Party, the government and the enterprise and to put a stop to the substitution of Party for government and the substitution of government for enterprise administration, to institute a division of responsibilities among different levels, types of work and individuals, increase the authority and responsibility of administrative bodies and managerial personnel, reduce the number of meetings and amount of paper work to raise work efficiency, and conscientiously adopt the practices of examination, reward and punishment, promotion and demotion. . . .

The plenary session holds that the whole Party should concentrate its main energy and efforts on advancing agriculture as fast as possible because agriculture, the foundation of the national economy, has been seriously damaged in recent years and remains very weak on the whole. . . . This requires first of all releasing the socialist enthusiasm of our country's several hundred million peasants, paying full attention to their material well-being economically and giving effective protection to their democratic rights politically. Taking this as the guideline, the plenary session set forth a series of policies and economic measures aimed at raising present agricultural production. The most important are as follows: The right of ownership by the people's communes, production brigades and production teams and their power of decision must be protected effectively by the laws of the state; it is not permitted to commandeer the manpower, funds, products and material of any production team; the economic organizations at various levels of the people's commune must conscientiously implement the socialist principle of "to each according to his work," work out payment in accordance with the amount and quality of work done, and overcome equalitarianism; small plots of land for private use by commune members, their domestic side-occupations, and village fairs are necessary adjuncts of the socialist economy, and must not be interfered with; the people's communes must resolutely implement the system of three levels of ownership with the production team as the basic accounting unit, and this should remain unchanged.

The Gorbachev Strategy
Thomas H. Naylor

In 1985 Mikhail Gorbachev rose to power in the Soviet Union and initiated major reform policies: glasnost *(political and cultural openness) and* perestroika *(economic restructuring). Major changes within the Soviet Union, in other eastern European countries, and in*

SOURCE: Reprinted by permission of the publisher, from *The Gorbachev Strategy* by Thomas H. Naylor (Lexington, Mass.: Lexington Books, D. C. Heath & Co., copyright 1988 D. C. Heath & Co.), pp. 48–49.

*international affairs apparently streamed from these reform policies. In the following se-
lection, Thomas H. Naylor of Duke University attempts to interpret the nature and objectives of these reforms.*

> **Consider:** *How Naylor interprets these reforms; what other interpretation might
> be made of these reforms; whether events since 1985 support Naylor's interpreta-
> tion.*

To achieve his overall objective of making the Soviet Union a more open society,
Gorbachev has formulated and is in the process of implementing a strategy of
radical reform consisting of ten specific strategies:

1. *Economy:* Decentralization of decision making of state-owned enterprises
   including such decisions as product mix, prices, output, wages, employment, investment, research and development, domestic and international
   sales and marketing, and incentives. Creation of new financial institutions
   to finance the expansion of Soviet enterprises. Authorization of private
   enterprises in the service sector of the economy.
2. *Agriculture:* Decentralization of state-owned farms and strengthening of
   agricultural cooperatives. Greater use of market incentives and an increase
   in the number of private farms.
3. *Technology:* A substantial increase in the commitment of resources to
   education and research and development in high technology fields—computers, process controls, robotics, genetic engineering, and space research.
   Creation of joint ventures with Western high-tech companies. Increased
   purchases of Western technology from such countries as West Germany,
   Japan, Israel, and Brazil.
4. *Consumption:* Increased investment in the manufacturing of consumer
   goods. Importation of high-quality consumer goods from the West.
5. *International Trade:* Decentralization of foreign trade to individual enterprises with the authority to trade directly with Western companies. Encouragement of joint ventures with the West. Participation in international
   trade and financial institutions.
6. *Democratization:* Decentralization of the Communist party, the Soviet
   government, and the Soviet economy. Increased democracy in the work-
   place. Greater freedom of political dissent. Improved possibilities to em-
   igrate from the Soviet Union.
7. *Foreign Policy:* Encouragement of increased political independence for
   Europe. A major effort to increase bilateral trade with Japan and China.
   The establishment of diplomatic relations with Israel and China.
8. *Third World:* Development of a face-saving strategy to get out of Afghanistan. Concentration of political and economic relations on the more afflu-
   ent Third World nations that offer the greatest promise for trade and
   technology.
9. *Arms Control:* Reduction in the level of anti-U.S. rhetoric and pursuit of

a strategy aimed at signing a major arms control agreement with the United States in 1990.

10.   *Culture:* Increased freedom of expression in speech, the press, literature, art, drama, movies, and religion. Permission for firms to go bankrupt and to fire incompetent employees. Tough disciplinary actions for alcohol and drug abuse, bribery, theft, and corruption.

After Communism: Causes for the Collapse
Robert Heilbroner

The rapid collapse of communism in the Soviet Union and eastern Europe has stunned most observers. Only in retrospect have reasons for this collapse been presented with any conviction. Scholars are now struggling to interpret what has happened. One of these is Robert Heilbroner, who has written extensively on economics, economic history, and current affairs. In the following selection, he focuses on the Soviet economic system, particularly the Soviet's central planning system as the key to the collapse.

> **Consider:** *Why the Soviet's central planning system might have worked well enough in the early stages of industrialization or for specific projects, but not well enough for a mature industrialized economy; why the collapse of communism in the Soviet Union has such widespread significance.*

Socialism has been a great tragedy this century, its calamitous finale the collapse of Communism in the Soviet Union and Eastern Europe. I doubt very much whether socialism has now disappeared from history, but there is no doubt that the collapse marks its end as a model of economic clarity. Moreover, I suspect that its economic failure may haunt socialism longer than the pathologies of Communism. Early on, one could see that the Soviets were headed toward political disaster, but much of that disaster seemed attributable to the hopeless political heritage of Russian history, not to socialism per se. It was the economic side of the Russian collapse that came as a shock. The prodigies of Russian prewar industrialization appeared to be an incontrovertible argument for the capacity of a planned economic system to achieve growth, and the argument appeared to be confirmed by the spectacular performance of the Soviets during the years of reconstruction immediately following the Second World War. Thus, there may have been discomfiture but there was not much surprise when the Soviet economy during the nineteen-fifties grew twice as fast as the American economy. Surprise did not appear until the nineteen-seventies, when the Soviet growth rate slipped to only half of ours, and consternation was not evident until the middle to late

SOURCE: Robert Heilbroner, "After Communism," *The New Yorker*, Sept. 10, 1990.

nineteen-eighties, when C.I.A. and academic specialists alike began to report something very close to zero growth. But collapse! No one expected collapse.

There is still no definitive account as to exactly why the Soviet economic system collapsed—one can never find the nail for whose want the shoe was lost. There were undoubtedly elements of this economic disaster with their roots in history: the bureaucrat is well known to Russian literature. Perhaps the final blow was delivered by *glasnost,* which released long-pent-up anger against economic conditions; or perhaps by the Soviet attempt to meet the Star Wars initiative—one hears many such guesses. All we know for certain is that the system deteriorated to a point far beyond the worst economic crisis ever experienced by capitalism, and that the villain in this deterioration was the central planning system itself. The conclusion one inevitably comes to is that to whatever extent socialism depends on such a system it will not work. . . .

The great problem of central planning lies buried in the procedures by which the economy is given its marching orders. As in a military campaign, which central planning resembles in many ways, production is brought about by a series of commands from the top, not by the independent decisions of regimental commanders, company captains, and platoon sergeants. This means that the economy "works" because—and only to the extent that—the quantity, quality, size, weight, and selling price of every nut, bolt, hinge, beam, tractor, and hydroelectric turbine have been previously determined. At the supreme headquarters, the numbers for gross national product are announced. In considerably lower and dingier offices, the numbers for nuts, bolts, and turbines are calculated, but it is apparent that if the plans for the latter are off, the plans for the former may be impossible to attain.

Planning thus requires that the immense map of desired national output be carved up into millions of individual pieces, like a jigsaw puzzle—the pieces produced by hundreds of thousands of enterprises, and the whole thing finally reassembled in such a way as to fit. That would be an extraordinarily difficult task even if the map of desired output were unchanged from year to year, but, of course, it is not: the chief planners change their objectives, and new technologies or labor shortages or bad weather or simply mistakes get in the way. In 1986, before *perestroika* was officially formulated, Gosplan, the highest planning commission in the Soviet Union, issued two thousand sets of instructions for major "product groups," such as construction materials, metals, and automotive vehicles. Gossnab, the State Material and Technical Supply Commission, then divided these product groups into fifteen thousand categories—lumber, copper, and trucks, for instance—and the various ministries in charge of the categories in turn subdivided them into fifty thousand more finely detailed products (shingles, beams, laths, boards) and then into specific products in each category (large, medium, and small shingles). These plans then percolated down through the hierarchy of production, receiving emendations or protests as they reached the level of plant managers and engineers, and thereafter travelled back up to the ministerial level. In this Byzantine process, perhaps the most difficult single step was to establish "success indicators"—desired performance targets—for enterprises. For many years, targets were given in physical terms—so many yards of cloth or tons of nails—but that led to obvious difficulties. If cloth was rewarded by the yard, it was woven loosely to make the yarn yield more yards. If the output of nails was determined by their number, factories produced huge numbers of pinlike nails; if by weight, smaller numbers of very heavy nails. The satiric magazine *Krokodil* once ran a cartoon of a factory manager proudly displaying his record output, a single gigantic nail suspended from a crane.

The difficulty, of course, was that the inevitable mismatches and mistakes could not be set to rights by the decisions of platoon sergeants or regimental commanders who were able to see that the campaign was not going as expected.

❁

I am not very sanguine about the prospect that socialism will continue as an important form of economic organization now that Communism is finished. This statement will come as a wry commentary to those who remember that Marx defined socialism as the stage that precedes Communism. But the collapse of the planned economies has forced us to rethink the meaning of socialism. As a semi-religious vision of a transformed humanity, it has been dealt devastating blows in the twentieth century. As a blueprint for a rationally planned society, it is in tatters.

Economic Revitalization of East Asia
Thomas B. Gold

More than any other part of the world, east Asia came out of the second world war in a state of extreme disruption and devastation. Japanese leaders had brought their people to the verge of starvation even before the massive American firebombing of Tokyo and the dropping of two atomic bombs. China had been at war with Japan since 1931 only to see the end of that war in 1945 followed by five years of brutal civil war. Taiwan, which had been bombed prior to 1945, had its resources stretched even more with the arrival of 2 to 3 million Chinese from the mainland as the Nationalists (Guomindang/GMD) were losing the war against the communists. Korea went through its own devastating war in 1950–1953.

Given this desolation, the region's lack of raw materials and sufficient foodstuffs, and the traditional Confucian (in China, Korea, Japan, and Vietnam) view of the merchant (who was at the bottom rung of the social ladder) as being immoral because of the pursuit of profits, economic recovery seemed very distant indeed. But Confucianism also placed

SOURCE: Thomas B. Gold, "Economic Revitalization of East Asia," In Myron L. Cohen, (ed.), *Asia in the Core Curriculum. Case Studies in the Social Sciences*, pp. 464–469.

*very high value on education, particularly rote memory. It also taught loyalty to, and
dependence on, a collective entity: family, enterprise, and the state.*

*In recent years Japan, Korea (at least South Korea), Hong Kong, Taiwan, and Singa-
pore—all Confucian states—have become enormously successful economically. There are
many complicated reasons for this, but one certainly is the shared characteristic of a
strong centrally run state. In this excerpt Thomas B. Gold, Professor of Sociology at the
University of California, Berkeley, examines how this attribute is linked to economic development.*

> **Consider:** *The relationship between economic growth and political democratiza-
> tion; the limitations of terms such as "socialist" and "capitalist" in describing eco-
> nomic systems.*

China, Japan, Taiwan, and South Korea **all share an economic model with a
central role for the state.** This is multi-faceted. The strong state role in socialist
China is well-known, but many are unaware of the major place of the state in the
market-economies of Japan, Taiwan, and South Korea. In each of these countries,
the state periodically produces plans for economic development; government
agencies collect data on the local and international economies and make predic-
tions as to their evolution. They target certain domestic sectors for special incentives (tax breaks and rebates, low-interest loans, access to foreign exchange, reduced import tariffs, etc.) in order to motivate local businesses to invest in those
target industries. The states have considerable control over the banking system
(through ownership of major shares in a number of banks and administration of
the postal savings systems), which facilitates implementation of fiscal policies. The
states also own many enterprises in key sectors, often as monopolies, enabling
them to direct certain materials to targeted companies. These are **indicative
plans,** not the command-type plans of a Soviet-style economy as in pre-reform
PRC. What is more, they are **market-conforming,** that is, they try to anticipate
market developments and assist private businesses to take optimal advantage of
future trends. In addition to these positive tactics, the states can use various
sanctions to elicit the desired response. By withholding incentives and licenses,
imposing punitive taxes, auditing books, and exercising various forms of political
coercion, the states can motivate recalcitrant businesses to conform. These are
economies attuned to the market and they have large vibrant private sectors, but
they are not strictly free enterprise economies as is often argued, because the
state, directly and indirectly, is a major actor. Its role has shrunk since the 1950s,
but it nonetheless continues to be a determinant.

An additional important role of the state that has had positive economic consequences has been its **massive investment in education in order to develop
human capital.** The literacy rate in Japan, Taiwan, and South Korea exceeds 90
percent. There is severe competition for advanced education, but the governments
have also invested in vocational training in order to provide a highly qualified
cadre of technicians and workers.

There are a number of reasons for the dominance of the state in East Asian economies. **In East Asian tradition, people expect the state to play a dominant role in their lives, helping to create prosperity and ensuring social harmony; failure to do so is considered grounds for rebellion.** There is the historical legacy of the Confucian bureaucracy placing constraints on the activities of merchants, although one of the revolutionary aspects of contemporary East Asia is the high social prestige given to private businessmen. Bureaucrats still enjoy high status and a certain degree of insulation from politics, enabling them to work according to objective criteria.

As part of the 1868 Meiji Reform in Japan, the central leadership took a forceful approach to developing the country's economy in order to make it wealthy and strong and thereby able to fend off Western imperialists. Japan took Taiwan, Korea, and Manchuria as colonies and implemented similar statist policies for their economies, introducing a structure which subsequent postcolonial governments adopted and continued. As in many underdeveloped economies, only the state had the necessary capital to establish key enterprises and build the infrastructure required for industrialization. This legacy of state-owned enterprises in crucial sectors has continued to the present.

Also, the governments of Taiwan and South Korea see themselves as under continued threat from their Communist enemies. This garrison mentality stimulates their efforts for economic development and legitimizes policies which interfere in private business decisions and activities in the name of national security. These governments are highly militarized and have created vast internal security networks, which frequently serve, through intimidation, to ensure compliance with state policies. It has also resulted in severe labor repression and the maintenance of labor peace, at least as long as incomes keep ahead of inflation. In China, the Communist party controls labor unions tightly. Defining itself as the party of the proletariat, it legitimizes labor repression by claiming that strikes work against the workers' own interests. . . .

Japan, Taiwan, South Korea, and now to a greater degree than ever, China, have mixed planned and market economies, and a powerful state sector alongside a vibrant private sector. **The old dichotomies of capitalism and socialism are breaking down.** Other developing economies of various political stripes are increasingly attempting to adopt aspects of the East Asian systems. . . .

Perhaps the major shortcoming of the East Asian development experience has been the strict and often brutal political authoritarianism that has accompanied rapid economic growth. It has been suggested that this authoritarianism facilitated, indeed, is indispensable to growth, and is a small price to pay for the tremendous economic reward it has brought. In order for the state to play a strong role in guiding the economy and channelling resources efficiently, the argument goes, it needs to have unquestioned authority and force. This reasoning runs counter to the assumption, popular in the 1950s, that economic development would be accompanied by political "modernization," meaning the introduction of Western-style democratic institutions and practices. Although postwar Japan has instituted a democratic electoral system, in the 1930s its industrialization was led by a militarized fascistic state.

The KMT[GMD] brought to Taiwan a militarized state with a far-flung internal security network. Comprised of a small cohort of mainland émigrés, it monopolized political power over 85 percent of the population who, while also Chinese, had lived on the island prior to its retrocession in 1945 from Japanese to Chinese control. Similar in structure to a Leninist communist party it penetrated Taiwan's society to stifle dissent and mobilize the people. It did not permit other parties and maintained its rule by martial law, dealing ruthlessly with its enemies.

The year 1987 proved to be a watershed for both Taiwan and South Korea. On Taiwan, the KMT abolished martial law and tacitly recognized the legitimacy of the opposition party, which until then had been illegal. It also began to step up exchanges with the Communist mainland, a sign of renewed confidence in itself and in its people. In January of 1988, President and KMT Chairman Chiang Ching-kuo died and was succeeded by Lee Teng-hui, a Taiwanese technocrat without military experience. The succession was peaceful, and the process of democratization and opening to the mainland continued and even accelerated. In South Korea, President Chun Doo-hwan bowed to public pressure to permit a constitutional change allowing the direct election of his successor. After a campaign in which two leading opposition figures opposed each other as well as Chun's hand-picked candidate, Roh Tae-woo, it was Roh who emerged victorious. He proceeded to speed up political liberalization and in 1988 did not prevent the public censure of his predecessor. In both Taiwan and South Korea, street demonstrations have increased, and there is a very visible radical component among Korean students. But in both societies, the process of political democratization has definitely begun; political modernization is catching up with economic and social development.

The Short Century—It's Over
John Lukacs

Historians have traditionally been interested in dividing their study and analysis of civilizations into eras or periods that make some sense—ideally that begin and end with some watershed developments and have some unifying characteristics. This is particularly difficult to do for our own time, for we lack some historical perspective. In the following selection, John Lukacs argues that in 1989 watershed events occurred in the west, bringing the twentieth century to an end and initiating the twenty-first century.

SOURCE: John Lukacs, "The Short Century—It's Over." *The New York Times,* February 17, 1991. Copyright © 1991 by The New York Times Company. Reprinted by permission.

Consider: *How Lukacs supports his argument; whether his argument works as well for the nonwestern world; what this might mean for the future.*

The 20th century is now over, and there are two extraordinary matters about this.

First, this was a short century. It lasted 75 years, from 1914 to 1989. Its two principal events were the two world wars. They were the two enormous mountain ranges that dominated its landscape. The Russian Revolution, the atom bomb, the end of the colonial empires, the establishment of the Communist states, the emergence of the two superpowers, the division of Europe and of Germany—all of these were the consequences of the two world wars, in the shadow of which we were living, until now.

The 19th century lasted exactly 99 years, from 1815 to 1914, from the end of Napoleon's wars to the start of the—so-called—First World War. The 18th century lasted 126 years, from 1689 to 1815, from the beginning of the world wars between England and France (of which the American War of Independence was but part) until their end at Waterloo.

Second, we know that the 20th century is over. In 1815, no one knew that this was the end of the Atlantic world wars and the beginning of the Hundred Years' Peace. At that time, everyone, friends as well as enemies of the French Revolution, were concerned with the prospect of great revolutions surfacing again. There were revolutions after 1815, but the entire history of the 19th century was marked by the absence of world wars during 99 years. Its exceptional prosperity and progress were due to that.

In 1689, the very word "century" was hardly known. The "Oxford English Dictionary" notes its first present usage, in English, in 1626. Before that the word meant a Roman military unit of 100 men; then it began to have another meaning, that of 100 years. It marked the beginning of our modern historical consciousness.

We know that the 20th century is over—not merely because of our historical consciousness (which is something different from a widespread knowledge of history) but mainly because the confrontation of the two superpowers, the outcome of the Second World War, has died down. The Russians have retreated from Eastern Europe and Germany has been reunited. Outside Europe, even the Korean and the Vietnam wars, the missile crisis in Cuba and other political crises such as Nicaragua were, directly or indirectly, involved with that confrontation.

In 1991, we live in a very different world, in which, both the U.S. and the Soviet Union face grave problems with peoples and dictators in the so-called third world. Keep in mind that the ugly events in Lithuania are no exception to this: They involve the political structure of the Soviet Union itself. Even its name, the Union of Soviet Socialist Republics, is becoming an anachronism, as once happened with the Holy Roman Empire.

Keep in mind, too, that no matter when and how the gulf war ends, the so-called Middle East will remain a serious problem both for the U.S. and the Soviet Union. Even in the case of a smashing American political or military victory, its beneficial results will be ephemeral. To think—let alone speak—of a Pax Americana in the Middle East is peurile nonsense.

Not only the configuration of great powers and their alliances but the very structure of political history has changed. Both superpowers have plenty of domestic problems. In the Soviet Union, this has now become frighteningly actual; in the U.S., the internal problems are different but not superficial. The very sovereignty and cohesion of states, the authority and efficacy of the governments are not what they were.

Are we going to see ever larger and larger political units? "Europe" will, at best, become a free-trade economic zone, but a Union of Europe is a mirage. Or are we more likely going to see the break-up of several states into small national ones? Are we going to see a large-scale migration of millions of peoples, something that has not happened since the last centuries of the Roman Empire? This is at least possible. The very texture of history is changing before our very eyes.

Are we on the threshold of a new Dark Ages? We must hope not. The main task before us is the rethinking of the word "progress." Like that of "century," the meaning of that word, too, is more recent than we have been accustomed to think. Before the 16th century, that is, before the opening of the so-called modern age (another misnomer, suggesting that this age would last forever) progress simply meant an advance in distance, not in time, without the sense of evolutionary improvement.

Thereafter, the word "progress" began to carry the unquestionable optimistic meaning of endless material and scientific promise, until, during the 20th century, it began to lose some of its shine, because of the increasingly questionable benefits of technology. At the beginning of the 20th century, technology and barbarism seemed to be antitheses. They no longer are. But technology and its threat to the natural environment are only part of the larger problem of progress, a word and an ideal whose more proper and true application is the task of the 21st century that has already begun.

A Feminist Manifesto
Redstockings

It is increasingly recognized that women, both individually and in organizations, have been struggling for changes for a long time. The effort to gain consciousness and understanding of what it means to be a woman—politically, socially, economically, and sexually—became central to women's struggles for change in the mid-twentieth century. During the 1960s and 1970s women's struggle for change spread and took on a new militancy. Throughout the West, women were arguing for change in what came to be

SOURCE: Redstockings, July 7, 1969, mimeograph.

known, especially in the United States, as the women's liberation movement. Numerous
women's organizations formed, and many issued publications stating their views.
The following selection is an example of one of the more radical statements of feminism. It
was issued in July 1969 by Redstockings, an organization of New York feminists.

Consider: *The primary demands of the Redstockings; how this group justifies its*
demands; how men might react to this selection.

I. After centuries of individual and preliminary political struggle, women are
uniting to achieve their final liberation from male supremacy. Redstockings is
dedicated to building their unity and winning our freedom.

II. Women are an oppressed class. Our oppression is total, affecting every facet
of our lives. We are exploited as sex objects, breeders, domestic servants, and
cheap labor. We are considered inferior beings, whose only purpose is to enhance
men's lives. Our humanity is denied. Our prescribed behavior is enforced by the
threat of physical violence.

Because we have lived so intimately with our oppressors, in isolation from each
other, we have been kept from seeing our personal suffering as a political condition. This creates the illusion that a woman's relationship with her man is a matter
of interplay between two unique personalities, and can be worked out individually.
In reality, every such relationship is a *class* relationship, and the conflicts between
individual men and women are *political* conflicts that can only be solved collectively.

III. We identify the agents of our oppression as men. Male supremacy is the
oldest, most basic form of domination. All other forms of exploitations and oppression (racism, capitalism, imperialism, and the like) are extensions of male
supremacy: men dominate women, a few men dominate the rest. All power
structures throughout history have been male-dominated and male-oriented. Men
have controlled all political, economic, and cultural institutions and backed up this
control with physical force. They have used their power to keep women in an
inferior position. *All men* receive economic, sexual, and psychological benefits
from male supremacy. *All men* have oppressed women.

IV. Attempts have been made to shift the burden of responsibility from men
to institutions or to women themselves. We condemn these arguments as evasions.
Institutions alone do not oppress; they are merely tools of the oppressor. To blame
institutions implies that men and women are equally victimized, obscures the fact
that men benefit from the subordination of women, and gives men the excuse
that they are forced to be oppressors. On the contrary, any man is free to renounce
his superior position provided that he is willing to be treated like a woman by
other men.

We also reject the idea that women consent to or are to blame for their own
oppression. Women's submission is not the result of brainwashing, stupidity, or
mental illness but of continual, daily pressure from men. We do not need to
change ourselves, but to change men.

The most slanderous evasion of all is that women can oppress men. The basis for this illusion is the isolation of individual relationships from their political context and the tendency of men to see any legitimate challenge to their privileges as persecution.

V. We regard our personal experience, and our feelings about that experience, as the basis for an analysis of our common situation. We cannot rely on existing ideologies as they are all products of male supremacist culture. We question every generalization and accept none that are not confirmed by our experience.

Our chief task at present is to develop female class consciousness through sharing experience and publicly exposing the sexist foundation of all our institutions. Consciousness-raising is not "therapy," which implies the existence of individual solutions and falsely assumes that the male-female relationship is purely personal, but the only method by which we can ensure that our program for liberation is based on the concrete realities of our lives.

The first requirement for raising class consciousness is honesty, in private and in public, with ourselves and other women.

VI. We identify with all women. We define our best interest as that of the poorest, most brutally exploited woman.

We repudiate all economic, racial, educational, or status privileges that divide us from other women. We are determined to recognize and eliminate any prejudices we may hold against other women.

We are committed to achieving internal democracy. We will do whatever is necessary to ensure that every woman in our movement has an equal chance to participate, assume responsibility, and develop her political potential.

VII. We call on all our sisters to unite with us in struggle.

We call on all men to give up their male privileges and support women's liberation in the interests of our humanity and their own.

In fighting for our liberation we will always take the side of women against their oppressors. We will not ask what is "revolutionary" or "reformist," only what is good for women.

The time for individual skirmishes has passed. This time we are going all the way.

The Philosophy of Existentialism
Jean-Paul Sartre

One of the most popular and provocative philosophies to emerge in the mid-twentieth century was existentialism. Although the origins of existentialism can be found in nineteenth-century writers such as Søren Kierkegaard and Friedrich Nietzsche, its most popu-

Source: Jean-Paul Sartre, *The Philosophy of Existentialism*, Wade Baskin, ed. Reprinted by permission of Philosophical Library, Inc. (New York, 1965), pp. 35–36.

lar exponent was the French novelist, playwright, philosopher, and political activist Jean-Paul Sartre (1905–1980). Sartre's interpretation of existentialism reflects the dilemma of a twentieth-century atheist who can no longer accept traditional ways for determining standards of conduct. The following excerpt is from a lecture given by Sartre in Paris in 1945. In it he is describing the nature of existentialism and responding to critics.

> **Consider:** *What Sartre means when he says that man [or woman] chooses himself [or herself]; the ethical implications of this philosophy.*

Man is nothing else but what he makes of himself. Such is the first principle of existentialism. It is also what is called subjectivity. The name we are labeled with when charges are brought against us. But what do we mean by this, if not that man has a greater dignity than a stone or table? For we mean that man first exists, that is, that man first of all is the being who hurls himself toward a future and who is conscious of imagining himself as being in the future. Man is at the start a plan which is aware of itself, rather than a patch of moss, a piece of garbage, or a cauliflower; nothing exists prior to this plan; there is nothing in heaven; man will be what he will have planned to be. Not what he will want to be. Because by the word "will" we generally mean a conscious decision, which is subsequent to what we have already made of ourselves. I may want to belong to a political party, write a book, get married; but all that is only a manifestation of an earlier, more spontaneous choice that is called "will." But if existence really does precede essence, man is responsible for what he is. Thus, existentialism's first move is to make every man aware of what he is and to make the full responsibility of his existence rest on him. And when we say that man is responsible for himself, we do not only mean that he is responsible for his own individuality, but that he is responsible for all men.

The word subjectivism has two meanings, and our opponents play on the two. Subjectivism means, on the one hand, that an individual chooses and makes himself; and, on the other, that it is impossible for man to transcend human subjectivity. The second of these is the essential meaning of existentialism. When we say that man chooses his own self, we mean that every one of us does likewise; but we also mean by that that in making this choice he also chooses all men. In fact, in creating the man that we want to be, there is not a single one of our acts which does not at the same time create an image of man as we think he ought to be. To choose to be this or that is to affirm at the same time the value of what we choose, because we can never choose evil. We always choose the good, and nothing can be good for us without being good for all.

If, on the other hand, existence precedes essence, and if we grant that we exist and fashion our image at one and the same time, the image is valid for everybody and for our whole age. Thus, our responsibility is much greater than we might have supposed, because it involves all mankind. If I am a workingman and choose to join a Christian trade-union rather than be a communist, and if by being a member I want to show that the best thing for man is resignation, that the kingdom of man is not of this world, I am not only involving my own case—I want to be resigned for everyone. As a result, my action has involved all humanity. To take a more individual matter, if I want to marry, to have children; even if this marriage depends solely on my own circumstances or passion or wish, I am involving all humanity in monogamy and not merely myself. Therefore, I am responsible for myself and for everyone else. I am creating a certain image of man of my own choosing. In choosing myself, I choose man.

Revolution and the Intellectual in Latin America
Alan Riding

The political boundaries of Latin American nations have produced national identities and rivalries. But over the course of the past century, a broader Latin American nationalism has survived and even flourished. Common language, interlocked histories, and cultures have led Latin Americans, and especially intellectuals, to articulate a common identity. This excerpt by Alan Riding, looks at the importance of this special identity for Latin American intellectuals, who are central political as well as literary figures.

> **Consider:** *Why intellectuals in Latin America are so concerned with political issues; why there is not a greater distinction between art and politics in Latin American culture.*

[I]ntellectuals exercise enormous political influence in Latin America. It is they who provide respectability to governments in power and legitimacy to revolts and revolutionary movements, they who articulate the ideas and contribute the images through which Latin Americans relate to power, they who satisfy the decidedly Latin need for a romantic and idealistic raison d'être. . . .

"Why is it like this?" Mario Vargas Llosa, the Peruvian novelist, asked in a recent essay. "Why is it that instead of being basically creators and artists, writers in Peru and other Latin American countries must above all be politicians, agitators, reformers, social publicists and moralists?"

The question may be even more puzzling to people in the United States, where the political influence of writers and other intellectuals is exercised far more subtly and indirectly, and politics mainly has to do with specific issues rather than ideologies. . . .

Intellectuals may not be the principal actors in the Latin drama, but they define the issues. Before causes win out, it is their ideas that triumph. Nothing less than the continent's long-range political evolution may be at stake.

The Latin intellectual's position grows out of the society in which he lives. In a

---

region characterized by weak social institutions, inadequate public education and little democratic tradition, intellectuals automatically belong to a prestigious elite. And because Latin American politics invariably revolves around personalities, men of talent are looked to for wisdom and leadership.

Taken together, the intellectuals of Latin America form a kind of unofficial parliament in which the major political events of the day are discussed, integrated into the regional agenda, or allowed to fade from the public consciousness. . . .

This kind of political eminence rarely brings wealth—few Latin writers can survive on their royalties and only García Márquez, whose books have been translated into many languages, can be called rich. But it does make writers into powerful political symbols, particularly if they have been recognized abroad, and few of today's top Latin American authors show many qualms about making full use of this power. . . .

While they come from different countries, the writers' audience is continental, not only because they project a strong sense of a common Latin American identity but because the issues they raise are familiar throughout the region. Almost without exception, they write widely syndicated columns and give frequent interviews—more often about politics than about literature—that are read across Latin America. They frequently gather at conferences that issue sweeping declarations on world issues. And while their political opinions may be challenged, their moral authority is rarely questioned. . . .

Thus, the Latin American intellectual owes his role not only to the fact that so relatively few others in his society are well educated: He is also heir to a general European tradition. What distinguishes him even from the European intellectual, however, is the special tradition of dogma that he inherited from Catholic Spain and that still weighs down political thought in the hemisphere.

For three centuries after the Spanish Conquest, most Latin intellectuals came from the ranks of the clergy and observed the limitations on free thought dictated by the Spanish Inquisition. Such minimal dissent as existed could only come from within the church. Priests, for example, were the first to protest the enslavement of the Indians in colonial Mexico. Yet whatever the intellectual debate at the time, it revolved around the prevailing Catholic dogma. Priests organized Mexico's independence movement against Spain, but their troops followed the standard of the Virgin of Guadalupe. Even the Liberal Reforms that swept across Latin America in the 19th century became almost dogmatic in their anticlericalism.

This doctrinaire past facilitated the transition to Marxism following the 1917 Bolshevik revolution in Moscow. In Latin America, Marxism became the new creed and intellectuals its new priests, while the state was assigned the church's old role of organizing society. "We are the sons of rigid ecclesiastic societies," says the Mexican novelist Carlos Fuentes. "This is the burden of Latin America—to go from one church to another, from Catholicism to Marxism, with all its dogma and ritual. This way we feel protected."

Reviving African Culture
Ali A. Mazrui and Michael Tidy

Modern African nationalists have expressed concern over continuing "cultural imperialism" whereby colonial regimes had set a cultural agenda for Africa that was rooted not in African but in Western experience. Many, intellectuals and scholars, have called for cultural emancipation or liberation, a return to traditional values, a greater use of African languages, and a development of new philosophies and ideologies based in the African experience. Others, however, seek a more balanced development of existing cultural forms, including continued use of European languages for international communication, higher education, and national unity. Ali Mazrui, one of the authors of this excerpt, is a well-known proponent of the rediscovery and fuller use of the African traditional background. He lays out some of his thoughts in the following selection.

> **Consider:** *To what extent the ideology of national culture is a practical idea; how Africans might work within a cultural policy that stressed both Western and African elements; Ali's concern for the integrity of national cultures.*

The cultural tyranny of a Eurocentric world culture that was imposed on Africa during the colonial period has largely withstood the fairly tame assaults launched against it by independent African governments and African writers. In the fields of language policy, education and even literature only limited efforts have been made so far toward cultural liberation.

One of the obstacles to cultural liberation has been an excessive emphasis on the part of writers and scholars on political and economic liberation as processes in themselves, divorced from the struggle for cultural independence. Much of the earlier literature on modernization in Africa concentrated on political development, and too readily assumed that the road to political development lay through Westernization. Political development was envisaged in terms of building institutions comparable to those of Western systems. More recently there has grown up a new rival literature based on the concept of dependency, in which the whole concept of development has been either rejected or drastically redefined. Where it has been redefined, development is now conceived in terms of a progressive reduction in economic dependence. . . . Although some writers have emphasized economic decolonization, cultural decolonization is more fundamental than many have assumed. Mental and intellectual dependency, a lack of readiness to break loose from the metropolitan power, and a compulsive urge to imitate and emulate the West are factors that have on the whole had grave economic and political consequences for societies which are still unwilling to take drastic decisions for their own transformation; they are also phenomena with deep cultural causes. . . .

SOURCE: Ali A. Mazrui and Michael Tidy, *Nationalism and New States in Africa.* (Heinemann Educational Books, Portsmouth, NH, 1984). Reprinted with permission.

Another obstacle to cultural liberation has been the confusion of the concept of modernization with Westernization. In fact, retraditionalization of African culture can take modernizing forms, especially if it becomes an aspect of decolonization. Retraditionalization does not mean returning Africa to what it was before the Europeans came. In hard assessment, it would be suicidal for Africa to attempt such a backward leap. But a move towards renewed respect for indigenous ways and the conquest of cultural self-contempt may be the minimal conditions for cultural decolonization.

Amílcar Cabral, the Guinea-Bissau freedom fighter, pointed out that the African Westernized élite led the struggle for political independence because, having experienced Western education, it was the sector which most rapidly became aware of the need to win freedom from foreign domination. But this élite was culturally alienated and therefore fell victim to a neo-colonialist mentality and it therefore needed to be "reborn." Cabral's solution to the problem of the rebirth of the élite was to return "to the source," to the culture of the mass of the people. Colonialism was short-lived, lasting only about 70 years in most of Africa, and the colonial social structure and European culture affected the rural masses very little. "Repressed, persecuted, humiliated, betrayed by certain social groups who have compromised with the foreign power, culture took refuge in the villages, in the forests, and in the spirits of the victims of domination." The culturally alienated élite must repossess much of the culture of the villages in order to achieve identification with the masses, understand their needs and problems and mobilize them for social and economic development.

Almost every African state has a long way to go on the road to cultural emancipation, to adopt a language policy of relevance to African culture, to transform its educational system, to develop literature and arts of relevant kinds, as well as to pursue an ideology which puts a premium on autonomy and to build a political system which gives weight to the culturally more authentic peasants.

Televised Violence

Most observers agree that television has had a great impact on the lives of people within Western civilization and throughout the world, but exactly what that impact has been is open to debate. This picture illustrates one of the most controversial issues that have been raised. It shows a television camera crew filming the live action in Vietnam. The images filmed by such crews were displayed on daily newscasts in America and elsewhere, giving civilians a virtual firsthand, up-to-the-minute, perhaps overly realistic, impression of what the war was like. However, critics argue that because such images became so common, because they were displayed just before and just after the most mundane of other television shows (typically, situation comedies) and because they were viewed so often from the comfort of a living room, the image of a very real war may have come to seem unreal. Indeed, one must wonder whether this picture itself is not part of a staged scene for a

Photo 14-2

movie (as was the case with a scene the audience sees being filmed in Apocalypse Now, *a major movie of 1979–1980).*

Consider: *Other ways in which the media in the twentieth century have affected people's perception and understanding of war.*

Football Hawk: The Japanese Comic Book
Noboru Kawasaki

*In contemporary Japan some of the most important forms of popular culture are comic books—*manga. *Japanese comic books are not like American ones; they are designed largely for adults of all social strata and convey a wide array of stories from pornography to sports. They were so popular that in 1984 one billion were published—twenty-seven for every household in Japan.*

Their popularity has much to do with the nature of Japanese society. There is little physical space, inhabitable land is at a premium, and houses are very small. In addition, school and after school tutoring leave children little time for play. For adults, the rules of society are extremely rigid. Comic books are thus easy forms of escape for everyone. Comic books are also avenues of transmitting traditional Japanese values, even if they are wrapped in new formats. For example, values of bushido, *the martial spirit of the samurai, are conveyed in fantasies concerning team sports. American football—*Amefukami—*is*

Photo 14-3

Frederick L. Schodt, *Manga! Manga! The World of Japanese Comics* (Kodansha International, 1988).

especially popular. Engaging in combat, men dressed in uniforms learn about team spirit, strategy, and tactics.

This drawing is from a comic book called Football Taka *(Football Hawk) by Noboru Kawasaki. It portrays a Japanese hero named Taka who is smaller than his American opponent but fearless nevertheless. He is shouting "die punk" as he charges. Taka represents the spirit of the* kamikaze *pilots who used their tiny planes against the behemoth American battleships.*

Consider: *The use of modern images and metaphors to transmit traditional values and how this perpetuates a culture.*

The Earth in Deficit
Thomas Berry

Over the past two decades, it has become increasingly apparent that modern civilization is exacting a price from nature. Scholars point out that the world's air and water are becoming polluted, the world's species are being diminished or destroyed, and the world's resources are being threatened. In the following selection, Thomas Berry, a Christian theologian, analyzes how serious these problems are, arguing that the earth is being put into deficit.

Consider: *What Berry means by the earth deficit; the causes for these ecological problems; possible solutions to these problems.*

The reality of our present economy is such that we must have certain forebodings not simply as regards the well-being of the human community but even of the planet itself in its most basic life systems. . . .

In the natural world there exists an amazing richness of life expression in the ever-renewing cycle of the seasons. There is a minimum of entropy. The inflow of energy and the outflow are such that the process is sustainable over an indefinite period of time—so long as the human process is integral with these processes of nature, so long is the human economy sustainable into the future. The difficulty comes when the industrial mode of our economy disrupts the natural processes, when human technologies are destructive of earth technologies. In such a situation the productivity of the natural world and its life systems is diminished. When nature goes into deficit, then we go into deficit. . . .

. . . the earth deficit is the real deficit, the ultimate deficit, the deficit so absolute in some of its major consequences as to be beyond adjustment from any source in heaven or earth. Since the earth system is the ultimate guarantor of all deficits, a failure here is a failure of last resort. Neither economic viability nor improvement

SOURCE: Thomas Berry, "Wonderworld as Wasteland: The Earth in Deficit," *Cross Currents*, Winter, 1985, pp. 408–410, 412.

in life conditions for the poor can be realized in such circumstances. They can only worsen, especially when we consider rising population levels throughout the developing world.

This deficit in its extreme expression is not only a resource deficit but the death of a living process, not simply the death of *a* living process but of *the* living process—a living process which exists, so far as we know, only on the planet earth. This is what makes our problems definitively different from those of any other generation of whatever ethnic, cultural, political or religious tradition or of any other historical period. For the first time we are determining the destinies of the earth in a comprehensive and irreversible manner. The immediate danger is not *possible* nuclear war but *actual* industrial plundering.

Economics on this scale is not simply economics of the human community; it is economics of the earth community in its comprehensive dimensions. Nor is this a question of profit or loss in terms of personal or community well-being in a functioning earth system. Economics has invaded the earth system itself. Our industrial economy is closing down the planet in the most basic modes of its functioning. The air, the water, the soil are already in a degraded condition. Forests are dying on every continent. The seas are endangered. Aquatic life forms in lakes and streams and in the seas are contaminated. The rain is acid.

While it is unlikely that we could ever extinguish life in an absolute manner, we are eliminating species at a rate never before known in historic time and in a manner never known in biological time. Destruction of the tropical rain forests of the planet will involve destroying the habitat of perhaps half the living species of earth.

Thus the mythic drive to control our world continues, even though so much is known about the earth, its limited resources, the interdependence of life systems, the delicate balance of its ecosystems, the consequences of disturbing the atmospheric conditions, of contaminating the air, the soil, the waterways and the seas, the limited quantity of fossil fuels in the earth, the inherent danger of chemicals discharged into natural surroundings. Although much of this has been known for generations, neither the study nor the commercial-industrial practise of economics has shown any capacity to break free from the mythic commitment to progress, or any awareness that we are in reality creating wasteworld rather than wonderworld. This mythic commitment to continuing economic growth is such that none of our major newspapers or newsweeklies considers having a regular ecological section, equivalent to sports or business or arts or entertainment, although the ecological issues are more important than any of these, more important than the daily national and international political news. The real history that is being made is interspecies and human-earth history, not inter-nation history. Our real threat is from the retaliatory powers of the abused earth, not from other nations.

Chapter Questions

1. The closeness of the last thirty years makes it difficult to know what trends and developments will be the most significant historically. Those selected for this chapter are just a few of the possibilities. What others might have been selected? What evidence would demonstrate their importance?

2. It is possible to argue that most of what is claimed to be new about the last thirty years is not really so new, that it is just our impression that it is new because we have been living through it. How might this argument be supported? How might it be refuted?

3. Using sources in this and the previous chapter, evaluate the significance of recent events in the communist and formerly communist states of the world.